NEW EVIDENCE ON UNEXPLAINED EARLY INFANT CRYING:
ITS ORIGINS, NATURE AND MANAGEMENT

Tell me why you're crying my son.
I know you're frightened like everyone.
Is it the thunder in the distance you fear?
Will it help if I stay very near?
I am here.

And if you take my hand my son,
all will be well when the day is done.
And if you take my hand my son,
all will be well when the day is done.
Day is done…

DAY IS DONE, by Peter Yarrow
© 1969 (Renewed), Pepamar Music Corp.
All Rights Reserved. Used by Permission.
WARNER BROS. PUBLICATIONS U.S. Inc., Miami, FL 33014

NEW EVIDENCE ON UNEXPLAINED EARLY INFANT CRYING:
ITS ORIGINS, NATURE AND MANAGEMENT

Edited by Ronald G. Barr, MDCM,
Ian St. James-Roberts, PhD,
Maureen R. Keefe, RN, PhD

Sponsored by
Johnson & Johnson pediatric institute L.L.C.
Shaping the future of children's health

Table of Contents

	Page
Participants	vi
Preface	ix

Julia A. Freedman

Introduction xiii
Ronald G. Barr, MDCM

Section 1. What is "Unexplained Early Crying"? 1
Abstracts 3
Infant Crying and Its Impact on Parents 5
Ian St. James-Roberts, PhD
The Possible Contribution of Temperament to Understanding the Origins and Consequences of Persistent and Excessive Crying 25
Nathan A. Fox, PhD and Cindy P. Polak
Infant Crying: Expectations and Parental Response 43
Lewis A. Leavitt, MD
Discussion 51

Section 2. Crying as a Developmental Phenomenon 55
Abstracts 57
Infant Crying: An Evolutionary Perspective 59
Myron A. Hofer, MD
Development of Crying: The Origin and Change Problems 71
Brian Hopkins, PhD
"Colic" is Something Infants Do, Rather than a Condition They "Have": A Developmental Approach to Crying Phenomena, Patterns, Pacification and (Patho)genesis 87
Ronald G. Barr, MDCM
Crying: Multiple Determinants of Perceived Meaning 105
James A. Green, PhD and Gwen E. Gustafson, PhD
Discussion 121

Section 3. The Challenge of Assessing Crying Complaints 129
Abstracts 131
Clinical Clues to Organic Etiologies in Infants with Colic 133
Siobhán Gormally, MD

Table of Contents (continued)

The Impact of Irritable Infant Behavior on Maternal Mental State:
A Longitudinal Study and a Treatment Trial 149
Professor Lynne Murray and Professor Peter Cooper

Assessing Crying Complaints: The Interaction with
Gastroesophageal Reflux and Cow's Milk Protein Intolerance 165
William R. Treem, MD

Discussion 177

**Section 4. Empirically Based Approaches to Management:
Behavioral Strategies** 183

Abstracts 185

Behavioral Treatment of Prolonged Infant Crying:
Evaluation, Methods and a Proposal 187
Dieter Wolke, PhD

Behavioral Management of Early Infant Crying in Irritable Babies 209
Professor Dymphna C. van den Boom

The REST Regimen: A Conceptual Approach to Managing
Unexplained Early Infant Irritability 229
Maureen R. Keefe, RN, PhD

Discussion 245

**Section 5. Is There Life After Unexplained Crying?:
Outcomes and Consequences** 255

Abstracts 257

From Colic to Toddlerhood 259
Liisa Lehtonen, MD

Life After Unexplained Crying: Child and Parent Outcomes 273
Cynthia A. Stifter, PhD

Clinical Perspectives on Unexplained Early Crying: Challenges and
Risks for Infant Mental Health and Parent-Infant Relationships 289
Mechthild Papoušek, MD, Harald Wurmser, PhD and Nikolaus von Hofacker, MD

Discussion 317

Section 6. Summary 323

Abstract 325

Summary 327
Ian St. James-Roberts, PhD

Participants

Gene Cranston Anderson, PhD, RN
*Edward J. and Louise Mellen Professor
of Nursing
Frances Payne Bolton School of Nursing
Case Western Reserve University
10900 Euclid Avenue
Cleveland, OH 44106-4094 USA*

Ronald G. Barr, MDCM
*Professor of Pediatrics and Psychiatry
McGill University
Head, Child Development Program
Montreal Children's Hospital
2300 Rue Tupper, D-280
Montreal, Quebec H3H 1P3 Canada*

Nathan A. Fox, PhD
*Professor
Institute for Child Study
Department of Human Development
University of Maryland
Room 4304, Benjamin Building
College Park, MD 20742 USA*

Edward Goldson, MD
*Pediatrician
Child Development Unit
The Children's Hospital
CDU-B140
1056 East 19th Avenue
Denver, CO 80218-1088 USA*

Siobhán Gormally, MD
*Consultant Pediatrician
Our Lady of Lourdes Hospital
Drogheda, County Louth, Ireland*

James A. Green, PhD
*Associate Professor
Department of Psychology #107
University of Connecticut
406 Babbidge Road, Box U-20
Storrs, CT 06269-1020 USA*

Megan R. Gunnar, PhD
*Professor
Institute of Child Development
University of Minnesota
216 Child Development
51 East River Road
Minneapolis, MN 55455-0345 USA*

Gwen E. Gustafson, PhD
*Associate Professor
University of Connecticut
406 Babbidge Road, Box U-20
Storrs, CT 06269-1020 USA*

Pamela High, MD
*Clinical Professor of Pediatrics
Brown University School of Medicine
Medical Director
Infant Development Center
Women and Infants' Hospital
101 Dudley Street
Providence, RI 02905-2499 USA*

Myron A. Hofer, MD
*Director
Division of Developmental
  Psychobiology
Columbia University
1051 Riverside Drive, Unit 40
New York, NY 10032-1013 USA*

Brian Hopkins, PhD
*Professor
Department of Psychology
Lancaster University
Lancaster LA1 4YF United Kingdom*

Participants (continued)

Maureen R. Keefe, RN, PhD
Dean
College of Nursing
Medical College of South Carolina
99 Jonathan Lucas Street
PO Box 250160, Room 203
Charleston, SC 29425-8900 USA

Lewis A. Leavitt, MD
Professor of Pediatrics
Director of Developmental Pediatrics
Medical Director
Waisman Center
University of Wisconsin
1500 Highland Avenue
Madison, WI 53705-2274 USA

Liisa Lehtonen, MD
Neonatology Fellow
Rainbow Babies & Children's Hospital
11100 Euclid Avenue
Cleveland, OH 44106-6010 USA

Barbara Medoff-Cooper, PhD, RN
Director
Center for Nursing Research
University of Pennsylvania School
  of Nursing
420 Guardian Drive
Philadelphia, PA 19104-6096 USA

Professor Lynne Murray
Department of Psychology
University of Reading
3 Earley Gate
Whiteknights
Reading, Berkshire
RG6 6AL United Kingdom

Professor Frank Oberklaid
Director
Centre for Community Child Health
University of Melbourne
Royal Children's Hospital
Flemington Road, Parkville
Victoria, 3052, Australia

Mechthild Papoušek, MD
Institute for Social Pediatrics and
  Youth Medicine
University of Munich
Heiglhofstrasse 63
D-81377 Munich
Germany

Ian St. James-Roberts, PhD
University Reader in Child
  Development
Thomas Coram Research Unit
Institute of Education
University of London
27 Woburn Square
London WC1H 0AA United Kingdom

Cynthia A. Stifter, PhD
Professor of Human Development
Pennsylvania State University
110 Henderson Building South
University Park, PA 16802-6504 USA

William R. Treem, MD
Chief
Pediatric Gastroenterology and
  Nutrition
Duke University Medical Center
116 Bell Building
Durham, NC 27710 USA

Participants (continued)

Professor Dymphna C. van den Boom
Developmental Psychology
Universiteit van Amsterdam
Wibautstraat 4
1091 GM Amsterdam
The Netherlands

Carole Welp, MEd
Director
Pointe St. Charles Early
  Childhood Center
Montreal, Quebec H3K 2RI Canada

Dieter Wolke, PhD
Research Professor, Psychology
Division of Psychology
University of Hertfordshire
Hatfield Campus
College Lane, Hatfield
Herts AL 10 9AB United Kingdom

Harald Wurmser, PhD
Institute for Social Pediatrics and
  Youth Medicine
University of Munich
Heiglhofstrasse 63
D-81377 Munich
Germany

Philip Sanford Zeskind, PhD
Research Professor of Pediatrics
University of North Carolina -
  Chapel Hill
Director
Neurodevelopmental Research
Department of Pediatrics
Carolinas Medical Center
1000 Blythe Boulevard
Charlotte, NC 28203-5871 USA

Preface

Johnson & Johnson is delighted to provide this year's edition of its highly regarded Pediatric Round Table series. These conferences have two primary goals: to foster the free exchange of the latest research in infant development and to disseminate those findings to all professionals working in the field of infant health.

This Pediatric Round Table focuses on a particularly challenging and frustrating subject for professionals and parents alike. *New Evidence on Unexplained Early Infant Crying: Its Origins, Nature and Management* brought together some of the world's most prominent scholars and healthcare professionals in the field of infant crying to share their ideas, experiences and observations. The faculty for this Round Table includes leaders in developmental psychoneurobiology, cry research, developmental psychology, pediatrics and nursing. They worked together to explore unexplained early infant crying from several different perspectives, including its relationship to other infant phenomena as well as its etiology, management and prognosis.

Several important findings emerged from this Round Table. Terminology remains elusive, as "colic" may impart an unwarranted emphasis on a gastrointestinal etiology for unexplained crying; an ideal term has yet to be identified. In addition, it has become evident that infants normally experience a period of increased crying. It is also the degree or level of crying, together with caregiver perceptions, that results in the interpretation of crying as a problem. Strategies for managing early infant crying are evolving as well, and readers may find new information in this edition to help guide caregivers in coping with this potentially challenging issue.

At the Johnson & Johnson Pediatric Institute, L.L.C., our continuing aspiration is to build and provide a library of current research and significant information about infant development that features the world's leading researchers and healthcare professionals. I trust that readers of *New Evidence on Unexplained Early Infant Crying: Its Origins, Nature and Management* will agree that this latest volume offers a valuable resource for healthcare professionals worldwide.

Julia A. Freedman
Executive Director
Johnson & Johnson Pediatric Institute, L.L.C.

New Evidence on Unexplained Early Infant Crying

Introduction

Introduction

Ronald G. Barr, MDCM

The "Unexplained Early Infant Crying" Dilemma

All infants cry, but the crying that occurs early in life—in the first 3 or 4 months after birth—is remarkable. For one thing, there seems to be more of it in the first few weeks, no matter what the most conscientious and committed parents do. For another, much of it does not make sense. It starts without warning, stops without warning and seems "independent" of anything we try to do. In this sense, it is "unexplained." Of course, anyone who has had the experience of being present when an infant is crying like this is not very comfortable with behaviors that are "unexplained."

For parents, it may sometimes be only a minor burden and irritant; often it is a major one, depending in part on what it means to them, what sorts of support are available, whether it can be managed, whether their healthcare services are helpful, whether their in-laws are complaining, and so on. Crying, after all, does not happen in isolation, but rather in the context of the infant's caregivers. For clinicians, it can also be a challenge, not because they have to live with the infant, but because they need and want to support new parents, reassure them if necessary and appropriate and help them turn this experience into a creative opportunity to get to know their challenging infant.

Not to be forgotten, it is a challenge for the infant as well because of what is sometimes referred to as "the crying paradox"—the fact that the same crying behavior (or amounts of crying) can function to bring about good or bad consequences, depending on how the crying is responded to in the context in which the infant is living.[1-3] Thus, on one hand, it can function to elicit essential caregiving responses, assuring the infant of nutrition and of close and attentive interaction between the mother and her new baby.[4-7] On the other hand, if it is considered "excessive," it can generate repeated visits to clinicians,[8] and cause mothers to discontinue breastfeeding.[9] In rare but, paradoxically all-too-common cases, it can be the proximate stimulus for Shaken Baby Syndrome, traumatic abuse or even death.[10-13] Who would have designed such an organism, coming equipped with a behavioral capacity that could be so essential for ensuring caregiving resources and so prone to compromising them or, in the extreme, eliminating them completely? In this sense, also, early infant crying is "unexplained."

Together with the Johnson and Johnson Pediatric Institute, Ian St. James-Roberts, Maureen Keefe and I were challenged to help bring together an internationally recognized group to collectively consider and try to synthesize what we know, and what we need to know about this "unexplained" early crying behavior. This was quite a challenge for a number of reasons.

First, to our surprise and delight, there has been a small explosion of interest in this topic from a variety of fields of study. We wanted to provide a venue to ensure that these new and potentially exciting findings could be brought forward and made available across disciplinary divides. Although this provided considerable grist for the symposium's mill, so to speak, we also quickly realized that we would not be able to adequately represent all aspects in the detail and depth deserved. Consequently, we had to choose some foci for the Round Table.

Second, we wanted the proceedings to be relevant and helpful to parents who might be challenged with infants who cried a lot, in common clinical discourse referred to as infants with "colic," "excessive crying" or "persistent crying." Because of the way science and behavioral investigation work, however, not all aspects of all findings are equally strongly confirmed by the appropriate empirical studies. We were faced with what might be referred to as a "translation" problem; namely, addressing the latest—but not necessarily completely confirmed—results and presenting them in a way that was relevant to the real needs of parents. Scientific conferences are one thing; parenting sessions and courses are another. We wanted to try for the best of both in the same context.

Third, we wanted to make the proceedings valuable for the many varieties of clinicians to whom frustrated parents turn for help when faced with crying babies who challenge their parenting skills. Different clinicians (nurses, front-line physicians, specialist physicians, etc) have different needs just as do different parents. Because of the international nature of the Round Table, we had to address the fact that the delivery systems for supportive pediatric care vary enormously from country to country, so that an approach that might be relevant in one might be far from relevant in another.

In the face of these challenges, we decided on a number of priorities for the Round Table that were reflected in the five sessions that form the core of this report. We focused on crying in the first 3 to 4 months of age. This represents two aims in one. Crying is probably the most salient, and the most likely behavior to cause clinical concerns but is not the only thing infants do or the only aspect of their behavior that can be problematic for new parents. Infants also feed and sleep, and problems may occur in all of these behavioral domains. Indeed reference to sleeping and feeding problems came up during the Round Table. However, we wanted to explore crying behavior in depth, so, although these other behaviors are discussed, they are discussed in the context of how they might help us understand crying. (For readers who might want to explore this issue further, there is a recent volume addressed to just this topic.[14]) Similarly crying does not occur only in the first 4 months of life, but continues in various circumstances as the infant grows older. The crying that occurs in the first few months, however, is different in regard to amount, pattern, clinical presentation and, quite possibly, function. As with other related behaviors, reference to crying problems after the first 3 months did come up for consideration. Indeed, a whole section is related to "Life after Unexplained Crying" of the first 4 months (Section V). However, we focused on discussing later crying in relationship to how it helped us understand crying in the first few months of life. (Again, for readers who might want to explore these relationships further, another recent volume addresses other developmental and clinical manifestations of crying during and after the first 3 months.[15])

One of the clear shifts in our understanding of clinically significant crying problems has come from studies that have taken as their primary focus the developmental changes in crying behavior in the first few months of life. We focused on findings from that domain of inquiry to see if we could determine where the field was, especially insofar as these developmental studies could inform us about the clinical manifestations of early unexplained crying. This perspective is introduced in each of the presentations in Section 1 (What is "Unexplained Early Crying"?) and is the primary focus in all of the presentations in Section 2 (Crying as a Developmental Phenomenon). Furthermore, it is complemented (in Section 2) by a fascinating contribution from Myron Hofer, who presents what is in many respects a unique evolutionary perspective of the significance of early infant crying, based on years of work on the contextual, behavior and biologic determinants of distress vocalizations in infant rat pups. This is not to say that more traditional clinical studies that try to understand colic from the point of view of pathology or organic conditions are not interesting or relevant. Indeed, many of the results of work from that perspective are critically reviewed and summarized in Section 3 (The Challenge of Assessing Crying Complaints), especially in the chapters by Siobhán Gormally and William Treem. The other chapter in that section by Lynn Murray and Peter Cooper addresses one of the most difficult of clinical dilemmas in the postpartum period, concerning the likely relationship between infant crying and postpartum maternal depression. This convergence of evolutionary, developmental and clinical perspectives provides an exciting, thought-provoking and truly "new" way of thinking about what early crying means and how we can address it in the context of early parenting and clinical decision making.

Perhaps the most attention in the clinical literature has been paid to the question of dietary approaches to infant "colic." Although this is an important issue, it is increasingly clear that dietary approaches will be appropriate only for a limited number of infants with clinically significant early unexplained crying, probably less than 5% (see Gormally, Section 3). Also, this topic has been thoroughly reviewed already in a number of publications.[14, 16-20] We wanted parents and clinicians to become aware of nondietary approaches to clinically significant crying concerns and of how strong (or weak) the evidence was in support of those approaches. In Section 5 devoted specifically to treatment questions, we concentrated on the evidence concerning behavioral approaches to clinically significant early unexplained crying.

We also wanted to focus on what the empirical evidence about crying behavior contributed to our understanding. We asked what is known about early crying that has been demonstrated to be true by one or more studies. There is great variety of opinions about crying, what its function is, what it means, what to do to stop it, etc. There are also a number of observations that many investigators can accept as empirically supported but the interpretation of which is controversial. The result is that many aspects of our understanding of early unexplained crying remain untested and/or controversial. We tried to focus on those aspects that had at least been subjected to empirical test and to keep opinion and anecdotal evidence to a minimum.

This is manifested in a number of ways throughout the volume. For example, in the first chapter, Ian St. James-Roberts limits his discussion to findings that have been confirmed by at least two independent studies of what we know about infant crying that makes it distressing to parents in Western caregiving settings. The question of treatment was particularly challenging, since there is much less available empirical evidence concerning successful interventions. Nevertheless, what is available is promising. This is addressed in a critical review by Dieter Wolke (Section 4). As the reader will note, one of the best tested and most successful interventions has been carried out in infants older than 3 months (see chapter by van den Boom in Section 4). Because of the quality of the empirical evidence in that study, we requested that Professor van den Boom present it and then speculate about the extent to which the lessons learned from that experience might be relevant to earlier crying problems. We also had the opportunity to hear about preliminary findings from a randomized study that is ongoing at the time of this report (see Keefe, Section 4). We have included a number of excerpts from the discussions that followed each section. Although space limitations made it impossible to include the complete proceedings, we were able to raise a number of important points that were stressed, revisited, sometimes reframed, and often debated and challenged during the discussions. These excerpts speak to the excitement generated by the new findings and provide another means for readers to consider the strength of the evidence and the possibility of alternative interpretations.

In summary, we hope that readers—whether parents, clinicians or investigators—will find this a unique, timely, thought-provoking and practical volume devoted to much of what is novel and exciting in our developing understanding of unexplained crying behavior in the first few months of age. This is a rapidly evolving area of interest. The findings presented here will not result in crying problems disppearing from the lives of parents and clinicians, but we think that the papers present a remarkable summary of what we currently know and what we need to know about developmental contributions to early infant crying, how developmental inquiries inform clinical decision making and what the empirically sustainable approaches to intervention are in as balanced, open and evidence-based a way as is currently possible. Despite the challenges posed in accomplishing these aims and the inevitable limitations of time and space, we were gratified to see how these themes were revisited time and again, from different perspectives and in different forms, but always with the common purpose of improving our understanding of this somewhat mysterious early increase in infant crying behavior. We hope that, although this crying behavior will still appropriately be described as "unexplained," this Round Table will have contributed to its being better understood by parents, healthcare professionals and anyone who has been intrigued or bothered by early infant crying.

References

1. Barr RG. The early crying paradox: a modest proposal. *Human Nature.* 1990;1:355-389.
2. Barr RG. Excessive crying. In: Sameroff AJ, Lewis M, Miller SM, eds. *Handbook of Developmental Psychopathology.* New York, N.Y.: Kluwer Academic/Plenum Press; 2000.
3. Barr RG. Infant cry behaviour and colic: an interpretation in evolutionary perspective. In: Trevathan WR, Smith EO, McKenna JJ, eds. *Evolutionary Medicine.* New York: Oxford University Press, 1999.
4. Ainsworth MDS, Bell SM. Some contemporary patterns of mother-infant interaction in the feeding situation. In: Ambrose A, ed. *Stimulation in Early Infancy.* London: Academic Press, 1969.
5. Konner MJ. Aspects of the developmental ethology of a foraging people. In: Blurton-Jones NG, ed. *Ethological Studies of Child Behavior.* Cambridge: Cambridge University Press, 1972.
6. Bowlby J. *Attachment and Loss.* New York: Basic Books; 1969.
7. Acebo C, Thoman EB. Role of infant crying in the early mother-infant dialogue. *Physiology and Behavior.* 1994;57(3):541-547.
8. Forsyth BWC, McCarthy PL, Leventhal JM. Problems of early infancy, formula changes, and mothers' beliefs about their infants. *Journal of Pediatrics.* 1985;106:1012-1017.
9. Bernal J. Crying during the first ten days of life. *Dev Med Child Neurol.* 1972;14:362-372.
10. Frodi A. Contribution of infant characteristics to child abuse. *American Journal of Mental Deficiency.* 1981;85:341-349.
11. Steele B, Pollack C. A psychiatric study of parents who abuse infants and small children. In: Helfer R, Kempe C, eds. *The Battered Child.* Chicago: University of Chicago Press, 1968.
12. Weston J. The pathology of child abuse. In: Helfer R, Kempe C, eds. *The Battered Child.* Chicago: University of Chicago Press, 1968.
13. Lummaa V, Vuorisalo T, Barr RG, Lehtonen L. Why cry? Adaptive significance of intensive crying in human infants. *Evolution and Human Behavior.* 1998;19:193-202.
14. St James-Roberts I, Harris G, Messer D, eds. *Infant Crying, Feeding and Sleeping: Development, Problems and Treatment.* Hemel Hempstead, Hert: Harvester-Wheatsheef, 1993.
15. Barr RG, Hopkins B, Green JA, eds. *Crying as a Sign, a Symptom, & a Signal: Clinical, Emotional and Developmental Aspects of Infant and Toddler Crying.* London: Mac Keith Press, 2000.
16. Miller AR, Barr RG. Infantile colic: Is it a gut issue? *Pediatric Clinics of North America.* 1991;38(6):1407-1423.
17. Barr RG. Colic and gas. In: Walker WA, Durie PR, Hamilton JR, Walker-Smith JA, Watkins JB, eds. *Pediatric Gastrointestinal Disease.* Hamilton, ON: B.C. Decker Inc., 2000.
18. Treem WR. Infant colic: a pediatric gastroenterologist's perspective. *Pediatric Clinics of North America.* 1994;41:1121-1138.
19. Sauls SH, Redfern DE eds. *Colic and Excessive Crying.* Columbus, Ohio: Ross Products Division Abbott Laboratories, 1997.
20. Wolke D. The treatment of problem crying behavior. In: St.James-Roberts I, Harris G, Messer D, eds. *Infant Crying, Feeding and Sleeping: Development, Problems and Treatments.* New York: Harvester-Wheatsheef, 1993.

New Evidence on Unexplained Early Infant Crying

Section 1:
What is "Unexplained Early Crying"?

Abstracts
What is "Unexplained Early Crying"?

Infant Crying and Its Impact on Parents
Ian St. James-Roberts, PhD

There is little consensus on how to measure infant crying, while different approaches identify hugely different amounts and features. This chapter offers a conceptual and methodologic guide which distinguishes between the crying, its perception by parents, and its impact as a problem for some parents and clinicians. Next, it summarizes what we know about the features of early infant crying which make it so distressing for Western parents. The prolonged, unsoothable and unexplained nature of some crying bouts seem to be key reasons for their concern. Lastly, the term "colic" and others which add to the confusion in this area are reviewed, and suggestions are made for reducing the confusion.

The Possible Contribution of Temperament to Understanding the Origins and Consequences of Persistent and Excessive Crying
Nathan A. Fox, PhD and Cindy P. Polak

Developmental psychologists have sought to understand the early origins, functions, and individual differences in infant crying, in part to determine whether this behavior has long-term consequences for the infant and for the infant-parent relationship. One subset of infants, who present with a temperamental disposition toward irritability and negative affect, may display characteristic behaviors that can persist for years. The type of caregiving that such children receive may modulate, at least in part, the degree to which early infant irritability predicts later social withdrawal.

Infant Crying: Expectations and Parental Response
Lewis A. Leavitt, MD

Cultural expectations, parental belief systems, and characteristics unique to individual infants all influence parental perceptions of infant crying. Infants who cry excessively may cause parents heightened distress and may have an effect on parents' responses to them. Helping parents develop skills to respond to their infants' signals may enhance parental self-efficacy.

Infant Crying and Its Impact on Parents

Ian St. James-Roberts, PhD

Introduction

Unexplained crying in young babies is a common and distressing problem for parents in Western societies.[1-5] It is costly for health services; one recent estimate being that parental inquiries about crying and sleeping in 1- to 3-month-old infants cost the British National Health Service £65 million during 1997.[6] In some cases, the crying is associated with more serious or protracted problems, including infant abuse,[7] maternal depression[8] and long-term child disturbances.[9, 10] These are compelling reasons for wanting to understand this phenomenon better.

This introductory chapter has 3 main aims. First, since there is little consensus on how to measure infant crying, it offers a conceptual and methodologic framework that distinguishes between measures of crying, its perception by parents and its impact as a problem for some parents and, consequently, clinicians. The importance of often-overlooked aspects of infant cry behavior, including fussiness and soothability, is highlighted. Secondly, this chapter summarizes what we know, with some degree of confidence, about the features of crying behavior in 1- to 3-month-old infants that make it so distressing for Western parents. The confidence criterion used is that the findings presented in this section have been replicated in at least 2 independent studies. Lastly, the term "colic," and other terms that have led to confusion in this area, is reviewed, and proposals are made for ways to navigate around them.

Measuring and "Reading" Infant Crying

One of the most striking findings about infant crying to have emerged in the last 10 to 12 years is illustrated in Table 1. When babies' crying is recorded continuously for 24 hours using a radio microphone and tape recorder, the

Table 1. Comparison of Parental Diary versus Audio-Recording Measures of 24-hour Total (Mean) Minutes of Crying[11, 12]

	Minutes of Crying by Method		
	Diary	Audio-Recording	% Difference of Diary Reports Recorded in Audio
Barr et al[11] (n = 10)	125 (48)	29 (15)	23
St. James-Roberts et al[12]			
Moderate criers (n = 55)	121 (85)	22 (16)	18
Persistent criers (n = 67)	220 (126)	44 (27)	20

number of minutes of recorded crying is about 20% to 25% of the amount parents record in behavior diaries.[11, 12] Parents record approximately 4 to 5 times as much crying as is tape-recorded. This is a remarkable finding for at least 2 reasons.

First, both diaries and tape-recording methods are relatively objective measuring devices. Parents complete behavior diaries prospectively: They fill them in more or less as infant crying and other behaviors happen. Consequently, it is unlikely that the difference between the findings is due solely to parental subjective "bias." Note, too, that this is not true just where parents report a lot of crying—the "inflation" by parental diaries is similar no matter how much a baby cries (Table 1[11, 12]).

Second, this difference provides an example of the importance of definition and method. The literature on infant crying is replete with vastly different data for the amount of time infants cry, as well as with studies that show reduced crying after changes in parental care, which cannot be replicated in subsequent research.[13-15] If it is possible to obtain up to a 5-fold difference in the amount of crying simply by measuring it in a different way, the level of confusion in the literature is hardly surprising. Until we reach a consensus on what we want to measure, why and what methods to use, different studies are not going to agree.

Fig 1. Levels in "reading" infant crying.

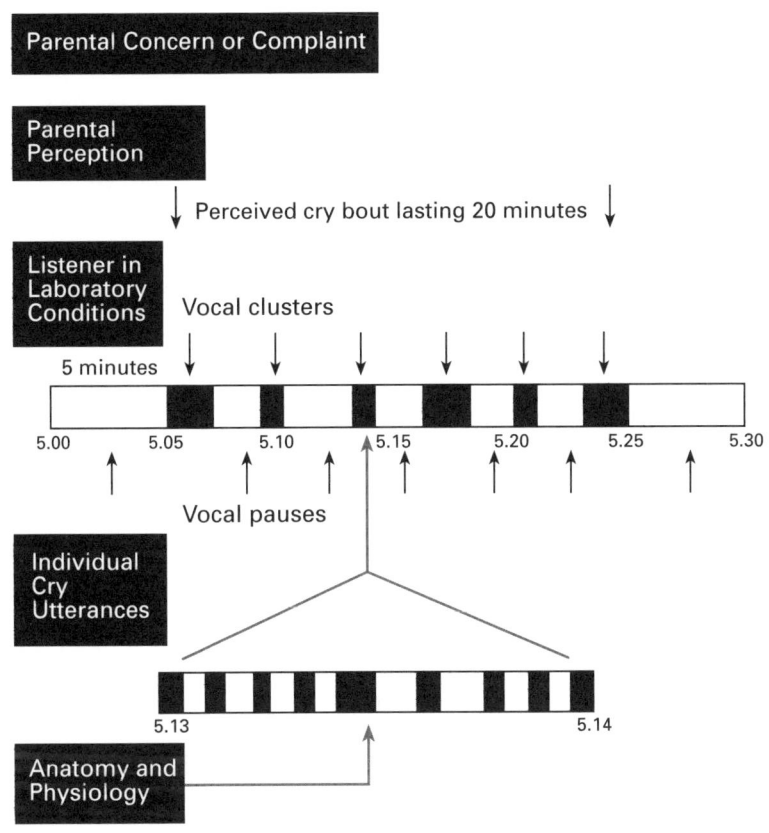

Time shown in minutes (5.13 to 5.14 equals 1 minute).

Fortunately, we know why parents report more crying than is audio tape-recorded. Since the reason throws light onto the discrepancy between crying and its perception by parents, it is illustrated in Fig 1. This emphasizes that crying can be analyzed at a number of different levels. Starting at the bottom of Fig 1, we could measure the actions of neurophysiological and muscular systems as they produce cry behavior and sounds. However, I'll begin at level 3—the level of precise listening—which refers to measures of crying by trained researchers who listen in the laboratory to continuous, 24-hour, voice-activated, audio recordings of crying. This is a method we have used to study infant crying both in general community samples and groups of infants selected because their parents approached professionals with concern about their babies' crying.[12, 15, 16] The methods we use are highly reliable, so that measurements of total 24-hour amounts of crying agree to within 1 minute.[12]

As Fig 1 illustrates, crying has a "burst-and-pause" structure. Audible crying clusters are more or less continuous sequences of vocalizations that last for a few seconds, or minutes, of time. The pauses in between also last for a few moments of time. They allow for respiration and metabolic recovery, and may also serve other purposes. The key point is that, at this level of measurement, trained listeners hear crying as cycling between short vocal clusters and intervening pauses.

In contrast, parents do not sit transcribing crying in controlled surroundings. They "overlook" the short pauses. Similarly, they are not commonly very interested in vocal clusters that last for a few seconds of time. Ascending to the level of perception in everyday settings, parents usually report crying "bouts"; that is, periods when babies remain unsettled and crying for minutes at a time. At this level, overlooking the pauses leads the 9 minutes of cry vocalizations in Fig 1 to be transformed into a 20-minute cry bout. As noted, however, most of this bout time consists of pauses between bursts of cry vocalizations, rather than the actual vocalizations. For practical reasons, we usually ask parents to record bouts of crying in 5-minute units. As long as we know the exact time of each audio-recorded cry vocalization, we can identify crying bouts in the same way; by defining a bout as a set of crying vocalizations separated from others by 5 minutes or more. Using this technique, trained listeners and parents agree about the amounts of time babies cry,[12] and professionals, too, can identify bouts of crying lasting some 10 to 20 minutes.[12, 17]

One implication is that, rather than thinking of parents as "cry analysts," it is probably more realistic to think of them as synthesizing or evaluating crying; that is, as putting together information from a variety of sources in order to understand their individual baby's condition and needs. For instance, 28 years ago Bernal acknowledged that parents often use contextual information, such as knowing how long it was since their baby was fed, in interpreting the reason for a bout of crying.[18] That is, when interpreting or "reading" crying, parents bring together information in the cry as well as other information available to them, including their own knowledge and ideas.

Progressing to the next level of parental concern or contact with professionals because of cry "problems," we can distinguish between parents' perceptions of the amount and sound of crying and their judgement that something is wrong. Even when parents agree about the amount of crying, one parent may seek help for the crying, turning it into a crying "complaint," whereas another parent may view the crying as normal. At this point, we have crossed the line between perception of, and parental reaction to the crying. Such reactions are likely to be influenced by parents' individual subjective characteristics and vulnerabilities, as well as by social expectations and norms. However, rather than measuring crying, we are assessing its impact on parents.

This view of parents as synthesizers who actively give meaning to crying contrasts somewhat with the major approach to infant crying accepted until recently by researchers, an approach that has tended to be analytic and reductionist in emphasis.

In Fig 1, the 1-minute cry cluster heard by the listeners between 5.13 and 5.14 is extracted and expanded to show that, at a microanalytic level, the individual vocal utterances and pauses between them can be analyzed more objectively and precisely than by even trained listeners. Computer acoustic analysis provides much greater detail, evaluating sounds in milliseconds. At this level, individual cry utterances last for the order of 1 to 2 seconds. Acoustic properties of cry utterances, such as fundamental frequency, can be measured exactly, as can breath intakes between utterances. This degree of objectivity and accuracy has been important in advancing our understanding of the sound quality of cries; in particular, identifying certain cries as indices of neurologic impairment.[19] We have also learned that the sound of cries affects parental responses.[20] Unfortunately, though, computer programs used in acoustic analysis can process only short periods, usually only a few seconds, of crying, or even single cry utterances in some studies, compared with the much longer periods parents report in diaries.

Acoustic analysis has provided valuable evidence about cry sounds, which are one type of information used by parents. However, at least 2 other sources are also available. The top line of Fig 2 shows the same audible cry clusters as Fig 1, but recognizes that vocalization does not occur in isolation; rather, parents have visible behavioral information available. Visible behaviors, such as facial grimaces and limb and body movements, are overlooked both by listening to audio-recordings and by acoustic analysis. Yet, parents refer to facial grimaces,

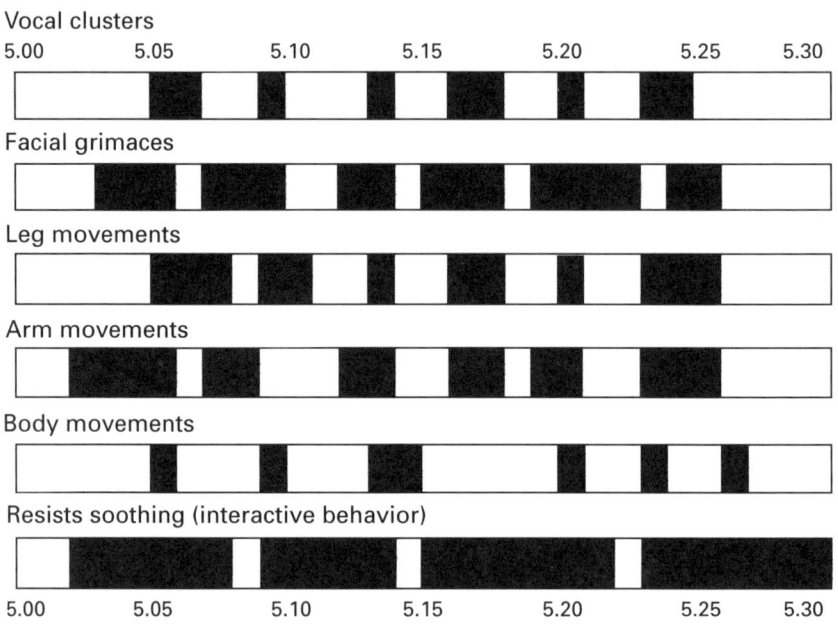

Fig 2. Visible or interactive, as well as vocal, behaviors during a crying bout.

Time shown in minutes (5.00 to 5.05 equals 5 minutes).

raised knees and clenched fists when identifying crying that concerns them.[12, 20] Furthermore, when parents have been instructed to distinguish between fussing and crying, much of the behavior they report in diaries is "fussing" rather than crying; indeed, about twice as much fussing as crying is usually reported.[11, 12] I will return to this distinction later, but if we assume that fussing signifies a baby who is not settled, but who is also not crying continuously either,[11] fussing may often identify cases in which parents are working hard to prevent crying. If this is true, we need to use methods of measurement, such as video recordings, that include fussing, rather than methods that overlook it. We may also learn that inaudible "fussing" helps explain why parents join 2 clusters of audible crying together into a single cry bout.

As Fig 2 illustrates, the baby's interactive, or elicited, behavior during crying is another inaudible aspect of crying behavior that has become a focus of attention recently. Interactive, or elicited, behaviors refer to the baby's responses when stimulated during fussing or crying. Growing evidence suggests that some infants' resistance to soothing maneuvers, such as cuddling and feeding, are important features in raising parental concerns and in understanding the concept of "unexplained crying", which is the focus of this Round Table.

Before developing this idea further, I will summarize the key points made thus far.

- The crying of 1- to 4-month-old infants comprises a complex set of audible and visible behaviors, including interactive qualities, such as resistance to soothing. It is helpful to distinguish different levels of cry analysis according to the purpose of study, since measures at lower levels will not be sufficient to understand phenomena at higher levels.

- For clinical purposes, parents provide the main source of information about infant crying, and parental concerns are the bases for clinical contact. With parental perceptions as our starting point, cry researchers can use more precise methods to understand the features of infant crying behavior that are most central to the formation of these perceptions. We also must distinguish between perceptions of crying behavior and measures of its impact on parents' responses and actions.

What do We Know About the Features of Infant Cry Behavior that Give Rise to Parents' Concerns?

The list that follows summarizes the findings we, as researchers, believe we know with confidence. Each finding has been replicated in at least 2 separate studies.

1. Parental concern about infant crying peaks within the first 3 or 4 months of infancy,[1, 2] which is the reason why this Round Table text focuses on this period. This concern mirrors the amounts infants cry in general and is known as the "crying peak."[1, 2, 21] It follows that much of the crying that concerns parents is due to developmental processes that occur in babies, in general, at this age. "High criers" cry more than most babies, but it is normal to fuss and cry a lot at this age. This concept will be developed later in the text.

   In early studies of American and Canadian babies, the crying peak occurred at approximately 5 to 6 weeks of age, but recent European studies have identified more crying at 3 weeks than at 6 weeks, as shown in

Fig 3. It has not yet been proven whether this is a European versus North American phenomenon, whether the age of the peak has changed recently or if there is a methodological reason for the different findings. This highlights one uncertainty; namely, the reason for the differences in the precise age at which the crying peak occurs.

Fig 3 also highlights another issue: how much babies normally cry.[22-26] Historically, researchers believed that between 2 hours and 2½ hours of diary-recorded fussing and crying per day was normal at the peak age for crying in Western infants, but several recent studies have found significantly lower amounts. These data derive from longitudinal, diary-based studies with relatively large, general-community samples, and the reason for these differences is not clear. In sum, all the studies agree that crying is greatest in the first 3 months of life. However, these trials neither agree on how much crying is considered normal in Western societies nor on the precise age when crying peaks. Furthermore, almost no comparable data exist for non-western societies.

2. The amount of time a baby cries provides a major basis for parental perceptions and concerns. Several studies have provided objective evidence that parental perceptions are generally accurate about differences between babies. Babies said by parents to cry a lot in fact usually do.[12, 16] Not all babies taken to clinicians because of their crying cry more than average, but many do.[27]

3. In the early months, babies tend to cry most in the late afternoon and evening. This is true whether they cry an average or a greater-than-average amount overall. This diurnal variation, or "evening crying peak," is one of the most reliable findings to have emerged from community-based studies.[1, 2, 14, 18, 21, 22, 28-30] It is not yet clear *why* babies fret and cry most in the evening. It is also arguable whether the evening peak is a major reason for parental concern. Babies who fuss and cry a lot tend to do so throughout the day, rather than just in the evenings.[1, 29] This implies that the evening peak could be a somewhat different phenomenon from high amounts of crying, in general.

4. Although a lot of infant crying is likely to increase parental concern, within-baby variability—from 1 day to the next—is also substantial.[22, 31] The practical implication of this observation is that diary or other measures based on single days are not representative of individual differences between babies. It is necessary to sample over several days.

Fig 3. Longitudinal, European diary-based studies of how much normal babies cry.[22-26]

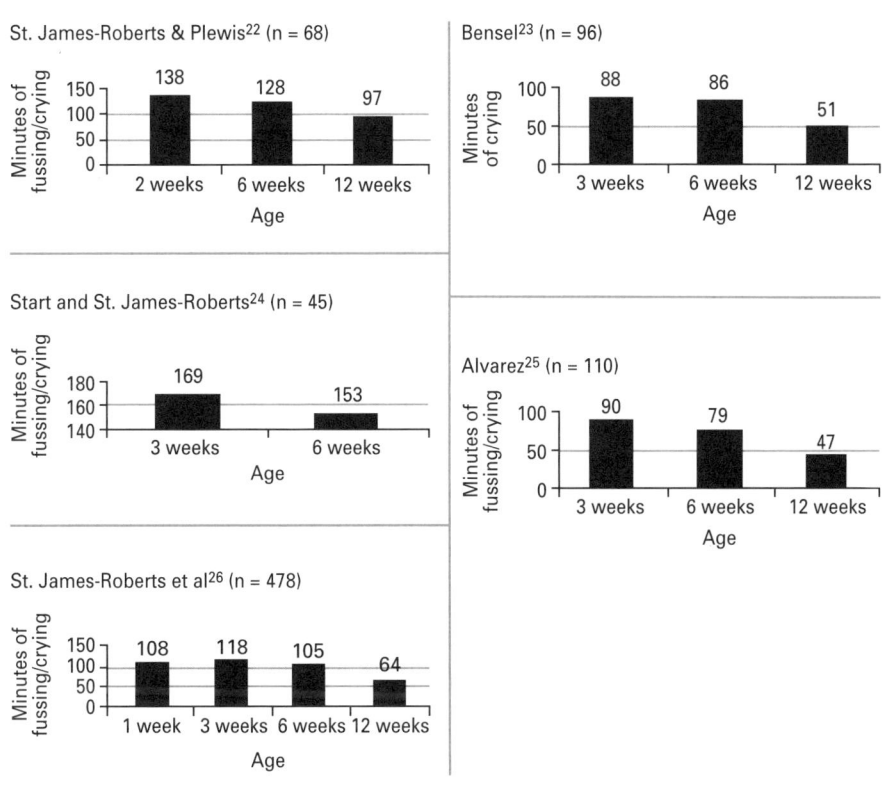

5. Diary-based studies of crying have shown that individual differences between babies are moderately stable. That is, there is a fairly consistent positive correlation between the amounts of fuss/crying in the early weeks of age and the amounts some months later, at around 5 months[32, 33]; on the order of 0.5. Generally, the amounts of crying reduce with age across infants, but rank differences in crying or fussing are quite stable in the first 6 months. As a result, interactions with some babies continue to be demanding, even beyond 3 months of age.

6. Both diary and audio-recording methods confirm that babies who cry a lot have longer cry bouts than other babies.[12, 34] These babies not only cry a lot, but, once they start, they continue to cry for a long time.

7. Babies who cry a lot show a higher ratio of crying-to-fussing behavior within individual bouts of crying compared with babies in general, so that their crying sounds relatively intense.[12, 35] Whether or not the crying sounds abnormal, so that it is distinct, for instance, from the crying of a baby who is intensely hungry or highly aroused for some other reason, remains more controversial.[12, 20, 36] The presentation by Green and Gustafson in this text provides an authoritative view about this issue.

8. Although it is true that babies who cry a lot cry relatively intensely, the majority of their crying is intermittent fussing or fretting, rather than highly intense crying.[12, 37] In their pioneering report, Wessel and colleagues referred throughout their paper to "fussy babies"[28]; this remains an appropriate term in most cases. Anecdotally, most cry researchers can report rare instances of babies who cried frenziedly for hours at a time. However, most young babies who cry a lot actually spend the majority of their crying time fussing, which is intermixed with periods of more continuous and intense crying.[12, 37]

9. An important reason why these babies fuss, rather than cry intensely, is because their parents spend extensive amounts of time soothing and preventing them from crying.[25, 33] This points to one of the most important features to have emerged recently about 1- to 3-month-old "high criers": Their crying is objectively difficult or impossible to soothe.[38, 39]

    This finding first emerged clearly from a naturalistic study of 67 infants selected because they fussed and cried for 3 or more hours per day. In 1995, my colleagues and I reported that both mothers and trained researchers using standard consoling procedures found that crying by infants in this group was difficult, and in some cases impossible to soothe, in contrast with other babies.[38] In a very recent elegant laboratory study, Prudhomme White and colleagues showed that young infants selected for high amounts of crying were more difficult to console when stressed or challenged, such as when undergoing standard baby examinations.[39]

10. First-born babies do not cry substantially more than later borns, so that parental inexperience does not seem to cause babies to cry a lot.[1, 2, 22] Family social-demographic factors and how parents feed their babies are

also poor predictors of how much babies will cry.[40-43] Although high amounts of crying may sometimes be due to parental shortcomings, we know that babies can fuss and cry a lot even when parents provide highly sensitive and responsive care.[25, 33] In short, babies can cry a lot in the first 3 months of age despite excellent parenting.

11. Finally, as the title of this Round Table text suggests, the prolonged and unsoothable nature of early infant fussing and crying remains unexplained. Parents do not know why babies cry this way, nor have experts provided them with a consensus explanation. This challenge provides the rationale for this Round Table text.

One of the most important bodies of knowledge to emerge from social psychology in the last 25 years is known as "learned helplessness." Coined by Seligman, this term refers to the response of adult humans and animals who are exposed repeatedly to uncontrollable, aversive stimulation, such as loud noise.[44] After a time in such circumstances, animals as well as humans cease to attempt to respond to the stimulation. They become anxious and depressed. Humans report feelings of anxiety and inadequacy.

Donovan and Leavitt have argued that the learned helplessness model provides a powerful conceptual framework for understanding why the features of early infant crying described previously are so disturbing for Western parents.[45] The crying of 1- to 3-month-old babies who cry a lot is aversive because of its acoustic characteristics, relative intensity and long bout duration. However, it is probably because such crying is so hard to soothe effectively and occurs for no apparent reason—that is, it is both unexplainable and uncontrollable by parents—that it has such a substantial impact. In the face of their inability to control or explain such behavior in their young, vulnerable babies, parents feel helpless and inadequate and may become anxious and even depressed over time.[8, 45]

If this formulation is supported by the findings presented elsewhere in this Round Table text, it will have important implications for the measurement of crying as well as for clinical interventions and their evaluations. First, it will become important to include separate measures of fussing and "hard-to-soothe" behavior within studies, to measure the more global construct of crying. Unless these are distinguished as separate behaviors within behavior diaries, we are at risk of developing interventions that reduce crying by turning it into fussing, while failing to measure whether babies are more readily soothed as a result of the intervention. In effect, the behaviors most relevant to parents may be overlooked. Second, if "hard-to-soothe" crying is a core feature of 1- to 3-month-old babies who cry a lot, it is imperative that we learn more about its nature and causation. Third, if babies of this age are objectively hard to soothe, interventions with parents should aim at helping them contain and cope with this specific feature of their young babies' behavior.

Terminology: Pitfalls and Guidelines

The word "colic" is conspicuously missing from the title of this Round Table text. This was deliberate and draws attention to one of our major sources of misunderstanding: the lack of a clearly defined and consistently applied terminology. The terms used are often vague or have multiple meanings, so that people use the same word to refer to different things, or different words to refer to the same thing. This is a significant source of confusion.

Table 2 lists some of the main "culprits" and acknowledges that we have added to this complexity by coining a new term, "Unexplained Crying," for this Round Table. Considering each of these in turn, I will suggest some ways in which we might reduce the associated confusion. Since the numerous terms represent different theoretical assumptions and orientations, reaching a consensus will likely be a lengthy process. However, in this discussion we can identify some of the major sources of confusion and make progress towards a shared terminology. To provide systematic guidelines, Table 3 lists Rutter's criteria for an effective system for classifying disorders in children.[46]

Table 2. Terms Used in Infant Crying Research: Pitfalls and Guidelines

- Fussing vs crying
- Excessive crying
- Colic
- Wessel's colic
- Persistent crying
- Unexplained crying
- Irritability
- Regulatory disorder

Table 3. Rutter's criteria for an Effective Classification Scheme for Child Disorders[46]

- Classification must be based on explicit, measurable properties, not abstract concepts; that is, it must be defined in operational terms.
- It must be reliable, so users can employ it in same way.
- It must be relevant and practicable within the context and by people who use it.
- It must provide comprehensive coverage, so that important disorders are not omitted.
- It must distinguish sensitively and accurately between different disorders.
- Differentiation should have external validity. It is not enough for conditions to be separate in theory; they must differ in terms of other variables, such as etiology, symptomatology, course or response to treatment.

The distinction between fussing and crying has already been mentioned several times, as has the reason for including both fussing and crying in studies. This is not to say that we have agreed on operational definitions: Some schemes treat fussing as a separate behavioral state, whereas others view it as a less-intense degree of crying. Hopkins and von Wulfften Palthe have argued that fussing is a more mature form of distress that arises as infants develop the ability to inhibit or regulate their behavior.[47] In agreement with that interpretation, Plewis and I have found that amounts of crying are stable in the early weeks, while fussing becomes more stable later.[22] The definition set forth by Hopkins and von Wulfften Palthe[47] includes "eyes open," whereas the one offered by Conroy, Wilsher and I, taken from audio-recordings, is based primarily on the intervals between vocalizations. Other discriminators of audible cry intensity, such as the amplitude of crying, are difficult to standardize in naturalistic studies because they depend on the distance of the infant from the microphone, while the ratio of vocalization to pauses has the advantage that it can be measured objectively.[48] However, none of the existing definitional schemes for "fuss versus crying" has overall advantages. More work is needed to identify the most sensitive, reliable and effective approaches, but there are strong reasons to recommend that fussing and "hard-to-soothe" crying are measured wherever possible in future studies, and that researchers make their definitions and methods explicit, so that we can explore and understand the differences clearly.

The term "Excessive Crying" (Table 2) fails to meet several of Rutter's criteria.[46] It has no precise meaning and it is a relational term—it implies that the crying is judged to be excessive by *someone*. A more-tolerant individual might not find the crying excessive. This term confounds the subjective appraisal with the crying, so that it is best avoided for scientific studies of crying behavior.

The word "Colic" (Table 2) is the source of a huge amount of confusion in this area of study. Most cry experts have probably been tackled after conference talks with the question: "But what is colic?" "Colic" is currently a poorly specified social concept, rather than a scientific term that refers to an agreed meaning or thing. In relation to Rutter's criteria,[46] it is not yet defined in agreed operational terms.

The term "Wessel's Colic," introduced by Barr, overcomes this problem at least partially, in that it draws on Wessel and colleagues' original definition of a fussy baby as: *"Fussing or crying lasting for a total of more than three hours per day and occurring on more than three days in any one week."*[28] This is a step forward, since it allows reliable selection and assessment of infants who are comparable, at least in terms of the amounts they cry. The drawback is that the definition is arbitrary: As Barr and colleagues have pointed out, it is not helpful to disregard an infant because he cries for only 2 hours and 55 minutes.[49] Moreover, this term raises practical measurement problems. In principle, it is necessary to keep behavior diaries for at least 1 week to meet this definition, while the extended "Rule of Threes," sometimes extrapolated from Wessel's original formulation,[28] requires babies to meet the above criteria for 3 successive weeks. British mothers, at least, are reluctant to collaborate with this. Moreover, if the most recent figures for amounts of crying are accurate, few babies will meet the Wessel et al criteria,[28] at least in 1990s mainland Europe. The principle of using a definition based on amounts of crying for research seems to be a helpful one, but the precise amount, as well as other criteria, may need to be adapted to suit the context and norms of a society.

Returning to the word "colic," in principle it should be possible to assign it any suitable definition. However, a pitfall is that the word "colic" carries significant etymologic and historic "baggage." Carey highlighted the origins of the word: from the Greek "kolikos," the adjective derived from "kolon."[50] Used in this way, "colic" goes beyond a simple description of crying as a behavioral syndrome to imply an explanation; that is, that the baby is crying because of gastrointestinal pain. Illingworth, who popularized the term "colic" in 1955, exemplified this view of colic when he referred in 1985 to "pain that is obviously of intestinal origin."[51] In historic usage, colic is a categoric term, inferring a distinct clinical condition—gastrointestinal pain—that a baby does or does not have, rather than referring to an amount or type of crying behavior. In spite of Illingworth's certainty, 15 years later we still do not know whether most 1- to 3-month-old babies who cry a lot have a digestive disorder, or if they are in pain. Indeed, there is not much evidence that such babies have a shared clinical condition of any sort. They seem to differ from most babies in degree: They cry longer, and more intensely, rather than forming a distinct clinical category.

One way to meet Rutter's criteria[46] would be to redefine "colic" from scratch, as a behavioral syndrome involving large amounts of crying, long crying bouts and "hard-to-soothe" behavior. This approach has the advantage that it refers to defined behaviors, rather than to an abstract concept. Likely drawbacks are the historic and etymologic associations of the word "colic," the related problem of persuading people to use the word in this new way and the lack of an operational definition. This new approach would need to be translated into specific measurements that could be used reliably for research and clinical purposes.

An alternative approach would be to abandon the word "colic" until clear evidence of a digestive disorder is established. The term "Persistent Crying" (Table 2) was introduced approximately 10 years ago with this in mind, and because at that time "colic" was often defined in terms of parental complaint. The aim was to distinguish between actual infant crying and the complaint about the crying in order to focus specifically on the infant's behavioral phenomena. The word "persistent" designated what seemed to be crying's cardinal properties; that it continued despite parental efforts and it recurred over time. Initially, this term lacked a specific operational definition, but more recently my colleagues and I have used it to refer to a 2-stage procedure.

Infants are first selected based on 3 or more hours of fuss/crying using the Crying Pattern Questionnaire, then the amount of crying is confirmed using 3 successive 24-hour behavior diaries.[12] Because of the practical difficulties in obtaining diaries for multiple days, my colleagues and I use the 24-hour total crying amount averaged over the available diaries to select cases. This procedure follows the common clinical strategy of using a quick screening measure followed by a more intensive assessment—and it has proven practical, at least in the UK. However, this approach, too, has limitations and we have not yet attempted to estimate the false-positive and false-negative rates associated with using the Crying Pattern Questionnaire.

The basis for the term "Unexplained Crying" (Table 2) has already been mentioned. It is the unexplained nature of the prolonged, unsoothable crying during the first 3 months of life that is at the heart of parental concern. This term has the advantage of no historical baggage, but it, too, lacks an operational definition and it is limited in that it is defined by exclusion. Moreover, knowing that a baby is not seriously ill or disturbed may well help parents to cope, but a term that designates the crying as unexplained seems unlikely to endear itself to parents or clinicians. While it is helpful to focus on "unexplained crying" to move our field forward, it may be unhelpful to promote the long-term usage of this phrase.

In general use, the word "Irritability" (Table 2) refers to fretful behavior, but it is also used more specifically to identify individual differences in responses to standardized, challenging stimulation. In our area, it has been used to refer to scores given during the Brazelton Neonatal Behavioral Assessment Scale (BNBAS) that identify an infant who is highly negatively responsive to handling and stimulation that other infants do not respond to as strongly.[8, 52] In this sense, "irritability" serves as a measure of reactivity, rather than of spontaneous behavior. Work done by Murray and colleagues noted only a weak correlation between irritability scores from the BNBAS and maternal questionnaire measures of infant behavior,[8] replicating an earlier finding by Wolke and I using the same methods.[53] Since babies selected for high amounts of diary-measured crying are fretful when handled and "hard-to-soothe" in other studies,[38, 39] irritability during BNBAS assessments would be expected to predict everyday fussing and crying. Hence, the failure to find it is puzzling. Why these relationships have not been found consistently needs further study in order to isolate the methodologic or other factors involved. In the meantime it seems prudent to distinguish reactive irritability from spontaneous crying, rather than to use the terms interchangeably.

The term "Regulatory Disorder" (Table 2) was first used in 1991 by DeGangi and colleagues to refer to a group of 11, 8- to 11-month-old infants who exhibited chronic disturbances of sleep, feeding, state control, self-calming and mood regulation.[54] Importantly for our purposes, these researchers explicitly excluded infants who had early crying or sleeping problems: Their definition included only infants whose problems persisted beyond 5 months of age. By definition, therefore, "Regulatory Disorder," as they defined it, cannot be measured in early infancy. Of course, we could use this term in other ways to describe infants who cry a lot, but it does not seem clear whether it is appropriate to do so. For instance, 3 studies have reported that infants who meet the "Rule of Threes" definition for high amounts of crying sleep less—about 1½ hours less during a 24-hour period—than their peers.[29, 55, 56] This may signify a regulatory disorder, but on the face of it is just evidence of a deficit, while if babies cry more in 24 hours they have to do less of something else. "Regulatory Disorder" seems to imply irregular organization, rather than just a deficit, but is not yet defined operationally.

A further use of the concept of "Regulatory Disorder" is to point to disorganization at an underlying level—such as at a physiologic level—on the assumption that this disorganization is the cause of the behavior measured. Crying could then be seen as a sign of physiologic disturbance. This use of "Regulatory Disorder" is plausible, but seems to go beyond currently available evidence. For example, studies of babies selected for high amounts of crying by Prudhomme White[39] and Barr and Gunnar[57] failed to find evidence of disturbances in some physiologic systems. In sum, it is not yet clear whether 1- to 3-month-old babies who cry a lot are regulatory disordered; this term will need to be defined and operationalized precisely if progress is to be made.

References

1. St. James-Roberts I, Halil T. Infant crying patterns in the first year: normal community and clinical findings. *Journal of Child Psychology and Psychiatry.* 1991;32:951-968.
2. Alvarez M, St James-Roberts I. Infant fussing and crying patterns in the first year in an urban community in Denmark. *Acta Paediatrica.* 1996;85:463-466.
3. Forsyth BWC, Leventhal JM, McCarthy PL. Mothers' perceptions of problems of feeding and crying behaviors. A prospective study. *American Journal of Diseases of Children.* 1985;139:269-272.
4. Rautava P, Helenius H, Lehtonen L. Psychosocial predisposing factors for infantile colic. *British Medical Journal.* 1993;307:600-604.
5. Canivet C, Hagander B, Jakobsson I, Lanke J. Infantile colic—less common than previously estimated? *Acta Paediatrica.* 1996;85:454-458.
6. Morris S, St. James-Roberts I, Sleep J, Gillham P. Economic evaluation of strategies for managing infant crying and sleeping problems. *Archives of Disease in Childhood.* In press.

7. Frodi AM. Contribution of infant characteristics to child abuse. *American Journal of Mental Deficiency.* 1981;85:341-349.
8. Murray L, Stanley C, Hooper R, King F, Fiori-Cowley A. The role of infant factors in postnatal depression and mother-infant interactions. *Developmental Medicine and Child Neurology.* 1996;38:109-119.
9. Forsyth BWC, Canny PF. Perceptions of vulnerability 3½ years after problems of feeding and crying behavior in early infancy. *Pediatrics.* 1991;88:757-763.
10. St. James-Roberts I, Conroy S, Wilsher K. Stability and outcome of persistent infant crying. *Infant Behaviour and Development.* 1998;21:411-436.
11. Barr RG, Kramer MS, Boisjoly C, McVey-White L, Pless IB. Parental diary of infant cry and fuss behaviour. *Archives of Disease in Childhood.* 1988;63:380-387.
12. St. James-Roberts I, Conroy S, Wilsher K. Bases for maternal perceptions of infant crying and colic behaviour. *Archives of Disease in Childhood.* 1996;75:375-384.
13. Taubman B. Parental counseling compared with elimination of cow's milk or soy milk protein for the treatment of infant colic syndrome: a randomized trial. *Pediatrics.* 1988;81:756-761.
14. Hunziker UA, Barr RG. Increased carrying reduces infant crying: a randomized controlled trial. *Pediatrics.* 1986;77;641-648.
15. St. James-Roberts I, Hurry J, Bowyer J, Barr RG. Supplementary carrying compared with advice to increase responsive parenting as interventions to prevent persistent infant crying. *Pediatrics.* 1995;95:381-388.
16. St. James-Roberts I, Hurry J, Bowyer J. Objective confirmation of crying durations in infants referred for excessive crying. *Archives of Disease in Childhood.* 1993;68:82-84.
17. St. James-Roberts I. What is distinct about infants' "colic" cries? *Archives of Disease in Childhood.* 1999;80:56-62.
18. Bernal J. Crying during the first 10 days of life, and maternal responses. *Developmental Medicine and Child Neurology.* 1972;14:362-372.
19. Zeskind PS, Lester BM. Acoustic features and auditory perceptions of the cries of newborns with prenatal and perinatal complications. *Child Development.* 1978;49:580-589.
20. Lester BM, Boukydis CFZ, Garcia-Coll C, Hole W, Peucker M. Infantile colic: acoustic cry characteristics, maternal perception of cry, and temperament. *Infant Behavior and Development.* 1992;15:15-26.
21. Barr RG. The normal crying curve: what do we really know? *Developmental Medicine and Child Neurology.* 1990;32:356-362.
22. St. James-Roberts I, Plewis I. Individual differences, daily fluctuations, and developmental changes in amounts of infant waking, fussing, crying, feeding, and sleeping. *Child Development.* 1996;67:2527-2540.
23. Bensel J. The course of early crying – individual versus group values. Poster presented at: Sixth International Workshop on Infant Cry Research; July 1-4, 1997; Lancaster, UK.
24. Start K, St. James-Roberts I. A randomised controlled trial of the effects of a cross-cut feeding teat on infant feeding, crying, waking and sleeping behaviour. *Professional Care of Mother and Child.* 2000;10:45,47.
25. Alvarez M. Maternal caregiving practices, response and flexibility attitudes, and early infant fussing and crying. Presented at: International Conference on Infant Studies; July 16-19, 2000; Brighton, England.
26. St. James-Roberts I, Sleep J, Morrius S, Owen C, Gillham P. Use of a behavioural programme in the first three months to prevent infant crying and sleeping problems. *Journal of Paediatrics and Child Health.* In press.
27. Barr RG, Rotman A, Yaremko J, Leduc D, Francoeur TE. The crying of infants with colic: a controlled empirical description. *Pediatrics.* 1992;90:14-21.
28. Wessel MA, Cobb JC, Jackson EB, Harris GS, Detwiler AC. Paroxysmal fussing in infancy, sometimes called "colic." *Pediatrics.* 1954;14:421-433.

29. Papoušek M, Papoušek H. Infantile persistent crying, state regulation, and interaction with parents: a systems view. In: Bornstein MH, Genevro JL, eds. *Child Development and Behavioral Pediatrics.* Mahwah, NJ: Lawrence Erlbaum Associates; 1996:11-31.
30. Brazelton TB. Crying in infancy. *Pediatrics.* 1962;29:579-588.
31. de Weerth C, van Geert P, Hoijtink H. Intraindividual variability in infant behavior. *Developmental Psychology.* 1999;35:1102-1112.
32. Baildam EM, Hillier VF, Ward BS, Bannister RP, Bamford FN, Moore WM. Duration and pattern of crying in the first year of life. *Developmental Medicine and Child Neurology.* 1995;37:345-353.
33. St. James-Roberts I, Conroy S, Wilsher K. Links between maternal care and persistent infant crying in the early months. *Child: Care, Health and Development.* 1998;24:353-376.
34. Stifter CA, Braungart J. Infant colic: a transient condition with no apparent effects. *Journal of Applied Developmental Psychology.* 1992;13:447-462.
35. Papoušek M, von Hofacker N. Persistent crying in early infancy: a non-trivial condition of risk for the developing mother-infant relationship. *Child: Care, Health and Development.* 1998;24:395-424.
36. Zeskind PS, Barr RG. Acoustic characteristics of naturally occurring cries of infants with "colic." *Child Development.* 1997;68:394-403.
37. Papoušek M, von Hofacker N. Persistent crying and parenting: search for a butterfly in a dynamic system. *Early Development and Parenting.* 1995;4:209-224.
38. St. James-Roberts I, Conroy S, Wilsher K. Clinical, developmental and social aspects of infant crying and colic. *Early Development and Parenting.* 1995;4:177-189.
39. Prudhomme White B, et al. Behavioral and physiological responsivity, sleep, and patterns of daily salivary cortisol production, in infants with and without colic. *Child Development.* In press.
40. Stahlberg MR. Infantile colic: occurrence and risk factors. *European Journal of Pediatrics.* 1984;143:108-111
41. Rubin SP, Prendergast M. Infantile colic: incidence and treatment in a Norfolk community. *Child: Care, Health and Development.* 1984;10:219-226.
42. Hide DW, Guyer BM. Prevalence of infant colic. *Archives of Disease in Childhood.* 1982;57:559-560.
43. Thomas DW, McGilligan K, Eisenberg LD, Lieberman HM, Rissman EM. Infantile colic and type of milk feeding. *American Journal of Diseases of Children.* 1987;141:451-453.
44. Seligman MEP. *Helplessness: On Depression, Development, and Death.* San Francisco, Calif: WH Freeman; 1975.
45. Donovan WL, Leavitt LA. Simulating conditions of learned helplessness: the effects of interventions and attributions. *Child Development.* 1985;56:594-603.
46. Rutter M. Classification. In: Rutter M, Hersov L, eds. *Child Psychiatry: Modern Approaches.* Oxford, England: Blackwell Scientific Publications; 1977:359-386.
47. Hopkins B, von Wulfften Palthe T. The development of the crying state during early infancy. *Developmental Psychobiology.* 1987;20:165-175.
48. Zeskind PS, Klein L, Marshall TR. Adults' perceptions of experimental modifications of durations of pauses and expiratory sounds in infant crying. *Developmental Psychology.* 1992;28:1153-1162.
49. Lehtonen L, Gormally S, Barr RG. 'Clinical pies' for etiology and outcome in infants presenting with early increased crying. In: Barr RG, Hopkins B, Green JA, eds. *Crying as a Sign, a Symptom, & a Signal.* London, England: MacKeith Press; 2000:67-95.
50. Carey WB. 'Colic'—primary excessive crying as an infant-environment interaction *Pediatric Clinics of North America.* 1984;31:993-1005.
51. Illingworth RS. Infantile colic revisited. *Archives of Disease in Childhood.* 1985;60:981-985.
52. van den Boom D. *Neonatal Irritability and the Development of Attachment: Observation and Intervention* [dissertation]. Leiden, The Netherlands: University of Leiden; 1988.
53. St. James-Roberts I, Wolke D. Differences between maternal and objective ratings of difficult neonatal behavioral style: implications for temperament research and clinical perspectives. *Journal of Reproductive and Infant Psychology.* 1983;1:53-60.

54. DeGangi G, et al. Psychophysiological characteristics of the regulatory disordered infant. *Infant Behavior and Development.* 1991;14:37-50.
55. St. James-Roberts I, Conroy S, Hurry J. Links between infant crying and sleep-waking at six weeks of age. *Early Human Development.* 1997;48:143-152.
56. Kirjavainen J, Huhtala V, Kirjavainen T, Lehtonen L, Korvenranta H, Kero P. Colicky infants have normal sleep structure. Presented at: *Pediatric Academic Societies, 1999 Meeting.* May 1-4, 1999; San Francisco, Calif.
57. Barr RG, Gunnar M. Colic: the transient responsivity hypothesis. In: Barr RG, Hopkins B, Green JA, eds. *Crying as a Sign, a Symptom, & a Signal.* London, England: MacKeith Press; 2000:41-66.

The Possible Contribution of Temperament to Understanding the Origins and Consequences of Persistent and Excessive Crying

Nathan A. Fox, PhD, and Cindy P. Polak

Introduction

A key task in the study of behavior and development is to define, as precisely as possible, the characteristics of the developmental process or the individual behavior pattern under investigation. Such precision ensures that investigators from different research centers are examining the same phenomenon and that discoveries about the etiology, correlates or consequences of behavior can be shared across sites. Prolonged or "excessive" crying in the first months of life is a behavior pattern that has eluded precise definition. In part, this is due to the apparent differences amongst cultures in the frequency of crying in early life.[1-4] What seems like a great deal of crying in one culture may not be viewed as excessive in another; "excessive" is a relative term. Further, there are legitimate disagreements among researchers regarding the nature or the pattern of cry behavior. Is crying in early infancy a function of some apparent physiologic condition (hunger, pain, excessive sensory stimulation),[5] or is excessive crying only that which lacks an obvious etiology?[6] Is crying that responds to methods of soothing or intervention different from crying that does not respond to intervention? These questions have engendered great debate amongst developmental psychologists seeking to understand the early origins, developmental trajectories and individual differences in infant crying.[7,8]

The phenomenon of prolonged crying in the first months of life is also of great interest to pediatricians and parents. The work of pediatricians rules out pathological conditions that may cause the crying and provides families with strategies for reducing the behavior. Parents are both concerned about and stressed by an infant who presents with prolonged crying. They are concerned that perhaps their infant is ill, in which case medical intervention may be necessary, and they are often stressed by the sudden, unexplained nature of their infant's crying. Although prolonged crying in the first postnatal months of life can create a stressful period for parents, in most instances such crying decreases after the third month of life. Overall, follow-up studies of infants who exhibit prolonged crying in early life (often called colic in the pediatric and developmental literatures) indicate that, in low-risk families, there are few long-term effects on the social development of the infant.[9-12] Babies who exhibit prolonged crying during the first months of life do not appear, as a group, to cry more than controls in the second half of the first year of life, nor are they identified as being more irritable in their behavioral response compared with controls.[10, 12]

There are, however, infants among those identified as early, prolonged criers who continue to cry a lot after the first 3 months of life. These infants may, in fact, have a different developmental trajectory from those whose crying diminishes. Continued excessive crying after 3 months of age may mean that whatever caused the behavior in the first place has not resolved for this group of infants. Alternatively, the etiology of their crying may differ from that of infants whose crying diminishes by 3 months.

The Role of Temperament in Understanding Early Crying

The continuity of crying behavior after 3 months of age suggests that this pattern may reflect a temperamental trait of the infant. Temperament refers to a behavior pattern that appears early in life and is relatively stable over the first postnatal year.[13, 14] Thomas, Chess and Birch described 9 such "patterns," or factors, of personality that were derived from intensive observation of infant behaviors during the first year (Table 1).[15] Among these personality factors were quality of mood, threshold of responsiveness and intensity of response. Infants who exhibit characteristic negative moods, low or high thresholds of responsiveness and a high intensity of response were categorized as "difficult." Infant difficulty was associated with sleep problems and later behavioral problems, as well.[15]

The continuity of behavior over time indicates that a behavioral pattern may be temperamental in nature. Infants who continue to cry past the 3-month period most certainly would be considered to be temperamentally difficult.

Table 1. Nine-point Personality Index[15]

Type of Child	"Easy"	"Slow to Warm Up"	"Difficult"
Activity Level *The proportion of active periods to inactive ones.*	Varies	Low to moderate	Varies
Rhythmicity *Regularity of hunger, excretion, sleep and wakefulness.*	Very regular	Varies	Irregular
Distractibility *The degree to which extraneous stimuli alter behavior.*	Varies	Varies	Varies
Approach Withdrawal *The response to a new object or person.*	Positive approach	Initial withdrawal	Withdrawal
Adaptability *The ease with which a child adapts to changes in his/her environment.*	Very adaptable	Slowly adaptable	Slowly adaptable
Attention Span and Persistence *The amount of time devoted to an activity, and the effect of distraction on the activity.*	High or low	High or low	High or low
Intensity of Reaction *The energy of response, regardless of its quality or direction.*	Low or mild	Mild	Intense
Threshold of Responsiveness *The intensity of stimulation required to evoke a discernible response.*	High or low	High or low	High or low
Quality of Mood *The amount of friendly, pleasant, joyful behavior, as contrasted with unpleasant, unfriendly behavior.*	Positive	Slightly negative	Negative

Reprinted with permission from Thomas A, Chess S, Birch HG. The Origin of Personality. Copyright © 1970 by Scientific American, Inc. All rights reserved.

It is not clear whether infants who display persistent crying in the first 3 months of life only are also considered "difficult" in temperament. Clearly, during the first months of their childrens' lives, parents view these infants as difficult; however, if crying behavior diminishes afterwards, such a label may not endure.

Although it may be difficult in the first few months to distinguish behaviorally infants who are difficult from those who are colicky, data suggest that the 2 groups do not share similar physiologic characteristics. In a recent study of 2-month-old infants, White and colleagues showed that although infants with colic could be differentiated from infants without colic, based on behavioral characteristics during a lab visit, there were no significant differences found between the groups in heart rate, vagal tone or cortisol.[16] The only difference found in physiologic responsivity between the 2 groups of infants was that those with colic displayed a blunted rhythm in cortisol production. Since colicky infants do not show the same physiologic characteristics as are associated traditionally with difficult temperament, it may be more appropriate to study this particular group as distinct from temperamentally difficult infants.

The notion that difficult temperament emerges from intrinsic behavioral characteristics of the infant has been challenged by several researchers. Bates suggested that the concept of difficult temperament is based only on caregiver perceptions of infant characteristics, and that it has little to do with actual infant behaviors.[17] Hubert and Wachs found a high degree of variability among parents' attributions of easiness or difficultness regarding their infants' behaviors, such that behavior patterns associated with easiness for one parent were often associated with difficultness for other parents[18]: For example, some parents perceived the curious/exploratory behavior of their infant as being difficult and demanding, while other parents associated this behavior with easiness. In fact, studies by Diener, Goldstein and Mangelsdorf[19] and by Zeanah, Keener and Anders[20] indicate that the strongest predictors of parental perceptions of infant temperament are their own prenatal expectations. Such findings raise the possibility that infants may be labeled as either difficult or easy based only on parental expectations rather than on objective observations of their infants' individual characteristics.

Irritability as a Temperamental Feature Associated with Persistent Crying

Another temperamental quality that could be related to excessive crying is irritability. Irritable infants are those who respond with negative affect, and with fussing, crying and motor arousal in response to sensory stimulation and handling. There are multiple items on the Brazelton Neonatal Behavioral Assessment Scale (BNBAS) that assess the infant's affective response to the sensory manipulations that take place over the course of being assessed by the BNBAS.[21] Factor analyses of these items have led to proposed clusters, or behavior categories, that describe each infant's orientation, range of state, motor responses, autonomic stability, regulation of state, response decrement and reflexes.[22] The range-of-state cluster contains items that assess the infant's response to the exam, including peak of excitement, rapidity of buildup, irritability and lability. Infants who score high on this cluster display excessive crying and fussiness when handled or when presented with sensory stimulation.

Irritable infants may or may not be a subset of those infants identified as displaying excessive and persistent crying in the first months of life. They are likely to display negative affect when presented with low levels of sensory stimulation or when handled. They present with a low threshold for response to sensory stimulation. Their responses are intense, and the affective quality of responses is negative. Given this pattern of behavior, irritable infants meet the definition of the "difficult" infant posed by Thomas, Chess and Birch.[15] Conversely, it is neither clear that their crying or fussing is persistent (in the absence of moderate to high levels of sensory stimulation or handling), nor is it necessarily the case that their crying or fussing is excessive. Rather, they are considered irritable because they respond with crying and fussing to routine handling and social interaction that would usually elicit positive affective responses. While these irritable infants appear to increase the stress levels of parents who care for them, it is not clear that these babies cry persistently over long periods of time.

Neonatal temperamental irritability may remain stable over the entire first year of life.[23] In a study by Fish and Crockenberg, a significant positive relationship was found between 5-day irritability and 9-month social behaviors (eg, an increase in the frequency of eye contact and smiling to mother), although no link was found between neonatal irritability and 9-month fussing and crying.[24] Work by Riese demonstrated a significant relationship between neonatal measures of irritability, resistance to soothing, activity while awake and reinforcement value with 9-month emotional tone, activity, attentiveness and social orientation to staff.[25, 26] In another study, Riese reported that irritable neonates were rated as more upset, less attentive to stimuli and less responsive to staff at 24 months, suggesting modest continuity of certain temperamental components from the neonatal period through the second birthday.[23] This evidence supports the possibility that temperamental irritability accounts for a subset of infants who present with persistent excessive crying in early life and whose distress continues past 3 months of age.

What are the long-term outcomes for irritable infants? Several areas of study provide relevant information. In the *attachment* literature, some work suggests that infant irritability is a risk factor for insecure attachment. Crockenberg, who examined the effects of infant irritability in low-income families who did and who didn't have social support systems, found a higher incidence of insecure attachment in high-risk families who didn't have social support than in families with irritable infants who had functioning social support networks.[27] van den Boom completed an intervention study with low-income families who had irritable infants.[28] Like the work by Crockenberg,[27] irritability was defined by elevated cluster scores on the BNBAS that was administered during the first 2 weeks of life.[28] The intervention was designed to increase maternal sensitivity and responsiveness to the irritable infant. Interestingly, van den Boom found that neonatal irritability was not stable across the first 5 months of life. She observed little stability in irritability scores from the neonatal period to 5 months. Nevertheless, van den Boom found that irritable infants in low-income families who did not receive the experimental intervention had a higher incidence of relationships that featured insecure attachment than did infants whose families participated in the intervention.

Researchers interested in *behavioral inhibition* have also examined the long-term outcomes of irritable infants. Kagan, Snidman, Arcus and Reznick[29] identified 3 possible origins of neonatal irritability. Individual differences in irritability are posited to result from differences in the reactivity of the amygdala, a region of the limbic system, the degree of visceral feedback to limbic sites, particularly to the central gray area, or the infant's preparedness to detect subtle differences in sensory stimulation. The first 2 proposed origins of neonatal irritability derived from the work of LeDoux and colleagues[30, 31] and Davis,[32] who focused on neural substrates of the fear system in animals. These investigators used a paradigm involving conditioned shock to examine the neural pathways involved in an animal's startle response. These researchers noted that animals (mostly laboratory rats) would startle when presented with a fast-rising, short-duration blast of white noise. In a now well-known paradigm, animals were conditioned to a tone with electric shock. After conditioning, the animals were again presented with the blast of white noise, this time paired with the tone. The magnitude of the startle response was greater to the white noise paired with the tone than to the noise alone. Both Davis[32] and the LeDoux teams[30,31] argued that the startle response could be potentiated by pairing it with a conditioned, fearful stimulus. They then examined the anatomic and physiologic pathways in the brain that were responsible for the potentiation effect. Their findings indicated that the central nucleus, a small area in the amygdala, was likely involved in the potentiation effect. Destroying the central nucleus abolished the effect. Output from the central nucleus innervates the autonomic nervous system via the lateral hypothalamus and activates motor activity via the central gray, 2 other structures within the limbic system (Fig 1[33]).

Kagan and colleagues[29] reasoned that inhibited children expressed similar behavioral and physiologic responses to those displayed by animals who show potentiated, or heightened, fear responses. Both hyperactivation of the central nucleus of the amygdala and visceral feedback to limbic sites, themselves outputs from the amygdala, could contribute to these responses. Kagan et al[29] reasoned further that behaviorally inhibited children *as infants* might display similar characteristics of heightened irritability (negative affect and heightened motor arousal) as a function of the activation of this fear system.

Data from the laboratory in the Department of Human Development at the University of Maryland support the notion that behaviorally inhibited children display many of the output responses that are a function of a hyperactivated fear system, including heightened autonomic arousal and elevated cortisol response. As evidence, in a study of inhibited 7 year olds, Schmidt and colleagues found that when challenged emotionally by the expectation that they would be speaking about their most embarrassing moment, these children showed a significant increase in heart rate and a decrease in heart rate variability.[34] In a different study, Schmidt and colleagues found that inhibited 4 year olds showed elevated basal morning salivary cortisol compared with cortisol levels in control children.[35] Schmidt and Fox also observed that inhibited infants exhibited a potentiated startle response following the approach of an unfamiliar adult.[36]

Fig 1. Different outputs of the amygdala control different conditioned fear responses.[33]

In the presence of danger or stimuli that warn of danger, behavioral, autonomic and endocrine responses are expressed and reflexes are modulated. Each of these responses is controlled by a different set of outputs from the central nucleus of the amygdala. Lesions of the central nucleus block the expression of all these responses, whereas lesions of the output pathways block only individual responses. Selected examples of central amygdala outputs are shown. CG, central gray; LH, lateral hypothalamus; PVN, paraventricular hypothalamus (which receives inputs from the central amygdala directly and by way of the bed nucleus of the stria terminalis); RPC, reticulopontis caudalis.

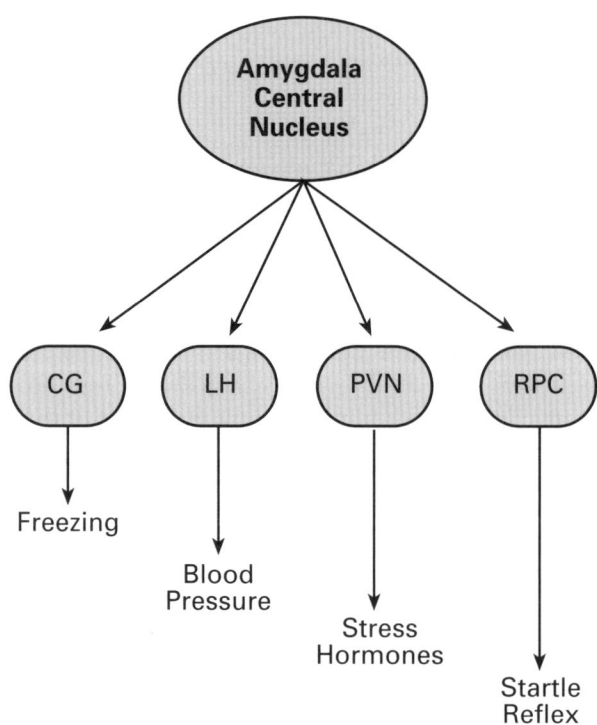

Reprinted with permission of Simon & Schuster from THE EMOTIONAL BRAIN by Joseph LeDoux. Copyright ©1966 by Joseph LeDoux.

Results of these studies[29, 34-36] indicate that behaviorally inhibited children in potentially stressful situations display physiologic responses similar to those described by Davis[32] and LeDoux and colleagues[30, 31] as outputs of the fear system. Of course, these parallels in response patterns do not prove that the brain structures or system characterized as subserving conditioned fear in rats underlies the behavior of inhibited children. Indeed, the behavioral origins of inhibition may reside not in a history of conditioning, but rather within a history of more general fear or anxiety when responding to environmental cues. Along these lines, it is interesting to note that Davis and colleagues[37, 38] have described a second fear system—this one associated less with conditioned fear and more with generalized anxiety. This second fear system is not associated with heightened activity of the amygdala, but rather with increased activity of an adjacent structure; the bed nucleus of the stria terminalis. Importantly, with regard to autonomic and other visceral responses, this structure has identical outputs to the same limbic nuclei.

The third possible origin of irritability, suggested by Kagan and colleagues,[29] was "preparedness to detect subtle differences in sensory or perceptual information." Such heightened sensitivity to environmental events would create a more vigilant state and mild degrees of novelty or stress might disturb the system to a greater extent than would be found among nonirritable children. The idea that heightened sensitivity leads to withdrawal and negative affect is one that has a long history in *personality psychology.*

Eyesenck was among the first to suggest that some individuals would tend toward introversion because of greater central arousal.[39, 40] Such heightened arousal would lead to lower thresholds for arousal, in general, and to lower sensory thresholds, in particular. Research with introverts confirms this notion: Compared with nonintroverts, introverted individuals are more sensitive to low auditory frequencies,[41, 42] they are more sensitive to pain,[43-45] to olfactory[46] and to visual thresholds,[47] and they have a lower tolerance for intense and prolonged stimulation. It is thought that the introverted individual's heightened sensitivity to a range of sensory stimuli creates a more vigilant state and leads to active withdrawal behavior as he or she attempts to lower an already high level of arousal.

Based on their review of research into sensory sensitivities in introverts, Aron and Aron identified 2 distinct groups of highly sensitive individuals.[48] People in one of these groups (comprising approximately one third of the total) tended to have higher scores than the others for social introversion and negative emotionality. The remaining two thirds of highly sensitive individuals also scored in the high range on these factors. Aron and Aron stated that those in the first group of highly sensitive individuals reported experiencing negative parenting and an unhappy childhood more often than did those in the latter group as well as those adults who displayed no particular heightened sensory sensitivity. This association is also stronger for males than for females. These findings from the adult personality literature provide some support for an association between increased negative emotionality/social withdrawal and heightened sensory sensitivity. Whether such associations exist in infancy or childhood and among inhibited children are unknown. Nevertheless, it is reasonable to continue to explore the possibility that heightened sensory sensitivity is an origin of irritability. Further, these data from adults illustrate the importance of examining the long-term social outcomes of irritable infants.

The Role of Infant Temperamental Irritability in Predicting Social Behavior

Research by Fox et al[49] has examined closely the social outcomes of infant irritability. We recently completed an outcomes study in which more than 400 families were screened initially when their infants were 4 months of age. The screening procedure consisted of observations of the infants' responses to a series of visual and auditory stimuli that increased in complexity and to a series of auditory stimuli that increased in decibel level. Infant behavioral response was coded into 3 general categories: positive affect, including smiles, cooing and positive vocalizations; negative affect, including crying, fretting/fussing and distress vocalizations; and motor arousal, including back arching and movements of the arms and legs. Infants who displayed a high degree of motor activity, high negative affect and low positive affect were known as the "irritable" group. During this same screening procedure, this group was compared with a group of infants who had high motor activity, low negative affect and high positive affect as well as to a group of infants who had low motor activity, low negative affect and low positive affect.

Study infants were seen individually at 14 months and 24 months in our laboratory for an assessment of behavioral inhibition. The assessment included observations of the infants' responses to an unfamiliar adult, to a novel robot toy and to challenging play situations (eg, crawling through a tunnel). We coded the infants' proximity-seeking behaviors toward their mothers, latency to approach the unfamiliar adult, latency to approach and touch the novel toy and latency to crawl through the tunnel. The variables were aggregated and standardized to create an index of behavioral inhibition.

These children returned at age 4 for a play session in which one behaviorally inhibited child, one noninhibited child and 2 children whose inhibition index was approximately at the mean were placed together. The 4 children played together for 15 minutes, which was followed by a cleanup session. Each child was then asked to stand and talk about their most recent birthday party, after which a cooperative game was played in which all 4 children were expected to participate. The observation period ended with another 15 minutes of free play. This session was coded using Rubin's Play Observation Scale, in which behaviors are coded every 10 seconds.[50] We were interested particularly in the childrens' reticent behavior, which was defined as unoccupied, onlooking behavior along with anxious behaviors, such as lip biting or rocking, during the free play sessions. Children who exhibited high levels of reticent behavior typically sat or stood on the periphery watching other children play. When approached by other children to interact they usually rejected such initiations.

Fig 2, which presents the longitudinal data for the 3 groups of infants selected at 4 months of age,[49] shows that "high negative" infants selected for temperamental irritability (high motor response, high negative affect, low positive affect) displayed a high degree of behavioral inhibition at 14 months of age. At 24 months and at 4 years of age, however, the mean for this group on the inhibition/reticence aggregate was no different than that of the "low reactive" (rated "low" on all measures) children. The standard error for the mean (±SE) of the "irritable" ("high negative") group was large, indicating that there was considerable individual variability within the group. Inspection of the individual developmental curves of the children in the "irritable" group revealed 2 distinct subtypes. The first subtype consisted of children who showed continuity over time, remaining inhibited and displaying a high degree of reticence over the 44-month study period. The second subtype of children, however, changed over time, moving from inhibited/reticent to noninhibited/nonreticent behavior over the course of the study.

This intriguing difference in outcomes within the "irritable" group led to an examination of factors that could have affected the continuity (or lack thereof) for children in this group.[49] Using the longitudinal data, the following 4 factors were explored: the attachment status of the infant at 14 months of

Fig 2. Mean scores on standardized measures of inhibition at 14, 24 and 48 months as a function of 4-month temperament group.

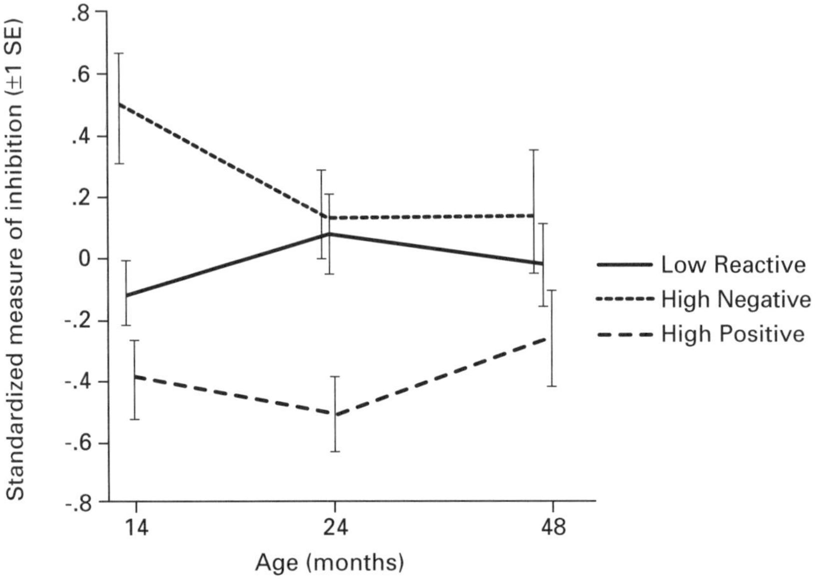

At 14 months, Low Reactive (n = 43), High Reactive (n = 44), High Positive (n = 36). At 24 months, Low Reactive (n = 44), High Negative (n = 44), High Positive (n = 37). At 48 months, Low Reactive (n = 39), High Negative (n = 44), High Positive (n = 35).

Reprinted with permission from Fox NA, Henderson HA, Rubin KH, Calkins SD, Schmidt LA. Continuity and discontinuity in behavioral inhibition and exuberance: Psychophysical and behavioral influences across the first 4 years of life. *Child Development.* 2001;72. Copyright © 2001 by the Society for Research in Child Development.

age; the gender of the child; family characteristics, including significant life events and parental divorce over the period of the study; and the child's daycare status during the first year of life.

When the infants were 14 months of age they were observed using the Ainsworth Strange Situation.[51] Videotapes of each infant's reaction to being in a strange room with or without their parent present and to the presence of an unknown adult with or without their parent present were coded, and infants were assigned an attachment classification according to Ainsworth's standardized scheme. Children who were classified as attached insecurely to the parent were further categorized by type of insecurity (either avoidant [A] or anxious/ambivalent [C]). If a child was classified as attached securely, the specific subtype within the secure (B) classification was assigned. Data analysis revealed no relationship between security of attachment and continuity of inhibition over the 44-month study period. Infants who remained inhibited as 4 year olds were no more or less likely to be attached securely than those infants who became noninhibited preschoolers.

Unlike attachment status, gender was related to continuity of inhibition in the preschool period. Girls from the high-negative, irritable group were more likely to change over the 44-month period than were boys. This gender difference in continuity of inhibition supports other reports in the literature. In a study of inhibited children over a 7-year period, Stevenson-Hinde and Glover reported that boys were more likely to remain inhibited than were girls.[52] These investigators speculated that inhibited boys were more salient and therefore drew more attention from their mothers. The added attention reinforced, rather than diminished, their inhibition. Girls who were inhibited drew less attention and less-protective parenting and seemed to benefit from this lack of attention, and they were less likely to remain inhibited over the course of the study. The implication from Stevenson-Hinde and Glover[52] is that the overindulgence that inhibited boys elicit from their parents reinforces their behavior in social situations. Supporting evidence comes from a study of 1-year-old boys, as reported by Park, Belsky, Putnam and Crnic.[53] These authors found that inhibited boys who remained inhibited beyond 2 years of age were more likely to have overprotective mothers, while inhibited boys who became less inhibited by age 2 had mothers who allowed them more autonomy and independence.

Stressful life events, including divorce, were among the family factors examined for associations with continuity or change in inhibition. Evidence from other studies—particularly by Crockenberg[27] and by van den Boom[28]—suggests that infant irritability may act as a significant additional risk factor in families already under stress. To address this issue, my colleagues and I computed a stress/risk index for each family based upon reported events.[49] We found no differences in family risk status between those families with infants who remained inhibited over time versus families in which the child changed.

The final factor we examined was the child's daycare status during the first year of life.[49] We computed the association between placement in daycare and change or continuity in inhibition over the 44-month study and found a significant association. Compared with "irritable" infants who were not placed in daycare in the first year of life, infants who went to daycare were more likely to become noninhibited preschoolers. What does this association mean? It is possible that infants who were placed in daycare were somehow inherently different than those who stayed at home. However, our data do not support this contention. Irritable infants placed in daycare did not differ from those who remained at home, based on levels of 4-month irritability or on other temperament variables. It seems more likely that specific aspects of the daycare experience or context facilitated a reduction in inhibited behavior among young children.

There are 2 possible explanations for the relationship between daycare experience and context and the reduction of inhibited behavior. Children in daycare must learn social skills to interact and "get along" successfully within the group. Exposure to a group setting provides the infant with this type of social interactive experience, which facilitates the development of social competence that may reduce the child's tendency toward social withdrawal. A second aspect of the daycare experience that may decrease inhibition concerns the immediacy of the caregiving response. Children in group care will often not receive the immediately responsive caregiving that they may experience at home. Caregivers in daycare settings necessarily interact with multiple children, and therefore usually cannot overindulge one child with attention. If anxious, intrusive caregiving maintains an inhibited behavioral pattern, then daycare would provide an environment where the child would experience a different pattern of caregiving responsivity.

This latter explanation fits well with the observations regarding continuity in inhibition for boys, as reported previously. This work[49] suggests that anxious, intrusive caregiving contributes to the maintenance of inhibited behaviors over time, whereas caregiving that allows for independence and autonomy is associated with change in inhibition status. Placing a child in daycare, where it is unlikely that he or she would experience intrusive, hovering attention, might provide the child with the degree of independence and autonomy needed to decrease inhibition. Further research, in which actual observations of caregiving interactions are undertaken, will provide the data necessary to address these issues.

Conclusions

Those who study persistent, excessive crying in early life do so to understand the etiology of this pattern and to identify its long-term consequences for the infant and for the infant-parent relationship. One approach to this issue conceptualizes a subset of these infants as presenting with a temperamental disposition toward irritability and negative affect. This subgroup of persistent criers would likely display irritability beyond the first 3 or 4 months of life. Longitudinal studies reveal that a significant percentage of these "irritable" infants display social withdrawal in the presence of novel social events beginning at approximately 1 year of age and lasting at least through the preschool years. The degree to which early temperamental infant irritability predicts later social withdrawal appears to be, at least in part, a function of the type of caregiving the child receives. Individuals who provide mental and physical health services to parents of infants who cry excessively beyond 3 months of age should consider the possibility that such behavior reflects the innate temperamental disposition of the child.

Acknowledgement

Work on this chapter was funded by a grant from the National Institutes of Health (HD#17899) to Nathan A. Fox.

References

1. Barr RG, Konner M, Bakeman R, Adamson L. Crying in !Kung San infants: a test of the cultural specificity hypothesis. *Developmental Medicine and Child Neurology.* 1991;33:601-610.
2. Richman AL, LeVine RA, New RS, Howrigan GA, Welles-Nystrom B, LeVine SE. Maternal behavior to infants in five cultures. *New Directions for Child Development.* 1988;40:81-97.
3. St. James-Roberts I, Bowyer J, Varghese S, Sawdon J. Infant crying patterns in Manali and London. *Child: Care, Health and Development.* 1994;20:323-337.
4. Prior M, Garino E, Sanson A, Oberklaid F. Ethnic influences on "difficult" temperament and behavioral problems in infants. *Australian Journal of Psychology.* 1987;39:163-171.
5. St. James-Roberts I. Infant crying: normal development and persistent crying. In: St. James-Roberts I, Gillian H, eds. *Infant Crying, Feeding and Sleeping: Development, Problems and Treatments: The Developing Body and Mind.* Hemel Hempstead, Hert: Harvester Wheatsheaf; 1993:7-25.
6. St. James-Roberts I. Explanations of persistent infant crying. In: St. James-Roberts I, Gillian H, eds. *Infant Crying, Feeding and Sleeping: Development, Problems and Treatments: The Developing Body and Mind.* Hemel Hempstead, Hert: Harvester Wheatsheaf; 1993:26-46.
7. St. James-Roberts I, Plewis I. Individual differences, daily fluctuations, and developmental changes in amounts of infant waking, fussing, crying, feeding, and sleeping. *Child Development.* 1996;67:2527-2540.

8. Lummaa V, Vuorisalo T, Barr RG, Lehtonen L. Why cry? Adaptive significance of intensive crying in human infants. *Evolution and Human Behavior.* 1998;19:193-202.
9. Stifter C, Braungart J. Infant colic: a transient condition with no apparent effects. *Journal of Applied Developmental Psychology.* 1992;13:447-462.
10. Raiha H, Lehtonen L, Korhonen T, Korvenranta H. Family functioning 3 years after infantile colic. *Journal of Developmental and Behavioral Pediatrics.* 1997;18:290-294.
11. Sloman J, Bellinger DC, Krentzel CP. Infantile colic and transient developmental lag in the first year of life. *Child Psychiatry and Human Development.* 1990;21:25-36.
12. Keefe MR, Kotzer AM, Froese-Fretz A, Curtin M. A longitudinal comparison of irritable and nonirritable infants. *Nursing Research.* 1996;45:4-9.
13. Fox NA, Henderson HA, Marshall PJ. The biology of temperament: an integrative approach. In: Nelson CA, Luciana M, eds. *The Handbook of Developmental Cognitive Neuroscience.* Cambridge, Mass: MIT Press. In press.
14. Goldsmith HH, Buss AH, Plomin R, et al. Roundtable: what is temperament? Four approaches. *Child Development.* 1987;58:505-529.
15. Thomas A, Chess S, Birch HG. The origin of personality. *Scientific American.* 1970;223:102-109.
16. White BP, Gunnar MR, Larson MC, Donzella B, Barr RG. Behavioral and physiological responsivity, sleep, and patterns of daily cortisol production in infants with and without colic. *Child Development.* 2000;71:862-877.
17. Bates JE. The concept of difficult temperament. *Merrill-Palmer Quarterly.* 1980;26:299-319.
18. Hubert NC, Wachs TD. Parental perceptions of the behavioral components of infant easiness/difficultness. *Child Development.* 1985;56:1525.
19. Diener ME, Goldstein LH, Mangelsdorf SC. The role of prenatal expectations in parents' reports of infant temperament. *Merrill-Palmer Quarterly.* 1995;41:172-190.
20. Zeanah CH, Keener MA, Anders TF. Developing perceptions of temperament and their relation to mother and infant behavior. *Journal of Child Psychology and Psychiatry.* 1986;27:499-512.
21. Als H, Tronick E, Lester BM, Brazelton TB. The Brazelton Neonatal Behavioral Assessment Scale (BNBAS). *Journal of Abnormal Child Psychology.* 1977;5: 215-231.
22. Jacobson JL, Fein GG, Jacobson SW, Schwartz PM. Factors and clusters for the Brazelton Scale: an investigation of the dimensions of neonatal behavior. *Developmental Psychology.* 1984;20:339-353.
23. Riese ML. Temperament stability between the neonatal period and 24 months. *Developmental Psychology.* 1987;23:216-222.
24. Fish M, Crockenberg S. Correlates and antecedents of nine-month infant behavior and mother-infant interaction. *Infant Behavior and Development.* 1981;4:69-81.
25. Riese ML. Procedures and norms for assessing behavioral patterns in full-term and stable pre-term neonates. *JSAS Catalog of Selected Documents in Psychology.* 1982;12:6.
26. Riese ML. Assessment of behavioral patterns in neonates. *Infant Behavior and Development.* 1983;6: 241-246.
27. Crockenberg SB. Infant irritability, mother responsiveness, and social support influences on the security of infant-mother attachment. *Child Development.* 1981;52:857-865.
28. van den Boom DC. The influence of temperament and mothering on attachment and exploration: an experimental manipulation of sensitive responsiveness among lower-class mothers with irritable infants. *Child Development.* 1994;65:1457-1477.
29. Kagan J, Snidman N, Arcus D, Reznick SJ. *Galen's Prophecy: Temperament in Human Nature.* New York, NY: Basic Books; 1994.
30. LeDoux JE, Iwata J, Cicchetti P, Reis DJ. Different projections of the central amygdaloid nucleus mediate autonomic and behavioral correlates of conditioned fear. *Journal of Neuroscience.* 1988;8: 2517-2529.

31. LeDoux JE, Sakaguchi A, Iwata J, Reis DJ. Interruption of projections from the medial geniculate body to an archi-neostriatal field disrupts the classical conditioning of emotional responses to acoustic stimuli. *Neuroscience.* 1986;17:615-627.
32. Davis M. Pharmacological and anatomical analysis of fear conditioning using the fear-potentiated startle paradigm. *Behavioral Neuroscience.* 1986;100:814-824.
33. LeDoux J. *The Emotional Brain.* New York, NY: Simon and Schuster; 1996.
34. Schmidt LA, Fox NA, Schulkin J, Gold PW. Behavioral and psychophysiological correlates of self-presentation in temperamentally shy children. *Developmental Psychobiology.* 1999;35:119-135.
35. Schmidt LA, Fox NA, Rubin KH, et al. Behavioral and neuroendocrine responses in shy children. *Developmental Psychobiology.* 1997;30:127-140.
36. Schmidt LA, Fox NA. Fear-potentiated startle responses in temperamentally different human infants. *Developmental Psychobiology.* 1998;32:113-120.
37. Davis M, Walker DL, Lee Y. Amygdala and bed nucleus of the stria terminalis: differential roles in fear and anxiety measured with the acoustic startle reflex. *Philosophical Transactions of the Royal Society of London. Series B: Biological Sciences.* 1997;352:1675-1687.
38. Walker DL, Davis M. Double dissociation between the involvement of the bed nucleus of the stria terminalis and the central nucleus of the amygdala in startle increases produced by conditioned versus unconditioned fear. *Journal of Neuroscience.* 1997;17:9375-9383.
39. Eyesenck HJ. *A Model for Personality.* New York, NY: Springer-Verlag; 1981.
40. Eyesenck HJ. Biological dimensions of personality. In: Pervin LA, ed. *Handbook of Personality.* New York, NY: Guilford Press; 1991:244-276.
41. Stelmack RM, Campbell KB. Extraversion and auditory sensitivity to high and low frequency. *Perceptual and Motor Skills.* 1974;38:875-879.
42. Stelmack RM, Michaud-Achorn A. Extraversion, attention, and auditory evoked response. *Journal of Research in Personality.* 1985;19:416-428.
43. Barnes GE. Extraversion and pain. *British Journal of Social and Clinical Psychology.* 1975;14:303-308.
44. Haier RJ, Robinson DJ, Braden W, Williams D. Evoked potentials augmenting-reducing and personality differences. *Personality and Individual Differences.* 1984;5:283-301.
45. Schalling D. Tolerance for experimentally induced pain as related to personality. *Scandinavian Journal of Psychology.* 1971;12:271-281.
46. Herbener ES, Kagan J, Cohen M. Shyness and olfactory threshold. *Personality and Individual Differences.* 1989;10:1159-1163.
47. Siddle DA, Morrish RB, White KD, Mangan GL. Relation of visual sensitivity to extraversion. *Journal of Experimental Research in Personality.* 1969;3:264-267.
48. Aron EN, Aron A. Sensory-processing sensitivity and its relation to introversion and emotionality. *Journal of Personality and Social Psychology.* 1997;73:345-368.
49. Fox NA, Henderson HA, Rubin KH, Calkins SD, Schmidt LA. Continuity and discontinuity in behavioral inhibition and exuberance: psychophysical and behavioral influences across the first four years of life. *Child Development.* 2001;72(1). In press.
50. Rubin KH. *The Play Observation Scale (POS).* University of Waterloo; 1989.
51. Ainsworth MD, Blehar MC, Waters E, Wall S. *Patterns of Attachment.* Hillsdale, NJ: Lawrence Erlbaum Associates; 1978.
52. Stevenson-Hinde J, Glover A. Shy girls and boys: a new look. *Journal of Child Psychology and Psychiatry, and Allied Disciplines.* 1996;37:181-187.
53. Park SY, Belsky J, Putnam S, Crnic K. Infant emotionality, parenting, and 3-year inhibition: exploring stability and lawful discontinuity in a male sample. *Developmental Psychology.* 1997;33:218-227.

Infant Crying: Expectations and Parental Response

Lewis A. Leavitt, MD

Introduction

Parents of newly arrived children have preconceived beliefs and expectations about their newborns. These beliefs and expectations derive from their own experiences, advice from family members, friends and professionals and cultural biases. How parents perceive their children based on these beliefs and expectations determines an important part of early parent-infant interaction.[1, 2]

For new parents, learning how to interact with their infant is very similar to the task of learning a new language. The infant presents a variety of motor and vocal signals that must be decoded. Parental success in decoding these signals is determined by assessing the infant's response to the parents' actions in response to the infant's signals.

Early Infant Crying

The infant cry is the most salient of infant signals. It is present upon the newborn's entry into the parent's life and is heard even when the parent is at some distance from the infant. Attending to the infant's cry very quickly becomes a core experience of parenthood. Barr and St. James-Roberts have demonstrated the pervasiveness of crying during the first 3 months of life (pages 87 through 104 and pages 5 through 23 in this text) and each has noted the degree of distress that crying may elicit from parents. In particular, infants who are at the "high end" of variation in crying activity may prove exceedingly stressful to their parents.[3, 4]

To understand the implications of "high crying activity" for parental behavior and the consequent implications of that parental behavior for infant and child development, it is instructive to review typical parental responses to infant cries and assess the important determinants of parental response.

Three Basic Levels of Response to Infant Crying

It may be helpful to think of parental response to infant crying as the outcome of a system of interactions that can be considered at 3 basic "levels" (Fig 1).

Fig 1. The influences that affect parent-infant interactions.

Level 1	Cultural
Level 2	Parental Belief Systems
Level 3	Infant Characteristics

Level 1 includes the influences of *culture*. Among different cultures there are contrasting expectations for infant behavior as well as appropriate parental responses expected for specific types of infant behavior. Whereas North American parents may view persistent crying as a negative, aversive infant activity, impoverished mothers in northern Brazil may perceive such activity as representing the positive characteristics of an infant who is strong and willing to fight for his or her own well-being.[5] Even within a single culture there may be contrasting expectations for infants who have specific characteristics. For example, the same vocalizations elicit different behavioral responses from adults depending upon whether they are told that the crying infant is premature, has Down syndrome or is a typically developing normal infant.[2,6,7]

Level 2 includes the *specific belief systems of individual parents*. Mothers develop beliefs and expectations about their infants based on their experiences within their cultures as well as their life histories. They develop styles of coping with everyday problems, including those of child care. In this paper I will review studies that show how differences at this level influence mothers' responses to infant cries.

Level 3 reflects the *characteristics of the individual infant*. Each infant's characteristics interact strongly with the parental beliefs, expectations and coping styles of level 2.

The key to understanding the family implications of "high crying activity" on the part of the infant is the interplay of culture (level 1) and maternal beliefs (level 2). It is the influence of culture (level 1) that transforms the interplay of maternal beliefs (level 2) and individual infant characteristics (level 3) from the realm of family behavior, parents interacting with a crying baby, to the realm of a medical entity, colic.

Within level 1, cultural tradition and medical and psychologic professionalism define and classify what is typical behavior and what is aberrant. This is not to say that "colic" is not objectively a significant problem for parents. My point is simply that cultural traditions may define or label different levels of crying as "excessive." These varying conceptions of the proper level of activity for infants may shift the cutoff points for what is deemed atypical or pathologic in a particular culture.

A Review of the Clinical Literature

In this regard it is helpful to consider the work of social anthropologists who have used the term "parental ethnotheories" to describe how parents in different cultures possess varying theories of how infants should behave and what this behavior means in terms of their future.[1] In North American and European cultures, pediatricians and child psychologists play an important role in molding and refining parental ethnotheories. There is, therefore, an interesting feedback that can occur amongst epidemiologic, medical and psychologic research on parents and parents' conceptualizations of "excessive crying" or "colic."

This feedback is very important for 2 reasons: First, colic, or the syndrome of excessive crying in early infancy, is usually a benign condition for the infant that is associated generally with good health and physical development. (This is discussed in greater detail by Barr, St. James-Roberts and Stifter in separate papers in this text.) Second, excessive crying may evoke maladaptive responses from *some* parents; these responses may prove to have longer-term consequences for child development. It is this second issue (at level 2) that will be emphasized in this paper.

As was stated previously, the infant cry is one of the most powerful and effective signals that elicits parent-infant interaction. Responding to a crying infant is, *par excellence,* the test of parental coping skills.[8, 9] For several decades, Donovan and I have studied how parental expectations and experiences affect their responses to infant cries.[8-15]

We have used both laboratory models of mother-infant interactions as well as observations of mother-infant interactions to examine influences on developing mother-infant relationships.[2, 10] Based on our laboratory work, Donovan and I have proposed a model of how a mother's sense of "self-efficacy," defined as how effective she believes she is at managing child-care tasks, affects mother-infant interactions and, in turn, infant development (Fig 2).[11]

We have tested the role of maternal perceptions of self-efficacy by utilizing experiments that require mothers to terminate infant cries by learning a pattern of button presses in a laboratory task.[2, 8, 11] When we have controlled mothers' successes in a first series of cries we find that mothers who are unsuccessful terminating cries in the first series are less successful terminating subsequent series of cries.

Fig 2. Maternal self-efficacy: how parental management affects mother-infant interactions and infant development.[11]

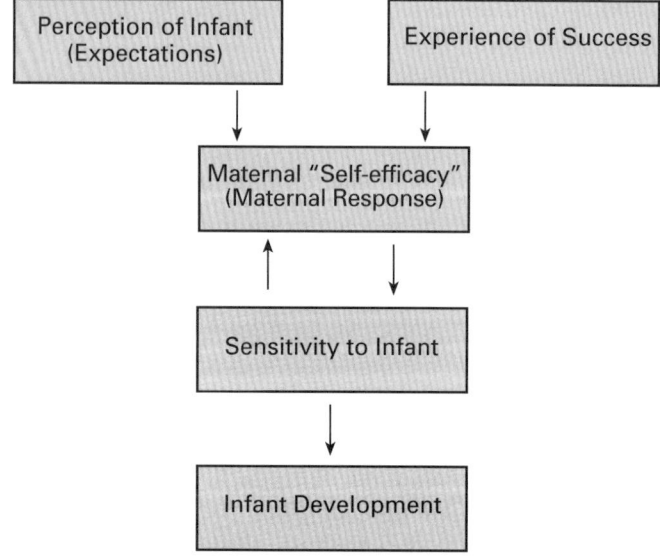

In these experiments we can arrange conditions so that the mother can very easily stop a baby's cry that she hears or make it difficult, or even impossible, for her to do so. We do this by computer control of a set of buttons that the mother can press to stop a tape-recorded baby's cry that she hears from a speaker. If we arrange conditions so that the mothers are unsuccessful in stopping cries in a laboratory session we find that these mothers become less successful in learning how to stop a baby's cry in a following laboratory session in which we have made the task easy.

The experience of not succeeding in the first session decreases mothers' performance in the second session. In other words, not having a recent experience of success in stopping a cry is associated with less-able performance in stopping a cry even when the conditions are set up to make success in stopping the cry easy to achieve. Of interest is that this less-able performance after an experience of "failure" can be improved. We found that by "reframing" maternal expectations the negative effect of lack of success can be removed. Following the experience of "failure" in the first laboratory session we inform the mothers that the second session involves a similar task, but their performance in this task is unrelated to the previous task. When we encourage the mothers to expect "success" in the second laboratory session, despite their lack of success in the first session, we are able to remove the negative effect of the recent experience of "failure."

With our colleagues Frodi and Lamb, Donovan and I have also studied mothers' and fathers' physiologic responses to infant cries.[6, 12] In the experiments, parents listened to the same cries that were described as coming either from a "normal, healthy" baby or as from a premature baby or a "difficult" baby. When labeled as coming from a difficult or premature baby, the same cries elicited greater heart rate, blood pressure changes and verbal descriptions associated with negative events than when labeled as coming from a normal, healthy baby. These "labeling" studies show that beliefs and expectations modify how parents respond to a baby's crying.

All of these studies emphasize the role of mothers' beliefs and expectations in determining how they respond to a baby's cry. Our findings suggest that beliefs and expectations combine with experience to form a sense of "self-efficacy." By self-efficacy, my colleagues and I are referring to an assessment of how successful parents have been and will continue to be in a given task; in this case, stopping an infant's cry. Donovan and I also examined the link between maternal self-efficacy and infant development in a series of studies that indicate how mothers assess their success in confronting infant cries. We found that when we manipulated how successful mothers were at terminating an infant cry in the laboratory, some mothers overestimated their success.[13] Mothers who overestimate their success are less physiologically responsive when they are listening to infant cries, less sensitive in discriminating cries acoustically and are less behaviorally sensitive when interacting with their children when they are toddlers.[14] Moreover, mothers who have an unrealistic sense of their efficacy—that is, those who overestimate their success in controlling cries—later use more negative behavioral interactions with their children in a task that requires toddler compliance. Toddlers of these mothers were more defiant when asked to comply with the task.

Implications of These Studies

What do these experiments and our model imply? For some mothers who experience an infant who cries a lot, there are pathways of developing mother-infant interactions that may result in less optimal child development.[8-10, 15] Some mothers may develop expectations of low success in childcare tasks. Expectations of low self-efficacy can lead to less effective mother-infant interactions. Another pathway is the development of an unrealistic evaluation of self-efficacy. Mothers who overestimate their own efficacy show less sensitivity to infant signals, and therefore have less effective mother-infant interactions. Subsequently, both of these pathways have negative consequences for infant development.

What do these studies imply for pediatric practice? Mothers' responses to infant crying are a formative component of parental care. Assisting mothers to develop skills in attending to infant signals that lead to pleasurable and successful interactions can help reframe perceptions of the infant, enhancing the experience of successful mother-infant interactions.

Conclusion

When an infant cries a great deal in the early months of life, fostering successful interactions with the child when he or she is *not* crying may provide a constructive, positive experience for the mother. Positive interactions may help mothers' assessments of self-efficacy and filter their perceptions of their infants in a more positive manner.

References

1. Harkness S, Super CM. *Parents' Cultural Belief Systems: Their Origins, Expressions, and Consequences.* New York, NY: The Guilford Press; 1995.
2. Leavitt LA. Mothers' sensitivity to infant signals. In: Warhol JG, Shelov SP, eds. *New Perspectives in Early Emotional Development.* Skillman, NJ: Johnson and Johnson Pediatric Institute; 1998:59-63.
3. Wessel MA, Cobb JC, Jackson EB, Harris GS, Detwiler AC. Paroxysmal fussing in infancy, sometimes called "colic." *Pediatrics.* 1954;14:421-443.
4. St. James-Roberts I, Hurry J, Bowyer J. Objective confirmation of crying durations in infants referred for excessive crying. *Archives of Disease in Childhood.* 1993;68:82-84.
5. Scheper-Hughes N. *Death Without Weeping: The Violence of Everyday Life in Brazil.* Berkeley, Calif: University of California Press; 1993.
6. Frodi A, Lamb ME, Leavitt LA, Donovan WL. Fathers' and mothers' responses to infant smiles and cries. *Infant Behavior and Development.* 1978;1:187-198.
7. Stevenson MD, Leavitt LA, Silverberg SB. Mother-infant interaction: Down syndrome case studies. In: Harel S, Anastosiow NJ, eds. *The At-risk Infant: Psycho-socio-medical Aspects.* Baltimore, Md: Paul H. Brookes; 1985:379-388.
8. Donovan WL, Leavitt LA. Simulating conditions of learned helplessness: the effects of interventions and attributions. *Child Development.* 1985;56:594-603.
9. Donovan WL, Leavitt LA. Physiologic assessment of mother-infant attachment. *Journal of the American Academy of Child Psychiatry.* 1985;24:65-70.
10. Donovan WL, Leavitt LA. Early cognitive development and its relation to maternal physiologic and behavioral responsiveness. *Child Development.* 1978;49:1251-1254.
11. Donovan WL, Leavitt LA. Maternal self-efficacy and infant attachment: integrating physiology, perceptions, and behavior. *Child Development.* 1989;60:460-472.
12. Donovan WL, Leavitt LA. Physiology and behavior: parents' response to the infant cry. In: Lester BM, Boukydis CFZ, eds. *Infant Crying: Theoretical and Research Perspectives.* New York, NY: Plenum Publishing; 1985.
13. Donovan WL, Leavitt LA, Walsh RO. Maternal self-efficacy: illusory control and its effect on susceptibility to learned helplessness. *Child Development.* 1990;61:1638-1647.
14. Donovan WL, Leavitt LA, Walsh RO. Maternal illusory control predicts socialization strategies and toddler compliance. *Developmental Psychology.* 2000;36:402-411.
15. Donovan WL, Leavitt LA, Walsh RO. Cognitive set and coping strategy affect mothers' sensitivity to infant cries: a signal detection approach. *Child Development.* 1997;68:760-772.

Section 1 Discussion: What is "Unexplained Early Crying"?

Moderated by Philip Sanford Zeskind, PhD
Research Professor of Pediatrics
University of North Carolina
Chapel Hill, North Carolina, USA

Zeskind: It is important to talk about crying in a developmental perspective. Development proceeds as a function of a dynamic and bidirectional interaction between the organism and its environment. We need to keep that in mind whenever we talk about infant crying and its effects on the environment and on the infant itself. The environment helps create the infant, and then the infant "feeds back" to help create the environment, meaning the parents and even the nonsocial environment, at subsequent periods in its development.

* * * * *

Ian St. James-Roberts described some very difficult issues that had not been adequately addressed previously. Nathan Fox talked about some of the infant's characteristics, and Lewis Leavitt discussed how those characteristics could impact the environment. This gives us a framework by which we can start to examine some of these bidirectional interactions. The title of this workshop is "Unexplained Early Crying"; that indicates that we do not know where it comes from or the conditions that bring it about. We need to look at crying as both an objective and a subjective phenomenon. Both types of measures that Ian St. James-Roberts talked about are very important. As Lewis Leavitt mentioned, the parents' sensitivity may play an important role, as well as their previous experience and developmental history. We need to explore all factors that differentially affect the perceptual set of the adult listener when we are helping parents deal with excessive or unexplained crying.

In my own research, I have looked at the effects of culture on perceptual set, gender and parenting experience. For example, parents with more than one child have big differences in perceptual set. The same cry can have very different effects in different environments, depending on the parents' perceptual set. From our studies on heart rate response in college students, we saw that even before people have children, they have experiences that create a perceptual set. When a child cries, one person may have a very different reaction from that of a person who has a different set of attitudes and beliefs. When parents hear crying, it is very different when they have been up, as Megan Gunnar suggests, night after night after night. They have a different perceptual set to that infant's cry.

* * * * *

Can the frequency of the cry play a role in perception? Yes. Does the infant bring something to it? Yes. Some of my work with Ronald Barr shows that cries of colicky babies in certain segments are higher in pitch, not in fundamental frequency.[1] Some higher-frequency harmonics have higher intensity, so that there is a subjectively higher-pitched sound. In this sense, the infant does bring something to the perception. It is interesting that Ian St. James-Roberts did not find acoustic differences in the cries of infants with and without colic.[2] What that might mean and how that can be resolved can be of interest.

It is not the phenomenon of crying in and of itself but the perception of that crying that may play an important role. A mother who had a crying child came to me with the child because she couldn't stand it anymore. It was interesting to see how she was holding the infant. The child flopped over her arm; at one point, the baby went "aah." The mother said, "See, see how he's crying all the time!" Another woman I was working with had a baby who seemed to cry all the time. I asked the mother if the crying bothered her. She said, "What, why?" So when we start talking about and understanding the phenomenon of unexplained crying and colic, we need to consider the concept of *goodness of fit* between the infant's characteristics and how parents perceive them. How many babies are there who have unexplained excessive crying and are not brought in? We would not know about them, because the baby was a "good fit" with the parent.

* * * * *

How much stimulation does it take an infant to start crying? It seems to be related to such issues as rhythmicity, latency, intensity and other measures. All these things are the foundations of descriptions of temperament. There is some relationship between temperament and reactivity to stimulation for crying. Exactly what that is is open for discussion. Importantly, these individual differences in behavior may arise from nonobvious experiences. Looking at heart rate spectra in infants, we found that subtle conditions and nonobvious experiences in the prenatal environment may "wire" the infant differently and that this results in different patterns of regulation. We also found that very subtle postnatal experiences, such as the formula used, result in different power spectra. The point is that, although we are talking about unexplained crying, we need to know what factors contribute to the "dysregularity" or "differences in reactivity." Of course, rhythmicity is basic to such processes as feeding, crying, sleeping, all those things that Ian St. James-Roberts and Dieter Wolke discussed several years ago.[3,4] They are all related, and this may be the reactivity of the infant that Nathan Fox discusses. The threshold for arousal may be related to the eventual phenotypic outcome called "unexplained crying," but we do not know yet what nonobvious experiences may be leading to that behavioral outcome.

St. James-Roberts: There seems to be evidence that babies who are not reactive are "dysregulated," so there is the concept of regulation and dysregulation, but also words like "reactive" or "threshold" or "sensitive." To what extent are these terms referring to similar or different things?

Fox: I think that we should attempt to operationalize these qualities in a very specific way. We do this with very specific sensory channels. I do not think it is appropriate to talk about "reactivity" of any individual infant across different sensory channels or in response to social versus nonsocial stimuli, but I think that we have to start somewhere. This problem has always existed in our field. We tend to provide definitions first and then search for the behavioral phenomena that meet those definitions. I am suggesting that we first start with the behavioral descriptions and be as specific as we can about them. Then, and only then, should we go back and create the labels that match those behavioral descriptions. Reactivity, threshold, latency and these other terms become very confusing, much like a list of the different ways in which excessive or unexplained fussiness or crying has been described.

* * * * *

Gunnar: We really are, in some sense, talking about a 2-by-2 table, or a space that has two questions: (1) whether you are reacting and (2) given the conditions, does it makes sense to react (or fail to react)? If someone is jabbing your heel with a lancet and you do not cry or show much reaction, this is probably of as much concern as reacting "too much." This issue is certainly important in my domain of looking at stress physiology. Both hyper- *and* hyporesponsiveness are reflections of problems associated with physical illness. We are focusing on unexplained crying, but of equal concern, I would think, is unexplained *lack* of crying.

* * * * *

Zeskind: This question is for Nathan Fox, since he triggered an interesting debate in terms of what occurs after 4 months. Were any of the children you studied previously identified as having been colicky babies?

Fox: No. Indeed, one of the criteria that we used for screening was whether the parent reported colic.

* * * * *

Wolke: One important point that has not been addressed is how crying problems actually differ from other problems in infancy, such as feeding and sleeping problems. What are the associations between feeding, excessive crying and sleeping problems?

* * * * *

Zeskind: When we talk about "unexplained" infant crying, we should be very careful. There may be things going on that could explain it and should be explored, such as whether the environment begins to wire the nervous system prenatally or whether there are subtle and nonobvious postnatal phenomena to which we are not yet attuned in the caregiving context.

References

1. Zeskind PS, Barr RG. Acoustic characteristics of naturally occurring cries of infants with "colic." *Child Development.* 1997;68(3):394-403.
2. St. James-Roberts I. What is distinct about infants' "colic" cries? *Archives of Disease in Childhood.* 1999;80:56-62.
3. St. James-Roberts I, Harris G, Messer D, eds. *Infant Crying, Feeding and Sleeping: Development, Problems and Treatment.* Hemel Hempstead, Hert: Harvester Wheatsheaf; 1993.
4. Wolke D. The treatment of problem crying behavior. In: St. James-Roberts I, Harris G, Messer D, eds. *Infant Crying, Feeding and Sleeping: Development, Problems and Treatments.* London, England: Harvester Wheatsheef; 1993.

New Evidence on Unexplained Early Infant Crying

Section 2:
Crying as a Developmental Phenomenon

Abstracts from Section 2: Crying as a Developmental Phenomenon

Infant Crying: An Evolutionary Perspective

Myron A. Hofer, MD

Studies of vocalization patterns in infant rats suggest several potential roles for this behavior, including modulating tracheal pressure as a mechanism for protection against cold. The communicative function of vocalizations likely evolved later, and multiple environmental and social signals mediate rat pup vocalization and maternal responses to such vocalizations. Considering the nature and origins of infant rat vocalization patterns from an evolutionary perspective may allow an appreciation of some of the mechanisms by which these behaviors developed and ultimately enhance our understanding of behaviors exhibited by human infants.

Development of Crying: The Origin and Change Problems

Brian Hopkins, PhD

Crying is a complex act that involves coordination of at least 3 systems: the respiratory system, responsible for the aerodynamic power required to produce sound; the laryngeal system, which acts to control the flow of air from the respiratory system; and the vocal tract, which controls and filters the resonance frequencies of the sounds generated by the larynx. In addition, facial movements and body position are integral parts of crying behavior. Analysis of these components of crying, both in the prenatal setting and after birth, may help elucidate key organizational principles that underlie appropriate development of the act of crying.

"Colic" is Something Infants Do, Rather than a Condition They "Have": A Developmental Approach to Crying Phenomena, Patterns, Pacification and (Patho)genesis

Ronald G. Barr, MDCM

While "colic" is frequently described as a distinct clinical syndrome, the behavioral patterns that correspond to early unexplained excessive crying may be more appropriately considered the upper end of a spectrum of individual differences in normally developing infants. Several lines of evidence suggest that individual differences in infants' abilities to regulate the crying state influence the expression of crying behaviors, such as prolonged bout length in infants with early excessive crying. It is likely that central opioid-dependent systems contribute to the regulation of crying in young infants, suggesting that intrinsic differences in central nervous system function influence this behavior.

Crying: Multiple Determinants of Perceived Meaning

James A. Green, PhD and Gwen E. Gustafson, PhD

Acoustic analysis alone does not provide complete information about crying; parental perceptions of infant distress are related to many more behavioral features than simply the sound of infants' cries. Nonvocal aspects of crying, including visual and tactile cues, clearly contribute to parents' and other adults' perceptions of the level of infant distress associated with crying. Increased understanding of the physiologic phenomena that mediate cry production suggests that infant crying represents an important component of the developing prelinguistic communication system between infant and parent.

Infant Crying:
An Evolutionary Perspective

Myron A. Hofer, MD

Introduction

Whenever we are faced with a condition that we must still refer to as "unexplained," despite years of research, it is time to reexamine our assumptions, to take a step back conceptually, in order to make a fresh start from first principles. It is in this spirit that I was asked to provide a paper for this conference and its proceedings, although I have not been studying the condition that is the topic of this text. Instead, I have been trying to learn more about the biological and psychological nature of the infant crying system itself. In order to do that I have been working with a simpler mammal, the laboratory rat, that provides a model system for discovering the basic principles of infant crying inherited from our early mammalian forebearers.

In taking an evolutionary perspective, we ask questions about the adaptive value of infant crying and its "ultimate causation," as well as about more proximate biological and psychological mechanisms. Taking this long view can help protect us from the unwitting assumptions that may be interfering with our ability to understand "unexplained infant crying" in humans and may provide new hypotheses and research methods with which to approach future research of this baffling condition.

Evolution of the Larynx

To consider the evolution of crying, it is first necessary to consider the evolution of the organ for crying, the larynx. Negus, the distinguished British anatomist and physiologist, published a monumental work in which he compared the larynxes of over 1500 different species, from primitive vertebrates to primates.[1] He concluded that the larynx evolved initially as a valve to protect the delicate membranes of early air-breathing fish; to ensure that food on its way to the esophagus, or other particulate matter entering the mouth, did not damage the membranes for gas exchange. As evolution progressed, air breathing became a more prominent and important physiologic function, and muscular development of the larynx began. Some muscles developed to keep the larynx open and promote airflow, while others worked to close it for protection. Later, cartilage developed to make the structure more rigid, to prevent airway collapse and further improve airflow. Thus, although we recognize the importance of the larynx in vocalization, it is important to keep in mind that it evolved initially as a valve to optimize airflow.

Furthermore, the anatomical structure of the larynx varies widely among modern mammals. Negus observed tremendous structural variation, ranging from a simple tube in the ox to an elaborate structure with delicate valve leaflets, actually vocal cords, in the lemur, a primitive primate with a limited vocal repertoire.[1] He also came to the interesting conclusion that, across species the degree of relative complexity of the larynx relates *not* to vocal capacity, but rather to the capacity for powerful and precise upper-arm movements. One functional example of this can be noted in humans: After each serve in tennis, there is often an audible grunt, or expulsion of air. During the serve, very precise upper-arm movements are required, causing the laryngeal valves to close in order to stabilize the thorax. When the serve is completed, the valves open and air is expelled.

Thus, while the larynx evolved originally to protect gas-exchange structures and later to decrease airway resistance, the vocal cords evolved as an adaptation within the larynx that improved limb function. There are likely to be other derivative functions of different aspects of laryngeal anatomy: For example, vocalization involves closing the larynx and using thoracic and abdominal muscles to force air through the vocal cords. This alters intrathoracic pressure, modulating central blood circulation and pulmonary gas exchange, which may play a role in the regulation of body temperature. As requirements for communication and the exchange of information became critical to more complex social species, functional adaptations associated with vocalization may have played a role in further shaping the evolution of the larynx: For example, a mother's need to infer accurately the state or condition of her infant may have facilitated the evolution of an association between crying and emotional states that underlies the "signal" function of crying.

The Connection Between Crying and Cold

Homeothermy, the maintenance of stable body temperature, was a critical capacity in the evolution of early mammals. Young offspring needed to stay in close proximity to the nest and to the mother to help maintain their body temperature. They also needed a means to signal their mothers to retrieve them from the cold if displaced from the nest. Infant crying appears to have evolved to play that role. Evolutionary adaptation of certain reptilian anatomical features in mammals resulted in the development of inner ear bones and an extra set of sensory hair cells, allowing the early mammals to hear much higher sounds than reptiles can hear. This allowed mammals to communicate with ultrasound, which their reptilian predators were unable to hear. This trait has been preserved in the ultrasonic frequency of many rodent vocalizations.

The evolution of infant crying may have had an earlier connection with the evolution of mechanisms for endogenous heat production in early mammals. In recent years, physiologists have established that hypothermia in small infant mammals results in cessations of heartbeat and respiration, leaving such animals essentially in a state of "suspended animation" from which they can recover readily due to their capacity to generate heat from specialized fat called brown adipose tissue (BAT). The high surface area:body mass ratio of infant rats allows rapid cooling in ice water and is used as a highly effective anesthetic in the laboratory. To our surprise, my colleague and I found that hypothermic infant rats vocalize in ultrasound while still comatose.[2] In our laboratory, we measure ultrasonic vocalizations (USVs) by infant rats using portable bat echolocation detectors that transduce ultrasound into the audible range. The mean USV rate of unresponsive hypothermic rat pups at about 20°C body temperature approximates that for normal rat pups who have just been separated from their mothers. Initially, there is no change in the USV rate of hypothermic rat pups when placed in contact with their mothers. As the pups warm beyond 25°C, however, they become responsive to sensory cues from her. This results in a decline and cessation of rat pup USV that is not seen when the gradually warming pups are alone. This "contact quieting" indicates that some level of consciousness has returned to the rat pups prior to full recovery.

Blumberg and Alberts[3] hypothesized that, in response to isolation in cool temperatures, the USV of normal infant rats serves to facilitate pulmonary oxygen transport to improve BAT oxygenation. Because of its very high mitochondria content, BAT acts as an internal heater. This tissue is innervated densely by sympathetic nerve fibers, it envelops all of the major blood vessels and, when activated, it has a very high oxygen requirement. Blumberg and Alberts noted that all vocalizations result in an increase in intrathoracic pressure as the larynx closes against the escaping breath. This phenomenon, known as "laryngeal braking," under some conditions enhances pulmonary oxygenation of the blood: For example, at birth the first cry is believed to increase alveolar water transport, ridding the lungs of amniotic fluid. Laryngeal braking, in the form of grunting, is known to play a role in ameliorating respiratory distress syndrome (RDS) in human infants, probably by preventing alveolar collapse.

To determine whether the USV production we had discovered in hypothermic rat pups was related functionally to oxygenation of BAT, and thus facilitated recovery from hypothermia, as predicted by the laryngeal braking hypothesis, Shair and I measured the temperature in intrascapular brown fat and at a control site in intact rat pups and in those who were unable to use laryngeal braking (eg, those with a denervated larynx or with a tracheostomy) who could not emit USV.[4] We observed that the core temperatures of intact rats rose faster than those of devocalized ones. However, there was no difference in the extent to which BAT generated heat in the vocal pups, as compared with the silent ones, such that USV-facilitated BAT oxygenation, if it took place at all, could not have been responsible for the more rapid warming. We also observed that approximately 20% of the devocalized animals ultimately did not recover, and at autopsy we found pulmonary edema. A human analogy may be found in mountaineers and skiers who fall into crevasses and are trapped for a time before being rescued. These hypothermic individuals often develop acute pulmonary edema during warming. Clinically, this is treated with positive end-expiratory pressure (PEEP) ventilation, which increases the alveolar pressure and reduces the development of lung edema. We observed that with each USV in the hypothermic rat pups, intrathoracic pressure increased significantly, producing a self-administered form of PEEP that would similarly minimize the development of pulmonary edema.[4] Our rat pups who could not vocalize, however, were unable to use this mechanism, and this might account for the high incidence of pulmonary edema and death in this group.

Thus, it would seem that hypothermic vocalization may have evolved to serve dual purposes. In addition to modulating tracheal pressure to prevent pulmonary edema, hypothermic USV could also serve a communicative function, stimulating the mother to leave the nest to look for the comatose, but vocalizing, pup and retrieve it to the nest. Indeed, in another trial, my colleagues and I found that rat mothers hearing these vocalizations left their nests and directed their searching behavior accurately toward the pups, even though hypothermic USVs are lower-pitched, longer in duration and have greater intervals between calls than do normal USVs.[5] We can infer from these findings that rat pup ultrasonic calls may have evolved first as the product of a physiological adaptation facilitating recovery from hypothermia, while their role in communication was likely to have evolved later, as a derivative function. The lesson here for unexplained infant crying in humans is that it may have evolved in a very different context, and served a long outdated function earlier in mammalian evolution.

From Communication to Emotion

In exploring the early communicative function of infant calls my colleagues and I found that infant rats provide a good animal model with which to study early attachment and the separation response, as well. Very young infant rats learn to identify their own mothers by smell. They vocalize readily in response to separation from the mother, a response that had been attributed simply to "cold" stress. But our research led us to another process: the separation-induced withdrawal of several specific sensorimotor regulators of USV that are intrinsic to the mother-pup interaction. First, we observed that moving a rat pup from the nest to a test chamber, where it was alone, resulted in a vigorous outburst of calling. But, if an anesthetized mother was in the test chamber, the pup immediately reduced, and then stopped, its calling.[6] This quieting appeared due simply to contact with the dam and is effective despite the novel environment. We then deconstructed the maternal contact experience into many individual stimuli in an attempt to identify the particular factors responsible for its regulating vocalizations so effectively. When we studied pup responses to various part surrogates for the mother, such as an anesthetized littermate, a flat piece of synthetic fur (with and without nest odor) or a clay model in the shape of a littermate (either warmed or unwarmed), we learned that the pup has multiple sensory functions that are involved in mediating maternal regulation of pup vocalization. This regulation is a central component of a complex homeostatic system that includes both the mother and the pup. In it there are at least 3 maternal regulators—thermal, tactile and olfactory stimuli. When these regulators were withdrawn, the pup vocalized, eliciting retrieval by the mother, thereby "completing the circle."[7]

The central brain pathways responsible for pup USVs can be analyzed similarly into their component neurotransmitter mechanisms. Interestingly, the profile of neurotransmitters involved in separation vocalization in infant rats is very similar to the neurotransmitter pattern shown to mediate human anxiety and presumably separation anxiety in children.[7,8] In this way the infant separation cry communicates information about the affective state of the infant. Evidence of this is as follows: Benzodiazepines, which are anxiolytics in humans, are powerful and selective inhibitors of rat pup vocalizations. In contrast, substances such as pentylenetetrazol or beta carbolines, which produce disintegrative anxiety in humans by acting on the gamma-aminobutyric acid (GABA) receptor complex, increase vocalizations drastically in infant rats. Oxytocin, which represents the "neurohormone of attachment," reduces pup calling rate. Opiate-like compounds within the brain play an important role in mediating infant contact quieting, while serotonin, adrenergic agonists and peptides, such as corticotropin-releasing factor (CRF) and substance P, are also involved in the regulation of both human affective states and rodent ultrasonic calls.

Evolutionary "Trade-offs" May Have Shaped Other Crying Responses

Recently, Brunelli and I discovered that if an isolated pup was allowed to interact briefly with a lactating female, the pup's subsequent vocalization rate upon reisolation, after removal of the dam, increased far beyond that observed when the pup was first isolated. This "maternal potentiation" effect is specific to interaction with the mother. Repeating the same experiment with littermates, instead of the dam, resulted in the same degree of quieting during contact, but USV rates returned to the pups' initial isolation level only after removal of the littermates. The potentiation effect implies that the pup is sensitive to its specific context immediately *prior* to separation and demonstrates that features of that context can regulate USV rates even after the context is no longer present. This response begins to resemble the complexity of human-infant crying responses, such as the sudden outcry typical of a toddler when his or her mother returns to the daycare center unexpectedly, and then departs again after a brief interaction.

A very different form of vocal response involves the suppression of isolation calling.[9] Unfamiliar adult male rats are predators of infant rats. Males from outside the colony can maximize their genetic transmission by killing young rat pups and mating with the mother. The odor of an unfamiliar adult male silences isolated infant rats, and the inhibition of USV continues for many minutes after pups are removed to another chamber far from the unfamiliar male.[10] In contrast, prepubescent unfamiliar males or familiar adult males do not elicit any inhibition of vocalization. This vocal response to a highly specific threat stimulus may represent an early fear state, as contrasted with the anxiety-like state elicited by the far less well-defined dangers inherent in the isolation situation. If so, the opposite direction of this effect on crying may be one of the clearest experimental distinctions yet observed between the closely related emotional states of fear and anxiety.

Both the inhibition of vocalization after removal of the unfamiliar adult male rat and the potentiation of isolation calling when the dam is removed are examples of vocalization patterns in response to prior contexts. In another study[11] my colleagues and I have investigated the time course of development of these context-sensitive effects. In the first 2 days after birth, the isolation calling and the contact quieting responses develop first. In contrast, the maternal potentiation and the male suppression effects develop later, after the first postnatal week, possibly related to maturation of the pups' ability to regulate the intensity of their responses according to the specific environmental contexts prior to the events.

How can we better understand the nature and origins of these vocal response patterns by thinking about them from an evolutionary perspective? If a rat pup has detected the odor of an unfamiliar male, it would be evolutionarily advantageous to inhibit all vocalizations to avoid detection by such a predator. The strength of the inhibition response would be regulated ideally by the proximity of the potential predator, and thus selection pressure may have favored evolution of the olfactory signal that we found to elicit the response. On the other hand, if a pup is parted suddenly from an active dam, it is highly likely that pup vocalizations will result in immediate retrieval of the pup. In this situation, the risk of attracting a predator is much less than the likelihood of eliciting maternal response. Therefore, maximal calling rates are relatively safe. In addition, my colleagues and I have found that vocalization rates following separation from an active mother are higher than if the dam is anesthetized.[12] One could hypothesize that an unresponsive mother is equivalent to a sleeping one and this context signals a lower likelihood of rapid maternal response relative to predator risk. It would seem that a less-than-maximal calling rate would be most adaptive in this situation, and that is precisely what occurs. If pups have been with littermates and the mother has been absent for more than 5 minutes, pup calling rates are even lower. This is consistent with a further reduced likelihood of maternal response relative to predator risk, but not yet the adverse risk-benefit ratio signaled by the odor of the predator itself.

A Genetic Approach: Evolution in the Laboratory

Infant-rat crying responses thus appear to be adaptively calibrated to the relative risk:benefit ratio signaled by the prior contexts in which they take place. My colleagues and I then wondered whether we could test these evolutionary ideas by asking if a selection process could indeed influence the characteristic USV rates of the infant isolation vocalization response over time in a population of rat pups. To explore this concept, we began a program of selective breeding of rat pups for high or low rates of crying in response to isolation, mimicking environments with either low or high numbers of predators, respectively. We began with a genetically heterogeneous strain from the National Institutes of Health that represents laboratory rats from all over the world. We selected the pups who had the highest USV rates in each litter and then bred them together as adults. After only 5 generations, there were marked differences in the characteristic crying rates from litters of these lines. Although we are just at the beginning of these studies, they could provide us with answers to some of the difficult questions this conference will be raising about the unexplained infant crying that occurs in a subgroup of human infants.

Summary and Perspective

I have approached infant crying as an evolving trait. From classic studies of the larynx, the organ of crying, we find that while it developed initially to regulate airflow, its structure in mammals became more complex as a mechanism to stabilize the thorax for upper arm movement, rather than to facilitate vocalization. Furthermore, we have learned about the role of vocalization in another derived function in which the laryngeal-thoracic act itself functions to maintain thoracic pressure and avoid pulmonary edema as rat pups warm after severe hypothermia. Crying as a communicative role appears to have been the most recent evolutionary step. Yet, even in a relatively simple mammal, such as the laboratory rat, crying is a highly regulated response that is controlled by many different environmental and social signals; cues that connect crying with the risks and benefits of this behavior in the environments within which mammals evolved. Recent research is beginning to elucidate the neurochemical pathways by which crying responses are transduced in the brain of the infant as well as to shed new light on the nature of the "emotional" states underlying crying.

Two other more complex forms of infant crying, maternal potentiation and inhibition by unfamiliar male scent, are described as adaptations within a set of opposing evolutionary selection pressures. The intensity of infant crying may thus be regulated by contextual cues representing the relative risk or benefit of the behavior at the time. A laboratory selective breeding study is the most recent focus of our attempts to understand how natural selection has shaped the evolution of this most interesting early behavior.

In this paper I have looked to illustrate how useful an evolutionary perspective can be in coming to an understanding of the development of infant crying and its regulation in an animal model system. In medicine, child development and psychology, in general, evolution is too often seen as irrelevant. Puzzling physiological responses or behaviors are simply viewed as "aberrant" or "pathologic," thus effectively removing them from any connection with evolutionary processes in the minds of researchers and clinicians. I believe that both medical and evolutionary approaches are useful: For example, fever is clearly an evolved response, having been shaped over eons by selective pressures at work in our coevolution with infectious agents. Yet fever can be excessive, and needs to be reduced in some instances. Evolutionary questions are being asked increasingly in psychiatry today: for example, about anxiety, depression and attention deficit-hyperactivity disorder. The responses to these issues are important because they can have clear implications for the healthcare professions in terms of the designation and management of many so-called disorders.

There are several reasons for applying an evolutionary perspective to unexplained infant crying: the convincing body of evidence for the robustness of infants with this condition; the absence of negative consequences later in development; and the similarity of its defining features in so many different countries and cultures. But before I go further in this direction, there are some reservations that must be kept in mind when attempting to account for traits on the basis of their possible adaptive role in evolution. First, traits need not be adaptive in order to evolve. New structures, physiology and behaviors may arise in other ways: They may be secondary consequences of selection for other traits; they may arise by random mutation and persist if there is no selective pressure against them; or they may be the products of self-organization in development.[13] Second, any adaptive function that we can propose for a trait at an earlier stage in evolution can only be a hypothesis until it is tested by specific predictions in new situations or actually observed over time in changing ecological conditions. Until that time they remain vulnerable to the label of a "just-so story." But, hypotheses are crucial for science, as long as we keep them in perspective.

How can we begin to consider the possible evolutionary origins of unexplained infant crying? First, we can ask whether its circadian timing and limited developmental window, from 4 weeks to 4 months, might indicate some unexpected physiological role within thermoregulatory, cardiac or respiratory system development, such as the link we found in our studies on rat pups. Second, we can look for novel regulators of the crying response that might have been lost in our evolution from our prehistoric ancestors. Here we should look for dynamic social contexts as well as simpler forms of sensorimotor, oral, gustatory, vestibular, olfactory, visual and thermal stimulation that may be human analogies to the regulators we found in our studies on rat pups. The timing, rhythm and patterning of stimulation would be important here, as well. Regulators of neural systems for crying behavior, such as those I have described, are powerful physiological control systems that go far beyond simple notions of "soothing." Third, from what we have learned about the neurochemical substrates of infant crying in animals, a pharmacologic approach to unexplained infant crying seems well worth investigating. It seems remarkable that we know so little about the pharmacologic substratum of unexplained infant crying in human infants. Any such intervention would be naturally time-limited to the 3- to 4-month period during which unexplained infant crying is confined. If fever is an analogous condition, perhaps there is an analogous "aspirin" for unexplained crying.

One of the most useful potential applications of evolutionary thinking stems from the role of infant crying as a communication within a social context. In her recent book, *Mother Nature: A History of Mothers, Infants, and Natural Selection*,[14] Sarah Hrdy describes the implication of current evolutionary theory for a better understanding of the unique features of the modern human mother. Two recent advances, kin selection and parent-offspring conflict theories, provide us with a new perspective on the current worldwide controversies over the "proper" role of the mother. The degree of maternal investment in newborn infants, Hrdy shows, has been closely related to the degree to which women have control over the expression of their reproductive potential during various historical periods and in differing cultures.[14] "Allomothering," caring for another's infant, is a common and powerful social resource in most societies because, in our evolutionary past, caring for infants with whom one shares genes tends to transmit those genes preferentially to the next generation. Closer to our topic, as Ronald Barr has suggested in his paper, a pre-historic baby that cried loudly and often would most likely have been the one that was picked up by others in the small band of closely related hunter-gatherers when the earthquake, warring tribe or famine struck. This would allow genes predisposing to loud babies, rather than silent ones, to survive into the next generation. As Hrdy states, the loudly crying infant is "a baby worth investing in."[14]

From the aforementioned, it is easy to see that evolutionary thinking can lead in several different directions. At this point it is not clearly evident which may be the most productive to follow. That is alright, because by now each person who has read this far is likely to have come to a different conclusion as to what aspect of the story might be useful to him or her. In time, the best of these directions will be selected by its end results, and we will all wonder why it took us so long to find the right answer.

References

1. Negus VE. *The Mechanism of the Larynx*. St Louis, Mo: CV Mosby Company; 1931.
2. Hofer MA, Shair HN. Ultrasonic vocalization by rat pups during recovery from deep hypothermia. *Developmental Psychobiology*. 1992;25:511-528.
3. Blumberg MS, Alberts JR. Ultrasonic vocalizations by rat pups in the cold: an acoustic by-product of laryngeal braking? *Behavioral Neuroscience*. 1990;104:808-817.
4. Hofer MA, Shair HN. Ultrasonic vocalization, laryngeal braking, and thermogenesis in rat pups: a reappraisal. *Behavioral Neuroscience*. 1993;107:354-362.
5. Brunelli SA, Shair HN, Hofer MA. Hypothermic vocalizations of rat pups (*Ratus norvegicus*) elicit and direct maternal search behavior. *Journal of Comparative Psychology*. 1994;108:298-303.
6. Hofer MA, Shair HN. Ultrasonic vocalization during social interaction and isolation in 2-week old rats. *Developmental Psychobiology*. 1978;11:495-504.
7. Hofer MA. Multiple regulators of ultrasonic vocalization in the infant rat. *Psychoneuroendocrinology*. 1996;21:203-217.

8. Brunelli SA, Hofer MA. Selective breeding for an infantile phenotype (isolation calling): a window on developmental processes. In Blass E, ed. *Handbook of Behavioral Neurobiology.* New York, NY: Plenum Press. In press.
9. Takahashi LK. Ontogeny of behavioral inhibition induced by unfamiliar adult male conspecifics in preweanling rats. *Physiology and Behavior.* 1992;52:493-498.
10. Shair HN, Masmela JR, Hofer MA. The influence of olfaction on potentiation and inhibition of ultrasonic vocalization of rat pups. *Physiology and Behavior.* 1999;65:769-772.
11. Hofer MA, Masmela JR, Brunelli SA, Shair HN. The ontogeny of maternal potentiation of the infant rats' isolation call. *Developmental Psychobiology.* 1998;33:189-201.
12. Hofer MA, Brunelli SA, Masmela J, Shair HN. Maternal interactions prior to separation potentiate isolation-induced calling in rat pups. *Behavioral Neuroscience.* 1996;110:1158-1167.
13. Kauffman SA. *The Origins of Order: Self-Organization and Selection in Evolution.* New York, NY: Oxford University Press; 1993.
14. Hrdy SB. *Mother Nature: A History of Mothers, Infants, and Natural Selection.* New York, NY: Pantheon Books; 1999.

Development of Crying: The Origin and Change Problems

Brian Hopkins, PhD

Introduction

Much research has been devoted to how the newborn controls voicing during crying, the diagnostic implications of variations in such voicing and the social significance of crying at various ages during early infancy. In contrast, there is a dearth of knowledge about how crying develops in normal infants, particularly with regard to qualitative changes. Even less is known about the developmental origins of crying in terms of its prerespiratory precursors that become established during prenatal life. The latter is referred to as the *origin problem* and the former as the *change problem*. Together, these comprise the major focus of this chapter.

The Origin and Change Problems

For the present purposes, the origin problem refers to events that predispose or prepare a developing organism to achieve a particular outcome (eg, being able to emit cry vocalizations). Each event is a necessary, but not sufficient, condition for the emergence of a new ability with a concomitant particular function. Thus, when that ability emerges the infant can perform functions that were not possible previously. One example is the ability of the human fetus to perform breathing movements by approximately 10 weeks of gestational age.[1] These movements, however, do not become functional in the sense of gas exchange in and out of the lungs until after birth, with the change from fetal to neonatal circulation. Antenatal breathing movements can then be seen as a necessary exercise that prepares the developing fetus to achieve the act of taking in and expelling air from the lungs as required by the transition to the extrauterine environment.

The change problem involves both description and explanation. The descriptive task is to answer one of the following questions—"How does change in a developing system occur?" or "What are the dynamics of change?"—by means of longitudinal studies, which are an infrequent feature of research about infant crying. Explaining the process by which crying develops requires teasing out the determinants of mechanisms of change—a task that can really be achieved only through experimental manipulations of theoretically justified **variables** in and around previously identified transitions in the development of crying. What must be explained is how transformations in the development of crying occur as a consequence of changes in the coordination of many different systems. What is missing is a requisite theory of crying that addresses such changes.

Crying is Not Just a Sound

Crying is not only a sound that has certain acoustic features, but is also a complex act, which, like speech, involves the coordination of at least 3 systems: the respiratory system (responsible for the aerodynamic power required to produce sound), the laryngeal system (acting to control the flow of air from the respiratory system) and the vocal tract (controlling and filtering the resonance frequencies of the sounds generated by the larynx). To complete the picture, these systems are coordinated with movements of the face and those of the articulators. Thus, the act of crying represents a very high-dimensional system with many degrees of freedom. The processes by which it reduces to a controllable, low-dimensional system with few degrees of freedom is far from being understood, but they must begin during prenatal development. At approximately 2 months to 3 months after birth, crying undergoes a major transformation (see "The Change Problem," as well as the following), such that it becomes distinctively different from the crying of the newborn.

This paper will attempt to provide some speculative answers to the following questions: What are the potential prenatal precursors that contribute to crying in the newborn? And, what is the nature of the transformation in crying that occurs a few months after birth? Before answering these questions, however, 3 sets of distinctions germane to the study of infant crying need to be considered briefly in order to set the scene: methodological distinctions, quantitative versus qualitative changes and distinctions relating to spontaneous versus elicited crying.

Infant Crying: Three General Considerations

Methodologic Differences

Much of our present knowledge about newborn cry production stems from acoustic analyses based on spectrography and high-speed digital computation, with insights into subsequent development based largely on parental diaries. While acoustic analyses detect microsegmental events, such as biphonations that cannot be identified readily by the unaided ear, and diaries provide an inexpensive means of obtaining quantitative measures of age-related changes in crying periods, neither can account for the nonvocal accompaniments of crying. The nonvocal components of crying, such as movements of the face and limbs, may, in fact, signal some of the most salient features of developmental change in crying.

Quantitative versus Qualitative Changes

This may be a potentially misleading distinction, as development can be described in terms of either quantitative or qualitative change depending on the temporal units used. Using global units of time (ie, months instead of weeks), development can appear to progress in a discontinuous fashion through a series of qualitatively different states or stages. With units of time that are spaced more closely, development seems to be a continuous and incremental process. The way in which development is described will also depend on the units of behavior considered. If we focus on only 1 unit, such as the relative amount of crying per 24 hours, then inevitably development will be depicted as consisting of continuous and quantitative changes. However, if multiple units of behavior are employed (eg, cry vocalizations, looking behavior and facial expression) and our interest is in how they become coordinated during development, our descriptive account will bear the imprint of qualitative change. Our challenge, then, is the more objective identification of the hallmarks that herald a transition to a new developmental state or mode of crying.

Spontaneous versus Elicited Crying

It has been claimed that spontaneous and elicited crying do not have unique acoustic properties, but rather reflect differences in the degree of discomfort experienced by the infant.[2,3] As such, it serves as another reminder that acoustic features alone cannot make unambiguous discriminations between different types of crying in normal infants.[4] Furthermore, both spontaneous and elicited crying display a marked degree of intraindividual variability during the first 6 months after birth.[5] While such within-subject variation probably characterizes crying in healthy infants, it once again suggests that acoustic parameters alone are not very revealing about developmental changes in "normal" crying.

The Origin Problem

Leonardo da Vinci (1452–1519) believed that the fetus could not vocalize and thus did not cry. Approximately 500 years later, this is still a widely held belief. Strictly speaking, this view is accurate, since amniotic fluid and the absence of air prevent inhalation and exhalation and thereby the production of sounds. The only reports of fetal cry sounds are in cases where the amniotic sac ruptures prematurely.[6] Referred to as *vagitus uterinus,* it occurs as a consequence of air entering the uterus, which, in turn, triggers breathing. More recently, an attempt to detect vocalizations from the intact, near-term fetus by means of digital sound processing combined with ultrasonography proved inconclusive.[7] However, given our knowledge of prenatal development in the human and other species, it is highly improbable that crying appears de novo in its entirety only after birth. It is more probable that some of the nonvocal accompaniments of crying are developed before birth. Subsequently, the transition to the extrauterine environment results in the establishment of the voicing component. What nonvocal behaviors develop prenatally and are part of the complex act of crying postnatally? Educated guesses have included breathing movements, movements of the tongue and possibly the larynx and movements of the mouth and other parts of the face, all of which are undoubtedly state-dependent for their expression in the near-term fetus.

Breathing Movements

Antenatal breathing movements, first described by Ahlfeld,[8] have been reported to undergo quantitative changes during the first half of pregnancy[9, 10] and in the last trimester.[11-13] On average, they have been noted to increase from 6% of recording time at 20 weeks to 30% after 30 weeks. In addition, the mean breath-to-breath interval displays a complex pattern of decreasing, increasing and then decreasing again at 36 weeks. At this age, there are distinct periods during which the movements are either regular or irregular, heralding the establishment of discrete behavioral states (see "Behavioral States"). Such changes indicate increasing central nervous system (CNS) control, with regulation of actions generated by the coordination of diaphragmatic, abdominal and intercostal muscles. These observations suggest that, together, coordinated muscle actions would function sufficiently to force air from the lungs into the vocal tract so as to make the vocal folds vibrate at some time after 20 weeks. Pediatricians know that the preterm infant of about 23 weeks' to 24 weeks' gestational age is capable of producing crying sounds[14-16] and associated facial movements, as well as a cry-specific posture,[17] confirming theoretic speculations. The cry-related synergies of the respiratory muscles still require further development after this age, as these sounds have a shorter duration and higher F_0 compared with those of full-term newborns.[18]

Jaw, Tongue and Swallowing Movements

Fetal breathing movements sometimes co-occur with jaw openings and swallowing during the first 20 weeks,[9] but it is not known if such co-occurrences develop systematically in the second half of pregnancy. Jaw openings (sometimes with tongue movements) and swallowing (together with sucking) appear, like breathing movements, during the first trimester.[1] Appearing initially as isolated events, jaw movements tend to occur repetitively by 20 weeks, with openings varying in duration from less than 1 second to 5 seconds.[9] Sucking and swallowing, resulting in the ingestion of amniotic fluid, involve not only tongue movements, but also displacements of the larynx. Thus, the movements that serve to modulate sounds after birth are established and subsequently exercised in a different functional context before birth. This proposition abides by the well-known principle of "preadaptation" in evolutionary biology.[19] According to this principle, a preadaptation is "…a previously existing structure, physiological process or behavior pattern which is already functional in another context and available as a stepping stone to the attainment of a new adaptation."[20] Developmentally, it means that a prenatal behavior can alter its function markedly as a consequence of a postnatal change in context, but without any major alterations in its underlying mechanisms.[21] Being germane to the origin problem, the principle allows us to formulate one way of establishing a pre- to postnatal continuity in the development of crying.

Facial Movements

Except for jaw openings, the developmental course of facial movements in the fetus is not well-documented. However, the facial musculature and its innervations are evident at 8 weeks[22] and complete by 18 weeks to 29 weeks of gestation.[23] In addition, all but one of the discrete facial actions seen in adults can be identified in preterm newborns during the last trimester.[24] Clearly, the development of facial expression must originate in prenatal life. But what about the expressive gestalt termed the "cry face"? Ultrasound recordings have been used to monitor facial expressions in the mid-third trimester fetus. Facial expressions resembling a "cry face" have been demonstrated.[25] Ongoing improvements in the resolution of detail of ultrasound images should enable ultrasonographic studies of facial movements earlier in gestation. Advances in capturing these and other fetal movements may also accrue from further developments in 3-dimensional dynamic ultrasonography. At present, it has a very narrow scanning width, which restricts its application to behavioral studies. Also necessary is a reliable and valid system for coding facial movements in the fetus as expressive gestalts used together with an appropriate classification of behavioral states.

Behavioral States

Four behavioral states have been classified in the human fetus that attain a stable organization only within the last month of a full-term pregnancy.[11] Behavioral states are categorized into active and inactive sleep and wake states on the basis of the presence or absence of body and eye movements and on 4 heart-rate patterns. Interestingly, this fetal classification does not include a crying state. However, ultrasound recordings of orofacial movements could provide a first step in identifying the prenatal homologue of the newborn crying state. Additional criteria could include hand movements (eg, the presence or absence of "fisting") and the patterning of fetal heart rate. Given the much lower incidence of wakefulness compared with sleep states in the near-term fetus,[11] crying would likely not appear as anything more than a fleeting state towards the end of pregnancy. Developmentally, however, evidence of cry acts before the last trimester should be expected, which, as they increase in duration, begin to assume state-like characteristics (eg, simultaneous changes in 2 or more criteria, as proposed by Nijhuis et al[11]).

The Change Problem

Described initially by Brazelton,[26] the so-called 6-week peak in crying is a quantitative change that has been replicated many times in the ensuing decades, mainly by means of data obtained from 24-hour diaries. Following this increase in duration, there is a gradual decrease in crying until approximately 4 months of age. Nevertheless, there are 2 qualifications to consider regarding the nature of this developmental trend. First, it does not refer to absolute durations of crying at any one age, but only to the fact that crying duration is distributed normally, assuming an "n-shaped" curve.[27] Second, what most infants emit vocally at the 6-week peak is fussing or fretting, rather than clear-cut crying.[28] According to Wolff,[29] fussing does not emerge until some time after 3 weeks of age, which may constitute the first major developmental transformation in the control and regulation of vocal output. To date, the emergence of fussing as a qualitative change and as a behavioral state distinct from crying remains a contentious issue.[30]

So, is there any other evidence that supports qualitative changes in the development of crying during early infancy? Two studies provide relevant insights. One study considers crying in the context of the sweeping changes that occur at 2 months to 3 months after birth,[31] while the other informs us about the nature of change after this age.[32] Together with Wolff,[29] these studies are rare examples of longitudinal trials looking at the development of both the vocal and nonvocal components of crying.

Hopkins and von Wulfften Palthe (1987)[31]

Every third week, from 3 weeks to 18 weeks, 14 infants were observed by means of audiovisual recordings in their homes while they were alone or during interactions with their mothers. In contrast with crying, fussing and cooing vocalizations were not present until 6 weeks of age. After 6 weeks, these vocalizations became intermingled in a state-like entity referred to as "interrupted fussing," which is defined as rapid alternations between fussing and cooing. Emitted only when infants were alone, this new form of vocal output was associated with at least 2 nonvocal behaviors: the eyes remained open and the hands manipulated each other mutually. Impressions not reported at the time for interrupted fussing included abrupt alternations between a "cry face" together with a fussing vocalization and smiling together with a cooing vocalization as well as movements of the head and eyes as if "searching" the immediate environment. Thus, at approximately 2 months to 3 months of age, there is a major transformation in crying that results from new coordinations between its component parts. The apparent sensitivity to differences in context during interrupted fussing has been found at approximately the same age in other studies of infant crying.[33, 34]

Gustafson and Green (1991)[32]

Auditory-based assessments were made in the homes of younger (n = 12) and older (n = 14) infants covering the age range of 3 months to just after 12 months. Four patterns of crying were identified; 3 patterns included nonvocal accompaniments in their definitions. One of these, the "elaborated" pattern, was observed at 6 months in a small proportion of infants; it was displayed by the majority of infants by the end of the first year. In this pattern, the onset of a cry bout co-occurred with looking at the mother, a gesture by the mother or both. This elaborated pattern revealed another qualitative change in crying subsequent to change at 2 months to 3 months. As elswhere with interrupted fussing, it was noted that elaborated crying was achieved through the temporal coordination of behaviors previously performed independently of each other. This interesting finding, based on auditory assessments, was subsequently replicated by these same investigators using audiovisual recordings.[35]

A Shared Problem and a Resolution

Neither study[31, 32] could identify objectively the nature of the respective changes involved. Such objectivity might be sought in "catastrophe theory," given its potential for detecting whether a developmental transition is linear or nonlinear, and if nonlinear whether it involves quantitative or qualitative change. Detection is possible through applying so-called "catastrophe flags" to the behavioral output of a system at its macrolevel of organization, at which level it is referred to as an "order parameter" or "collective variable." There are 8 flags for detecting the onset and offset of a transition.[36, 37] Three of these flags signal an upcoming transition (ie, critical fluctuations, divergence of linear response and critical slowing down), while the remaining 5 flags become apparent during the transition itself (ie, sudden jump, divergence, bimodality, inaccessibility and hysteresis). Four flags require experimental manipulation of a relevant control parameter for their detection (divergence of linear response, critical slowing down, divergence and hysteresis), while the remainder can be revealed in the spontaneous behavior of the system.

Using these catastrophe flags to detect developmental transitions and this sort of change requires a combination of longitudinal research to detect the timing of a transition by means of those flags associated with a system's spontaneous behavior and experimental studies around the age of a transition to detect the nature of the change. By itself, a sudden jump in an order parameter cannot reveal unequivocally whether the change is instantaneous or a continuous acceleration.[38] To make this distinction, the presence of other flags, such as critical fluctuations, bimodality, critical slowing down and divergence of linear response, is required. The strongest evidence for qualitative change is when the system not only demonstrates critical fluctuations, but, more importantly, when it reacts to a perturbation with divergence and hysteresis. In terms of infant crying, catastrophe flags might be used to test whether the appearance of interrupted fussing represents a transition to a qualitatively different stable state. As with any other behavior, the proper use of these flags depends on capturing an appropriate order parameter—by no means a trivial problem, as it must be a relational measure that is scaled continuously (eg, the relative phase between limb movements, as discussed in detail by Kelso[39]). A candidate order parameter for crying might include phase relationships between the respiratory movements of the diaphragm and intercostal muscles, as recorded by surface electromyography (EMG),[40] or the temporal relationships between brow and orofacial movements, assuming they can be measured in a continuous fashion.

The main function of a dynamic systems approach, such as catastrophe theory, is to expose the organizational principles, rather than the mechanisms, that underlie the temporal evolution of an order parameter by means of its analytic tools.[41] It should be completely neutral as to the domain-specific contents of an order parameter and as to the nature of the control parameter that induces a particular developmental change in infant crying. Control parameters responsible for change at the macrolevel may differ from one age to the next, residing in the neural control of the vocal tract at one age[42-44] and in the control of respiration, the articulators or perception at other ages.[45] They not only induce change, but act as constraints or rate-limiting factors on the attainment of a new developmental state.[46] It is the maintenance, breaking and remaking of such constraints that are responsible for stability when a system is not undergoing a transition, for instability during a transition, as well as for the emergence of a new state after a transition has been achieved that typify a developmental process. An important, but neglected, constraint on the development of crying is posture.

Posture and the Development of Crying

The Newborn

The supine crying newborn assumes an opisthotonic-like posture in which the arms are flexed and adducted and the trunk is rigid and partially extended, causing the head to become retroflexed.[29, 31] The turbulence and pitch in the spontaneous crying of the newborn could be due to this posture.[47] Greater variability in cry spectra and more rapid variations of pitch in preterm infants of 35 weeks' to 36 weeks' gestation, compared with full-term newborns, have been attributed to their poorer postural stabilization in the supine position.[48] From the gestational age of 35 weeks onward, the head is maintained primarily to the right side of the body in the supine position.[49] Allied with flexed and adducted arms, this position facilitates ipsilateral hand-mouth contact,[50] thereby enabling the self-regulation of crying. Observations that newborns terminate a crying bout with hand-mouth contact, but not with contacts to other parts of the face, support this interpretation.[51]

Beyond the Newborn Period

Little is known about the codevelopment of posture and crying after the newborn period. However, there are 2 major anatomic changes that occur at approximately 3 months of age that alter the infant's posture that promote an adult-like control of respiration during sound production. One is the achievement of vertical alignment between the head, neck and torso.[52] The other is a change in the relative orientation of the rib cage in relation to the spine. In the neonate, the rib cage is aligned perpendicularly with the spine. At approximately 3 months of age, the configuration changes so that the rib cage is directed downward and outward, with the angle between it and the spine similar to that seen in the adult.[53] With this change, the actions of the intercostal and abdominal muscles become coordinated so that a constant level of subglottal air pressure can be preserved. As a consequence, the infant acquires a "hold-back" mechanism, ensuring that nearly all cries can be produced during the expiratory phase of tidal breathing.[29, 54]

Both changes are associated with a reorganization of the inspiratory-expiratory cycle and with the emergence of new variations in voicing, such as cooing and interrupted fussing. In addition, they parallel changes in self-regulation of the duration of crying. Beyond the newborn period, at about 2 months of age, the ability to terminate a crying bout by means of hand-mouth contact disappears.[51] The loss of this ability co-occurs with a change in posture that results in the newborn's upper limb flexion giving way to increased arm extension. Consequently, the arms are further away from the face. When the infant is able to alternate the arms between extension and flexion at approximately 3 months of age, hand-mouth contact reestablishes itself as a means of ending a crying bout. These qualitative changes in motor control correspond with the n-shaped normal crying curve: The 6-week peak coincides with an inability to terminate crying by way of hand-mouth contact, and the subsequent decline in cry duration coincides with the reappearance of this functional synergy.

Discussion

The Origin Problem

To date, the prenatal origins of crying have been accorded little theoretical or empirical attention. While fraught with technical difficulties, ultrasound recordings of the prerespiratory components of crying during the third trimester of pregnancy can be compared with similar observations of spontaneous crying of healthy preterm infants of the same gestational age. In this way it should be possible to determine behavioral expressions in the fetus that are indicative of crying and observe whether they co-occur in a state-like constellation. Comparisons between fetuses and preterm infants of the same gestational age could also help resolve another issue; namely, if the additional extrauterine experience of preterm infants results in a crying peak before term age.[55]

The Change Problem

Qualitative changes in the development of crying and the constraint-breaking mechanisms that may explain such changes have similarly received little theoretical or empirical attention. Cry researchers need to account more fully for crying in terms of its nonvocal accompaniments and develop a more complete understanding of the temporal coordinations between vocal and nonvocal components. Whether the application of dynamical systems approaches, such as catastrophe theory, will be beneficial in these respects is still an open question, but some encouraging signs indicate that it should be a profitable step.[56, 57]

Posture has been identified as a potentially important constraint on the development of crying, at least when the infant is supine. At 2 months to 3 months of age, supine posture changes from being lateralized and body-referenced to becoming more symmetric and spatially oriented.[58] This change exerts profound influences on the patterning of limb movements during crying as well as on respiratory control of voicing, but these influences are not yet properly identified. Whether similar or different effects operate when the newborn or young infant is in a semiupright position requires further investigation. The finding that interrupted fussing was emitted only when the infant was supine and alone, but not when upright and faced with the mother, will likely encourage additional study.[31]

Crying Involves Not Only Action, But Also Perception

This chapter essentially represents an action-based account of infant crying. However, the development of crying must involve recursive links between auditory perception and laryngeal action. At least one study suggests that this sort of coupling between perception and action is already present at birth.[59] Using the technique of delayed auditory feedback (DAF) and eliciting crying by snapping a rubber band against the sole of the infants' feet, Cullen and colleagues found that a delay interval of 200 ms produced a noticeable disturbance, but one restricted to the expiratory duration of cries, which was reduced on average by 100 ms. This effect confirms the claim that DAF results only in short-lasting cessations of crying in young infants.[60] How this form of perception-action develops beyond the newborn period in humans is unknown.

Conclusions

These observations may have clinical relevance. Acoustic analyses of elicited pain cries continue to be utilized as a standardized method for early detection of CNS disturbances. However, spontaneous, rather than elicited, crying could be a more sensitive indicator of nervous system integrity. Experimental animal models involving asphyxiation support this hypothesis. These studies consistently demonstrate that while responses can still be elicited from animals who have terminal conditions, the quality, rather than the quantity, of their spontaneous movements is noticeably different from that of intact counterparts. This represents another compelling argument for a closer study of the nonvocal accompaniments of spontaneous infant crying.

Taken together, findings reviewed here suggest an approach toward understanding developmental transitions in crying of clinical groups of infants, and perhaps even fetuses. If, as argued, the crying of compromised infants lacks in some way the normal variability of expression, then their capacity to embark upon and complete a developmental transition to a new mode of crying may be limited severely. This impairment could be manifested by a marked delay or a different way to achieve the transition. In the worst-case scenario, the infant may never transition to the next developmental phase (eg, to the elaborated crying described by Gustafson and Green[32]). The clinical relevance of this recommendation will depend on detecting the timing and organizational features of developmental transitions in the crying of healthy infants. To achieve such a "gold standard" requires a strategy of research that is conspicuously different from the approaches we have used to study infant crying in the past.

References

1. de Vries JIP, Visser GHA, Prechtl HFR. The emergence of fetal behaviour. I. Qualitative aspects. *Early Human Development.* 1982;7:301-322.
2. Murray AD. Infant crying as an elicitor of parental behavior: an examination of two models. *Psychological Bulletin.* 1979;86:191-215.
3. Porter FL, Miller RH, Marshall RE. Neonatal pain cries: effect of circumcision on acoustic features and perceived urgency. *Child Development.* 1986;57:790-802.
4. Barr RG. The enigma of infant crying: the emergence of defining dimensions. *Early Development and Parenting.* 1995;4:225-232.
5. Fuller BF, Horii Y. Differences in fundamental frequency, jitter and shimmer among four types of infant vocalizations. *Journal of Communication Disorders.* 1987;19:111-117.
6. Blair RG. Vagitus uterinus: crying *in utero. Lancet.* 1965; 2(7423): 1164-1165.
7. Ischii T, Horiguchi S, Kato T, Waturi N, Hirose M, Hirota K. If the fetus can vocalize, how can we detect it? *Biology of the Neonate.* 1991;60:52-61.
8. Ahlfeld D. Uber bisher noch nicht beschriebene bewgungen des kindes. *Verhandlungen der Deutschen Gesellschaft für Gynäkologie.* 1988;2:203-210.
9. de Vries JIP, Visser GHA, Prechtl HFR. Fetal motility in the first half of pregnancy. In: Prechtl HFR, ed. *Continuity of Neural Functions from Prenatal to Postnatal Life.* Oxford, England: Blackwell Scientific Publications; 1984:46-64.
10. de Vries JIP, Visser GHA, Prechtl HFR. The emergence of fetal behaviour. II. Quantitative aspects. *Early Human Development.* 1985;12:99-120.
11. Nijhuis JG, Prechtl HFR, Martin CB Jr, Bots RSGM. Are there behavioural states in the human fetus? *Early Human Development.* 1982;6:177-195.
12. Patrick J, Campbell K, Carmichael L, Natale R, Richardson B. Patterns of human fetal breathing during the last 10 weeks of pregnancy. *Obstetrics and Gynecology.* 1980;56:24-30.
13. Trudinger BJ, Knight PC. Fetal age and patterns of human fetal breathing movements. *American Journal of Obstetrics and Gynecology.* 1980;137:724-728.
14. Carmichael L. The onset and early development of behavior. In: Mussen PH, ed. *Carmichael's Manual of Child Psychology.* New York, NY: John Wiley & Sons; 1970:447-564.

15. Gesell A, Amatruda CS. *The Embryology of Behavior.* New York, NY: Harper; 1945.
16. Peiper A. *Cerebral Function in Infancy and Childhood.* New York, NY: Consultants Bureau; 1963.
17. Humphrey T. Function of the nervous system during prenatal life. In: Stave U, ed. *Perinatal Physiology.* New York, NY: Plenum Press; 1970:651-683.
18. Michelsson K. Cry analyses of symptomless low birth weight neonates and of asphyxiated newborn infants. *Acta Paediatrica Scandinavica Supplement.* 1971;216:1-45.
19. Mayr E. *Evolution and the Diversity of Life: Selected Essays.* Cambridge, Mass: Belknap Press; 1976.
20. Wilson EO. *Sociobiology: The New Synthesis.* Cambridge, Mass: Belknap Press; 1975.
21. Hopkins B. The development of early non-verbal communication: an evaluation of its meaning. *Journal of Child Psychology and Psychiatry, and Applied Disciplines.* 1983;24:131-144.
22. Crelin ES. *Anatomy of the Newborn: An Atlas.* Philadelphia, Pa: Lea and Febiger; 1969.
23. Gasser RF. The development of the facial muscles in man. *American Journal of Anatomy.* 1967;120:357-375.
24. Oster H. Facial expression and affect development. In: Lewis M, Rosenblum LA, eds. *The Development of Affect.* New York, NY: Plenum Press; 1978:43-75.
25. Birnholz JC, Farrell EE. Ultrasound images of human fetal development. *American Scientist.* 1984;72:608-613.
26. Brazelton TB. Crying in infancy. *Pediatrics.* 1962;29:40-47.
27. Barr RG. The normal crying curve: what do we really know? *Developmental Medicine and Child Neurology.* 1990;32:356-362.
28. St. James-Roberts I, Conroy S, Wilsher K. Clinical, developmental and social aspects of infant crying and colic. *Early Development and Parenting.* 1995;4:177-189.
29. Wolff PH. The natural history of crying and other vocalizations in early infancy. In: Foss BM, ed. *Determinants of Infant Behavior.* Vol. 4. London, England: Methuen; 1969:81-109.
30. Barr RG. Introduction: crying in context. *Early Development and Parenting.* 1995;4:157-159.
31. Hopkins B, von Wulfften Palthe T. The development of the crying state during early infancy. *Developmental Psychobiology.* 1987;20:165-175.
32. Gustafson GE, Green JA. Developmental coordination of cry sounds with visual regard and gestures. *Infant Behavior and Development.* 1991;14:51-57.
33. Franco F. Differences in manner of phonation of infant cries: relationship to communicative context. *Language and Speech.* 1984;27(pt 1):59-78.
34. D'Odorico L, Franco F, Vidotto G. Temporal characteristics in infant cry and non-cry vocalizations. *Language and Speech.* 1985;28:29-45.
35. Green JA, Gustafson GE. Perspectives on an ecological approach to social communicative development in infancy. In: Dent-Read C, Zukow-Goldring P, eds. *Evolving Explanations of Development.* Washington, DC: American Psychological Association; 1997:515-546.
36. Gilmore R. *Catastrophe Theory for Scientists and Engineers.* New York, NY: John Wiley & Sons; 1981.
37. Hartelman PAI, Maas HLJ, Molenaar PCM. Detecting and modeling developmental transitions. *British Journal of Developmental Psychology.* 1998;16:97-122.
38. van der Maas HLJ, Hopkins B. Dynamical systems theory: so what's new? *British Journal of Developmental Psychology.* 1998;16:1-13.
39. Kelso JAS. *Dynamic Patterns: The Self-Organization of Brain and Behavior.* Cambridge, Mass: MIT Press; 1995.
40. Prechtl HFR, van Eykern LA, O'Brien MJ. Respiratory muscle EMG in newborns: a non-intrusive method. *Early Human Development.* 1977;1:265-283.

41. Hopkins B, Butterworth G. Dynamical system approaches to the development of action. In: Bremner JG, Slater A, Butterworth G, eds. *Infant Development: Recent Advances.* Hove, England: Psychology Press; 1997:75-100.
42. Golub HL, Corwin MJ. Infant cry: a clue to diagnosis. *Pediatrics.* 1982;69:197-201.
43. Golub HL, Corwin MJ. A physioacoustic model of the infant cry. In: Lester BM, Boukydis CF, eds. *Infant Crying: Theoretical and Research Perspectives.* New York, NY: Plenum Press; 1985:59-82.
44. Lester BM. A biosocial model of infant crying. In: Lipsitt L, ed. *Advances in Infant Behavior and Development.* Norwood, NJ: Ablex; 1984:167-212.
45. Hopkins B. Development of crying in normal infants: method, theory and some speculations. In: Barr RG, Hopkins B, Green J, eds. *Crying as a Sign, a Symptom, and a Signal.* London, England: MacKeith Press; 2000:176-209.
46. Soll DR. Timers in developing systems. *Science.* 1979;203:841-849.
47. Stark RE, Nathanson SN. Spontaneous cry in the newborn infant: sounds and facial gestures. In: Bosma JF, ed. *Fourth Symposium on Oral Sensation and Perception: Development in the Fetus and Infant.* Bethesda, Md: US Government Printing Press; 1974:323-347.
48. Tenold JL, Crowell DH, Jones RH, Daniel TH, McPherson DF, Popper AN. Cepstral and stationary analyses of full-term and premature infants' cries. *The Journal of the Acoustical Society of America.* 1974;56:975-980.
49. Hopkins B, Rönnqvist L. Human handedness: developmental and evolutionary perspectives. In: Simion F, Butterworth G, eds. *The Development of Sensory, Motor and Cognitive Capacities in Early Infancy:* From Perecption to Cognition. Hove, England: Psychology Press; 1998:189-233.
50. Hopkins B, Lems W, Janssen B, Butterworth G. Postural and motor asymmetries in newlyborns. *Human Neurobiology.* 1987;6:153-156.
51. Hopkins B, Janssen B, Kardaun O, van der Schoot T. Quieting during early infancy: evidence for a developmental change? *Early Human Development.* 1988;18:111-124.
52. Baken RJ. *Clinical Measurement of Speech and Voice.* Boston, Mass: Little, Brown; 1987.
53. Hixon TJ. Respiratory function in speech. In: Minifie F, Hixon TJ, Williams F, eds. *Normal Aspects of Hearing, Speech and Language.* Englewood Cliffs, NJ: Prentice-Hall; 1973:73-125.
54. Lieberman P. *On the Origins of Language: An Introduction to the Evolution of Speech.* New York, NY: Macmillan; 1975.
55. Barr RG, Chen S, Hopkins B, Westra T. Crying patterns in preterm infants. *Developmental Medicine and Child Neurology.* 1996;38:345-355.
56. Barr RG, Beek PJ, Calinoiu N. Challenges to nonlinear modelling of infant emotion regulation in real and developmental time. In: Savelsbergh GJP, van der Maas HJ, van Geert PLC, eds. *Non-linear Developmental Processes.* Amsterdam, The Netherlands: Royal Nethelands Academy of Arts and Sciences; 1999:15-37.
57. Wolff PH. *The Development of Behavioral States and the Expression of Emotions in Early Infancy: New Proposals for Investigation.* Chicago, Ill: University of Chicago Press; 1987.
58. Geerdink JJ, Hopkins B, Hoeksma JB. The development of head position preference in preterm infants beyond term age. *Developmental Psychobiology.* 1994;27:153-168.
59. Cullen JK Jr, Fargo N, Chase RA, Baker P. The development of auditory feedback monitoring. I. Delayed auditory feedback studies on infant cry. *Journal of Speech and Hearing Research.* 1968;11:85-93.
60. Menyuk P. *The Acquisition and Development of Language.* Englewood Cliffs, NJ: Prentice-Hall; 1971.

"Colic" is Something Infants Do, Rather than a Condition They "Have": A Developmental Approach to Crying Phenomena, Patterns, Pacification and (Patho)genesis

Ronald G. Barr, MDCM

Introduction

The phenomena that scientists and medical clinicians study are incredibly complex, with many degrees of freedom. With extensive study, we can delineate and understand, to some extent, the complexities of isolated physiological "subsystems," such as blood pressure or inflammation. By appreciating the complexities of these relatively straightforward systems, we can imagine how much more complex it is to understand the behavior of a whole organism. In the face of this complexity, the challenge is twofold: First, we need to find levels of descriptions of behavior that make a difference in understanding how the organism is organized; then, these descriptions should guide us towards potential mechanisms that underlie the behavior.

In our attempts to understand behavior, investigators have sometimes been classified as "splitters" or "lumpers" when it comes to finding an appropriate level of description. Temperament researchers debate whether there are 9 temperament dimensions, as Thomas, Chess and Birch have proposed,[1, 2] or 6, according to Bates, Rothbart and Derryberry.[3-5] In the field of crying research, an analogous tendency may be manifest in whether investigators consider descriptions of daily duration and patterns of crying or acoustic analyses of single cry bouts to be the most useful levels of analyses. Of course, all levels of description are important to some extent; they tell us different things. In this presentation I argue that a "midlevel" analysis of cry phenomena, which is neither extremely splitter nor extremely lumper, may provide insight into a developmental account of the early increased crying problems that are sometimes clinically known as "colic."

"Colic" as a Condition that Infants "Have"

In clinical practice and most pediatric textbooks, colic is usually described as a distinct clinical syndrome (ie, a collection of behavioral symptoms and signs) that implicates something wrong with, or abnormal in, the infant. The symptoms and signs are usually focused on 3 dimensions,[6] as listed in Table 1.

Table 1. Defining Dimensions of "Colic Syndrome"[6]

- Age-dependent and diurnal characteristics
  - Crying increases at 2 weeks of age, peaks during second month and declines to baseline by approximately the fourth month of life
  - Crying clusters in late afternoon and evening
- Behavioral characteristics
  - Prolonged crying bouts
  - Resistance to soothing
- Paroxysmal nature of crying bouts
  - Crying bouts seem to be spontaneous
  - Unrelated to environmental events
  - Starts and stops suddenly

The first dimension is that the colic syndrome has characteristic age-dependent and diurnal features. Typically, crying begins to increase at about 2 weeks of age, reaches a peak sometime in the second month and declines to baseline by the fourth month. Within the day, crying tends to cluster during the late afternoon and evening. In fact, the peak is primarily (though not solely) due to crying that clusters in the late afternoon and evening.

The second is that the syndrome is typified by a number of behavioral characteristics. The most common are that some of the crying bouts are prolonged and are resistant to soothing, including by feeding. Others are present, but are more variable, including a pain facies, flexing of the legs over the abdomen and arching of the back.

The third is that these bouts are often considered "paroxysmal." This term means different things to different people, but includes the feelings that crying bouts appear to be spontaneous, unrelated to other events in the environment and sometimes seem to start and stop suddenly, without warning.

Despite considerable study, the etiology (or etiologies) of the colic syndrome remain(s) unclear. Current estimates by various authors suggest that something less than 5%, or up to 10%, depending on the setting, are likely to be associated with organic diseases.[6-8]

Colic as a Developmental Phenomenon

In recent years, several studies have contributed to a shift in thinking about what colic syndrome represents. Rather than being a distinct clinical entity separate from the crying of normal infants, the behavioral features are thought to represent manifestations of crying typical of normally developing infants. Further, differences in the amounts or intensity of these features reflect individual differences characteristic of this period in development. We have tried to capture this shift in thinking by using the phrase incorporated in the title of this paper; namely, that *colic is something normal infants* **do**, *rather than a condition they* **have**. Many lines of evidence have contributed to this shift in thinking. One is the relative absence of organic diseases accounting for the syndrome, which has been well-reviewed elsewhere,[6,7,9,10] and will not be repeated here. Herein I will focus on 2 of the defining dimensions of the syndrome and review evidence that they may represent developmentally appropriate behaviors in normally developing infants.

The first concerns the so-called "peak" pattern—or better, the "crying curve"—characteristic of the first 3 months of life. Far from being specific to infants with colic, this crying pattern may be characteristic of virtually all infants in the first few months of life. Interestingly, Wessel and colleagues made this very point in their original 1954 article from which the widely used "rule of threes" definition of colic was derived.[11] They wrote that "the time distribution and frequency of diurnal regularity are similar for the mild fussy periods of the 'contented babies,' and for the more prolonged periods of the 'fussy infants.'"[11] Since then, several studies in nonclinical, nonreferred, Western caregiving settings have confirmed that this crying pattern is typical of normally developing infants. In 1962, Brazelton plotted cry patterns derived from parental diary recordings that clearly showed the early peak pattern.[12] Subsequently, a very similar pattern was demonstrated in a diary study of infant behavior in Montreal (Fig 1).[13] Those who have reviewed this literature carefully will note that not all samples in all studies have shown all of the elements of the "crying curve." However, most investigations have shown some elements of it, and many of the discrepancies can be explained on the basis of methodological differences between the studies.

Indeed, the robustness of this pattern has led cry researchers to consider the possibility that this pattern of crying may represent a behavioral universal of human infant development; that is, that human infants share a propensity for increased crying that is characteristic of all groups of infants in the human species, if not of all infants.[14] The following 5 lines of evidence support this possibility:

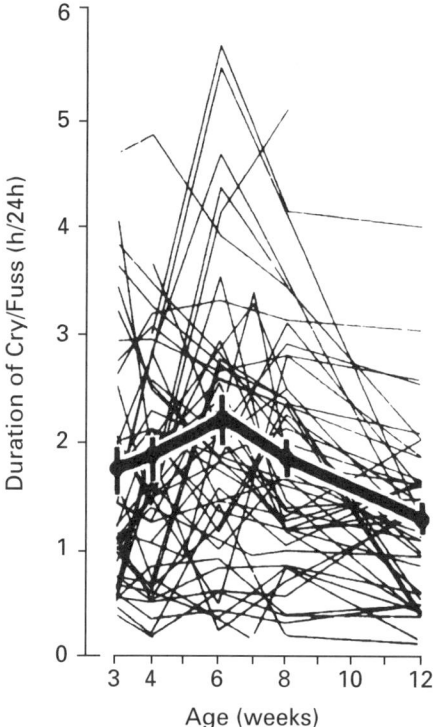

Fig 1. Total daily cry/fuss duration from week 3 to week 12 of 50 infants, with superimposed mean and SEM values for the whole group.

Reprinted with permission from Barr RG. *Developmental Medicine and Child Neurology.* 1990;32:356-362.

- First, this pattern has been documented in most samples of infants raised in Western caregiving settings, as mentioned previously.
- Second, similar crying patterns have been observed in cultures in which caregiving is radically different from that in the Western model.
- Third, this curve is observed in otherwise well infants born prematurely.
- Fourth, investigators have noted the concordance of this crying pattern with a wide variety of disparate behavioral and biological functions in normally developing humans.
- Fifth, similar curves of crying (sometimes referred to as "distress separation") may be preserved across several mammalian species.

With regard to the second line of evidence, the cross-cultural evidence is thinner than the evidence from within Western cultures, and sometimes it is more difficult to evaluate. My colleagues and I have reported behavioral observations in the !Kung San hunter-gatherers.[15, 16] !Kung San caregiving is usually characterized by close physical and temporal proximity of mothers and their infants. This style of caregiving has been described as "indulgent." Some of the more important aspects of !Kung San caregiving can be summarized in 5 caregiving dimensions, as shown in Table 2. Both skin-to-skin contact and carrying occur constantly, due to the sling (or "kaross") that is used to keep the infant with its mother. Feeding is described as "continuous," since it is characterized by frequent (approximately 4 times an hour), short (1 minute to 2 minutes each) and prolonged (2 to 3 years) breastfeeding. The infants are usually kept upright in the sling, rather than lying down. Finally, caregivers respond within 10 seconds to over 90% of infant signals. On the basis of what we know from laboratory-based studies,[16] these caregiving dimensions

Table 2. Dimensions of !Kung San Caregiving

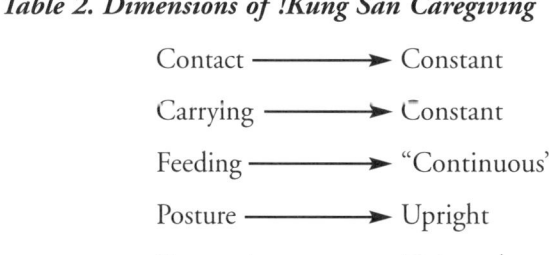

should be calming. Despite this, the crying curve is clearly present in the !Kung San infants, as well.

Cross-cultural replications of a behavioral pattern could be considered a natural experiment whereby we exploit differences in caregiving to show that the pattern is not dependent on differences in caregiving. Another type of natural experiment is the behavior of relatively well preterm infants, since they have additional extrauterine experience. We described the crying pattern of premature Dutch infants.[17] In these infants, too, the crying peaked at 6 weeks' corrected age; that is, an average of 14 weeks after they were born (at 32 weeks' gestation; Fig 2). Furthermore, as in the previous samples, this peak pattern was due primarily to evening, rather than to daytime or nighttime, crying. Malone reported similar findings in Irish infants.[18]

Fig 2. Duration of crying behavior in preterm infants as a function of age (geometric mean ±1 SEM). Numbers in brackets indicate the number of infants contributing to the mean at each age.[17]

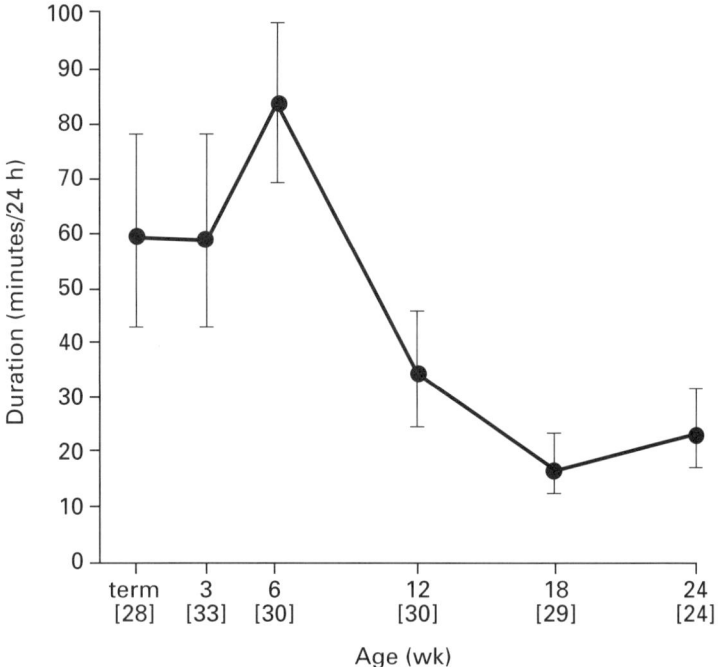

Reprinted with permission from Barr RG, et al. *Developmental Medicine and Child Neurology.* 1996;38: 345-355.

Such "n-shaped" curves are not restricted to crying behavior, but rather are found for a remarkably diverse set of behavioral and biological functions in normally developing newborns. This suggests that this pattern reflects a central and quite important period of developmental reorganization not limited to crying, and certainly not to "abnormal" crying. Numerous examples have been identified: I shall refer to 2 of these. One is the quantity of incomplete lactose absorption that can be tracked by repeated breath samples analyzed for hydrogen gas (Fig 3).[19] The reason that breath samples semiquantitatively index incomplete lactose absorption is that, after lactose passes through the small intestine (where most of it is absorbed), it is used as a substrate for the metabolic processes of resident bacteria in the colon, and hydrogen gas is a by-product of this bacterial metabolism. Hydrogen gas diffuses into the bloodstream and is excreted in a single pass into the breath of infants. In a longitudinal study, my colleagues and I[19] (and others[20]) have demonstrated that this incomplete lactose absorption (represented by hydrogen gas) tends to increase to the second month of life, and then decrease, in a curve very reminiscent of the crying curve. Another example is infant habituation to visual stimuli. Hood and colleagues,[21] as well as Slater and colleagues[22] and Bornstein, Brown and Slater,[23] showed that there is a distinct "n-shaped" curve in different indices of habituation in response to repeated presentations of a visual stimulus. In sum, the typical pattern of crying is neither peculiar nor specific to either colic or to crying behavior, but rather to a remarkably general pattern for several behavioral and biological functions in infants.

The fifth, and admittedly more speculative, line of evidence concerns the question of whether such crying curves are conserved as a reflection of normal development across species. Arguing for similarities across species is fraught with difficulties, not the least of which is the assumption that similarities in crying patterns might represent a behavioral *homology* (ie, a shared genetic relatedness, such as human arms and bat wings) or a behavioral *analogy* (ie, a shared function, but without shared genetic relatedness, such as the wings of birds and bees). However, as Panksepp[24] has argued, pervasive homologies at neuroanatomical and neurochemical process levels have been impressive. Further, they are more likely in regard to basic emotions (as compared, for example, with cognition), especially with regard to general operational principles. Arguably, this is truer in very young infants, prior to the appearance of more clearly cognitive functions that are more dependent on higher cortical functions.

Fig 3. Pattern of breath hydrogen excretion related to month of sampling for 4-hour average, peak and prefeeding measures. Means and standard deviations are shown after antilog conversion from log-transformed hydrogen values.[19]

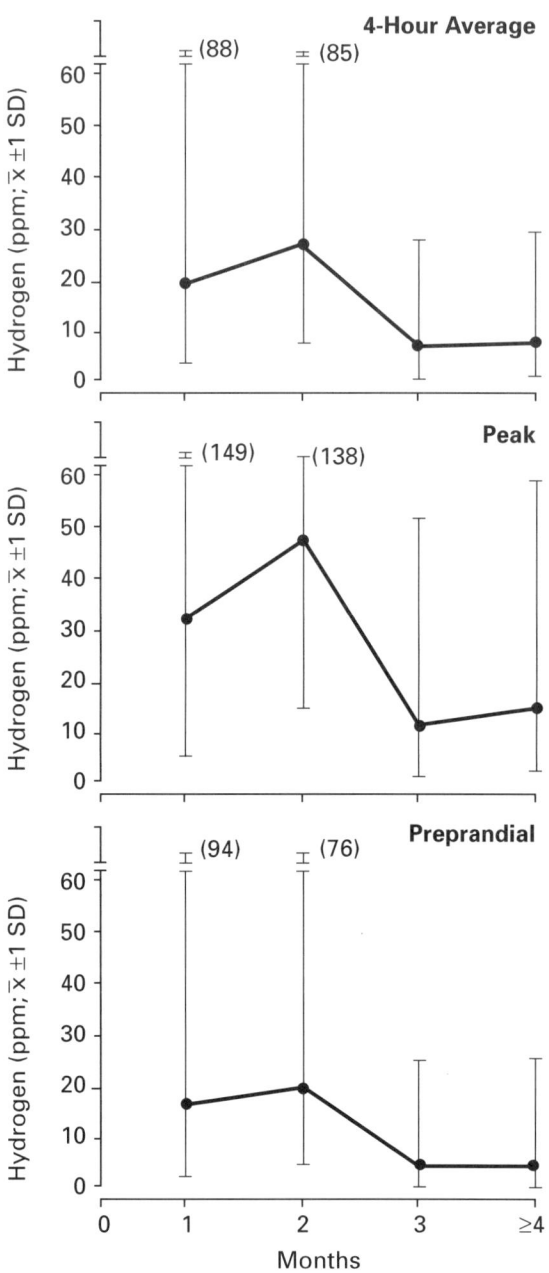

Reproduced with permission from Barr RG, et al. *The Journal of Pediatrics.* 1984;104:527-533.

One example comes from an early study in guinea pigs. Pettijohn reported a curve of separation distress calls as a function of age.[25] Calls were also different as a function of the presence of the mother (perhaps analogous to an "indulgent" !Kung San setting?) in a familiar or an unfamiliar place, or separation from the mother (perhaps analogous to a "separation" Western setting?) in a familiar or unfamiliar place. In the presence of the mother there was little or no distress, but in the absence of the mother there was a distinct, age-related crying curve, and crying was greater in an unfamiliar place. Another example comes from studies of "separation distress" in laboratory rats, as Hofer has described in this text. Interestingly, in papers on the ontogeny of infant rat isolation calls,[26, 27] Hofer and colleagues have described a "curve" over the first 23 days of life, composed, in part, of a curve with an early peak at 7 days for "isolation distress" calls and, in part, of a "maternal potentiation" call starting at 7 days to 9 days, peaking at 11 days and disappearing by 23 days. Finally, in a recent set of observations from captive infant chimpanzees observed with their mothers, Bard described rates of soothing responses stimulated by infant cries as a function of month of age that described a curve very analogous to that observed in humans.[28]

In sum, early crying curves are fairly robust phenomena in Western caregiving contexts, cross-cultural contexts, preterms with additional extrauterine experience and in other species. While much remains to be learned, these similarities may lead to insights into both the function and mechanisms of what is a remarkably widespread phenomenon in mammalian species. *At the very least, this pattern of crying is far from specific to human infants, particularly those with colic in whom something is thought to be wrong or abnormal. The typical pattern of crying is much more likely to reflect more basic aspects of normal growth and development.*

One Level of "Splitting": The Bout Length versus Frequency Dissociation

To this point, crying (or distress vocalizations in nonhuman species) has been described only at a fairly broad level of description—in terms of total daily duration or overall rates of crying. However, some observations (in humans, at least) suggest that additional insight may be possible by recognizing a distinction within this level of description; specifically, the distinction between bout length and frequency of crying. Interestingly, this dissociation has come up in at least 4 of our studies, despite the fact that we have been using relatively molar measures, such as diaries and behavioral observations in the field.[13, 15, 29, 30] The dissociation of these 2 aspects of crying may provide an important clue to our understanding of the development of early increased crying in normal infants—*and* in infants with colic.

In the study of the !Kung San mentioned previously,[15] the radically different caregiving did not abolish the early crying curve. However, crying was affected in other ways. The frequency of cry/fret events was very similar across ages and no different from that seen in similarly collected observational data sets in Dutch and American samples. However, the overall duration of cry/fret events was reduced by about 50%.[15] This observation implies that a frequency/bout length dissociation may be meaningful and that the determinants of each may be different. More specifically, caregiving context may be important for some aspects of crying, such as bout duration, but less so for others, like pattern and frequency.

Similar patterns of dissociation have been observed in other work. The study done by Hunziker and me in 1986 was designed to assess the effects of carrying/holding on infant crying.[13] In this randomized controlled trial, half of the mothers were asked to increase the amount of carrying and holding of their infants (to a minimum of 3 hours per day) starting in the child's fourth week of age. This increase clearly had an effect on "lumped" total daily duration of crying and fussing in this study, reducing daily duration by 43% during the sixth week, the time of peak crying. However, the increased carrying had no effect on the frequency of cry/fuss bouts at any time during the study. Consequently, the effect of increased carrying was to reduce bout length, rather than frequency of cry bouts. These results converge with the !Kung San findings,[15] implying that bout length and frequency are dissociable, and that the determinants of each may not be the same.

Both of these studies[13, 15] were performed in nonselected samples, so only a fraction of the infants in each group would have met traditional criteria for "colic." Consequently, it was of some interest to see whether this distinction might be relevant to the behavioral phenomenology of colic, especially in light of the second standard textbook criterion of colic; namely, the prolonged and unsoothable crying bouts that are traditionally thought to define the syndrome. In a 1992 study of the characteristics of crying that make it a problem for parents,[29] my colleagues and I compared the diary-recorded crying and fussing of 3 groups of infants. We included infants whose parents complained to their pediatricians about crying *and* met Wessel's criteria for colic,[11] infants whose parents complained but did *not* meet Wessel's criteria for colic and infants whose parents did not complain about crying problems. As expected, indeed, by definition, the daily duration of crying was significantly greater in infants meeting Wessel's criteria than in either of the other 2 groups.[29] Interestingly, however, there was no difference among the groups in the frequency of cry/fuss bouts; rather, the differences in bout length of crying and fussing were responsible for the variation in overall cry duration. We had a chance to look at this again in a recent study comparing diary-recorded crying, fussing and unsoothable crying in infants with and without colic at 6 weeks of age and at 4 months of age.[30] In this study, infants *with* colic had more frequent bouts of distress (fussing, crying or unsoothable crying) than did infants *without* colic both at 6 weeks of age and at 4 months of age, a result that was different from the 1992 study. However, infants with colic had longer bout lengths only at 6 weeks, but this difference in duration of bouts had disappeared completely by 4 months of age.

The results of these studies[29,30] converge with those of the first two[13,15] in showing that the frequency/bout length dissociation is viable and that this level of "splitting" will be very important to our understanding of the phenomena of early increased crying behavior. Furthermore, these studies show that this dissociation may be particularly important, even critical, in understanding the individual differences that contribute to the behavioral syndrome of colic. We propose that, in order to understand individual differences in early increases in crying, the focus might be better placed on the regulation of crying once it has started, rather than on what causes the infant to cry. This implies that empirical paradigms that provide us with the opportunity to know how infants regulate their crying, once started (the "pacification" of the title of this presentation), should be a productive avenue for understanding the mechanisms of early increased crying, in general, and for the clinical syndrome of colic, in particular. In the upcoming section, I address one possible such mechanism.

What *Pacification* by Sucrose Taste Can Tell Us About the (Patho)genesis of Early Increased Crying

Blass and colleagues, extrapolating from work on separation distress vocalizations in infant rats, were the first to introduce the phenomenon of the "sucrose response" into human developmental psychobiology.[31-33] This is a robust, striking phenomenon that has been reproduced in several laboratories, including our own.[34-36] In our paradigm, 2- to 3-day-old infants were watched prior to a feed until they cried continuously for 15 seconds, at which point 2, 250-μL drops of 24% sucrose solution were administered to each infant's tongue. The behavioral responses consisted of 2 distinct components: First, within 10 seconds, the infants virtually stopped crying and their facial muscles relaxed, and this calming persisted for 2 minutes to more than 5 minutes (Fig 4)[34]; and, mouthing rapidly increased, and then began to decline and disappear by the second or third minute.

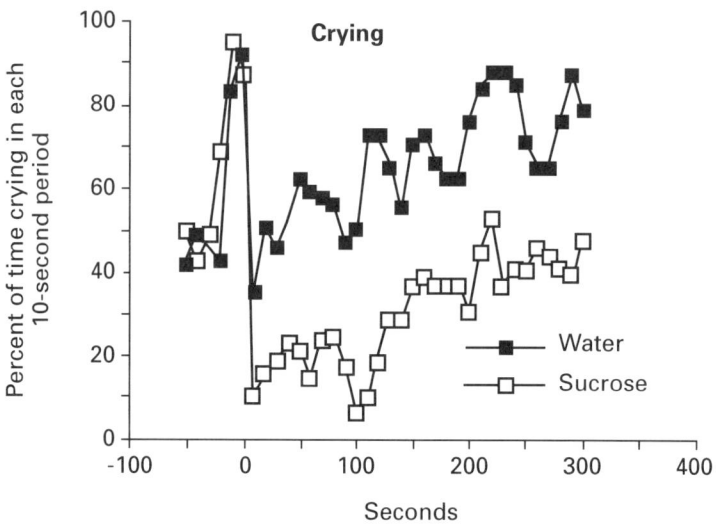

Fig 4. Responses to sucrose and water tastes in newborn infants before a feed. Percentage of time spent crying in 10-second time periods before and after intraoral delivery of 250 μL of water (closed squares) or 24% sucrose solution (open squares). Liquid was delivered at time 0.[34]

Reprinted with permission from Barr RG, et al. *Developmental Medicine and Child Neurology.* 1994;36: 608-618.

This response is intriguing for several reasons.[37, 38] First, this sucrose calming effect, or "orogustatory" effect, is different functionally from that seen with pacifiers, known as "orotactile calming." Sucrose calming persists after the stimulus has stopped; pacifier calming does not. Crying returns soon after the pacifier stimulus is removed. This suggests that there are 2 functionally separable calming systems. Also, work in infant rats (and many other species) suggests that the "orogustatory" effect is dependent on a functionally intact central opioid system, whereas other forms of tactile calming are not. And, in at least 2 studies in human infants (one of infants of methadone-dependent mothers; the other in stressed postmature infants; both of whom should have compromised opioid systems), the sucrose response was absent or attenuated, while the pacifier response was intact. These findings imply that the sucrose taste calming response activates one of 2 separable calming systems, each dependent on different central pathways.

Using other tastants, my colleagues and I demonstrated that the property of sucrose that mediates this change is the sweetness or, possibly, the positive hedonic value of the tastant, not the fact that it is a carbohydrate.[35, 36] In addition, by comparing the responses to several tastants, as well as pacifiers, we proposed that this response is likely to be composed of 2 components: First, there is an early "stimulus-bound" phase that occurs while the stimulus is present in the mouth. This phase can be defined operationally by the presence of mouthing, and is neutral as to whether the stimulus is taste or contact and whether it has positive, negative or neutral hedonic value. Next, there is a "poststimulus" phase, which persists after the stimulus and occurs postmouthing. This "poststimulus" phase is dependent on a taste that has positive hedonic value. Therefore, the originally observed sucrose-versus-water difference (Fig 4[34]) was probably composed of a combination of these 2 responses. We have proposed that it is this latter phase (after the first minute) that requires a functioning central opioid dependent system.[37]

To investigate whether the taste response may be able to be used as a "biobehavioral probe" for candidate control systems related to the early crying curve and colic, we performed 2 additional studies.[34, 39] In the first study, 6-week-old infants were studied with the same paradigm.[34] If this response was related to the crying curve, then the dramatic calming effect seen in newborns might be weaker in 6-week olds. Indeed, we saw that while a sucrose/water difference was still detectable, it is much less strong and apparently limited to the first 1 minute or 2 minutes. It is important to appreciate that there are many possible reasons for this reduced response, in addition to the implied developmental interpretation that this system is less available for activation during the peak of the crying curve.

In the other study,[39] we compared the response to a sucrose challenge of 6-week-old crying infants who met a "modified" Wessel's definition of colic with those that did not meet Wessel's definition. In this study, the sucrose taste stimulus was increased to 3 doses of 50% sucrose solution, given 30 seconds apart, versus equal volumes of water. There was no difference in response to water. However, in response to sucrose, infants without colic showed an early reduction in crying and a late-phase reduction, as well. Infants with colic showed an equivalent early-phase response, but a much reduced (or absent) late-phase response (Fig 5). Both showed an increased,

Fig 5. Percent of time crying after given water (solid symbols) and sucrose (open symbols) in infants with (circles) and without (squares) colic before taste administration (period 0) and in each minute after stimulus administration (periods 1 through 4) when tastes are administered to crying infants before a feeding.[39]

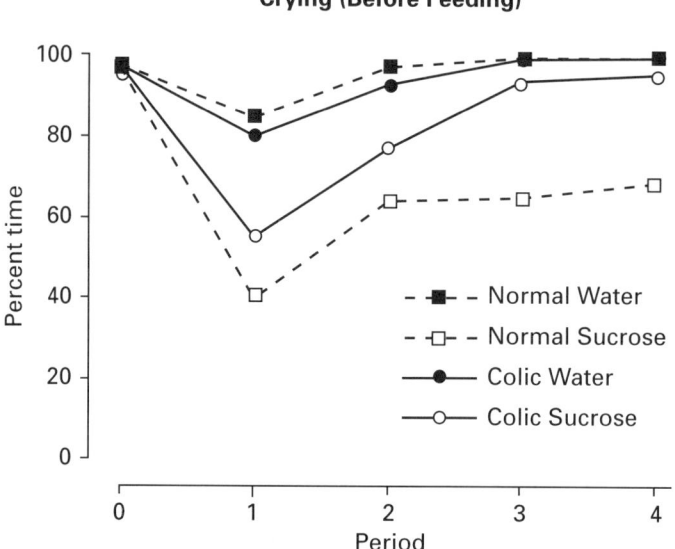

Reproduced with permission from Pediatrics Online, Vol. 103, No. 5, Figure1, Copyright 1999.

brief and equivalent mouthing response, implying that the differences in crying response were not due to the sucrose being more salient in one of the 2 groups.

These intriguing findings may provide insight into central control systems that are important in regulating the bout length and, consequently, the unsoothability of early infant crying. This paradigm specifically addresses the regulation of crying, since it is designed to put the infants in a similar crying state at the time that the taste is provided. Furthermore, these findings address central nervous system (CNS) processes, not gastrointestinal (GI) processes. Also, at least in this paradigm, the differences appear to be limited to "late-phase" responses. This may indicate that this particular soothing system, possibly dependent on central opioid-dependent mechanisms, has special value for understanding how infants with colic differ from those who do not have colic. Finally, our observations suggest that it is not that some infants respond and others do not, but rather that there are more effective responses in some than in others. In short, we believe that the sucrose response is tapping developmentally appropriate individual differences in response to sucrose taste.

Summary

Taken together, the findings presented here suggest the following tentative conclusions with regard to the phenomenology of early, unexplained increased crying:

- The symptoms and signs that typically define the behavioral syndrome of "colic" are more appropriately considered the upper end of a spectrum of individual differences in normally developing infants. This interpretation may represent an important shift in our understanding of this challenging clinical problem.

- It may be useful to make the distinction between frequency and bout length when considering crying phenomenology. This approach provides unique insights into the early increase in crying that are not apparent when only overall quantitative measures, such as total daily distress, are used.

- The prominence of bout length in early increased crying and colic phenomenology focuses attention on regulation of the crying state and suggests that further investigation of the determinants of soothing may provide insights into the genesis (rather than the pathogenesis) of excessive crying.

- Central opioid-dependent systems are likely candidates as contributing mechanisms related to the phenomenology of early infant crying and colic. If confirmed, this, too, is an important shift in our thinking; namely, *that individual differences in crying are likely to reflect differences in CNS functioning rather than GI functioning.* Although the potential role of GI determinants is by no means ruled out, these findings do suggest that if attention is limited only to that system, some keys to our understanding of this phenomenon may be missed.

Furthermore, it is important to emphasize that these findings do not lead to the conclusion that "colic does not exist." Rather, colic is robustly real, regardless of what laboratory research discovers about its origins, processes and mechanisms. Our observations challenge the myth that some infants "have" colic and some do not, and that colic is caused by GI disease or abnormality. Although these have always been *attributions*, they have not been definitions of the behavioral syndrome. As with blood pressure, it may be appropriate to change our thinking towards considering colic as the end of a spectrum of individual differences in normal functioning that nevertheless generates clinical concern and clinical consequences. Whether, or when, we treat hypertension or colic is an important issue, but it is a different issue than whether or not it is continuous or discontinuous with normal development—or whether it is a myth.

References

1. Thomas A, Chess S, Birch H. *Temperament and Behavior Disorders in Children.* New York, NY: New York University Press, 1968.
2. Thomas A, Chess S. *Temperament and Development.* New York, NY: Bruner/Mazel, 1977.
3. Bates JE. *Infant Characteristics Questionnaire, Revised Dissertation.* Bloomington, Ind: Indiana University, 1984.
4. Rothbart MK, Derryberry D. Development of individual differences in temperament. In: Lamb ME, Brown AL, eds. *Advances in Developmental Psychology. Vol 1.* Hillsdale, NJ: Lawrence Erlbaum Associates; 1981.
5. Rothbart MK. Temperament and development. In: Kohnstamm GA, Bates JE, Rothbart MK, eds. *Temperament in Childhood.* New York, NY: John Wiley & Sons; 1989.

6. Gormally SM, Barr RG. Of clinical pies and clinical clues: proposal for a clinical approach to complaints of early crying and colic. *Ambulatory Child Health.* 1997;3:137-153.
7. Treem WR. Infant colic. A pediatric gastroenterologist's perspective. *Pediatric Clinics of North America.* 1994;41:1121-1138.
8. *Colic and Excessive Crying.* Columbus, Ohio: Ross Products Division, Abbott Laboratories; 1997.
9. Miller AR, Barr RG. Infantile colic. Is it a gut issue? *Pediatric Clinics of North America.* 1991;38:1407-1423.
10. Barr RG. Colic. In: Walker WA, Durie PR, Hamilton JR, Walker-Smith JA, Watkins JB, eds. *Pediatric Gastrointestinal Disease: Pathophysiology, Diagnosis, and Management.* 2nd ed. St Louis, Mo: Mosby; 1996.
11. Wessel MA, Cobb JC, Jackson EB, Harris GS, Detwiler AC. Paroxysmal fussing in infancy, sometimes called "colic." *Pediatrics.* 1954;14:421-434.
12. Brazelton TB. Crying in infancy. *Pediatrics.* 1962;29:579-588.
13. Hunziker UA, Barr RG. Increased carrying reduces infant crying: a randomized controlled trial. *Pediatrics.* 1986;77:641-648.
14. Konner MJ. Spheres and modes of inquiry: integrative challenges in child development research. In: Zelazo PR, Barr RG, eds. *Challenges to Developmental Paradigms: Implications for Theory, Assessment and Treatment.* Hillsdale, NJ: Lawrence Erlbaum Associates; 1989.
15. Barr RG, Konner M, Bakeman R, Adamson L. Crying in !Kung San infants: a test of the cultural specificity hypothesis. *Developmental Medicine and Child Neurology.* 1991;33:601-610.
16. Barr RG. The early crying paradox: a modest proposal. *Human Nature.* 1990;1:355-389.
17. Barr RG, Chen S, Hopkins B, Westra T. Crying patterns in preterm infants. *Developmental Medicine and Child Neurology.* 1996;38:345-355.
18. Malone A. The crying pattern of preterm infants. ISSBD Programme, 4, 1997.
19. Barr RG, Hanley J, Patterson DK, Wooldridge J. Breath hydrogen excretion in normal newborn infants in response to usual feeding patterns: evidence for "functional lactase insufficiency" beyond the first month of life. *The Journal of Pediatrics.* 1984;104:527-533.
20. Douwes AC, Oosterkamp RF, Fernandes J, Los T, Jongbloed AA. Sugar malabsorption in healthy neonates estimated by breath hydrogen. *Archives of Disease in Childhood.* 1980;55:512-515.
21. Hood BM, Murray L, King F, Hooper R, Atkinson J, Braddick O. Habituation changes in early infancy: longitudinal measures from birth to 6 months. *Journal of Reproductive Infant Psychology.* 1996;14:177-185.
22. Slater A, Brown E, Mattock A, Bornstein MH. Continuity and change in habituation in the first 4 months from birth. *Journal of Reproductive Infant Psychology.* 1996;14:187-194.
23. Bornstein MH, Brown E, Slater A. Patterns of stability and continuity in attention across early infancy. *Journal of Reproductive Infant Psychology.* 1996;14:195-206.
24. Panksepp J. *Affective Neuroscience: The Foundations of Human and Animal Emotions.* Oxford, England: Oxford University Press, 1998.
25. Pettijohn TF. Attachment and separation distress in the infant guinea pig. *Developmental Psychobiology.* 1979;12:73-81.
26. Hofer MA, Masmela JR, Brunelli SA, Shair HN. The ontogeny of maternal potentiation of the infant rats' isolation call. *Developmental Psychobiology.* 1998;33:189-201.
27. Hofer MA, Brunelli SA, Masmela J, Shair HN. Maternal interactions prior to separation potentiate isolation-induced calling in rat pups. *Behavioral Neuroscience.* 1996;110:1158-1167.
28. Bard KA. Crying in infant primates: insights into the development of crying in chimpanzees. In: Barr RG, Hopkins B, Green JA, eds. *Crying as a Sign, a Symptom, & a Signal.* London, England: MacKeith Press, 2000.
29. Barr RG, Rotman A, Yaremko J, Leduc D, Francoeur TE. The crying of infants with colic: a controlled empirical description. *Pediatrics.* 1992;90:14-21.
30. Barr RG, Paterson JA, MacMartin LM, Calinoiu N, Young SN. What is colic?: a test of the early difficult temperament hypothesis [abstract]. *Pediatric Research.* 2000;47: Abstract 23a.

31. Blass EM, Hoffmeyer LB. Sucrose is an analgesic agent in 1-3 day-old human infants. *Society for Research in Child Development.* 1989;6:189.
32. Blass EM, Fillion TJ, Rochat P, Hoffmeyer LB, Metzher MA. Sensorimotor and motivational determinants of hand-mouth coordination in 1-3-day-old human infants. *Developmental Psychology.* 1989;25:963-975.
33. Smith BA, Fillion TJ, Blass EM. Orally mediated sources of calming in 1 to 3-day old human infants. *Developmental Psychology.* 1990;26:731-737.
34. Barr RG, Quek VS, Cousineau D, Oberlander TF, Brian JA, Young SN. Effects of intra-oral sucrose on crying, mouthing and hand-mouth contact in newborn and six-week-old infants. *Developmental Medicine and Child Neurology.* 1994;36:608-618.
35. Graillon A, Barr RG, Young SN, Wright JH, Hendricks LA. Differential response to intraoral sucrose, quinine and corn oil in crying human newborns. *Physiology & Behavior.* 1997;62:317-325.
36. Barr RG, Pantel MS, Young SN, Wright JH, Hendricks LA, Gravel R. The response of crying newborns to sucrose: is it a "sweetness" effect? *Physiology & Behavior.* 1999;66:409-417.
37. Barr RG, Young SN. A two-phase model of the soothing taste response: implications for a taste probe of temperament and emotion regulation. In: Lewis M, Ramsay D, eds. *Soothing and Stress.* Mahwah, NJ: Lawrence Erlbaum Associates; 1999.
38. Blass EM, Ciaramitaro V. A new look at some old mechanisms in human newborns: taste and tactile determinants of state, affect, and action. *Monographs of the Society for Research in Child Development.* 1994;59:1-81.
39. Barr RG, Young SN, Wright JH, Gravel R, Alkawaf R. Differential calming responses to sucrose taste in crying infants with and without colic. *Pediatrics.* 1999;103:e68.

Crying: Multiple Determinants of Perceived Meaning

James A. Green, PhD and Gwen E. Gustafson, PhD

Introduction

Parental perception is central to the phenomenon of colic, or unexplained, persistent crying in very young infants. Parents bring the complaint of excessive crying to the attention of the clinician; therefore, it is their perception of infant behavior that initiates clinical contact. Further, most research studies of "colic" rely on parental reports of the amount, or characteristics, of crying in the "colicky" infant. Indeed, in many studies of colic, infants are included solely on the bases of parental reports.[1,2]

Given the most common criteria for defining "colic," namely, those of Wessel,[3] the practical reasons for relying on parental reports are obvious. Few researchers or clinicians are willing or able to spend the time required to determine if an infant cries for more than 3 hours per day for more than 3 days per week. Defining colic in this manner would be especially difficult for researchers who use direct observations or audio recordings, rather than parental reports, to measure infant crying.

If we are to accept that clinical complaints of colic and research about its characteristics are both based on parental reports, it becomes important to address: (1) the features of crying that relate to parents' perceptions of distress; (2) the relationship among infants' distress, the cry sound and crying behavior; and (3) the interaction between parents' beliefs about crying and their perceptions of distress in infants. In this presentation, research bearing on these issues will be discussed and conclusions will be drawn about the complex relationships between infants' cry acts and parents' responses to them.

A Paradigm for Cry Perception Studies

Fig 1 depicts a model of the various components of infant crying and parental perception. Most investigations of cry perception, including those from our laboratory in the Department of Psychology at the University of Connecticut, have proceeded to focus only on the shaded areas in Fig 1. Cries are recorded and then played back to adult listeners at a later time. Listeners respond to the cries, usually by rating them on some characteristic(s), but sometimes by making a behavioral response.

The paradigm shown in Fig 1 is deceptively simple; yet, there are numerous ways to elaborate on either end. For example, on the left, or "cry act," end, one can vary the eliciting condition of the cry (eg, with a heel stick, a loud noise or hunger), the age of the infants producing the cries, the medical histories of the infants or the parts of the cry act that are presented (eg, sound alone, video or acoustically altered sound). On the right, or "response" side, possible variables include the nature of the rating required (eg, yes/no judgments of the type of cry or scaled ratings of the intensity of the cry), the types of behaviors recorded (eg, autonomic responses, caregiving behaviors or arbitrary behaviors signaling a change in perception) and the type of listener (eg, parent, nonparent or neonatal nurse). The basic statistical approach is

Fig 1. A model of cry production and perception; the shaded areas represent much of the literature on cry perception.

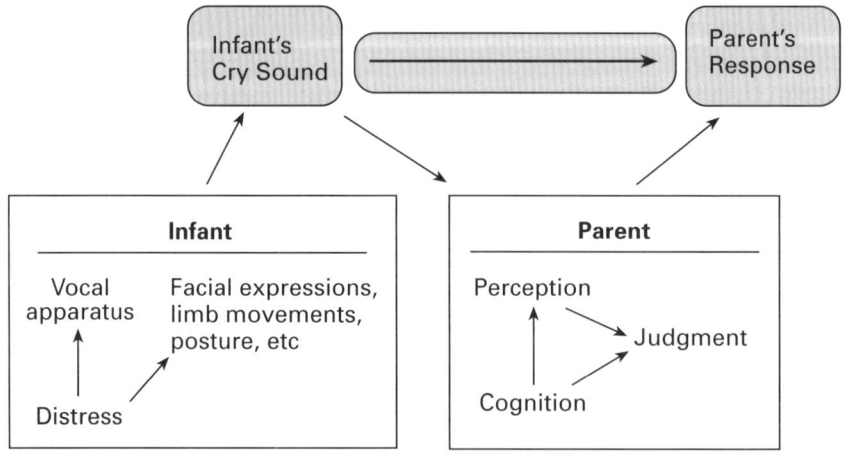

to determine whether differences in the cry act relate to differences in responses at levels above those expected by chance.

Although this paradigm will be elaborated upon, even this simple version leads to the following 2 key questions about perceived distress in cry sounds. First, which features of crying are most related to the perception of distress, and second, what are the special features of the cries of infants with colic that might relate to the perception of distress?

Acoustic Features of Cries and Perceived Distress

Certainly the *sound* of the cry act is the perceptual feature that has been studied most frequently. The word "crying" virtually demands an image that is acoustic in nature, and the acoustic component of crying is almost synonymous with crying itself. To study the cry act, then, one must know something about the acoustics of sound waves.

A pure tone or sine wave (Fig 2[4]) can be described fully by its frequency (ie, the number of times it completes a cycle in 1 second) and its amplitude (ie, the amount of "excursion" of each cycle from baseline). In general, the

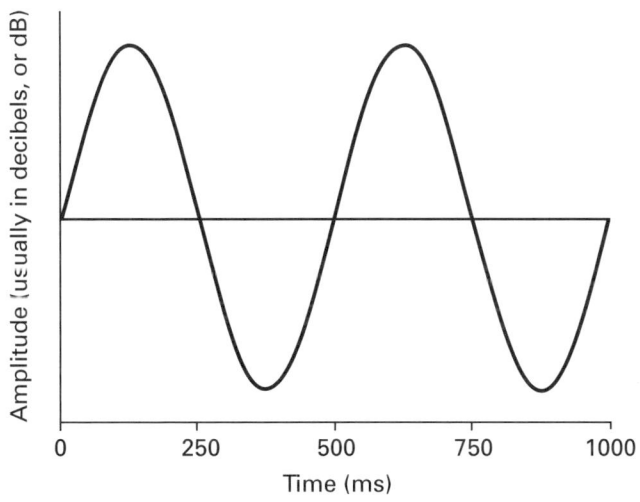

Fig 2. Two complete cycles of a sine wave, with a frequency of 2 Hz or cycles per second.[4]

Reproduced with permission from *Crying as a Sign, a Symtom, & a Signal: Clinical, Emotional, and Developmental Aspects of Infant and Toddler Crying.* Copyright 2000, MacKeith Press.

frequency of such a wave is perceived as "pitch" and the amplitude is perceived as "loudness." The greater the number of cycles per second, the higher the pitch of the tone; the larger the excursions, the louder the tone.

Cries, unfortunately, are not "pure" tones; they are complex sounds. For a typical cry from a human neonate, a plot of time versus amplitude of the cry (Fig 3) shows impressive irregularity.[4] Fortunately, such complex sounds can be decomposed into many separate frequencies, each with its own associated amplitude. A frequency-by-amplitude plot (Fig 4) for a small segment of this same cry shows energy in frequencies ranging from 100 Hz to 5000 Hz.[4] For even a single, 1-second cry sound, there are complex changes in the distribution of energy over time that make the acoustic analysis of cry sounds a very challenging endeavor.

Fig 3. The waveform of the expiratory segment from a single cry.[4]

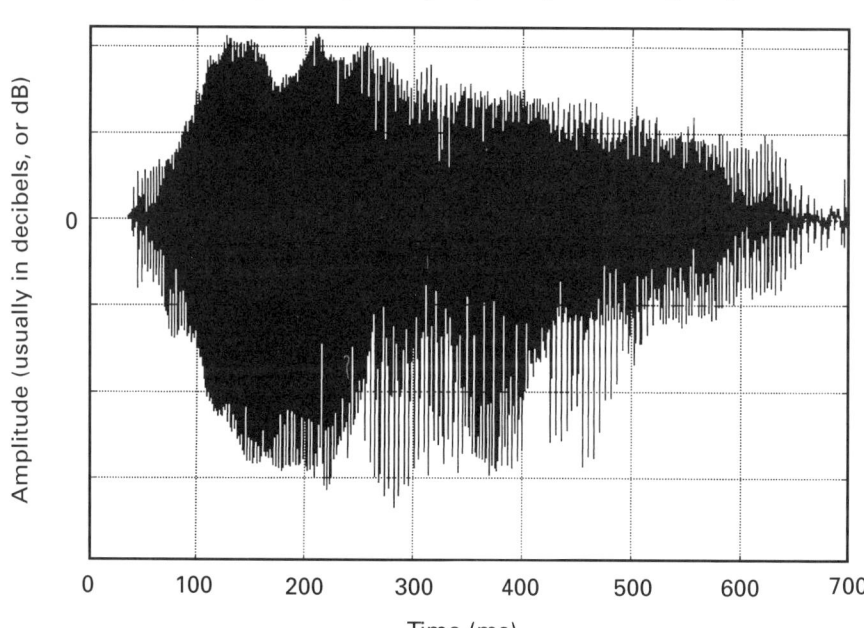

Reproduced with permission from *Crying as a Sign, a Symtom, & a Signal: Clinical, Emotional, and Developmental Aspects of Infant and Toddler Crying.* Copyright 2000, MacKeith Press.

Fig 4. *Top: the very beginning of the expiration shown in Fig 3 expanded to show more detail. Bottom: the spectrum obtained from a fast Fourier transform (FFT) of the shaded portion of the waveform at top. Note the peaks in the spectrum at the fundamental frequency of 464 Hz and at several harmonics (or multiples) of it.*[4]

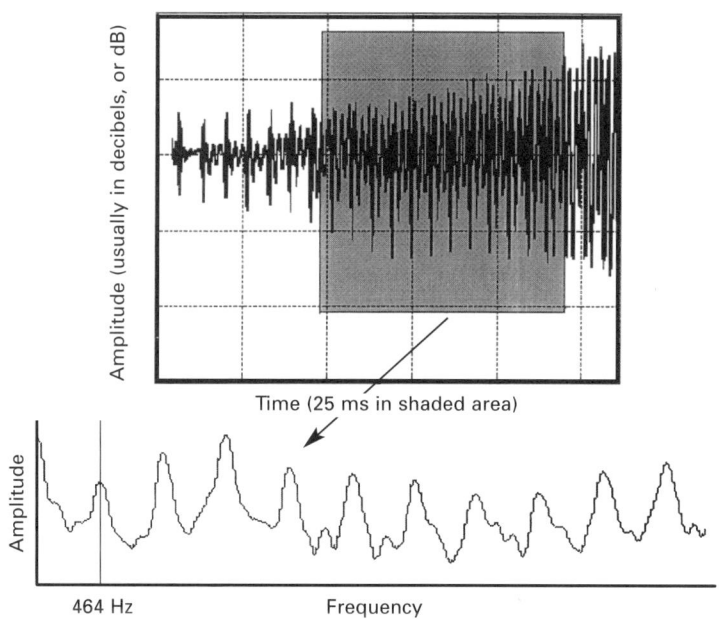

Reproduced with permission from *Crying as a Sign, a Symtom, & a Signal: Clinical, Emotional, and Developmental Aspects of Infant and Toddler Crying.* Copyright 2000, MacKeith Press.

In the 1960s and 1970s, before computer-generated plots were available, the sound spectrogram was the major tool used for analyzing cry sounds. Spectrograms provided remarkable visual representations of the cry sound. They were produced by an analog device, with time plotted on the x-axis and frequency plotted on the y-axis (Fig 5).[4] Amplitude was encoded as the darkness of the frequency lines. To capture the rich information displayed in the spectrograms, elaborate coding schemes were developed, the best example of which was given by Michelsson et al.[5] Many of the acoustic features that these investigators found useful for distinguishing normal from abnormal cries involve changes in the distribution of frequencies over time. These features include shift, vibrato, double harmonic break and glide, as shown in Fig 6.[5] This kind of patterning over time, however, is difficult to quantify.

Fig 5. A sound spectogram of the expiration shown in Fig 3. The "stripes" at the beginning show clearly the fundamental sound frequency (approximately 464 Hz) and its harmonics.[4]

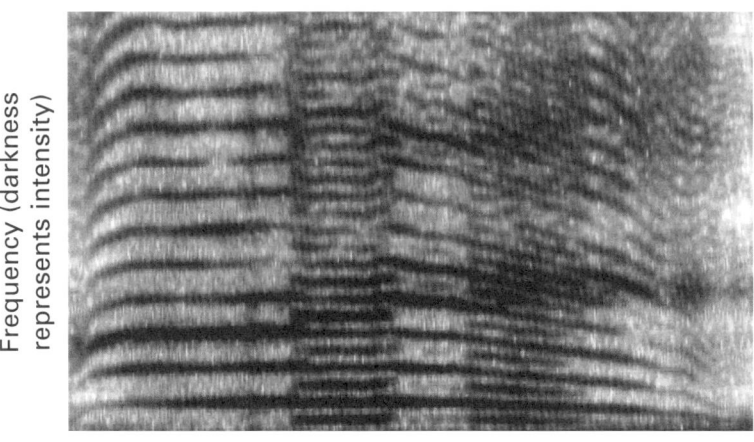

Reproduced with permission from *Crying as a Sign, a Symtom, & a Signal: Clinical, Emotional, and Developmental Aspects of Infant and Toddler Crying*. Copyright 2000, MacKeith Press.

Fig 6. A schematic spectogram illustrating the acoustic features studied by Michelsson et al[5] *in term and preterm infants: 1=shift; 2=maximum pitch; 3=minimum pitch; 4=biphonation; 5=double harmonic break; 6=vibrato; 7=glide; 8=furcation.*

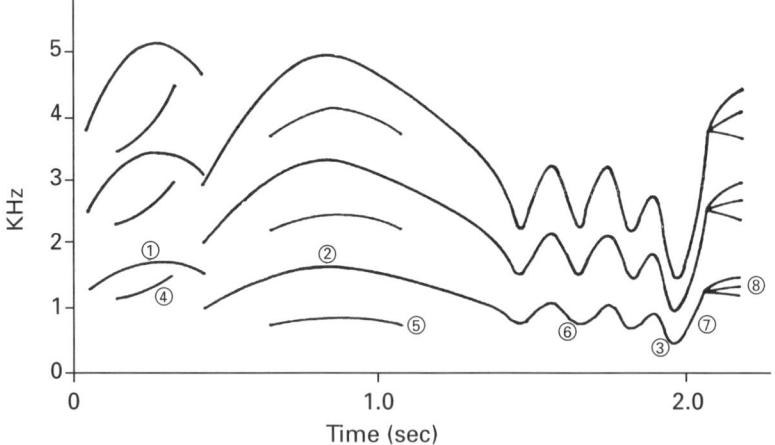

Reproduced with permission from *Crying as a Sign, a Symtom, & a Signal: Clinical, Emotional, and Developmental Aspects of Infant and Toddler Crying*. Copyright 2000, MacKeith Press.

In the 1980s and 1990s, cry researchers began to use computers to quantify information about the cry sound. In computer analyses, recorded cry sounds are digitized (ie, their amplitudes are measured repeatedly, usually at the rate of about 25,000 times per second), and then frequency and temporal information are estimated from the sampled cries.

The fast Fourier transform (FFT) is the algorithm used most commonly for creating a frequency-by-amplitude display. Typically, the FFT is performed on a small window, or "slice," of the cry (25 ms or 40 ms), such that many FFTs are required to analyze even a single cry sound. A 1-second cry sound, for example, comprises 40, 25-ms time segments. Many displays must be generated, therefore, to capture changes in frequencies over time. These plots must then be integrated and the information reduced in a meaningful way. So, while digitization and computer analysis added precision to cry measurement, variability was also added, as many parameters must be set to perform the FFTs necessary to analyze a cry sound. The optimal way to set these parameters is unclear, and the problem is not addressed in the same way by all researchers. Further, although the shift to digital analysis techniques allows for better quantification of many parameters, it does not handle dynamic cry features well. The dynamic features that were identified as diagnostically useful by researchers using spectrographic analysis are discarded in most digital analyses.

Digital analysis techniques tend to focus on static summary features, such as average fundamental frequency, peak or maximum frequency (ie, frequency with the greatest amplitude), percent dysphonation (aperiodic vibration of the vocal folds) and total duration of the cry. Most digital analysis systems pay particular attention to various measures of the fundamental frequency (F_0) of the cry. F_0 is the frequency at which the vocal cords vibrate at any given point during the cry sound. Especially salient aspects of the F_0 include the minimum and maximum value during the cry, the melody type (eg, falling, rising or rising-falling) and the occurrence of very-low-frequency voiced sounds (known as "glottal rolls" in the spectrographic literature).

In sum, the acoustic analysis of cry sounds remains largely unstandardized, as emphasized by Raes, Dehaen and Despontin.[6] Not only are there fundamental distinctions between spectrographic and digital analyses, but independent laboratories may employ different techniques for measuring the same cry feature.

The acoustic features of cries that are found most often to be related to their perceived distress are the fundamental frequency, the amount of dysphonation, the length of the cry and the amount of energy in higher frequencies. As pitch, dysphonation and length of cry increase so, too, does perceived infant distress. Increased energy in higher cry frequencies is also related to perception of increased distress.

Unfortunately, these general conclusions represent a vast oversimplification; specific findings vary greatly across studies. Recall from the discussion of the investigation of cry perception that methodologies vary greatly, so that variability in results across studies may be due to differences in the sets of cries used in any given study, differences in the characteristics of the listeners (eg, neonatal nurses versus parents) and differences in the tasks demanded of the listeners (eg, ratings versus behavioral responses). For example, if a particular study employs a set of cries in which dysphonation varies greatly, this feature will be particularly salient to listeners and it will likely emerge as a correlate of perceived distress *for that set of cries*. Furthermore, results across studies suggest that no single acoustic feature alone accounts for perceived distress in infants' cries.

Acoustic Features of "Colic" and Other "Types" of Cries

Can colic cries be distinguished acoustically from noncolic cries? Several papers have addressed this important question. One of these papers was published in 1997 by Zeskind and Barr,[2] while another was published 5 years earlier by Lester and colleagues.[1] Both groups noted a few significant differences between the cry sounds of infants whose parents reported excessive crying and those whose parents did not. These group differences involved the fundamental frequencies of cries[1] and dysphonation.[1,2] The distributions of these acoustic features, however, overlapped to such an extent that infants could not be identified as belonging to one group or the other based solely on acoustics. Furthermore, most of the acoustic features measured in these 2 studies[1,2] did not differ between the groups. St. James-Roberts[7] also presented data that suggested only minimal differences in cry acoustics between infants with and without colic. Given these results, a reasonable conclusion is that focusing on acoustics alone to determine what is special about the cries of infants who have colic is likely to lead to disappointment. A combination of acoustic and nonacoustic features of cries may be more useful in characterizing these cries. (This will be discussed later in this paper.) Finally, it is important to note that each of these studies[1,2,7] used different sampling procedures, and that these procedures are not adequately captured by labeling the infants as having colic.

The search for an acoustically distinct "colic" cry is reminiscent of the search for "cry types" unique to eliciting condition (eg, pain, hunger, fatigue and startle). In both cases caregivers have told us that there is "something there," yet our acoustic analyses have failed to yield any unique or distinctive features. In the case of putative "cry types," some resolution of this difference is provided by the more recent notion that cry acoustics and the perception of distress by caregivers may be graded by the infant's level of distress or arousal. The sometimes apparent link between the sound of the cry and its specific cause (eg, an inoculation) does not reflect the existence of a unique cry type, but rather the general principle that causes differ in their suddenness of onset, their intensity and their persistence. A recent, comprehensive review of "cry types" and the graded signal literatures can be found in work done by us and Wood.[8] A theoretical solution for the disparity between everyday perception and acoustic analysis would be a welcomed addition to the literature on colic.

Nonvocal Aspects of Crying

Although the defining quality of crying is, in some ways, the sound, other aspects of crying are salient, as well, and these features may be especially relevant to explorations of colic or excessive crying. Specifically, visual cues and tactile cues may contribute to perceived distress. A study performed in our laboratory at the University of Connecticut addressed the joint contribution of facial and vocal cues to the perception of cry and noncry sounds.[9]

Thirty-two nonparent adults were asked to judge whether each of 36 videotaped segments represented an infant making a fuss, a cry, a laugh or a positive vocalization.[9] To complicate this otherwise straightforward identification task, half of the 36 stimuli were mismatched for facial and vocal cues; that is, they represented either a cry face with a noncry sound edited over it or a noncry face paired with a cry sound. The individual contributions of facial and vocal cues to perceived distress could be determined by placing the 2 types of information in direct competition.

Results of this study, shown in Table 1 represent trials in which the cry sound was played with either a cry face or a noncry face, as well as a control condition in which the sound was played by itself.[9] These data show that adults were able to identify sounds alone as cry sounds, and they were very good at identifying cry sounds paired with cry faces as cry events. However, the noncry face proved to be a strong enough stimulus to reduce performance to chance levels when it was paired with a cry sound. The inability to identify cry sounds consistently in the presence of competing visual information was found for stimuli from 3-month-old infants and 12-month-old infants. Finally, in the absence of any visual information, the sound of the cry alone carried enough information for nonparents to identify cry sounds at levels above chance. These data suggest that crying is a *multimodal* event and that caregivers have information in addition to sound to use when interpreting infant crying.

Table 1. Proportion of Adults (n = 32) Correctly Identifying a Cry Sound.[9]

Condition	3-month-old infants	12-month-old infants
Cry sound and cry face	.91	.93
Cry sound and noncry face	.36	.68
Cry sound alone	.75	.92

Note: Chance response level was .50. Data from Green et al.[9]

To continue this inquiry, Irwin performed a more-detailed examination of infants' voices, faces and bodies as sources of information about distress.[10] Specifically, Irwin asked, "Which cry features permit discrimination of high distress from low distress?" Nonparent adults were asked to rate the distress level of videotaped events that displayed either face alone, body alone, sound alone or all 3 together. As shown in Table 2, results confirmed that adults can use sound alone, as well as information from faces and bodies, to discriminate infants who were highly distressed from those who were not so distressed. Further, adults could use the face alone to discriminate distress levels. However, movements of the infant's body alone generally were not sufficient to

Table 2. Cry act features that discriminate high versus low distress episodes.

Feature	3-month-old infants	12-month-old infants
Sound Alone	Yes (4.7 vs 2.5)	Yes (5.8 vs 2.6)
Face Alone	Yes (4.6 vs 1.8)	Yes (4.0 vs 3.0)
Body Alone	No	Yes (3.1 vs 2.0)
All 3 Together	Yes (5 vs 2.1)	Yes (5.5 vs 2.3)

Note: "Yes" indicates a statistically significant difference between high and low distress episodes on a 7-point scale. Mean ratings for the high and low conditions are in parenthesis. Data adapted from Irwin.[10]

discriminate distress levels, especially at 3 months. As Irwin noted, however, video images of an infant's body do not provide the same information that one gains when holding a real, crying baby. It is likely that *tactile* cues would be sufficient to discriminate the level of distress in real, live crying infants. Indeed, many descriptions of colic episodes include descriptions of the infant in tactile terms—flexed legs, hard abdomens and general rigidity.

Results of these 2 studies support the idea that nonvocal cues contribute to adults' perceptions of an infant's level of distress.[9, 10] It is reasonable to suggest, then, that a better understanding of the phenomenon of excessive crying will emerge as we come to appreciate crying as the multimodal event that parents perceive.

Physiologic Models of Cry Production

Although crying is not simply an auditory event, there are both historic and theoretic reasons for the primacy of acoustics in the cry literature. In brief, acoustical information has been thought to provide a window on the functioning of the central nervous system (CNS). According to several models of cry production, the sound of the cry should be closely related to autonomic functioning. All of the extant models imply that the vagal system is the primary source of variations in cry acoustics. Deficits in either brain stem functioning or higher brain functioning may affect vagal control of the cry, producing abnormalities in cry acoustics, especially in fundamental frequency.

In 1980, Golub suggested that respiratory influences are independent of laryngeal and nasopharyngeal influences on cry acoustics.[11] Based on this model, Golub proposed at least 3 "tests" to discriminate infants at varying degrees of medical risk. Indeed, some acoustic features of cries are sensitive to some medical conditions. However, these features are not specific enough to be used as routine screening devices; that is to say, these features are present in a significant proportion of infants whose development is typical.[12] Porges, Doussard-Roosevelt and Maiti proposed another model of cry acoustics in which vagal tone is related to the fundamental frequency of cry sounds.[13] Lester and Zeskind described a model that adds "arousability" to the crying state as an additional feature of cry analysis.[14] In their view, arousability should reflect sympathetic influences of the CNS independent of parasympathetic influences on cry acoustics.

Note that the complete model of cry production and perception shown in Fig 1 includes a component for the physiological underpinnings of the cry (labeled "distress" in the figure). Each physiologic model described posits that CNS changes are central to the recruitment of the vocal apparatus to produce cry sounds. Clearly, better conceptualizations of arousal, both in a physiologic and in a psychologic sense, are needed. There are likely theoretic as well as measurement issues involved, especially in linking measures of physiologic arousal to measures of psychologic arousal (sometimes termed "distress" in the cry literature). Considerable evidence indicates that we must move beyond linear models, such as those conveyed in path diagrams, to better understand these 2 domains and their interrelations. Our recent work, with McGhie, exploring changes in cry acoustics over time in relatively long bouts of crying,[15] represents an example of this approach.

Parents' Cognitions About Crying

The model of cry production and perception presented in Fig 1 involves cognitive and judgment processes that influence parental responses to a cry. It is often assumed implicitly that there is a direct link between a cry sound and the response, but this assumption is an oversimplification. The cognitions and perceptions of the parent, caregiver or nonparent adult are tied together in a complex manner that influences judgments about responding.

There are 2 studies, in particular, that relate to this issue. Work from our laboratory at the University of Connecticut (unpublished data, 1994) explored adults' cognitions about cry sounds. Nonparent adults were asked how alike they *thought* cries elicited under 10 different circumstances would sound. The 10 different circumstances yielded 45 possible pairs of hypothetical cry sounds that participants then rated on a 7-point scale of degree of similarity.

Multidimensional scaling was used to represent the paired-comparison data (Fig 7). Note that the farther apart cry sounds are in this geometric space, the more dissimilar they were believed to be by the participants. Nonparent

Fig 7. A multidimensional scaling solution for the paired comparisons of 10 cry "causes" (from unpublished data, 1994).

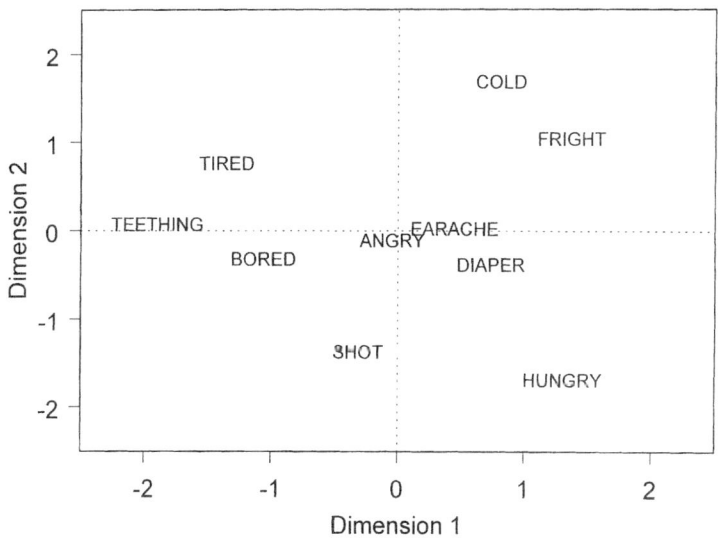

adults had a very well-defined set of cognitions about how cries were *supposed* to sound. Cries from teething, tired and bored infants are far away from the cries of cold or frightened infants. Acute pain from a vaccination (injection) occupies a fairly unique position in this space, as does "hunger." Certainly, a set of cognitions about how cries are *supposed* to sound would influence how a real, live cry is perceived—and what might be a possible response. An elegant study on expectations and perceptions of crying is waiting to be done.

In a study completed recently regarding the influence of adults' beliefs on their response to infant crying, nonparent adults listened to a series of 30-second samples of crying.[16] Listeners who had been told that the infant was tired and needed a nap waited longer before indicating that they would care for the infant than did listeners who were given no information. Caregiving context combined with acoustical information in the crying tend to affect latency to intended response.

Studies by Donovan, Leavitt and Walsh also illustrated that caregivers' cognitions about crying are critical components of cry perception.[17, 18] Their work on perceived controllability of cry sounds is particularly germane to the literature on excessive crying because of the oft-repeated adjective "inconsolable" found in the literature about colic. Infants with colic are believed or are thought to be inconsolable. It is imperative to consider the beliefs and cognitive systems of caregivers in understanding the variability inherent in the label "excessive crying."

Conclusions

The response to a given cry depends on much more than the actual sound of the cry itself. To summarize the work reviewed here, we offer the following: There is no single acoustic feature of cry sounds that determines perceived distress; "colic" cries are not distinguishable from other cries on the basis of acoustic features; crying must be considered a multimodal event, with facial expressions and body postures influencing perception; more sophisticated, probably nonlinear, models of the cry production system are needed, as are better measuring systems for the concepts of arousal and distress; and, the decision to respond to a cry is the end point of a complex interplay of cognitions and beliefs about crying and the available perceptual information.

In addition to being an important clinical problem, unexplained excessive infant crying may also hold relevance for understanding basic developmental processes. Significant changes occur in the act of crying itself as the infant moves through the first year of life.[19, 20] These alterations in crying modify the evolving communication system between parent and infant, and thus may affect parental perceptions and responses. In other words, infant crying is part of a prelinguistic communication *system* long before the infant's first words are spoken. Theoretical issues related to the development of this communication system could likely be informed by the literature on infants who cry excessively.

Parental perception is clearly a key part of the issue of unexplained crying. This is not to imply that unexplained crying, or colic, exists only in parents' heads. Rather, it is to emphasize that an improved understanding of parents' perceptions of distress will likely provide better tools to both researchers and clinicians who seek to explain what is now called "unexplained excessive infant crying."

References

1. Lester BM, Boukydis CFZ, Garcia-Coll CT, Hole W, Peucker M. Infant colic: acoustic cry characteristics, maternal perception of cry, and temperament. *Infant Behavior and Development.* 1992;15:15-26.
2. Zeskind PS, Barr RG. Acoustic characteristics of naturally occurring cries of infants with "colic." *Child Development.* 1997;68:394-403.
3. Wessel MA, Cobb JC, Jackson EB, Harris GS, Detwiler AC. Paroxysmal fussing in infancy, sometimes called "colic." *Pediatrics.* 1954;14:421-434.
4. Michelsson K, Sirviö P, Wasz-Höckert O. Sound spectrographic cry analysis of infants with bacterial meningitis. *Developmental Medicine and Child Neurology.* 1977;19:309-315.
5. Michelsson K. Cry analyses of symptomless low birth weight neonates and of asphyxiated newborn infants. *Acta Paediatrica Scandinavica Supplement.* 1971;216:1-45.
6. Raes J, Dehaen F, Despontin M. Towards a standardized terminology and methodology for the measurement of durational pain cry characteristics. *Early Child Development and Care.* 1990;65:127-138.
7. St James-Roberts I. What is distinct about infants' "colic" cries? *Archives of Disease in Childhood. Fetal and Neonatal Edition.* 1999;80:56-61.
8. Gustafson GE, Wood RM, Green JA. Can we hear the causes of infants' crying? In: Barr RG, Hopkins B, Green JA, eds. *Crying as a Sign, a Symptom, & a Signal.* London, England: MacKeith Press; 2000: 8-22.
9. Green JA, Gustafson GE, Irwin JI, Kalinowski LL, Wood RM. Infant crying: acoustics, perception and communication. *Early Development and Parenting.* 1995;4:161-176.
10. Irwin JI. *The Cry as a Multiply Specified Signal of Distress* [dissertation]. Storrs, Conn: University of Connecticut; 1998.
11. Golub HL. *A Physioacoustic Model of the Infant Cry and Its Use for Medical Diagnosis and Prognosis* [dissertation]. Boston, Mass: Massachusetts Institute of Technology; 1980.
12. Green JA, Irwin JI, Gustafson GE. Acoustic cry analysis, neonatal status, and long-term developmental outcomes. In: Barr RG, Hopkins B, Green JA, eds. *Crying as a Sign, a Symptom, & a Signal.* London, England: MacKeith Press; 2000:137-156.

13. Porges SW, Doussard-Roosevelt JA, Maiti AK. Vagal tone and the physiological regulation of emotion. *Monographs of the Society for Research in Child Development.* 1994;59:167-186.
14. Lester BM, Zeskind PS. A biobehavioral perspective on crying in early infancy. In: Fitzgerald HE, Lester BM, Yogman MW, eds. *Theory and Research in Behavioral Pediatrics.* Vol 1. New York, NY: Plenum Press; 1982:133-180.
15. Green JA, Gustafson GE, McGhie AC. Changes in infants' cries as a function of time in a cry bout. *Child Development.* 1998;69:271-279.
16. Wood RM, Gustafson GE. Infant crying and adults' anticipated caregiving responses: acoustic and contextual influences. *Child Development.* In press.
17. Donovan WL, Leavitt LA, Walsh RO. Maternal self-efficacy: illusory control and its effect on susceptibility to learned helplessness. *Child Development.* 1990;61:1638-1647.
18. Donovan WL, Leavitt LA, Walsh RO. Cognitive set and coping strategy affect mothers' sensitivity to infant cries: a signal detection approach. *Child Development.* 1997;68:760-772.
19. Gustafson GE, Green JA. Developmental coordination of cry sounds with visual regard and gestures. *Infant Behavior and Development.* 1991;15:51-57.
20. Hopkins B. Development of crying in normal infants: method, theory, and some speculations. In: Barr RG, Hopkins B, Green JA, eds. *Crying as a Sign, a Symptom, & a Signal.* London, England: MacKeith Press; 2000:176-209.

Section 2 Discussion: Crying as a Developmental Phenomenon

Moderated by Megan R. Gunnar, PhD
Professor, Institute of Child Development
University of Minnesota
Minneapolis, Minnesota, USA

Gunnar: Perhaps part of the reason that crying is so mysterious and bizarre is that we are struggling with our central dogma about crying. As I view our *central dogma,* the ultimate question is, Why do human infants cry? Obviously human infants cry because crying is a social signal that communicates that the baby is in need and recruits caregivers to do something about what is wrong. The Round Table sessions held so far raise the question of whether that ultimate purpose of crying explains *all* of why babies cry. There have been many indications of *other* possible functions that this early infant crying might be serving. One way to think about why the dogma might not be satisfactory is to ask "If I were God, if I were nature, if I were evolution, would I have come up with *this* early crying system?"

What would crying look like if the central dogma did cover all the functions of crying? I will offer you my theories, and then I will remind us all of how everything we have said today makes it inexplicable that babies cry the way they do.

If I were God, babies would cry only if they were in need. They would cry in a way that very clearly and accurately communicated what was causing the crying and what they actually needed us to do. They would soothe as soon as we met that need, and they would soothe only when we met that need; so they would not stop crying without intervention, and, conversely, they would stop when we did do the right thing.

Today, we have heard excellent examples of how early infant crying fails to meet many of those criteria. For example, James Green stated that, in fact, the cry is a fairly poor signal of what the infant needs. We have theories, even before we become parents and listen to a lot of crying, about how similar or different these cries *ought* to sound. We actually believe the central dogma even before we have children. In fact, what is so inexplicable to us in the early weeks is that our children somehow did not read the book! "They are crying and they are not doing this, and I cannot tell, and something is wrong. Call the pediatrician. Don't our infants understand?"

What these cries do convey, if we analyze the acoustics, seems to be something about urgency; at least, that is how we perceive them. Some cries are the "drop-everything-and-run" kind that we think of as pain cries. They mean that there is something wrong and we had better move fast, rather than the type of cries where you can wash the last dish ("I'll be there in a minute, dear") before you go. So there is an urgency dimension. There may also be something about health and illness that we are picking up somewhat accurately, when a sick baby sounds somewhat different from a baby with a healthy, lusty cry. This does not, however, tell us what illness the baby might have, only that the baby is not healthy.

We heard from Brian Hopkins that there is a lot of soothing. We also heard that sometimes you cannot soothe these infants. This is a big problem for parents, and also for our central dogma about crying. What Brian Hopkins demonstrated is that there is soothing without intervention. Even more interestingly, it seems to follow some lawful development patterns. Why would a baby soothe when we do not do anything if the function of the cry is to convey a need? We heard from Ronald Barr that infants with colic cry whether in need or not, and whether sick or not. Because we perceive the cries of colicky infants as clearly indicating urgency or pain, we have been confused for a long time. In fact, in 95% of cases, there is probably absolutely nothing wrong with the baby, and much of that baby's crying does not seem to be related to any need that we could possibly discern. It may not even be related to how aroused that baby is. Barbara White, a PhD student in our department, was very interested in infants with colic and whether their crying was linked to greater physiologic arousal,[1] leading to the question of whether their greater crying tells us something about how physiologically aroused they are. To answer the question, we brought "Wessel's colic" babies into the laboratory. By diary recordings, they were crying more. They were 8 weeks of age when they were brought into the lab. To get them to cry, we used a paradigm that we had used in other studies that we knew elevated glucocorticoids in this age; namely, we gave them a mock well-baby exam with four periods: baseline; measurement of height, weight and head circumference; a rest period; and a doctor exam period. We videotaped the babies and had observers who were blind to colic status.

At baseline, colic babies were crying a little bit, more than noncolic babies but not much more. In the morning, which is not prime colic time, they appeared similar to noncolic babies. As soon as the nurse started the measurements, distress increased for all the babies but more so for those with colic. During the rest period, the noncolic babies quieted down, as did the colic babies, but not as much. During the physical exam, the colic infants cried again and cried more. Overall, the infants with colic were fussing and crying twice as much as the infants without colic. Furthermore, when we looked at how intense the crying was, we found what has also been reported in home diaries: about 65% of the distress of our noncolic babies was fussing. Very little was really intense crying. For our colic babies, less of their crying was fussing, and more of it consisted of intense kinds of crying.

We also looked at consolability using a standard consolability paradigm. More than half of the colic babies who had cried to the required level could not be consoled.

The answer to the question of whether colic behavior is an honest measure of how physiologically aroused a baby is seems to be no. They cried more, but they did not differ in heart rate, vagal tone or cortisol response; despite the fact that they were crying twice as much, it was more intense and they were less consolable. The physiologic systems that should mobilize energy and shift the blood flow around to prepare the body to sustain that greater distress did not show any significant differences between the groups.

One conclusion we might come to is that nature has done a poor job of creating a cry system that shows distress only when the baby is actually in need, conveys what it is the baby needs and actually tells us something about the physical state or the physiologic arousal of that child. The discussions in this session focused us on the need to think developmentally and particularly to return to this question of function as we think developmentally, to try to understand why nature did such a poor job of creating this system that was supposed to help us care for our babies better.

Zeskind: Are the changes between the physical exam and baseline for the colicky infants different from those of the control infants?

Gunnar: The colic babies started out with slower heart rates and ended up with higher heart rates, but at no point was the within-period comparison significantly different.

Zeskind: Would you say that is a significant trend? Could you conclude that colic babies were more aroused than they were at baseline, whereas control babies were not?

Gunnar: Certainly, in this sample. But I am not comfortable about unpredicted interactions with a sample of only 20 colic and 20 noncolic infants. At this point, I think it tells us that they are more similar than different, given the magnitude of the differences in the behavior. I would certainly want to replicate the interaction before I said that they come in less aroused.

All of these measures are correlated with how much the baby is crying, and they are correlated similarly, about $r = .5$ in each group. So they are coupled in about the same way, but one group is crying so much more. The baby with colic is sustaining all of that with less actual physiologic arousal to go along with it, but the coupling between systems is the same within the groups.

Faculty Member: Colic babies are, in fact, crying twice as much as controls, but in terms of the total number of intervals that you are coding, they are not. In other words, my vision of colic is that they would be off scale compared with controls, and they really are not.

Gunnar: It is 60% of the time versus 40% of the time during the physical exam. That is quite a bit.

Faculty Member: Another thing to remember is that both the heart rate and vagal tone are reflecting energy metabolism. It may be the case that there is a threshold here, so that if you have a crying infant, you are going to get to an increase in heart rate, which reflects their level of crying.

Gunnar: It is possible. I looked at cortisol measurement in the home. Here you will see a difference, but not what one would expect. If the baby were using more energy because he or she was crying more, the cortisol level should be higher. The babies with colic at home were crying an average of 5 hours a day and the noncolic infants were crying an average of about 1 to 1½ hours a day. The control babies showed a very nice circadian rhythm. High in the morning, way down in the evening. The colic babies had a flatter slope. Overall, during the daytime they would have been producing less cortisol, even though they were crying much, much more.

* * * * *

Another difference with the colic babies is that they were sleeping less. They have, by definition, less awake time during the day when they are not fussing and crying. When you look at the slope of the hypothalamic-pituitary-adrenal rhythm, it is also linked to sleep. For the noncolic infants, it predicts how much time they are awake and not fussy during the day. So, if a baby has a better circadian organization at a younger age, that baby sustains more time awake without being fussy. None of the colic babies showed a good daily slope. Some noncolic babies did not have a terribly marked rhythm either, but it is very unpredictable at that age.

Almost all of the infants with colic were showing this kind of flat rhythm. Either it was not mature or the colic infants were awake so much at night that they could not have a morning rise.

* * * * *

Hofer: You said that if the central dogma is correct, nature is doing a poor job, and I would agree with that, but which would you throw out if you were going to throw something out? My answer to that is the central dogma, but then you would have to agree that nature is not doing a poor job. The solution to this yields a different central dogma, because what is selected in signals is not only what works in a cooperative environment but what works in a hostile and competitive environment. Crying qualifies as a deceptive signal—that is, an exaggeration of need. Then there is an "arms race" in which, through evolution, we have to learn to become more discerning about the signals so that we can distinguish an honest signal from a display that is manipulative.

Gunnar: That would allow us, in a sense, to keep the central dogma that it is a social signal. It is just not an honest social signal, but one that still has all the crying serving one function.

Hofer: Nature is doing an excellent job. Nature is doing what it always has done, which is to give us a variety of different ways of dealing with one another and with living together. Colicky infants have one strategy; other infants have another strategy.

Wolke: One thing crying leads to is a letdown reflex. We have to see the connection to the physiologic letdown reflex. If you observe what women do after holding a crying baby, you will see that they feed it. We have found that colic babies rarely fail to thrive. In fact, they usually thrive quite well because they are fat. We monitored 1500 children's births. We found that what distinguished the failure-to-thrive children was that although they cried early on, they also slept through the night early, so they did not produce the crying signal. There is a second mechanism. Infanticide is extremely rare in humans. In Britain, the last figure was something like 35 infants killed per year. Even if a baby is crying a great deal, the chance that the mother will kill the baby is very low; but the cost of not getting enough to eat is relatively high: The rate is about 3% in Britain. In other societies, it is much higher. So I think we have to see this in an evolutionary perspective. We cannot look at it just from a 21st-century perspective, but rather we must look back at the larger picture over time, at what the mechanisms were.

Gunnar: So the early crying is only "inexplicable" if we think about it in a rich, nourishing environment. If we put a crying infant into a more threatened environment, it becomes much less inexplicable. It is only during the last century and only in some countries that infants are not in that threatened situation.

Hopkins: I was just speculating about this question of the functional significance of crying. We tend to talk about central dogma in terms of eliciting functions. We could think about what Darwin speculated about crying. He said that in evolution crying has been symbiotic with functions that were there to serve feeding, so the mechanisms of feeding, swallowing, and so on have evolved and are useful but also served another function, namely, crying. Exactly the same organs are used. Crying is something special in humans. I think the qualities of voicing in the human baby are quite different from those of the chimpanzee, within the primate species. Maybe another step one could take is to think about a functional continuity, in some respects, between crying and speech development. Many processes that go on during crying, such as controlling of respiration, and maybe even articulation, serve to facilitate speech development as well.

Gunnar: We could add another, secondary function that might have to do with stimulating the organization of the vocal respiratory apparatus that humans need to talk. Some of our unexplained crying could be due to exercise.

Hopkins: Wasn't that part of Hunziker and Barr's study,[2] the idea that carrying the baby cut down on crying so that crying may be a source of self-stimulation, or autogenic stimulation? The argument is that if they are not being carried, they compensate by crying and that gives them the exercise of the vestibular system that they might otherwise not have.

In other words, crying is a form of self-stimulation, and when they are carried around by their mothers, they do not need to produce as much stimulation. The only problem with the data for that hypothesis is that they are incredibly nonspecific, because the increased carrying includes true vestibular stimulation, and it also includes direct contact, smell and probably more face-to-face interaction; so you may not be able to categorize it as vestibular stimulation or generic stimulation.

Gunnar: It may be interesting that we begin to see this increase in amounts of fussing and crying at about the same time that REM sleep is beginning to be organized and there is a drift toward nighttime sleep and away from daytime sleep. The high amounts of REM that babies produce may be serving some of this stimulation-of-the-brain function. To some extent we may be seeing a replacement for the fussiness.

Faculty Member: There have been three carrying studies,[2-4] and only one of those has found that infants cry less when carrying is increased. In searching for a function for crying, we need to understand why babies miraculously and suddenly do not need whatever this function is at whatever age we think it stops at, sometime around 12 weeks. Do they need any of these things any longer? Why is there a miraculous switch-off?

Actually, it does not stop. Babies continue to cry in response to a variety of experiences both internal and external. Could one simplify things and say that infants are moving through a period of transition? There is variability in maturation, and this is reflected in many ways. As long as there is no pathology, this could reflect a maturational process that we have all agreed comes to some kind of closure at about 3 months. Enzymes change, breathing changes, a variety of parameters change. Why not crying? Do we have to propose some bigger functions?

* * * * *

Gunnar: Nathan Fox, you looked at cross-cultural temperament. To the extent that we have good temperament data on Asian populations, is it very different than in Western populations?

Fox: Invariably, they are less intense and less active and have higher thresholds of reactivity. To the extent that you think temperament controls vulnerability to crying, the Asian cultures have less vulnerability.

* * * * *

Van den Boom: From the evolutionary point of view there is one function—survival; but since that is no longer an issue in our community, we have come up with other theories creating new functions.

* * * * *

Wolke: Why does unexplained crying stop at 3 months? The only time in life when you double your weight is in the first 3 months of life. This is a very risky period, the highest-risk period, when your body and brain need to grow. You have to make sure that this is one of the functions of crying.

A related function is sleeping. Basically, the longest period of sleeping follows the longest period of waking. To stretch that period of waking for some babies, they cry for longer in the evening. They only start sleeping through the night if there is a long period of waking. That is why we do not allow a baby to sleep from 5 to 6 PM and then ask them to go to bed again at 7. It is clear from the patterning that there is a change taking place for the long period of waking. For some children, that can be easy; for others, that may mean more crying.

References

1. White BP, Gunnar MR, Larson MC, Donzella B, Barr RG. Behavioral and physiological responsivity, sleep, and patterns of daily cortisol production in infants with and without colic. *Child Development.* 2000;71:862-886.
2. Hunziker UA, Barr RG. Increased carrying reduces infant crying: a randomized controlled trial. *Pediatrics.* 1986;77:641-648.
3. St. James-Roberts I, Hurry J, Bowyer J, Barr RG. Supplementary carrying compared with advice to increase responsive parenting as interventions to prevent persistent crying. *Pediatrics.* 1995;95:381-388.
4. Walker A, Menahem S. Intervention of supplementary carrying on normal baby crying patterns: a randomized study. *Developmental and Behavioral Pediatrics.* 1994;3:174-178.

New Evidence on Unexplained Early Infant Crying

Section 3:
The Challenge of Assessing Crying Complaints

Abstracts from Section 3: The Challenge of Assessing Crying Complaints

Clinical Clues to Organic Etiologies in Infants With Colic
Siobhán Gormally, MD

The Clinical Pie Model for Crying is a novel tool to categorize crying patterns in infants. It attempts to differentiate between infants with normal crying patterns, those with organic etiologies to explain their crying patterns, and three additional categories based on modifications of Wessel's criteria. An extensive literature review identified 11 clinical entities that can mimic colic; five of them are supported by strong evidence. Clinical clues or "red flags" that alert healthcare professionals to the possibility of potential organic conditions underlying excessive or extreme crying behavior are discussed.

The Impact of Irritable Infant Behavior on Maternal Mental State: A Longitudinal Study and a Treatment Trial
Professor Lynne Murray and Professor Peter Cooper

Neonatal irritability is characterized, at least in part, by excessive crying and resistance to soothing, resulting in significant strain on new mothers. Irritable infant behavior may precipitate clinical depression in vulnerable mothers, particularly in those lacking personal and social support. A preventive intervention approach was developed and implemented, leading to fewer maternal problems with infant crying at 2 months for women who did not ultimately become depressed. In preliminary analyses, depressed women did not benefit from the intervention in the same way.

Assessing Crying Complaints: The Interaction With Gastroesophageal Reflux and Cow's Milk Protein Intolerance

William R. Treem, MD

Considerable research has evaluated the degree to which 2 organic etiologies—gastroesophageal reflux-induced peptic esophagitis and cow's milk protein intolerance—contribute to infant colic. Gastroesophageal reflux may be a significant causative factor in about 5% of infants with colic, particularly those with vomiting, feeding refusal and other characteristic signs and symptoms. About 10% of infants with colic cannot tolerate cow's milk protein. After confirmatory workup, dietary modification, including elimination of cow's milk protein from the diet, may benefit this subset of infants.

Clinical Clues to Organic Etiologies in Infants with Colic

Siobhán Gormally, MD

Introduction

When the pediatrician is faced with the diagnostic dilemma of a crying, or so-called "colicky," infant under 5 months of age, there are 3 important questions that must be addressed:

- How can the clinician categorize the complaint of crying in this infant?
- What is the likelihood that this infant's crying pattern is secondary to underlying pathology?
- If pathology is present, are there any clinical clues in the infant's history or examination to alert the clinician to the possibility of organicity?

This chapter will attempt to answer these questions. In addition, a new model for crying complaints in nonfebrile infants less than 5 months of age will be discussed. And, the issue of organicity will be addressed in an evidence-based manner.

Categorization of Crying Complaints

A new system to categorize crying complaints in nonfebrile infants less than 5 months of age was published in 1998.[1] It takes the form of a clinical pie chart, as shown in Fig 1. The square surrounding the pie chart represents *all* nonfebrile infants less than 5 months of age, regardless of their amount of crying. Infants inside the circle exhibit a crying pattern that causes sufficient concern for parents to seek advice from a clinician. In contrast, the crying of infants outside the circle does not cause parents to seek professional assistance. The features of this pie chart represent "best current estimates" and may require revision as more data become available.

Fig 1. Crying complaints in nonfebrile infants <5 months of age.[1]

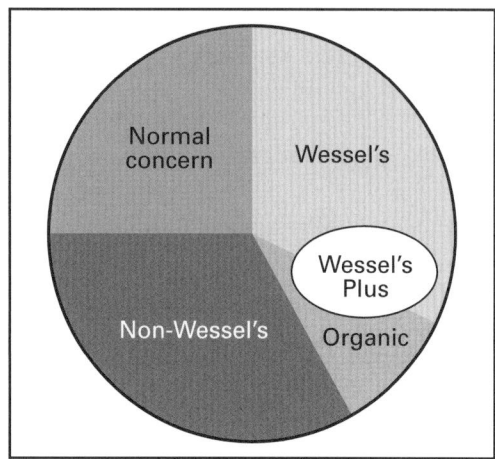

Reprinted with permission from Gormally SM, Barr RG. Of clinical pies and clinical cues: proposal for a clinical approach to complaints of early crying and colic. *Ambulatory Child Health*. Copyright © 1997 by Blackwell Science Ltd.

The clinical pie model for crying incorporates 5 separate categories of infants: those who have a normal crying pattern; those who fulfill Wessel's criteria[2]; those who fulfill non-Wessel's criteria; those who meet Wessel's Plus criteria; and those with organic disease. Approximately 25% of infants who are brought to a clinician because of parents' concern about their crying can be expected to have neither abnormal quality nor abnormal quantity of crying; that is, they are perfectly normal. The amount of concern generated by crying in infants often depends on the experience, anxiety level and general personalities of the caregivers. The infants who fit into this category are therefore often firstborns and their doctor's visit is simply a reflection of their parents' inexperience and desire for reassurance that all is well.[3] Infants who fulfill Wessel's classic criteria account for one third of the pie chart,[2,4] and infants with non-Wessel's colic account for an additional one third. Non-Wessel's colic refers to infants whose crying has a particular pattern and quality but does not meet Wessel's criteria in terms of *quantity* of crying.[5-7] The Wessel's Plus group includes those who meet Wessel's criteria as a minimum but who *also* exhibit typical behavioral manifestations, such as arching, drawing up of legs, abdominal distension, flushed facies and more.[8,9] These infants account for approximately 10% of the circle. The Wessel's Plus group overlaps with the final group, which includes infants whose crying or colic is due to organic disease.

Infants with a Crying Pattern Secondary to Organic Disease

A 9-month-old male was brought to the clinic at Our Lady of Lourdes Hospital by distraught parents, both of whom were healthcare professionals. Beginning at 1 month of age, this infant had severe episodes of inconsolable crying, especially late in the evening and at night, awakening, on average, 4 times nightly. His colicky episodes were associated with abdominal distension and discomfort and intermittent, loose and watery bowel movements. The infant had been seen previously by 3 doctors, all of whom made a diagnosis of "colic." Various preparations, including lactose, simethicone, gripe water and antacids, had been prescribed with little effect. The parents had also instituted behavioral modification, but to no avail. Examination revealed a well-nourished infant with mild flexural eczema who was otherwise normal. An underlying diagnosis of cow's milk protein intolerance (CMPI) was suspected. This was supported by a complete blood count that revealed eosinophilia, an elevated immunoglobulin E (IgE) and leukocytes in the stool. A predigested hydrolysate formula was prescribed. Within 1 week, all symptoms resolved.

Despite differences in definitions, most pediatricians accept that colic is a behavioral syndrome seen in a heterogeneous group of infants, and that underlying organic disease is responsible for colic in only a very small group. Nevertheless, some clinicians believe that colic is a distinct and likely pathologic entity,[10] as illustrated by the case just mentioned. This position is based on (a) scattered case reports of infants with a presumed diagnosis of colic who eventually are shown to have an organic basis for their crying behavior; (b) the ongoing, and as yet unresolved, controversy concerning the possible role of food intolerance (protein and carbohydrate) in colic; and, (c) review articles and book chapters that include exhaustive but often unsubstantiated lists of conditions that can present as "colic" despite the fact that many of these diagnoses have never been reported to present in true "colic" fashion.

In an effort to elucidate the issues concerning organicity, a comprehensive review of the literature[1] was performed, which focused on the frequency of organic etiologies in nonfebrile infants with colic. Also, clinical clues or key findings were identified in the literature that could be used as diagnostic tools to identify specific pathology, when present.

Main Findings of Literature Review

A detailed search of MEDLINE for the years 1966 to 1999 was performed. Search headings used were "crying" and "colic" for infants under the age of 1 year. Similar cues were used for searches of PUBMED and The Cochrane Controlled Trials Register. In addition, the search strategy was supplemented by checking the references from all papers to identify missing publications.

In reviewing the literature it became obvious that authors attributed the term "colic" to 3 distinct and very different clinical groups. The first group was comprised of *febrile* infants with excessive crying, usually of recent onset, who clearly did not fit into any accepted definition of colic. The second group included *nonfebrile* infants who had a crying pattern not dissimilar to that of colic but who presented beyond the classic 4-month cutoff period for colic. (These older, acute, nonfebrile infants also pose a diagnostic challenge for the pediatrician. Although not addressed in this review, this group was the subject of an interesting and informative case series by Poole in 1991.[11]) The third group encompassed infants who genuinely appeared to have a *colic behavioral syndrome*. This group did not include those who also had fever, were greater than 4 months of age or in whom the crying was clearly of acute (less than 24 hours) onset. However, because the clinical descriptions of the crying were certainly variable and often less than complete, a "best judgment" decision as to the presence of a colic syndrome was made by the authors.[1]

The search strategy yielded more than 100 articles that included clinical trials, case reports, case series, letters and topic reviews. All papers were assessed individually and were included in the study based on merit of definition used, age limitation and trial design.

This evidence-based evaluation of the relationship between organicity and colic was complicated by several factors, including *a lack of a uniform definition of colic* and by *clinical trials that were fraught with methodological problems, including selection bias and nonblinding.*

However, eventually, 51 original studies and case reports and 13 major reviews were considered of sufficient quality to be included in the analysis. Based on the scientific data provided, the evidence for implicating a specific pathologic etiology for colic was categorized into either "strong," "moderate" or "weak" evidence (Table 1).

Table 1. Evidence Supporting Pathology in Conditions Presenting as Colic

Strong[12-45]	Moderate[46-51]	Weak[11, 14, 16, 52-68]
Cow's milk protein intolerance	Gastroesophageal reflux disease/Gastroesophageal reflux	Lactose intolerance
Fructose intolerance		Eye pathology
Maternal drug ingestion	Shaken baby syndrome	Central nervous system abnormalities
Congenital heart disease	Infantile migraine	Urinary tract infection

Strong Evidence

"Strong evidence" could be provided by a well-planned, controlled clinical trial or a single comprehensively described case report. Strong evidence supported a role for 5 specific pathologic entities leading to colic: cow's milk protein intolerance, fructose intolerance, maternal drug ingestion, infantile migraine and congenital heart disease (CHD).

Cow's Milk Protein Intolerance. Intolerance of cow's milk protein is a well-recognized entity, yet its role in colic remains unclear. It has been the subject of 6 excellent review articles.[12-17] It has also been the subject of at least 14 clinical trials,[18-31] including a series of interesting original papers from Malmö, Sweden, wherein the papers' authors concluded that CMPI was implicated in colic.[20-23] Despite sophisticated study designs, the papers generated considerable debate, including several objections based on methodological grounds.[32-36]

Of all the clinical trials on CMPI, there were only 2 papers in which explicit entry criteria, detailed crying diary recordings, good definitions of colic and a multiple, double-blind, randomized design were utilized.[23, 31] In 1989, in a hospital-based study, Forsyth reported a decrease in colic in infants on the first change from cow's milk formula to a casein hydrolysate formula.[25] However, the effect of the change in formula decreased over the 17 days of the study. Consequently, only 12% (2 of 17) of the infants had a clinically meaningful change in crying with several formula changes. While this study supported an etiologic role for CMPI in colic, it also suggested that such a role is likely to be restricted to a small group of babies.

The larger community-based study by Hill and colleagues[31] complemented the crossover study by Forsyth.[25] It supplied strong evidence supporting a role for CMPI in severe colic, but the investigators suggested that these infants frequently have other coexisting symptoms. A recent article by Lucassen et al in *BMJ*,[14] which assessed the methodologic quality of diet treatment trials in colic, concluded that the pooled effect of eliminating cow's milk protein was 0.22, indicating that a hypoallergenic formula has a clear effect in some children with colic.

Strong evidence to support the remaining 4 pathologic conditions is based on case reports and case series, implying that they are real, but nonetheless exceedingly rare, causes of colic.

Isolated Fructose Intolerance. Fructose is a monosaccharide used as a "natural" sweetener in unprocessed foods. In 1990, Wales et al comprehensively described a single case of isolated fructose intolerance in a healthy term girl who presented with many features of a "colic syndrome."[37] The infant had received fennel and black currant drinks daily from 1 week of age and later received orange juice and bananas. From 7 weeks of age she had severe screaming attacks after feedings and required hospitalization on 2 occasions. These episodes were associated with excessive gas, intermittent diarrhea, arching and abdominal distension. There was no improvement with the introduction of a cow's milk protein-free diet. Because of the temporal relationships with fruit and fruit juices and the persistence of symptoms beyond 4 months of age, she was evaluated for fructose malabsorption by hydrogen breath test and jejunal biopsy. Symptoms disappeared completely on a fructose-exclusion diet, only to reemerge with a fructose challenge test.

Maternal Drug Ingestion. Maternal drug ingestion can potentially contribute to an infant manifesting a colic-like syndrome in either the prenatal, perinatal or postnatal period.

Prenatal. Prenatal maternal ingestion of narcotics or methadone is well recognized among neonatologists as a cause of excessive neonatal irritability and crying. This was well described by Finnegan[38] in the late 1970s. However, it is often not appreciated that the onset of withdrawal symptoms can be delayed beyond 2 weeks of age and can continue until the infant is 6 weeks to 8 weeks of age. Symptoms can include excessive crying, irritability, sweating, hypertonicity and diarrhea.[38, 39] Because of this, it may be difficult to distinguish colic from withdrawal from the effects of maternal drug ingestion.

Perinatal. The possibility that colic-causing substances are transferred through breast milk has been debated for many years. A report by Thomas suggested a possible association between drugs used during maternal labor and colic.[40] However, this investigator did not define colic or indicate how the infants were fed. His suggestions[40] were later discredited by Whichelow in a paper that satisfactorily defined the term "colic."[41] This letter in *Lancet*[41] reported an equal incidence of colic in breast-fed infants regardless of whether the mothers had received analgesia or oxytocin during labor.

Postnatal. Very rarely, maternal drug ingestion in the postnatal period causes symptoms of colic in breast-fed infants. In 1993, Lester et al reported a case of a 6-week-old breast-fed infant who had been well at birth.[42] At 2 weeks of age his mother began to use fluoxetine hydrochloride (Prozac) while breastfeeding. Soon after, the baby began to develop severe colicky symptoms that would have placed him in the Wessel's Plus group. The symptoms of excessive crying and irritability were reduced when the mother switched to a commercial formula, only to return again when breastfeeding was reinstituted. A significant concentration of fluoxetine hydrochloride was detected in the infant's serum. Clinical clues to the presence of an organic basis for this infant's colic were discernible from a diary in which the mother carefully recorded the coexistence of other symptoms, including watery diarrhea, abdominal distension, drawing up of legs and vomiting.

Infantile Migraine. In 1994, Katerji and Painter described a child with Wessel's Plus-type colic beginning at 2 weeks of life.[43] Crying episodes lasted 1.5 hours to 4 hours, during which she would "…cry inconsolably.… arch her back, twist her trunk, [and] extend her legs."[43] By 4 months of age the infant's symptoms persisted. In addition, by this time other atypical characteristics, including staring, lid retraction (Collier's sign), vomiting, lack of diurnal variation in cry and failure to thrive (FTT), became apparent. Extensive gastrointestinal (GI) and neurologic examinations and investigations were performed that proved normal. On direct questioning, a significant family history of migraine emerged—in her father, and in her paternal uncle, aunt, grandfather and great-grandfather. Cyproheptadine hydrochloride (Periactin) therapy was therefore begun empirically. All symptoms resolved within 1 week.

Congenital Heart Disease. Anomalous origin of the left coronary artery (ALCA) from the pulmonary artery is an exceedingly rare phenomenon; it occurs in 1 of 300,000 children.[45] Diagnosis can be difficult. Symptoms range from those of pneumonia to bronchiolitis and heart failure. There are 2 case reports of ALCA mimicking colic that presented in the first 2 weeks of life as excessive crying in otherwise healthy infants.[44, 45] Mentioned initially in 1933 by Bland, White and Garland,[44] ALCA was more comprehensively described in 1998 by Mahle.[45] Symptoms of colic became worse after meals, with severe crying spasms, abdominal distension and severe irritability.[45] There was no improvement following the introduction of a hypoallergenic formula. New clinical findings of tachycardia and tachypnea after 4 months of age enabled the correct diagnosis of ALCA to be established. It was postulated that the excessive postprandial symptoms occurred as a result of myocardial ischemia secondary to a "coronary steal phenomenon"; that is, the arterial blood bypassed myocardial capillaries to preferentially vascularize the gut, resulting in angina-like symptoms in the infant.

Moderate Evidence

There is moderate evidence to support the association of gastroesophageal reflux disease (GERD) and Shaken Baby Syndrome with the clinical appearance of colic.

Gastroesophageal Reflux Disease. Prior to the last 10 years, GERD was virtually unknown. Now it is arguably the cause of a large spectrum of symptoms ranging from an acute life-threatening event (ALTE), to pseudo-seizures to colic. The evidence to support GERD as the cause or underlying etiology in colic is, at best, moderate and includes results from 2 retrospective studies[46, 47] and one more recent prospective study.[48]

In a study in 1995 by Heine et al, only 1 of 24 excessively irritable infants who were less than 3 months of age had significant gastroesophageal reflux (GER), as determined by pH monitoring.[46] The diagnosis was suggested clinically by frequent vomiting. Interpretation of the retrospective study by Berezin et al is more difficult due to lack of information about patient selection.[47] Only 18 patients were accumulated over a 6-year period. Of the patients in the study group who were less than 3 months of age, 22% had endoscopic or histologic evidence of esophagitis. The only clinical parameter that helped differentiate infants with esophagitis was their increased frequency of regurgitation of feeds; this occurred, on average, 3.2 times per day compared with 0.5 times daily in infants who had a normal esophagus. A study by Berkowitz, Naveh and Berant in 1997, entitled "'Infantile colic' as the sole manifestation of gastroesophageal reflux," purported to be a prospective trial of GERD in infants with colic.[48] The investigators performed pH monitoring in 26 "colic" infants ranging in age from 2 months to 9 months (mean, 4.8 months). They subsequently treated 16 babies who had pH evidence of reflux with cisapride (Propulsid) and cimetidine (Tagamet) and reported clinical improvement. The majority of infant subjects were outside the proper age group for colic. In addition, this was not a randomized, controlled or blinded study. Furthermore, the presence or absence of other GI symptoms was not recorded.

Shaken Baby Syndrome. Nonaccidental injury (NAI) is an emotionally laden area in pediatrics. Crying is certainly a recognized precipitating event for potentially fatal child maltreatment.[49] However, the suggestion that colic can be the presenting complaint for NAI is somewhat perturbing.[49-51] Case reports, such as the one by Singer and Rosenberg,[51] are cited often. They described a 3-month-old infant who presented with a crying pattern that could be consistent with a diagnosis of colic by the nature of its duration and frequency. However, the remainder of the clinical picture was clearly atypical for colic. The infant's crying pattern had only become established at 10 weeks of age. Her continuous crying was so intense that she was unable to properly feed, and she was losing weight. She presented to an Emergency department at about 14 weeks of age. Faint limb bruise marks and retinal hemorrhages were probably present when she was first seen, although these findings were not noted until she was seen a second time in the Emergency Department in a moribund state, 9 hours later.

Weak Evidence

Weaker evidence exists for the possibility that lactose intolerance, eye pathology, central nervous system (CNS) abnormalities and urinary tract infection are implicated in colic.

Lactose Intolerance. A primary role for lactose intolerance in colic seems attractive because it is consistent with the following clinical pattern observed in infants: (a) colic occurs with equal frequency in cow's milk- and breast-fed infants; (b) crying peaks in the afternoon and evening after a day of ingesting carbohydrates; and, (c) colic usually resolves spontaneously at 4 months of age, coinciding with increased physiologic expression of gut lactase enzyme. Unfortunately, many studies purporting to support a role for carbohydrates in colic are flawed by methodologic problems and a lack of a clear definition of infant subjects.[16, 52-54] All but one of the more scientifically valid studies mitigate *against* a role for carbohydrates in colic.[55-62] In 1989, Hyams and colleagues were unable to demonstrate a difference in breath hydrogen excretion in infants with colic defined by prospective cry diaries.[55] Two other studies failed to show a decrease in crying or fussing behavior in infants with colic with decreased lactose intake[56] or addition of a lactase enzyme.[57] This is further supported by 2 negative studies that assessed the efficacy of simethicone in colic.[58, 59] The diet-trial review article by Lucassen et al in *BMJ* in 1998 concluded that there is no evidence that low lactose formula milks are effective in colic.[14] However, Lucassen et al[14] omitted a well-designed study by Kearney et al, also published in 1998.[60] These investigators performed a randomized, double-blind, crossover trial of lactase in the management of a group of 13 infants with Wessel's colic.[60] They showed a reduction in crying time in excess of 1 hour when milk formulas were incubated for 24 hours with lactase drops. This study design[60] addressed many of the previous studies' shortcomings. However, the authors did not mention the presence of any other specific symptoms, such as diarrhea or a family history of allergies.

Eye Pathology. In textbooks of emergency pediatric medicine, corneal abrasions and foreign bodies are often cited as possible causes of colic in infants. However, it is unlikely that these infants had colic syndrome. Much quoted papers, such as those by Poole in 1991[11] and Harkness in 1989,[63] describe infants who were well previously but who presented with *acute*-onset crying usually lasting less than 24 hours in duration. A single case of congenital glaucoma presenting in a colic-like manner was identified by Talbot et al[64] in the literature review. Unfortunately, this report is limited by an incomplete description of the infant, who, at 13 weeks of age had an 8-week history of crying. Crying bouts lasted up to 5 hours and were associated with the drawing up of legs. The physical examination was normal, except for large corneas at 13 weeks of age and photophobia at 17 weeks of age.

Central Nervous System Abnormalities. There is little in the literature to support brain tumors and subdural hematomas presenting as colic. There is, however, a report of a child with a Chiari brain malformation who began to cry excessively at 2 weeks of age.[65] He was initially diagnosed with colic despite the absence of an evening crying peak, crying persisting beyond 4 months of age and associated arching of his back. At 12 months of age a Chiari type-1 malformation was detected by magnetic resonance imaging (MRI) scan. Posterior fossa decompression was accompanied by complete resolution of crying.

Urinary Tract Infection. Urine examination is one of the most common investigations performed on infants with colic. This practice is based on the principle that urinary tract infection is a "hidden" cause of illness that is often detected easily by urinalysis. There have been 2 case series purporting to assess the prevalence of urinary disease in colicky infants.[66, 67] Both are flawed by a lack of description of the colic symptoms and by the absence of case controls. Browne and Lillystone retrospectively reviewed 1770 cases of colic presenting over a 10-year period.[67] They documented renal disease in 6 cases of severe colic that had not responded to conventional therapy. Their failure to acknowledge that the prevalence of asymptomatic bacteriuria (defined as a bag collection urine specimen with greater than 100,000 cfu/mL) is 1.4% in neonates and up to 3% in older infants weakens their conclusions considerably.[68]

Conclusions

Shortcomings in definitions and trial designs preclude the possibility of making definitive statements about organicity in infants with colic and excessive crying. The following generalizations, however, can be made:

An organic basis for *"true"* colic—that is, a behavioral syndrome of early crying that increases and then decreases in the first few months of life—is relatively rare and probably accounts for 5% to 10% of cases.[12-17, 69-71] A total of 11 entities that can mimic colic have been identified. Five presented with "strong evidence." The evidence for 8 of these conditions was based solely on case reports or case series. While virtually any disease in infants can present as *crying*, those that present with a complete *colic behavioral syndrome* are rare.

Our literature review implies that certain clinical clues or "red flags," either in the medical history or clinical examination, will suggest an underlying organic condition (Table 2). These "red flags" include infants whose crying is extreme, prolonged and high pitched, and whose crying patterns lack diurnal rhythm. Crying beyond 4 months of age is of concern. Other important symptoms include frequent regurgitation, vomiting, diarrhea, weight loss and/or failure to thrive. A positive family history of migraine (± atopy) may be useful. Discrete inquiries should be made of the parents regarding the possibility of maternal drug ingestion.

Table 2. Key Clinical Clues for Identifying Organic Disease as Etiology in Infants Presenting with Colic

Extreme or high-pitched cry
Lack of diurnal rhythm
Persistence of symptoms after 4 months of age
Presence of frequent regurgitation, vomiting, diarrhea, weight loss
Positive family history of migraine
Maternal drug ingestion
Positive physical examination

Clinical examination can also serve as an important source for diagnostic clues. It is imperative that examination of the infant includes careful skin and eye inspections, palpation of all large bones and thorough neurological, GI and cardiovascular assessments.

Areas for Future Research

There is no doubt that colic is an extremely difficult and painstaking phenomenon to study. Therefore, significant deficits still exist in our current understanding of this condition. The literature review cited in this chapter highlights the need for good quality community-based studies, uncontaminated by referral bias, to examine the prevalence of organicity in infants presenting with a colic-type syndrome. It is imperative that such studies be prospective, use a tight definition of "colic" and include age-matched, normal, control infants. Further research is also required to determine whether the "organicity" clinical clues or "red flags" derived from retrospective data can withstand the rigors of prospective studies.

References

1. Gormally SM, Barr R. Of clinical pies and clinical clues: proposed pie as a clinical approach to complaints of early crying and colic. *Ambulatory Child Health.* 1998;3:137-153
2. Wessel MA, Cobb JC, Jackson EB, Harris GS, Detwiler AC. Paroxysmal fussing in infancy, sometimes called "colic." *Pediatrics.* 1954;14:421-424.
3. St. James-Roberts I, Halil T. Infant crying patterns in the first year: normal community and clinical findings. *Journal of Child Psychology and Psychiatry, and Allied Disciplines.* 1991;32:951-968.
4. Barr RG, Rotman A, Yaremko J, Leduc D, Francoeur TE. The crying of infants with colic: a controlled empirical description. *Pediatrics.* 1992;90:14-21.
5. Barr RG. The normal crying curve: what do we really know? *Developmental Medicine and Child Neurology.* 1990;32:356-362.
6. St. James-Roberts I. What is distinct about infants' "colic" cries? *Archives of Disease in Childhood.* 1999;80:56-62.
7. Zeskind PS, Barr RG. Acoustic characteristics of naturally occurring cries of infants with "colic." *Child Development.* 1997;68:394-403.
8. Illingworth RS. Infantile colic revisited. *Archives of Disease in Childhood.* 1985;60:981-985.
9. Lester BM, Boukydis CFZ, Garcia-Coll CT, Hole WT. Symposium on infant colic: introduction. *Infant Mental Health Journal.* 1990;11:320-333.
10. Jones JA. Can fussy babies be spoiled? *Pediatrics.* 1985;76:854-855.
11. Poole SR. The infant with acute, unexplained, excessive crying. *Pediatrics.* 1991;88:450-455.
12. Kerner JA Jr. Formula allergy and intolerance. *Gastroenterology Clinics of North America.* 1995;24:1-25.
13. Is colic in infants associated with diet? *Nutrition Reviews.* 1988;46:374-376.
14. Lucassen PLBJ, Assendelft WJJ, Gubbels JW, van Eijk JTM, van Geldrop WJ, Knuistingh Neven A. Effectiveness of treatments for infantile colic: systematic review. *British Medical Journal.* 1998;316:1563-1569.
15. O'Neill M. A gastrointestinal perspective on colic. *The Canadian Journal of Pediatrics.* 1993;5:297-300.
16. Miller AR, Barr RG. Infantile colic. Is it a gut issue? *Pediatric Clinics of North America.* 1991;38:

1407-1423.
17. Treem WR. Infant colic. A pediatric gastroenterologist's perspective. *Pediatric Clinics of North America.* 1994;41:1121-1138.
18. Thomas DW, McGilligan K, Eisenberg LD, Lieberman HM, Rissman EM. Infantile colic and type of milk feeding. *American Journal of Diseases of Children.* 1987;141:451-453.
19. Evans RW, Fergusson DM, Allardyce RA, Taylor B. Maternal diet and infantile colic in breast-fed infants. *Lancet.* 1981;1(8234):1340-1342.
20. Lothe L, Lindberg T, Jakobsson I. Cow's milk formula as a cause of infantile colic: a double-blind study. *Pediatrics.* 1982;70:7-10.
21. Lothe L, Lindberg T. Cow's milk whey protein elicits symptoms of infantile colic in colicky formula-fed infants: a double-blind crossover study. *Pediatrics.* 1989;83:262-266.
22. Jakobsson I, Lindberg T. Cow's milk as a cause of infantile colic in breast-fed infants. *Lancet.* 1978; 2(8087):437-439.
23. Jakobsson I, Lindberg T. Cow's milk proteins cause infantile colic in breast-fed infants: a double-blind crossover study. *Pediatrics.* 1983;71:268-271.
24. Kahn A, Mozin MJ, Casimir G, Montauk L, Blum D. Insomnia and cow's milk allergy in infants. *Pediatrics.* 1985;76:880-884.
25. Forsyth BWC. Colic and the effect of changing formulas: a double-blind, multiple-crossover study. *The Journal of Pediatrics.* 1989;115:521-526.
26. Oggero R, Garbo G, Savino F, Mostert M. Dietary modifications versus dicyclomine hydrochloride in the treatment of severe infantile colics. *Acta Paediatrica.* 1994;83:222-225.
27. Taubman B. Parental counseling compared with elimination of cow's milk or soy milk protein for the treatment of infant colic syndrome: a randomized trial. *Pediatrics.* 1988;81:756-761.
28. Iacono G, Carroccio A, Montalto G, et al. Severe infantile colic and food intolerance: a long-term prospective study. *Journal of Pediatric Gastroenterology and Nutrition.* 1991;12:332-335.
29. Campbell JP. Dietary treatment of infant colic: a double-blind study. *Journal of the Royal College of General Practitioners.* 1989;39:11-14.
30. Hill DJ, Hosking CS. The colic debate. *Pediatrics.* 1995;96:165-166.
31. Hill DJ, Hudson IL, Sheffield LJ, Shelton MJ, Menahem S, Hosking CS. A low allergen diet is a significant intervention in infantile colic: results of a community-based study. *The Journal of Allergy and Clinical Immunology.* 1995;96:886-892.
32. Carey WB. Cow's milk formula and infantile colic [letter]. *Pediatrics.* 1989;84:1124-1125.
33. Miller JJ, Brand JC, McVeagh P. Breath hydrogen excretion in infants with colic [letter]. *Archives of Disease in Childhood.* 1990;65:248.
34. Taubman B. Colic or milk allergy [letter]. *Pediatrics.* 1989;84:938-939.
35. Forsyth BWC. A partially blind study [letter]. *Pediatrics.* 1983;71:667.
36. LeBlanc MH. Soy formula doesn't help colic [letter]. *Pediatrics.* 1983;71:299-300.
37. Wales JK, Primhak RA, Rattenbury J, Taylor CJ. Isolated fructose malabsorption. *Archives of Disease in Childhood.* 1990;65:227-229.
38. Finnegan LP. Pathophysiological and behavioural effects of the transplacental transfer of narcotic drugs to the foetuses and neonates of narcotic-dependent mothers. *Bulletin on Narcotics.* 1979;31: 1-58.
39. Sweet AY. Narcotic withdrawal syndrome in the newborn. *Pediatric Reviews.* 1982;3:285-291.
40. Thomas DB. Aetiological associations in infantile colic: an hypothesis. *Australian Paediatric Journal.* 1981;17:292-295.
41. Whichelow MJ. Infant colic and drugs during labor [letter]. *Lancet.* 1981;1(8223):777.
42. Lester BM, Cucca J, Andreozzi L, Flanagan P, Oh W. Possible association between fluoxetine hydrochloride and colic in an infant. *Journal of the American Academy of Child and Adolescent*

Psychiatry. 1993;32:1253-1255.
43. Katerji MA, Painter MJ. Infantile migraine presenting as colic. *Journal of Child Neurology.* 1994;9:336-337.
44. Bland EF, White PD, Garland J. Congenital anomalies of the coronary arteries: review of an unusual case associated with cardiac hypertrophy. *American Heart Journal.* 1933;8:787-801.
45. Mahle WT. A dangerous case of colic: anomalous left coronary artery presenting with paroxysms of irritability. *Pediatric Emergency Care.* 1998;14:24-27.
46. Heine RG, Jaquiery A, Lubitz L, Cameron DJ, Catto-Smith AG. Role of gastro-oesophageal reflux in infant irritability. *Archives of Disease in Childhood.* 1995;73:121-125.
47. Berezin S, Glassman MS, Bostwick H, Halata M. Esophagitis as a cause of infant colic. *Clinical Pediatrics.* 1995;34:158-159.
48. Berkowitz D, Naveh Y, Berant M. "Infantile colic" as the sole manifestation of gastroesophageal reflux. *Journal of Pediatric Gastroenterology and Nutrition.* 1997;24:231-233.
49. Showers J, Apolo J, Thomas J, Beavers S. Fatal child abuse: a two-decade review. *Pediatric Emergency Care.* 1985;1:66-70.
50. Ludwig S, Warman S. Shaken baby syndrome: a review of 20 cases. *Annals of Emergency Medicine.* 1984;13:104-107.
51. Singer JI, Rosenberg NM. A fatal case of colic. *Pediatric Emergency Care.* 1992;8:171-172.
52. Barr RG. Colic. In: Walker WA, Durie PR, Hamilton JR, Walker-Smith JA, Watkins JB, eds. *Pediatric Gastrointestinal Disease: Pathophysiology, Diagnosis, Management.* 2nd ed. St Louis, Mo: Mosby-Year Book; 1996:241-250.
53. Laws HF II. Effect of lactase on infantile colic [letter]. *The Journal of Pediatrics.* 1991;118:993-994.
54. Moore DJ, Robb TA, Davidson GP. Breath hydrogen response to milk containing lactose in colicky and noncolicky infants. *The Journal of Pediatrics.* 1988;113:979-984.
55. Hyams JS, Geertsma MA, Etienne NL, Treem WR. Colonic hydrogen production in infants with colic. *The Journal of Pediatrics.* 1989;115:592-594.
56. Stahlberg MR, Savilahti E. Infantile colic and feeding. *Archives of Disease in Childhood.* 1986;61: 1232-1233.
57. Miller JJ, McVeagh P, Fleet GH, Petocz P, Brand JC. Effect of yeast lactase enzyme on "colic" in infants fed human milk. *The Journal of Pediatrics.* 1990;117:261-263.
58. Danielsson B, Hwang CP. Treatment of infantile colic with surface active substance (simethicone). *Acta Paediatrica Scandinavica.* 1985;74:446-450.
59. Metcalf TJ, Irons TG, Sher LD, Young PC. Simethicone in the treatment of infant colic: a randomized, placebo-controlled, multicenter trial. *Pediatrics.* 1994;94:29-34.
60. Kearney PJ, Malone AJ, Hayes T, Cole M, Hyland M. A trial of lactase in the management of infant colic. *Journal of Human Nutrition and Dietetics.* 1998;11:281-285.
61. Liebman WM. Infantile colic. Association with lactose and milk intolerance. *JAMA: The Journal of the American Medical Association.* 1981;245:732-733.
62. Barr RG, Clogg LJ, Wooldridge JA, Tansey CM. Carbohydrate change has no effect on infant crying behavior: a randomized controlled trial. *American Journal of Disease of Children.* 1987;141:391.
63. Harkness MJ. Corneal abrasion in infancy as a cause of inconsolable crying. *Pediatric Emergency Care.* 1989;5:242-244.
64. Talbot EM, Pitts JF, Dudgeon J, Lee WR. A case of developmental glaucoma presenting with abdominal colic and subnormal intraocular pressure. *Journal of Pediatric Ophthalmology and Strabismus.* 1992;29:116-119.
65. Listernick R, Tomita T. Persistent crying in infancy as a presentation of Chiari type I malformation. *The Journal of Pediatrics.* 1991;118:567-569.
66. Du JN. Colic as the sole symptom of urinary tract infection in infants. *Canadian Medical Association*

Journal. 1976;115:334-337.
67. Browne G, Lillystone D. Renal disease presenting as severe unremitting colic. *The Medical Journal of Australia.* 1991;154:93-94.
68. Travis LB, Brouhard BH. Infection of the urinary tract. In: Rudolph AM, Hoffman JIE, Rudolph CD, eds. *Rudolph's Textbook of Pediatrics.* 1996:1388-1392.
69. Geertsma MA, Hyams JS. Colic—a pain syndrome of infancy? *Pediatric Clinics of North America.* 1989;36:905-919.
70. Sferra TJ, Heitlinger LA. Gastrointestinal gas formation and infantile colic. *Pediatric Clinics of North America.* 1996;43:489-510.
71. Lester B, Barr RG, eds. *Ross Roundtable on Infant Colic.* Columbus, Ohio: Ross Laboratories; 1996.

The Impact of Irritable Infant Behavior on Maternal Mental State: A Longitudinal Study and a Treatment Trial

Professor Lynne Murray and Professor Peter Cooper

Introduction

Conventional wisdom suggests that difficult infant behavior in the first few weeks of life, such as excessive or persistent crying or irritability, is due to parental inexperience, insensitive parenting or lack of parental effort. Yet, considerable research has shown that this is not the case.[1] Moreover, there is evidence that such difficult infant behavior places a considerable burden on caretakers, resulting, for example, in more frequent consultations with medical services in the first 3 months of an infant's life.

Some central questions arise from this line of inquiry: What is the extent of the impact of difficult infant behavior on parents? Does difficult infant behavior, including excessive or persistent crying, precipitate clinical depression in the mother? Furthermore, if infant behavior has an impact on maternal psychological status, can preventive treatments be developed that directly focus on infant behavioral issues? Two research studies that address these questions will be discussed.

The Impact of Infant Characteristics on Maternal Mental State

In the US and in the UK, approximately 10% of mothers experience a depressive disorder in the months following childbirth. Depression has pervasive effects on interpersonal functioning, and in many cases difficulties extend to the mother's relationship with her infant.[2] Depressed mothers interact with their infants in characteristic ways. Typically, such mothers are either withdrawn or disengaged from their infants, or their interactions are agitated, intrusive and hostile. To date, the literature on postnatal depression has emphasized the impact of the maternal mood disorder on the infant; that is, a direction of effect from parent to child. Indeed, there is substantial evidence that children of mothers who have experienced postnatal depression have a range of adverse developmental outcomes, several of which are linked to disturbances in maternal communication with the infant.[2] Several studies from the late 1980s suggested, however, that infants of depressed mothers might be intrinsically difficult to manage[3-5]; furthermore, there were suggestions that infant behavioral difficulties such as irritability or excessive crying may contribute to the mother's mood disorder. Certainly, depressed women are more likely to report problems with infant crying and demands for attention than those who are well,[2] but independent observations of infants of depressed mothers also suggest that these infants may be particularly difficult. Whiffen and Gotlib,[3] for example, observed that 2-month-old infants of depressed women deteriorated more rapidly under the stress of developmental testing than did infants of well women. Cutrona and Troutman[4] found an association between the presence of difficult infant behavior at 3 months of age, as assessed by both direct observations of infant crying and maternal crying records and reports, and the persistence of maternal depression. Also, Field and colleagues[5] found that 3- to 6-month-old infants of depressed mothers were more negative and fussy than other infants; notably, when research nurses interacted with these infants, the nurses began to behave in a more depressed fashion.

The results of these studies are clearly consistent with the idea that certain infant characteristics contribute to the onset of maternal mood disorder. Indeed, such an inference is in line with models of depression that emphasize the role of aversive and uncontrollable events—in this case difficult infant behavior—in creating a sense of helplessness.[6] Nevertheless, because each of these studies[3-5] assessed infants only *after* the onset of the maternal mood disorder, it is equally plausible that the infants had gradually become difficult to manage over the first few months as a result of their exposure to disturbed maternal functioning associated with depression.

A strict test of the influence of infant behavior on maternal mood requires that neonates be assessed *prior* to the onset of maternal mood disorder. Given that the incidence of postpartum depression is only approximately 10%, it has not been feasible, until recently, to mount a prospective study: This would require a full population screen entailing a large number of redundant assessments of infants of women who remain well in order to study sufficient numbers of infants of women who subsequently become depressed. With the development of a predictive index for postnatal depression,[7] prospective investigation has become feasible. Such a tool permits the antenatal recruitment of women who are at increased risk for depression whose infants can be assessed in the neonatal period before the onset of the depressive disorder. The risk factors for depression that comprise this index include a previous history of affective disorder, the mother's prior experience of pregnancy (ie, whether or not planned, and her subsequent emotional state) and poor social support and living conditions.

Using this index to identify a study group, the role of individual infant characteristics in the onset and persistence of postnatal depression was examined.[8] Because of previous research findings, we were particularly interested in the dimension of "irritability"; this refers to infants who respond to the slightest stimulation, become easily and intensely distressed and are hard to soothe and console. Lastly, to determine the longer-term significance of irritable neonatal characteristics, a follow-up assessment of the presence of infant behavior problems was made at 18 months.*

In this study, a consecutive series of primiparous women attending the 32-week antenatal clinic at the Cambridge (UK) Maternity Hospital[8] was screened with the Predictive Index for Postnatal Depression.[7] Subsequently, those women who were identified as being at high risk, and who delivered full-term, healthy infants, were approached on the postnatal wards for recruitment. Of the 238 women who were invited to participate in the study, 188 (79%) agreed to take part. A smaller number of women at low risk for depression were also recruited as a control group. Of the 46 low-risk women who were approached, 43 (93%) agreed to participate. The control group was studied to establish whether maternal risk status itself influenced neonatal functioning and to examine whether there was any difference in the effects of infant characteristics according to risk status. Because infant functioning in the days immediately following birth may be influenced by the nature of the labor and delivery, including medication administered to the mother,[9] the initial assessment of the neonate was delayed until 10 days postpartum. Then, at 8 weeks and at 18 weeks, the mother's mental state was assessed, and the relationship between neonatal characteristics and the subsequent onset and persistence of maternal depression was examined.

*A full account of this study is given in *Developmental Medicine and Child Neurology.* 1996;38: 109-119.

Mothers completed the Maternity Blues Scale[10] and the Mother and Baby Scale[11] in the first postpartum week. These instruments were used to evaluate any influence of the mother's emotional state on the neonate in the days following delivery as well as the mother's feelings of confidence in handling her infant. The Mother and Baby Scale[11] measures maternal perceptions of unsettled and irregular infant behavior, irritability and alertness during feeds and overall infant difficulty, as well as maternal self-confidence. In addition, obstetric and pediatric records were examined for information of potential relevance to neonatal functioning.

At 10 days a researcher administered the Brazelton Neonatal Behavioral Assessment Scale (NBAS)[12] to the infants in their homes, and the assessment was repeated at 15 days. The researcher also examined the infants to rule out neurologic abnormalities. The NBAS, a standardized assessment tool in which the neonate's behavior is elicited in relation to a range of stimuli, yields scores on measures of orientation, motor behavior, the range and regulation of state, autonomic stability, reflexes and irritability. In this study,[8] the measure of irritability employed was the average of the responses to 3 NBAS items: peak of excitement, rapidity of buildup and the irritability item itself.

At the time of the neonatal assessment, the researcher also interviewed the mothers using the Structured Clinical Interview for DSM diagnoses (SCID)[13]; if a mother had already become depressed, she and her infant were excluded from further participation in the study. Eight women from the high-risk group and one from the low-risk sample had evidence of depression by the time of initial neonatal assessment and were excluded. The remaining infants had not, therefore, been exposed to any influence of maternal depression at the time of the neonatal assessment.

At 6 weeks postpartum the Edinburgh Postnatal Depression Scale[14] was administered, and at 8 weeks and 18 weeks full mental-state assessments, again using the SCID, were conducted by a second researcher who was unaware of all previous assessments.

Main Findings

By 8 weeks, 32% of the high risk-group of women had become depressed, as had 19% of the low-risk group. (This was actually a surprisingly high rate for the low-risk hospital population as a whole.)[8]

Before focusing on the relationship between infant characteristics in the neonatal period and the subsequent development of maternal depression, we examined the associations between neonatal behavior and other factors in the postnatal period that may be relevant to the onset of depression, such as the mother's emotional state, her self-confidence and her perceptions of her infant.[8] That is, although mothers who were already depressed at 10 days were excluded from the study, it was important to confirm that neonates' behaviors at the time of the assessments were not simply a function of more subtle aspects of maternal feelings and mood at that time. In fact, there was little association between the objective measure of infant functioning and maternal perceptions and mood: The NBAS measure of irritability was correlated only weakly with maternal perceptions of irritability on the Mother and Baby Scale (.15), and there was a similarly weak relationship (.14) between the NBAS rating of irritability and maternal mood in the first days postpartum, as assessed by the Maternity Blues Scale. By contrast, mothers' perceptions of their infants as being difficult correlated strongly with their level of confidence (.52) and their "Blues" scores (.30).

We then looked for differences in the various measures administered in the neonatal period between the high- and low-risk groups.[8] The groups were quite similar; the rate of neonatal irritability was 17% in both groups. Taken together, these preliminary investigations indicate that the behavior of the neonates, as measured by the NBAS, was neither a function of current maternal experience nor of postnatal depression risk status.

Neonatal Behavioral Assessment Scale

The scores from the 10-day NBAS assessment were examined in relation to the occurrence of subsequent postnatal depression at 2 months. As predicted, neonatal irritability was positively associated with subsequent maternal depression, with the best prediction of depression being achieved by simply distinguishing the most irritable 25% of infants from the remainder. However, this relationship between neonatal irritability and depression applied only to women who were already at high risk for postnatal depression; in the low-risk group its impact was not significant.

Maternal Perceptions of the Infant

Having established that objectively assessed irritability on the NBAS predicted maternal depression, we then examined whether mothers' perceptions of their infants in the first few days postpartum were similarly predictive.[8] Three dimensions on the Mother and Baby Scale are associated with depression: the perception of unsettled and irregular infant behavior, perceived infant irritability during feeds and low maternal self-confidence. These effects were comparable in both high- and low-risk mothers. Specifically considering these 3 dimensions, irritability during feeds and maternal self-confidence were not useful to predict outcomes. However, the perception of unsettled and irregular infant behavior predicted maternal depression most accurately. As with the neonatal assessment results, the association between maternal depression and perceived unsettled and irregular behavior was further investigated. Again, the most useful classification distinguished between infants perceived to be in the *worst* 25% and all others.

Postnatal Blues

The effect of the Maternity Blues Scale score on subsequent postnatal depression was highly significant.[8] Overall, a difference of 5 points in the total score increased the odds of depression by a factor of 1.77.

Multivariate Analysis

As noted previously, there was little relationship between the infants' performance on the neonatal assessment and the mothers' "Blues" scores and perceptions of the infants in the first postnatal week. A final analysis was conducted to be certain that the apparent impact of objectively measured neonatal responses on the risk of postnatal depression was not confounded by aspects of maternal functioning in the first few days after delivery. The impact of neonatal irritability on subsequent maternal depression was considered simultaneously with maternal "Blues" scores and maternal perceptions of infants' unsettled and irregular behaviors. This analysis revealed that the effects of neonatal irritability and motor behavior remained significant even after taking account of maternal blues and perceptions of the infant.

Other Potential Confounding Effects

Before concluding that infant characteristics definitely influenced maternal mental state, it was important to look for potentially confounding effects.[8] First, we needed to consider the possibility that some third, as yet unidentified factor, operating either through the uterine environment or during delivery, may account for both depression and irritable infant behavior. For example, although human studies are lacking, there is evidence from animal research that pregnant mothers exposed to stress give birth to offspring who have elevated basal cortisol levels and increased adrenocorticotropin responses to stress, a possible equivalent of an irritable profile.[15] Thus, a range of maternal, obstetric and infant perinatal variables was investigated, which included smoking during pregnancy, bleeding, high blood pressure or preeclamptic toxemia, induced or accelerated labor, use of analgesia, suboptimal length of labor, fetal distress, method of delivery, 5-minute APGAR score, delayed or irregular neonatal respiration or use of artificial respiration and infant gender. Each of these maternal and infant factors was examined with relation to both postnatal depression and high neonatal irritability. No significant associations emerged.

Lastly, we addressed the possibility that maternal caretaking practices associated with incipient depression may have influenced neonatal behavior.[8] Several lines of evidence suggest that this was not the case. First, as noted previously, there was little relation between the measures of maternal mood, maternal perceptions of and feelings about the infant and actual infant behavior. In addition, levels of infant irritability were reduced between day 10 and day 15 postpartum with increasing exposure to maternal caretaking. Most importantly for this argument, infant irritability improved to the same extent in infants regardless of whether mothers became depressed. Had neonatal behavior on these dimensions been a function of incipient maternal depression, it might have been expected—contrary to our findings—that irritability would have increased in the infants of women who became depressed, but not in those remaining well. Evidence published in 1996 indicates considerable continuity between fetal functioning (eg, heart rate and variability) and reported neonatal temperament.[16] As such behaviors are predictive of later difficulties in behavioral organization,[17] there may be an intrinsic physical basis for individual infant differences.

In sum, we could find no support for a third factor account of the association between infant characteristics and maternal depression.[8] This points to one conclusion: Neonatal factors have a significant impact on maternal mental state.

To investigate the persistence of depression, all mothers who had become depressed by 8 weeks postpartum were followed-up at 18 weeks. Infants' scores on the NBAS were considered in relation to whether or not the mother's depression had remitted, but no significant relationships were identified. In contrast, the degree of support that the mother received from her partner was highly relevant: Women who had poor support were far more likely to experience depressive episodes that persisted.

Lastly, we sought to evaluate the longer-term significance of initially irritable neonatal behavior.[8] Mothers were interviewed about infant behavior problems, including excessive crying when their children were 18 months of age. No relationship was found that linked irritable neonatal behavior and later infant behavior problems; postpartum depression, however, was a relevant variable. Mothers who had been depressed reported significantly higher rates of infant difficulties than mothers who had remained well.

A Preventive Intervention for High-Risk Mothers

There are important clinical implications of the finding that mothers of irritable infants are at significantly increased risk of depression in the postnatal months, especially those without good personal and social supports. In particular, it suggests that early intervention to address difficult infant behaviors may be important, particularly for mothers who are already at high risk for depression. These considerations, together with the evidence from other interventions with irritable infants,[18] form the basis for the preventive intervention we conducted recently. As follow-up data for the study population are still being collected, the results presented here are preliminary.

The sample for the intervention study consisted of primiparous women who were screened with the predictive index in pregnancy at the Reading (UK) antenatal clinic and who were identified as being vulnerable to depression. Of the 156 women recruited into the intervention group, 147 (94%) completed the treatment; 95 women were recruited into the control group. Follow-up assessments were made for 139 of those receiving the intervention, and for 82 of the controls. Women who received the preventive intervention were given additional support late in pregnancy and in the first 8 weeks postpartum in their home by a community nurse (known as a "health visitor" in the UK). The control group received routine primary care. Routine care from a health visitor in the UK typically involves no antenatal contact, but a home visit on the tenth day after delivery. Subsequently, home visits may occur when clear problems are identified, but contact generally shifts to mother-and-baby clinics at the local health center. These clinics rely on the mother's initiative to attend. Several studies suggest, however, that women who are depressed are less likely to utilize these clinics than those who are well.

The antenatal visits in the preventive intervention generally occurred during the 35th and 37th weeks. During these visits the study health visitors used a counseling approach to establish a supportive, trusting relationship with the mother, to identify any areas of particular vulnerability and to discuss preparations for infant care (eg, plans for the birth, method of feeding and arranging support). The first postnatal session took place on the third day after the birth. This meeting usually consisted of a debriefing on the labor and delivery.

On the 6th and 11th days, again within the context of an overall counseling approach, the health visitor conducted a modified version of the NBAS. This was a central aspect of the intervention; its purpose was to highlight the infant's individual characteristics and to support the parents in understanding their infant's behavior. This sympathetic "profiling" of any difficulties in the infant's behavioral organization, such as irritability (in this context, less pejoratively called "sensitivity"), was designed to prevent a vulnerable mother from slipping into negative, or depressive, cognitions in 2 ways: The first concerned the way in which the mother viewed herself and her potential feelings of responsibility for the infant's difficulty (eg, blaming herself because her infant cried persistently). The second concerned negative cognitions about the infant, such as thinking of the infant as being inherently bad or even malevolent. Rather, in helping parents notice the systematic nature of their infant's behavior in relation to his or her environment, it was hoped to engage their sympathy and understanding and give them a greater sense of control.

In addition to helping parents better understand the nature of irritable or sensitive infant behavior, the neonatal assessment was also designed to help parents appreciate the infant's capacity for positive social engagement. As well as noting the infant's general social capacity, the health visitor demonstrated the infant's preferential responsiveness to the parent (eg, turning to the sound of the mother's voice). This part of the infant assessment was designed to facilitate a benign, rather than a negative, cycle of parent-infant interaction.

Subsequent weekly home visits were conducted until the eighth postpartum week. These visits similarly combined counseling support for the mother with consideration of the infant's behavioral and developmental profiles, facilitating the adoption of appropriate management strategies. At the end of the 8 weeks, the normal pattern of health visitor contacts resumed.

The health visitor aimed to help the mother become aware of 4 aspects of her infant's behavior with regard to excessive crying. The first was to recognize early signs of distress. By noticing signs of distress, such as grimacing, frowning, turning away from stimulation, back arching and squirming, the mother would potentially be better able to change the environment before the infant's negative state escalated. Secondly, the mother was encouraged to identify situations that repeatedly provoked the infant's distress, and, if possible, to take steps to avoid them. For example, the mother was encouraged to swaddle an infant who was easily aroused from light sleep by large startle movements. The third area concerning crying that the intervention addressed was the observation of any self-soothing capacities in the infant, so that the mother would be better able to facilitate such behaviors. For example, if the infant was comforted by sucking his or her fist, but had difficulty finding it, the health visitor would demonstrate how swaddling made the infant's fists more accessible. Finally, the health visitor helped the mother identify the particular parental soothing techniques that appeared most effective for the infant; for example, increasing stimulation of various kinds, or reducing it to a minimum by taking the infant to a quiet, darkened room. In short, the treatment aimed to develop a profile of the individual infant's strengths and difficulties, as well as to assist parents in finding appropriate management strategies for their particular infant.

Main findings

The first follow-up assessment was conducted at 2 months postpartum, immediately after the intervention was completed. The assessment included measures of maternal mental state, the mothers' perceptions of the care they had received from their health visitors (whether delivering the index intervention or routine primary care) and maternal reports of difficulties in infant behavior.

The questionnaire reports indicated that the preventive intervention was highly acceptable. Women who received the study treatment were significantly more likely than those receiving routine care to report that they found their health visitor to be sympathetic, to give good advice and to help with practical problems of infant care. Mothers also reported that the intervention had been beneficial in helping them communicate with their infant and helping them appreciate their infant's abilities (Fig 1).

Fig 1. Mothers' perceptions of health visitors' care.

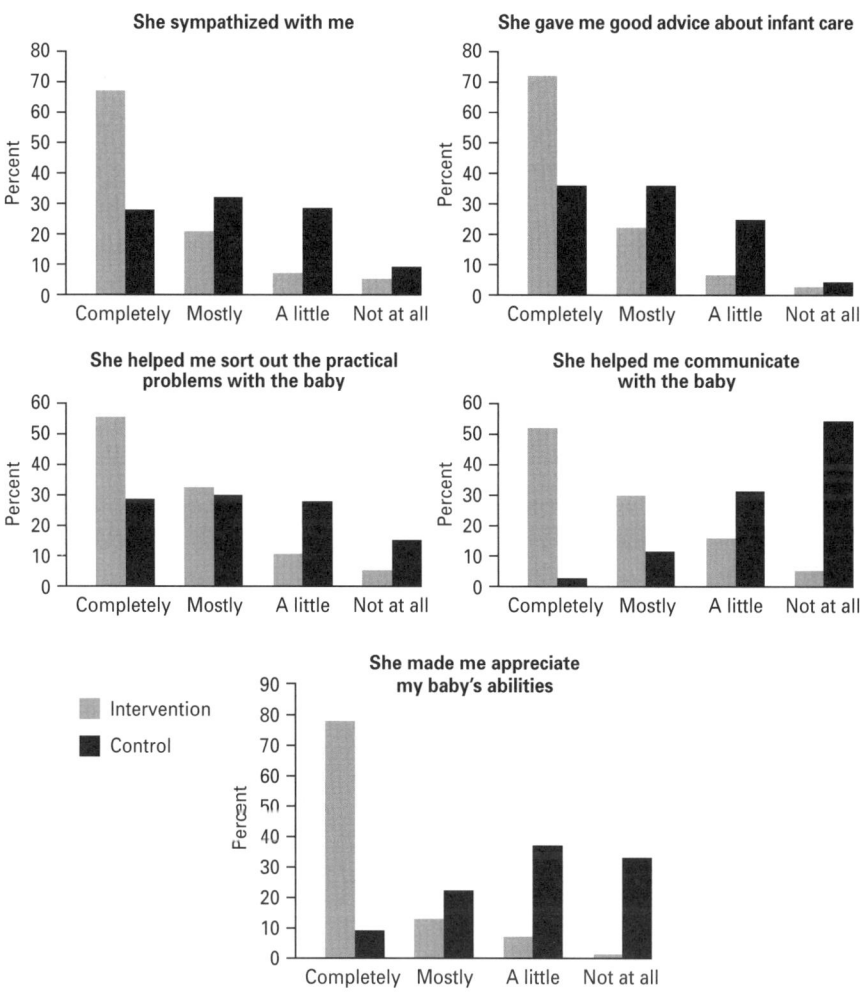

We also used a questionnaire to evaluate the impact of the intervention on infant crying. All mothers completed a form to assess the extent to which they perceived the infants' crying as a significant problem (Fig 2). Overall, mothers who received the intervention showed only a tendency to report fewer problems with crying than mothers who received routine care. However, for women who were not depressed at 2 months, the effect of the intervention for perceived problems with infant crying was significant: Those who received the intervention were less likely to report difficulties than were mothers in the control group. In contrast, the intervention was of no benefit to women who were depressed. In addition, depressed mothers were much more likely than nondepressed mothers to report that their infants' crying represented a significant problem.

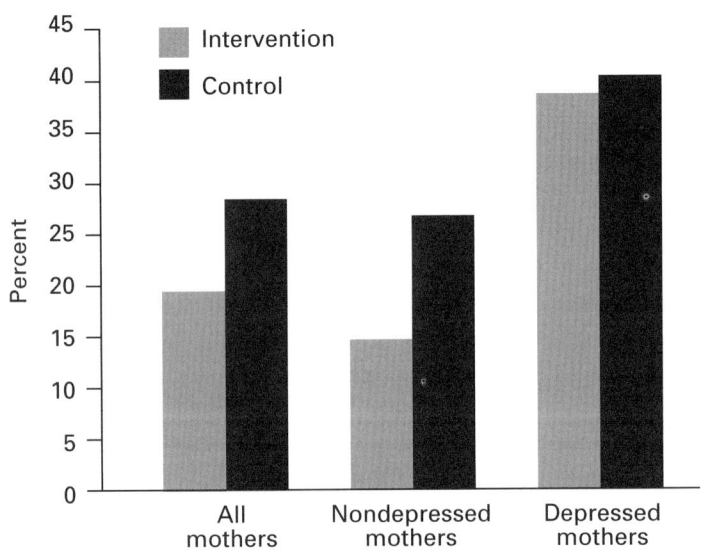

Fig 2. The impact of treatment on infant crying: proportion of mothers reporting significant infant crying problems.

Discussion

The first study showed a significant impact of neonatal behavior on maternal mental state.[8] For women who were already at elevated risk of depression, having an infant who was easily distressed and hard to soothe contributed significantly to the onset of depressive disorder in the first 2 months postpartum. Neither antenatal nor perinatal risk factors that were potentially common to both neonatal and maternal outcomes could explain this association, nor could maternal adjustment during the first postpartum week. This result is consistent with previous research showing that parental experience and caretaking practices do not explain individual differences in difficult infant behavior such as persistent crying during the first few weeks of life. In addition, this prospective study extends the findings of previous work documenting concurrent associations between maternal depression and difficult infant behavior.

Irritable infant behavior and excessive crying are likely to diminish after 2 months.[19] Our study indicated that there was no direct influence of neonatal difficulties on the persistence of maternal mood disorder beyond the age of 2 months. Rather, when depression persisted, it was usually associated with a low level of personal support from the woman's partner. As a result, women whose partners were sympathetic and available were more likely to have recovered from depression by 18 weeks than those who were in conflict with the child's father. Regarding longer-term infant outcomes, there was similarly no evidence for a direct impact of irritable neonatal behavior on the development of later behavior problems. This finding is consistent with studies showing only weak links between newborn irritability and difficult behavior in late infancy.[1] Nevertheless, the fact that postnatal depression, itself influenced by neonatal characteristics, was associated with behavior difficulties at 18 months underscores the clinical significance of neonatal irritability: That is, insofar as neonatal irritability contributes to the onset of maternal depression, it is indirectly detrimental to child outcome. This conclusion is central to the case for interventions targeted at difficult infant behavior in the early postpartum weeks.

Our second study evaluated a preventive intervention designed to address these infant difficulties. As follow-up data have not yet been collected, results presented here are preliminary. Although final interpretation is pending, preliminary conclusions can be drawn. First, it is clear that the preventive intervention was highly acceptable to the women who received it. By using a counseling approach, the intervention aimed to be emotionally supportive. In addition, by providing individualized profiles of each infant's sensitivities and strengths, parents were helped to feel more in control in their caretaking, and feelings of self blame for difficult infant behaviors were avoided. This approach is in marked contrast to that often seen in routine care, where health professionals' time for contact is limited. In that situation, the emphasis is often on imparting information within the context of an essentially normative view of the infant. This approach may undermine the confidence of a vulnerable mother, and she may rapidly conclude that any infant difficulties are due to her own incompetence. Indeed, on all dimensions concerning their own care and their infants' care, mothers rated the study intervention, which was delivered by health visitors who had received additional training, as vastly better than routine care.

The picture is more complicated regarding mothers' experiences of infant crying problems. The clearest finding was for women who did not experience postpartum depression. Among this group, women who received the index intervention[7] were significantly less likely than those receiving routine care to report that their infant's crying presented them with difficulty. In contrast, the intervention was of no benefit for the minority of women who were postnatally depressed. Until our analyses are complete, the interpretation of this finding remains unclear. One issue is whether the reported crying difficulties are genuine. It is possible that, being depressed, these women generally perceived their experience negatively, regardless of the objective circumstances. However, the broader literature on the nature and rate of crying in infants whose parents regard the crying as excessive and who consult their medical practitioners suggest that parental perceptions are generally accurate. Data from another study we are conducting suggest that this may apply even in the context of maternal depression. In this second study we used diary records to provide a more robust measure of infant crying and found that depressed women recorded significantly longer overall crying times than well mothers. Assuming that the reports of infant crying by depressed mothers in the intervention study are reliable, there are 2 possible causal interpretations that are consistent with these findings. First, maternal depression could have arisen in the context of overwhelming personal and social adversity, causing maternal caretaking to become so disturbed by the mood disorder as to disrupt infant behavior and lead to excessive crying. Although previous research has shown that variations in caretaking within a certain range do not account for individual differences in infant crying, the disturbance in maternal functioning in the context of clinical depression may have been sufficiently severe to have had a deleterious impact on infant behavioral organization. Second, neonatal behavioral difficulties may have been so marked as to provoke maternal depression. Later, these severe difficulties may become manifest in maternal reports of excessive crying. Further analysis of our data will reveal the contexts in which episodes of depression developed, allowing us to determine the extent to which either or both of these interpretations apply. However, regardless of the origin of maternal depression, it appears that a more intensive intervention than that delivered in the current study will be necessary to alleviate the problems depressed mothers experience with associated infant crying.

Conclusions

These studies suggest that neonatal irritability, characterized, in part, by excessive crying and resistance to soothing, may place considerable strain on new mothers, particularly those lacking in personal and social supports. In some cases, mothers may become clinically depressed. When the mother's relationship with her partner is particularly difficult, depression may persist, and the infant may exhibit behavior problems in the second year. These findings underscore the need for improved interventions. The current preventive intervention in our study combined an intensive primary care approach with counseling and an individual profiling of infant strengths and difficulties. Such a program, designed to help vulnerable mothers cope with their young infants, was highly acceptable in our clinical trial. Women who received such an intervention who did not become depressed generally appeared to benefit, as they experienced fewer problems with infant crying at 2 months. On the other hand, women who became depressed despite this primary care intervention by health visitors will require more intensive help to cope with infant crying problems.

Acknowledgments

This research was supported by the Medical Research Council and the NHS Executive.

References

1. St. James-Roberts I. Explanations of persistent infant crying. In: St. James-Roberts I, Harris G, Messer D, eds. *Infant Crying, Feeding and Sleeping.* Hemel Hempstead, Hert: Harvester Wheatsheef; 1993:26-46.
2. Murray L, Cooper PJ, eds. *Postpartum Depression and Child Development.* New York, NY: Guilford Press; 1997.
3. Whiffen VE, Gotlib IH. Infants of postpartum depressed mothers: temperament and cognitive status. *Journal of Abnormal Psychology.* 1989;98:274-279.
4. Cutrona CE, Troutman BR. Social support, infant temperament, and parenting self-efficacy: a mediational model of postpartum depression. *Child Development.* 1986;57:1507-1518.
5. Field T, Healy B, Goldstein S, et al. Infants of depressed mothers show "depressed" behavior even with nondepressed adults. *Child Development.* 1988;59:1569-1579.
6. Seligman MEP. *Helplessness: On Depression, Development, and Death.* San Francisco, Calif. Freeman Co; 1975.
7. Cooper PJ, Murray L, Hooper R, West A. The development and validation of a predictive index for postpartum depression. *Psychological Medicine.* 1996;26:627-634.
8. Murray L, Stanley C, Hooper R, King F, Fiori-Cowley A. The role of infant factors in postnatal depression and mother-infant interactions. *Developmental Medicine and Child Neurology.* 1996;38:109-119.
9. Lester BM, Als H, Brazelton TB. Regional obstetric anesthesia and newborn behavior: a reanalysis toward synergistic effects. *Child Development.* 1982;53:687-692.
10. Kennerley H, Gath D. Maternity blues. I. Detection and measurement by questionnaire. *British Journal of Psychiatry.* 1989;155:356-362.
11. St. James-Roberts I, Wolke D. Convergences and discrepancies, among mothers' and professionals' assessments of difficult neonatal behaviour. *Journal of Child Psychology and Psychiatry, and Allied Disciplines.* 1988;29:21-42.
12. Brazelton TB, Nugent JK. *Neonatal Behavioral Assessment Scale.* 3rd ed. Cambridge, Mass: Cambridge University Press; 1995.
13. Spitzer RL, Williams JBW, Gibbon M, First MB. *Structured Clinical Interview for DSM-III-R – Patient Edition (with Psychotic Screen).* New York, NY: American Psychiatric Press; 1989.
14. Cox JL, Holden JM, Sagovsky R. Detection of postnatal depression. Development of the 10-item Edinburgh Postnatal Depression Scale. *British Journal of Psychiatry.* 1987;150:782-786.
15. Glover V. Maternal stress or anxiety in pregnancy and emotional development of the child. *British Journal of Psychiatry.* 1997;171:105-106.
16. DiPietro JA, Hodgson DM, Costigan KA, Johnson TR. Fetal antecedents of infant temperament. *Child Development.* 1996;67:2568-2583.
17. Sewell J, Tsitsikas H, Bax M. Comparison of the Brazelton NBAS with health visitors' assessments of the nursing couple. *Developmental Medicine and Child Neurology.* 1982;24:615-625.
18. van den Boom DC. The influence of temperament and mothering on attachment and exploration: an experimental manipulation of sensitive responsiveness among lower-class mothers with irritable infants. *Child Development.* 1994;65:1457-1477.
19. St. James-Roberts I. Infant crying: normal development and persistent crying. In: St. James-Roberts I, Harris G, Messer D, eds. *Infant Crying, Feeding and Sleeping.* Hemel Hempstead, Hert:Harvester Wheatsheef; 1993:7-25.

Assessing Crying Complaints: The Interaction with Gastroesophageal Reflux and Cow's Milk Protein Intolerance

William R. Treem, MD

Introduction

The classic image of "colic" includes a shrieking infant who has a tense, distended abdomen, and who alternately arches her back and draws up her legs. Because these infants are often relieved by the passage of flatus and by rhythmic movements, many parents and physicians are convinced that colic is the result of abdominal pain. In 2 studies of infants who met rigorous criteria for colic based on parent diary recordings during a baseline period, my colleagues and I found that these parents also reported the typical description of symptoms included in most accounts of the classic image of colic.[1, 2] Each of the 54 study infants, between the ages of 2 weeks and 8 weeks, cried with a sudden onset and as if in pain, cried for periods longer than 15 minutes in duration, and were considered hard to console.[1, 2] Passing gas was considered a problem for 89% of these infants, and feeding and sleeping problems were noted in approximately 50% of the infants. At physical examination, 86% of these infants were hypertonic and approximately 50% had abdominal distension and were crying, drawing up their legs and flushing. Arching was observed in only 20%.

Proposed gastrointestinal (GI) causes of infant colic have generally been categorized into 4 main groups, including the following: excessive gas, bowel distension and spasm; abnormal intestinal motility related to immature development of the neuroenteric nervous system and gut peptide-receptor interactions; gastroesophageal reflux (GER)-induced peptic esophagitis; and cow's milk protein intolerance (CMPI) that provokes intestinal inflammation and motility disturbances. This presentation will focus on the latter 2 of these proposed etiologies and cite evidence both for and against the relationship of GER and CMPI as they relate to excessive crying in infancy. Conclusions based on this evidence, as well as recommendations for identifying infants with colic who may benefit from therapeutic interventions for these 2 GI problems, will be provided.

Gastroesophageal Reflux and Infant Colic

Gastric acid refluxed into the esophagus, leading to the development of peptic esophagitis, has been proposed as a mechanism of GER-induced crying. Indeed, crying itself was thought to potentiate GER via contraction of the abdominal wall, a Valsalva maneuver and an increased abdominal-thoracic pressure gradient, favoring reflux. When infants swallow air during crying, gastric contents may be displaced with air, contributing to reflux. However, Orenstein showed that episodes of GER are actually more frequent when babies are awake and quiet than when they are crying.[3] In this trial, 19 infants with GER were studied using 4-hour intraesophageal pH recordings in 3 states—crying, awake and quiet, and asleep. Overall, these infants experienced 11 episodes of GER per hour when crying, 17 per hour when awake and quiet and only 2 episodes per hour when asleep. During crying, an intraesophageal pH less than 4.0 was documented 21% of the time. When infants were awake and quiet, intraesophageal pH was less than 4.0 nearly twice as frequently, or 41% of the time.

In infants, GER appears to be a "physiologic" phenomenon. Fully 50% of 2-month-old infants regurgitate at least twice per day, and an intraesophageal pH less than 4.0, up to 5% of the total duration of continuous pH monitoring, is accepted as normal until 1 year of age. Most infants who have "physiologic" GER are considered "happy spitters" who will grow out of their GER between 8 months and 12 months of age and will no longer manifest any symptoms or signs of pathologic GER.

In contrast, infants with pathologic GER (sometimes referred to as gastroesophageal reflux disease [GERD]) usually present with other symptoms in addition to vomiting. Parents of infants who had suspected GERD who were referred to the gastroenterology unit of a children's hospital were asked to respond to a validated questionnaire regarding their infants' symptomatology.[4] As shown in Fig 1, results from the questionnaire indicated the following:

Fig 1. Is irritability (crying) really a symptom of GERD?[4]

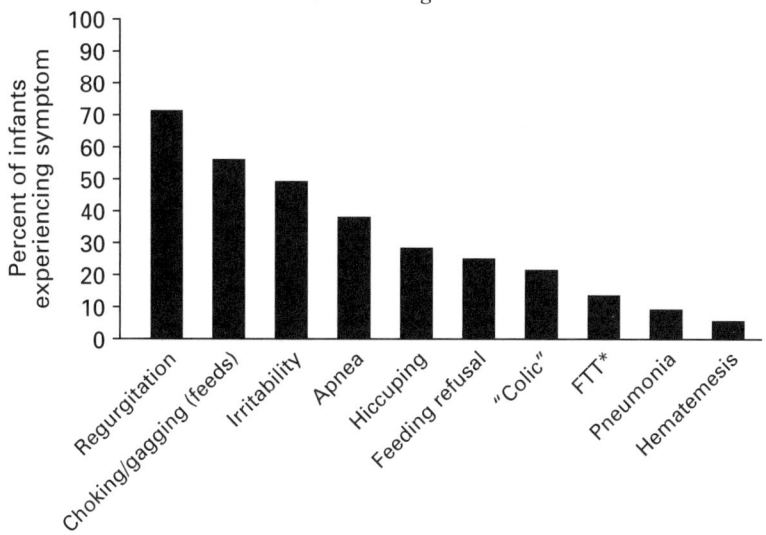

*FTT = failure to thrive

choking/gagging occurred in 57% of these infants; irritability in 49%; apnea in 38%; hiccuping in 28%; feeding refusal in 25%; "colic" in 22%; failure to thrive (FTT) in 12%; pneumonia in 8%; and hematemesis in 6%.

Can the cardinal manifestations of colic—excessive crying and irritability—be indicative of GER even in the absence of significant vomiting? Using split-screen recordings of continuous intraesophageal pH monitoring and continuous video-monitoring of 10 infants between the ages of 2 weeks and 32 weeks, Feranchak, Orenstein and Cohn investigated behaviors that were directly linked to the onset of an episode of reflux.[5] Crying and frowning or grimacing were associated with 17% of episodes of reflux and only 3% of periods without reflux ($P < .001$) in this small group. Other behaviors that were less commonly associated with episodes of GER included belching, yawning, mouthing and stretching. Sneezing, hiccuping, coughing and gagging were not correlated with the onset of reflux. In another study, 26 infants with "colic," but without vomiting, were referred to a pediatric gastroenterology unit to undergo prolonged intraesophageal pH monitoring.[6] Sixteen (61%) of these infants showed excessive GER. In addition, for these 16 infants, treatment with medical antireflux therapy resulted in a resolution of symptoms. However, most of these infants were not within the usual age group for colic (median age, 4.8 months) and most had been exposed to other therapies for colic prior to their referral.

Results of a larger study done in Australia suggested that GERD is an uncommon cause of irritability in infants under 3 months of age but, when it does occur, it is always associated with significant vomiting.[7] Seventy infants (median age, 3.8 months; 23 under 3 months of age) referred to a gastroenterology unit for excessive crying and irritability were included. All 70 infants underwent prolonged intraesophageal pH monitoring for suspected GER. By definition, a positive pH probe demonstrated pH less than 4.0 for greater than 10% of the total time of the study. Eleven of the 70 infants satisfied this criterion for a positive study. Ten infants were older than 3 months of age and only one was younger. In this group, only 4.2% of irritable infants studied who were younger than 3 months of age had GER, as compared with 22% of infants who were older than 3 months of age. In addition, all of the infants with positive pH probe studies exhibited vomiting, while all 18 infants who didn't exhibit vomiting had negative pH studies. There was no correlation between arching, sleep disturbance or feeding difficulties with the presence of GER.

Another crucial issue related to the association between colic and GER is the identification of symptoms that are predictive of peptic esophagitis in infants with GER. Sixty-two infants with a median age of 6.5 months were selected for study from a group of 126 infants with GER.[8] Endoscopic examination revealed that 34 infants had evidence of peptic esophagitis, while 28 did not; vomiting was almost universal in both groups (100% versus 96%). Excessive crying (85% with esophagitis versus 58% without), sleep disturbance (79% versus 21%) and failure to thrive (41% versus 11%) were significantly increased in the esophagitis group. In a smaller study of 18 younger infants (4 weeks to 11 weeks of age) diagnosed with colic based on crying more than 3 hours per day, peptic esophagitis was found in 5 of the infants.[9] Eighty percent of the group with esophagitis presented with vomiting, compared with 46% of the infants who presented without esophagitis. In addition, infants with esophagitis regurgitated more frequently than infants without esophagitis; 3.21 times per day compared with 1.01 times per day ($P < .001$). In the group with esophagitis, treatment with antireflux medication resulted in a significant decrease in crying time from 3.73 hours per day pretreatment to 1.24 hours per day posttreatment; such pretreatment had no effect on the duration of crying in infants who did not have esophagitis.

In contrast, other studies showed that vomiting, irritability, crying and/or fussiness do not predict the presence of peptic esophagitis in infants with GER. In 40 infants younger than 7 months of age (median age, 3.8 months), neither vomiting nor fussiness and crying could discriminate between the 20 infants with peptic esophagitis and the 20 infants with normal biopsies, as shown in Table 1.[10] Regurgitation is so common in infants, particularly in those with GER, that it is a sensitive indicator, but not at all specific, for peptic esophagitis. Irritability (fussiness) was neither sensitive nor specific for esophagitis; it was present in 55% of both groups of infants. In contrast, periods of arching and refusing feeds, even when hungry, were associated with esophagitis. Neither of these characteristics was sensitive, as each was present in only 55% and 40% of infants with esophagitis, respectively, but specificity for both was in the range of 80% to 85%. Hyams and colleagues similarly found that irritability did not predict esophagitis in infants with GER.[11] In

Table 1. Symptoms of Infantile Reflux Esophagitis Using Validated Techniques for Symptoms and Histopathology[10]

	Percent of infants positive for the symptom				
	Arching	**Refusal of feedings**	**Choking/ gagging**	**Regurgitation**	**Fussiness (Irritability)**
Esophagitis (n = 20)	55%	40%	55%	80%	55%
Normal (n = 20)	20%	15%	30%	70%	55%
X^2: P<	.05	.10	NS	NS	NS
Sensitivity	.55	.40	.55	.80	.55
Specificity	.80	.85	.70	.30	.45

their study of 40 infants between the ages of 2 months and 12 months who were tested for GER, no parameter from the pH probe study predicted esophagitis. Only 15% of infants with peptic esophagitis had hematemesis or occult blood in their stools.

Feeding resistance is a term used to describe an infant who cries, turns his or her head away, arches, retches, thrusts the nipple out with his or her tongue and at times becomes diaphoretic (ie, perspires) when feeding. This resistance is thought to be due to pain provoked by GER at the time of feeding in an infant who has established peptic esophagitis. Results of some studies suggest that feeding resistance is uncommon in neurologically intact infants with GER. It is no more prevalent in infants with GER and peptic esophagitis than in those with GER and normal esophageal biopsies.[12] Dellert and colleagues retrospectively studied 25 infants with GER and feeding resistance, culled from a larger group of 600 infants (less than 20 months of age), referred to a pediatric gastroenterology unit.[12] Among these 25 infants, none had craniofacial, esophageal or neurologic problems. These infants were matched with 25 similar infants with GER, but without feeding resistance. Comparative analyses showed no differences in the age at onset or at diagnosis, the incidence of vomiting or irritability or the presence of peptic esophagitis, which was approximately 40% in each group. However, while FTT was prevalent in the group with feeding resistance, it was almost absent in the control group (72% versus 8%, $P < .001$).

Taken together, these studies suggest that pathologic GER is a significant factor in approximately 5% of infants under 3 months of age who have colic. The absence of vomiting suggests that GER is not related to crying and irritability. When colic is accompanied by certain characteristic symptoms and signs, such as feeding refusal, FTT, heme-positive stools or emesis, the persistence and worsening of vomiting after 3 months of age and a reduction in crying and irritability with empiric antiacid therapy, the likelihood that GER is involved in the pathogenesis of colic is increased.

Cow's Milk Protein Intolerance and Infant Colic

Eosinophilic infiltration of the mucosa of the esophagus, stomach, small intestine and/or colon can be provoked by exposure to cow's milk proteins, and ameliorated by their avoidance, even in very young infants. This is considered strong evidence that cow's milk proteins can produce mucosal inflammation, edema, dysmotility, enteric blood and protein loss leading to pain that could manifest primarily as "colic."[13] There are several lines of evidence to link CMPI with colic: Cow's milk proteins can be detected in human breast milk; infants with colic show increased intestinal absorption of macromolecular proteins; and, colic recurs when cow's milk proteins are reintroduced into the diets of infants who have responded previously to their removal. An ample number of studies indicate that there is a subgroup of infants with colic who have CMPI and who subsequently improve with the removal of cow's milk proteins from their diets. However, there are considerable controversies over the proportion of infants with colic who will respond to this intervention and over the reliability of clinical clues to detect them.

Three cow's milk proteins have been implicated in the pathogenesis of colic: beta-lactoglobulin, alpha-casein and bovine immunoglobulin G (IgG). The first 2 proteins are found in much greater concentrations in cow's milk-based formulas than in human breast milk. As a result, they are less likely to account for the equal prevalence of colic in formula-fed and breast-fed infants. However, bovine IgG is found in roughly equivalent amounts in breast milk and in cow's milk-based formulas. In addition, it is interesting to note that bovine IgG is found in higher concentrations in the breast milk of mothers who have colicky infants than in their counterparts who have non-colicky infants.[14] The neonatal intestine expresses Fc receptors that bind bovine IgG, allowing its absorption by small bowel enterocytes and providing access to the immunologically competent lymphocytes of the lamina propria, initiating the allergic reaction.

Absorption of potentially immunogenic macromolecules appears to be increased in infants with colic. The intestinal uptake of human alpha-lactalbumin is increased in children who have cow's milk protein allergy who are given human breast milk. This increased gut permeability is similar to that seen in preterm infants. It may reflect subtle injury by cow's milk proteins to the surface epithelium of the intestine or an underlying genetic predisposition to macromolecular absorption similar to that seen in first degree relatives of patients with Crohn's disease. Lothe, Lindberg and Jakobsson demonstrated that, after ingestion of a breast milk meal, levels of human alpha-lactalbumin were increased in both breast- and formula-fed infants with colic compared with their noncolicky counterparts.[15] Although this finding implies a difference in gut permeability, there was significant overlap between controls and colicky infants, especially in the breast-fed group. Also, the level of alpha-lactalbumin did not predict those infants with colic who had a clinical response to the removal of cow's milk proteins from their diets.

There are several clinical studies that show a beneficial effect of the removal of cow's milk proteins from the diets of colicky infants, as well as the subsequent recurrence of symptoms upon rechallenge. Investigators from Sweden performed a double-blind, randomized, crossover study with 24 infants whose colic had previously responded to the open substitution of a hydrolyzed casein formula instead of a cow's milk protein formula.[16] When cow's milk whey protein was introduced into their hypoallergenic formula, 18 of the 24 infants showed increased crying, disturbed sleep and increased hiccuping and gas formation. The primary overall criticism of this study focuses on the selection of the infants included. Infants in this study may represent only a subgroup of colicky babies. These infants had already failed standard counseling and trials of medication. A majority of these infants presented with vomiting. In addition, these were infants with an extreme degree of crying (mean, 5.6 hours per day), and some of them were older than 12 weeks at the time of the double-blind challenge. The investigators estimated that the 18 infants who reacted to whey protein represented 9% of all colicky infants born in Malmö, Sweden, over the 6-month study period and 1.5% of all infants born during this time. These percentages correlate well with the figure of 2% usually quoted as the overall incidence of cow's milk protein allergy in infants prospectively studied in Denmark[17] and Holland.[18]

A more-recent study from Australia by Hill et al avoided this selection bias by enrolling healthy infants with colic (ages 4 weeks to 16 weeks) who had been seen by community pediatricians.[19] Formula-fed infants were randomized to receive either a casein-hydrolysate formula or a cow's milk formula. For breast-fed infants, mothers were randomized to an active elimination diet or a normal diet. Thirty-three (61%) of the 54 enrolled infants fed the hypoallergenic formula or taking breast milk from their mothers on an active elimination diet had a reduction in crying/fussing, but 21 did not. Also, 43% of the infants improved on a control diet. Although the difference was statistically significant ($P = .047$), this study[19] also shows the large placebo effect common to many studies of therapeutic interventions for colic. In this study, significant improvement was defined by the investigators as a 25% reduction in crying/fussing. Interestingly, the mothers did not recognize the same degree of improvement with diet intervention. This implies that the statistically significant level of reduction in crying/fussing accepted as meaningful by the investigators may not have been clinically significant. If the infants who did not complete the study were included in an intention-to-treat analysis, dietary intervention would have resulted in no improvement. The study designs of this and other trials of the elimination of cow's milk protein have been criticized. According to Forsyth, multiple crossover study designs would combat the large placebo effect and the trend toward improvement in colic over time.[20]

An increase in atopic conditions in previously colicky infants may provide evidence to link colic to CMPI. A study by Iacono et al evaluated 70 infants referred to a pediatric gastroenterology unit at an Italian medical center for the treatment of colic.[21] After the introduction of a soy protein formula, 50 infants (71%) experienced a significant reduction in crying. Severe crying recurred with 2 nonblinded challenges with cow's milk protein. However, in this study there appears to be a selection bias toward infants with atopy. The 70 infants included in this study, selected from a pool of 240 infants with colic, were those who had the most severe crying. Many of these infants had vomiting, a strong family history of atopy and had developed diarrhea and blood in their stools when challenged with cow's milk protein. Furthermore, approximately 30% of the original 70 infants showed vomiting, diarrhea, asthma, rhinitis and/or eczema when rechallenged later in the first year of life. Castro-Rodriguez and colleagues used another approach.[22] They prospectively followed almost 1000 infants for 13 years to determine the relationship between atopic disorders and colic. Initially, 9.2% of these infants were considered to have colic at their 2-month well-baby visits. This is almost exactly the same incidence of colic observed in a study by Canivet et al.[23] They found that with 3, 6 and 11 years of follow-up, there was no increased incidence of allergic rhinitis, eczema or asthma in the colicky group compared with controls. Fig 2 illustrates this point after 13 years of follow-up.[22]

Despite these ambiguous results, it is well known that milk protein-induced eosinophilic gastroenteritis can affect very young infants (ages 1 week to 8 weeks), resulting in irritability, feeding intolerance, vomiting and, less commonly, diarrhea.[24] Streaks of blood can be seen in the stools of some infants, and often the stool is positive for occult blood. A significant minority of infants exhibits peripheral blood eosinophilia. Eosinophils may infiltrate the

Fig 2. Is colic associated with later atopy?[22]

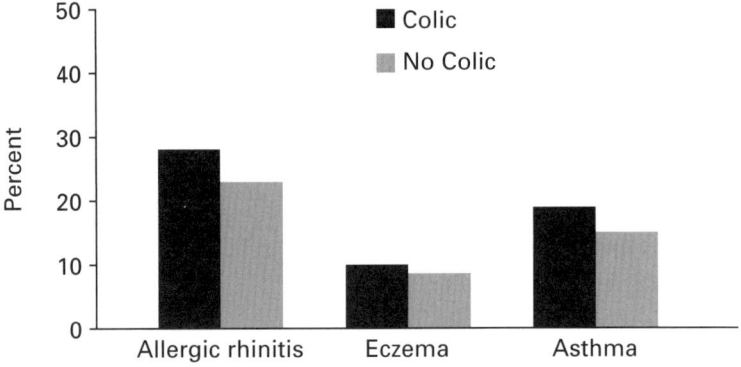

Methods: n = 983 enrolled at birth, and followed for 13 years
9.2% incidence of colic (diagnosis by physicians)

colon or, more rarely, the stomach, duodenum or esophagus. Anemia and hypoalbuminemia are rare. Most often, these infants have negative skin tests and RASTs (radioallergosorbent tests) and normal IgE (immunoglobulin E) levels at the time of presentation. In many cases there is a family history of atopy, asthma or eczema.

Taken together, these data suggest that there is a subset of approximately 10% of infants with colic who cannot tolerate cow's milk protein. These infants benefit from elimination of this protein from their diets. Often, these infants can be identified by at least one of the following: the presence of other GI symptoms, such as vomiting and diarrhea; streaks of blood or occult blood in their stools; a strong family history of atopy, asthma or eczema; the presence of peripheral blood eosinophilia; and a lack of response to behavioral or medical interventions. Infants who show any of these characteristics may benefit from dietary modification. A casein-hydrolysate formula may be tried for formula-fed colicky infants, and mothers of breast-fed colicky infants may want to eliminate cow's milk proteins from their diets. These changes may result in clinical benefit and reduction in crying for colicky infants with CMPI.

References

1. Treem WR. Infant colic. A pediatric gastroenterologist's perspective. *Pediatric Clinics of North America.* 1994;41:1121-1138.
2. Treem WR, Hyams JS, Blankschen E, Etienne N, Paule CL, Borschel MW. Evaluation of the effect of a fiber-enriched formula on infant colic. *The Journal of Pediatrics.* 1991;119:695-701.
3. Orenstein SR. Crying does not exacerbate gastroesophageal reflux in infants. *Journal of Pediatric Gastroenterology and Nutrition.* 1992;14:34-37.
4. Orenstein SR, Cohn JF, Shalaby TM, Kartan R. Reliability and validity of an infant gastroesophageal reflux questionnaire. *Clinical Pediatrics.* 1993;32:472-484.
5. Feranchak AP, Orenstein SR, Cohn JF. Behaviors associated with onset of gastroesophageal reflux episodes in infants. Prospective study using split-screen video and pH probe. *Clinical Pediatrics.* 1994;33:654-662.
6. Berkowitz D, Naveh Y, Berant M. "Infantile colic" as the sole manifestation of gastroesophageal reflux. *Journal of Pediatric Gastroenterology and Nutrition.* 1997;24:231-233.
7. Heine RG, Jaquiery A, Lubitz L, Cameron DJ, Catto-Smith AG. Role of gastro-oesophageal reflux in infant irritability. *Archives of Disease in Childhood.* 1995;73:121-125.
8. Ryan P, Lander M, Ong TH, Shepherd R. When does reflux oesophagitis occur with gastro-oesophageal reflux in infants? A clinical and endoscopic study, and correlation with outcome. *Australian Paediatric Journal.* 1983;19:90-93.
9. Berezin S, Glassman MS, Bostwick H, Halata M. Esophagitis as a cause of infant colic. *Clinical Pediatrics.* 1995;34:158-159.
10. Orenstein S, Putnam PE, Shalaby TM et al. Symptoms of infantile reflux esophagitis, using validated techniques for symptoms and histopathology. *Gastroenterology.* 1994;106:A153.
11. Hyams JS, Ricci A Jr, Leichtner AM. Clinical and laboratory correlates of esophagitis in young children. *Journal of Pediatric Gastroenterology and Nutrition.* 1988;7:52-56.
12. Dellert SF, Hyams JS, Treem WR, Geerstma MA. Feeding resistance and gastroesophageal reflux in infancy. *Journal of Pediatric Gastroenterology and Nutrition.* 1993;17:66-71.
13. Whitington PF, Whitington GL. Eosinophilic gastroenteropathy in childhood. *Journal of Pediatric Gastroenterology and Nutrition.* 1988;7:379-385.
14. Clyne PS, Kulczycki A Jr. Human breast milk contains bovine IgG. Relationship to infant colic? *Pediatrics.* 1991;87:439-444.
15. Lothe L, Lindberg T, Jakobsson I. Macromolecular absorption in infants with infantile colic. *Acta Paediatrica Scandinavica.* 1990;79:417-421.
16. Lothe L, Lindberg T. Cow's milk whey protein elicits symptoms of infantile colic in colicky formula-fed infants: a double-blind crossover study. *Pediatrics.* 1989;83:262-266.
17. Host A, Halken S. A prospective study of cow milk allergy in Danish infants during the first 3 years of life. Clinical course in relation to clinical and immunological type of hypersensitivity. *Allergy.* 1990;45:587-596.
18. Schrander JJP, van den Bogart JH, Forget PP, Schrander-Stumpel CT, Kuijten RH, Kester AD. Cow's milk protein intolerance in infants under 1 year of age: a prospective epidemiological study. *European Journal of Pediatrics.* 1993;152:640-644.
19. Hill DJ, Hudson IL, Sheffield LJ, Shelton MJ, Menahem S, Hosking CS. A low allergen diet is a significant intervention in infantile colic: results of a community-based study. *The Journal of Allergy and Clinical Immunology.* 1995;96:886-892.
20. Forsyth BWC. Colic and the effect of changing formulas: a double-blind, multiple-crossover study. *The Journal of Pediatrics.* 1989;115:521-526.
21. Iacono G, Carroccio A, Montalto G, et al. Severe infantile colic and food intolerance: a long-term prospective study. *Journal of Pediatric Gastroenterology and Nutrition.* 1991;12:332-335.

22. Castro-Rodriguez JA, Stern D, Halonen M, et al. Relation between infantile colic and asthma/atopy. A prospective study in an unselected population. *Pediatrics*. In press.
23. Canivet C, Hagander B, Jakobsson I, Lanke J. Infantile colic—less common than previously estimated? *Acta Paediatrica*. 1996;85:454-458.
24. Vandenplas Y, Quenon M, Renders F, Dab I, Loeb H. Milk-sensitive eosinophilic gastroenteritis in a 10-day-old boy. *European Journal of Pediatrics*. 1990;149:244-245.

Section 3 Discussion: The Challenge of Assessing Crying Complaints

Moderated by Edward Goldson, MD
Pediatrician
Child Development Unit
The Children's Hospital
Denver, Colorado, USA

Goldson: I think that Lynne Murray's work has reinforced the need to consider this constellation of behaviors within context and under a variety of circumstances. The medical community can become "organicized" with medical models; behavioral science looks at it differently, and the basic sciences look at it in yet another way. They are extraordinarily complex. One of our challenges is to understand complex symptoms and signs in a very broad perspective.

Although we agree on many issues, terminology is problematic. We speak to families using the language in the cry literature. Somebody is hurting—they are distressed, and they are coming to us for help. The symptom that they present with is crying. Nine-month-olds cry, and 12-month-olds cry, but crying in these infants is a very different phenomenon from what occurs in the first 3 months, or what we call "colic." So I was delighted when I read the papers by Siobhán Gormally and Ron Barr,[1] that attempt to generate a model, a way of looking at this particular phenomenon. We are not referring to a child who has been perfectly healthy and comes in because he is crying and has an ear infection. We are discussing persistent crying. What is persistent? What is excessive? Wessel has given us a beginning framework.[2] I would like to consider variations on the model, which I believe will be helpful clinically.

One subgroup is what we call "colic." Data suggest that this type of increased crying is a universal phenomenon with variations, some in duration, some in intensity, but it occurs in all infants under all circumstances. It is normal. We have defined part of "normal" as being healthy, gaining weight and a variety of factors that are fine, but at the same time, the infant cries a great deal, is irritable and unhappy and "is driving mommy and daddy crazy." The next group of infants are those with organic, or some underlying, pathophysiology. They do not have symptoms of colic. They are different. Siobhán Gormally and Will Treem have presented this very elegantly because these children have something physiologically wrong. They are not gaining weight, they are vomiting or they are losing blood. They may have seizures or other symptoms that present as a crying complaint. A very young child with severe eczema or a child with hydrocephalus are two examples. Some premature infants with chronic lung disease present with persistent crying. They are not colicky because they are not healthy infants. Then there is that very important group of normal babies who happen to cry but do not meet the criteria. The parents need reassurance that their child is "okay." In most cases, I would argue that a positive diagnosis of colic can be made.

* * * * *

Social workers can be extraordinarily helpful because they view the world differently. They will ask other questions and become engaged with families in a very different context from what I might as a pediatrician with a 20-minute block of time. Framing this as a heuristic model and perhaps combining it with what Ron Barr and Siobhán Gormally have put together, where else could we go? How do we integrate those findings so that we can respond to the needs of families?

Wolke: You now run into a problem. You've got nonorganic and organic, but there are also infants who are "mixed" organic and nonorganic who, for example, also have feeding problems due to delayed maturation.

Goldson: I am concerned about this issue. I believe this dichotomy of organic and nonorganic was driven to some extent by the child abuse problem, where organic and nonorganic causes were separated. If it was nonorganic, it was due to a "bad" mother and very often resulted in a poor assessment of the child. These types of "all-or-none" classifications are problematic. With colic we should clearly define what we are discussing and acknowledge that there will be a gray zone.

Wolke: The interesting aspect is that the organic cases of failure to thrive are much more likely to improve. This could happen with colic as well. The interesting point is that the perception by most experts is that if it is organic, it is persistent.

* * * * *

Fox: I would like to take the opposite position. Being able to identify, as two of our three speakers have, the very small group of infants who have organic pathology or pathophysiology, is important. Viewing the colicky infant or the excessively crying infant as a different individual or species is also a very important aspect of the taxonomy. The problem is that there is a range of individual differences in infants, which spans from infants who do not cry at all, and whom Stella Chess may have called "slow to warm up," to infants who are, as Barbara Medoff-Cooper said, "crabby and irritable" and show negative emotion across a wide range of contexts. I understand that as pediatricians you need to help parents in terms of dealing with these differences, but that pathologizing is not clear to me. On the other hand, what are the alternatives other than trying to explain the normal temperamental variation in infants and actually identifying particular children as falling within that normal variation?

Faculty Member: From the clinical perspective, what is the advantage of separating colic from complaints of normal crying if we are considering this to be a healthy infant who just cries a lot?

Oberklaid: Wessel's criteria are useful for research, but I do not know whether it is a different population of infants.

Barr: It has been useful as a benchmark to have comparable populations to study, at least on the basis of the primary presenting complaint. Whether infants who meet Wessel's criteria (or other criteria) also have organic disease or not has been raised from time to time. That is another fascinating area of investigation. It may well be that there is a subgroup of infants who meet Wessel's criteria who also have organic disease and another subgroup who do not. That is an empirical question. The point is that if you want to start with a benchmark for clinical studies, I do not think using Wessel's criteria is a problem.

What is important to change is the concept that there are both organic colic syndromes and nonorganic colic syndromes. Perhaps this could be accomplished in the following way. There is colic syndrome that is associated with organic disease, but organic disease does not necessarily cause all of the colic symptoms. I would argue that it exacerbates whatever crying that infant is going to do anyway. The pattern is going to be the same, and probably the characteristics are going to be the same. The crying bouts are going to be more intense, longer in duration, probably with a higher curve. If I were making one change to the conference topic, I would say we should discuss organic disease that can present as a "colic-like symptom complex" rather than organic versus nonorganic colic.

* * * * *

Gunnar: Yet we need to tell parents something. We could say, "Well, your child is on the high end of a normal continuum and therefore is a 'sensitive,' 'difficult,' whatever the term might be, infant." That advice is legitimate if this period of increased distress at 3 or 6 weeks is predictive of later behavior. "Temperament" has a connotation that this is not going to be resolved in 2 weeks. If you tell parents, "Just hold your breath and in a few weeks this is going to be a different child," that is not temperament. If it is not characteristic of the way this child is going to be forever, then even the label that the child is on the upper end of the normal continuum and temperamentally different is problematic.

* * * * *

Hofer: The emphasis seems to be on the child as the patient, whereas here, when you make the diagnosis of colic, I believe what you are saying is that the crying is a problem, but not for the infant. The problem is for the mother, because the mother has to deal with her feelings and her responses. And she gets relatively short shrift in an ordinary pediatric setting, because the mother is not the person to whom the pediatrician is paying attention. So, because we have compartmentalized medicine, we do not have much to offer the person who needs it most at the point when the diagnosis is made.

* * * * *

Treem: I would challenge the group to come up with what I would call the "Rome criteria" for colic. Our colleagues in adult gastroenterology have done a better job than pediatric gastroenterology, at least until recently. They defined irritable bowel syndrome as a positive diagnosis, which can be based on criteria such as clinical symptoms, history, physical exam and certain minimal laboratory tests. Irritable bowel syndrome is defined by a clear set of positive clinical criteria. We need to be able to make a positive diagnosis of colic based on clinical criteria.

Faculty Member: There is the colic symptom checklist. Barry Lester put together a series of symptoms that can be checked off as "yes" or "no." It may be valuable.[3, 4]

Barr: Along the lines that Will Treem raised, there is a "Rome group" book on pediatric functional disease.[5] I wrote the chapter on colic. We tried to accomplish what he is suggesting, although it is not nearly as far along or as well worked out as he is requesting.

References

1. Gormally SM, Barr RG. Of clinical pies and clinical clues: proposal for a clinical approach to complaints of early crying and colic. *Ambulatory Child Health*. 1997;3:137-153.
2. Wessel MA, Cobb JC, Jackson EB, Harris GS, Detwiler AC. Paroxysmal fussing in infancy, sometimes called "colic." *Pediatrics*. 1954;14:421-434.
3. Lester BM, Boukydis CFZ, Garcia-Coll CT, Hole WT. Symposium on infantile colic: introduction. *Infant Mental Health Journal*. 1990;11:320-333.
4. Lester BM, Boukydis CFZ, Garcia-Coll CT, Hole WT, Peucker M. Infantile colic: acoustic cry characteristics, maternal perception of cry, and temperament. *Infant Behavioral Development*. 1992;15:15-26.
5. Barr RG. Infant colic. In: Hyman PE, ed. *Pediatric Functional Gastrointestinal Disorders*. New York, NY: Academy Professional Information Services, Inc.; 1999.

New Evidence on Unexplained Early Infant Crying

Section 4: Empirically Based Approaches to Management: Behavioral Strategies

Abstracts from Section 4: Empirically Based Approaches to Management: Behavioral Strategies

Behavioral Treatment of Prolonged Infant Crying: Evaluation, Methods and a Proposal
Dieter Wolke, PhD

Althrough there have been numerous attempts to evaluate dietary and behavioral interventions for colic, such analyses are complicated by varying definitions of colic and different criteria for judging the effects of the interventions. Behavioral interventions are effective and generally readily accepted by parents and do not require mothers to stop breastfeeding, as dietary treatments may. Identification of the optimal approach for treating crying problems requires an appreciation of the age and developmental stage of the child and engagement of the parents as competent partners in the treatment process.

Behavioral Management of Early Infant Crying in Irritable Babies
Professor Dymphna C. van den Boom

The major outcome of most interventional studies of excessive crying is reduced crying, but this measure provides little information about the long-term effects of the intervention or the quality of the parent-child relationship. In a study of 100 irritable infants, an intervention to improve the quality of interaction between mother and child was evaluated. The intervention effectively enhanced maternal responsiveness and improved mother-child interactions across multiple domains; furthermore, sustained beneficial effects of the intervention were noted through the third year. These findings highlight the importance of a developmental approach to intervention.

The REST Regimen: A Conceptual Approach to Managing Unexplained Early Infant Irritability

Maureen R. Keefe, RN, PhD

"Irritable infant syndrome" is a behavioral disorder characterized by recurrent episodes of fussiness, crying, restlessness and diminished soothability. It is thought to be related to infants' inability to self-regulate their state, and it subsequently may disrupt the synchrony of the parent-infant dyad. The REST Regimen Intervention Program uses an integrative approach to the management of infant irritability, with components specifically designed for both infants and parents. A randomized clinical trial now under way will evaluate the efficacy of the REST regimen in reducing excess infant irritability and providing relief from parental distress associated with an excessively irritable infant.

Behavioral Treatment of Prolonged Infant Crying: Evaluation, Methods and a Proposal

Dieter Wolke, PhD

Dietary versus Behavioral Management Treatment of Colic

Direct comparison of diet change and behavioral management as colic treatments is complicated by variable definitions of colic and by the different methodologies required by dietary and behavioral trials. In a recent commentary, it was said that behavioral interventions have been unfairly judged by criteria developed for drug studies.[1] A new look at the evidence suggests that, in general, behavioral interventions are more effective than dietary treatments and they are more acceptable to parents.

Definitions of Colic or Prolonged Crying

Although some descriptions of colic include a flushed face, drawn-up legs, gas and difficulty passing stools, along with the classic symptom of high-pitched, inconsolable crying,[2, 3] these symptoms may not be defining characteristics of colic.[4, 5] Furthermore, some evidence suggests that the acoustic cry features of infants with colic differ from the cries of infants who do not have colic, although this is widely debated.[6-8] Other findings suggest that "colic" infants mostly fuss and fret, rather than cry, persistently.[9] The lack of a standardized, widely accepted definition of colic complicates critical comparisons of treatment studies[10] because the subjects in different studies may not represent the same population.

In an attempt to standardize the application of the term "colic," many investigators have adopted the "Rule of Threes," derived from Wessel, Cobb, Jackson, Harris and Detwiler.[11] This rule defines colic as fussing and crying lasting for a minimum of 3 hours per day, on at least 3 days per week for the previous 3 weeks. Some empiric evidence suggests that this definition provides a meaningful distinction between colicky and noncolicky infants[12] and that parents whose infants fulfill a *modified* "Rule of Threes" are more likely to seek help.[13] Unfortunately, it is difficult to accurately assess behavior for a 3-week baseline period, forcing researchers to rely upon retrospective parental reports that show that excessive fussing and crying have been present for at least 3 weeks. These reports may be influenced by parental personality and mental health, so that crying descriptions reflect parental perceptions and interpretations as well as objective infant behavior.[14-21] To minimize this issue, adapted Wessel criteria have been developed. These guidelines require that the infant has fussed or cried on at least 3 days for more than 3 hours per day during systematic recordings at baseline.[4, 22, 23] Furthermore, fulfillment of the modified Wessel criteria depends on the duration of the baseline diary assessment period (ie, 3 days, 4 days or 7 days).[23-25]

While adoption of the modified Wessel criteria to define colic solves certain problems, this definition is not perfect. One problem that may affect its acceptability is the existence of secular or cohort trends in many areas of physical or psychologic development (eg, increase in height or IQ scores).[26-28] When these forces are at work, norms become outdated and must be adjusted. Given changes in lifestyle, nutrition, feeding and caretaking behavior, secular trends may occur in fuss/cry behavior resulting in changes in fuss/cry amounts. Therefore, it may be somewhat problematic to use criteria reported in 1954[11] to define "colic."

Perhaps a more fundamental problem concerns the application of Wessel's criteria across cultures. Because infant fuss and cry amounts may vary among countries, using the same cutoff point (modified Wessel criteria) to define "colic" across cultures may include different groups of infants. As an example, assume that the fuss/cry averages are 130 minutes (SD ±50) in country A, but only 90 minutes (SD ±40) in country B. The infants who fuss or cry for more than 180 minutes on 3 days in country A are those who fuss or cry greater than 1 SD (on 3 days), compared with same-aged peers. In contrast, those in country B who cry for more than 180 minutes are infants who cry or fuss greater than 2.25 SD, compared with same-aged peers. Because the same arbitrary value is used to define colic in both countries, 16% of the infants in country A would be considered to have colic, compared with less than 2% of the infants in country B.

Cross-study comparisons would be strengthened if the same inclusion criteria were adopted by all researchers. Rather than the arbitrary cutoffs of the current definition for colic,[3, 29] *a universal definition of prolonged crying should be developed according to country-specific norms and distribution characteristics of fuss/cry amounts.* Researchers must decide whether "prolonged criers" are those above the 83rd percentile (>1 SD), above the 90th percentile (>1.5 SD), above the 97th percentile (>2 SD) or any other criterion—as long as the criterion discriminates meaningful groups and is the same across cultures. A universal definition would bring colic research in line with other areas of investigation, such as behavior-problem research. This universal definition would specify infants whose crying and fussing exceed the average range for same-aged peers. The old term "colic" suggests a false etiology (see article by Treem in this text), and may be more accurately replaced by "prolonged fussing and crying" for future use.

The "Best" Efficacy Studies of the Treatment of Colic/Prolonged Crying

If an appropriate, universal definition of prolonged crying is adopted, critical comparisons of studies should improve. Even without such a definition, large-scale reviews of colic treatment studies have been completed.[16, 30, 31] Reviews published by Lucassen and colleagues[29] and by the Wolke research group[16] will guide the present discussion of the effectiveness of dietary and behavioral treatments for prolonged crying. Although pharmacologic and naturopathic interventions for prolonged fussing and crying have been examined experimentally,[32-35] these will not be discussed here.

The Systematic Review by Lucassen et al[29]: A Summary

Lucassen and colleagues completed a systematic search of MEDLINE, EMBASE and the Cochrane Trials Register for published reports on colic and crying.[29] Of the 50 complete reports identified, 23 were excluded. Some trials were dismissed because they did not have a control group[36] and others because they included mainly infants with normative crying.[37, 38]

Lucassen and colleagues rated the remaining 27 trials on a 5-point scale according to 3 quality criteria: adequacy of randomization, double-blinding and completeness of follow-up. These 3 factors are critical to the internal validity of any experimental study and have been widely used to judge pharmacological clinical trials.[1, 39] Randomization is used to prevent selection bias before treatment is introduced, thereby ensuring the pretreatment comparability of the treatment and control groups. In a double-blind study, both the treatment subjects and the treatment providers are unaware of the exact treatment being provided (ie, sugar pill versus treatment drug). Double-blinding, when applicable, is used to control for any a priori bias due to perceived preference of the therapist or patient for a particular treatment. Double-blinding also guards against *performance bias* or systematic differences in the care provided apart from the intervention being evaluated. Ensuring the completeness of follow-up controls for *exclusion bias,* which involves selective withdrawal of certain patient groups from the trial.

When Lucassen and coworkers applied these quality criteria, 9 of the 27 trials received a low score (0-1).[40, 41] Of the remaining 18 trials that received higher scores, 7 involved dietary changes, 6 assessed pharmacological treatments, one involved herbal tea treatment[32] and 4 trials assessed behavioral interventions.[22, 36, 42, 43] Lucassen and colleagues drew the following major conclusions from their review: "A definite diagnosis of infantile colic should be followed by a one week trial of substituting cows' milk with hypoallergenic formula milk. Dietary intervention should be combined with behavioural interventions: general advice, reassurance, reduction in stimuli, and sensitive differential responding (teaching parents to be more appropriately responsive to their infants with less overstimulation and more effective soothing. Anticholinergic drugs are not recommended because of their serious side effects."[29]

Critical Reflections on the Conclusions Drawn by Lucassen et al[29]

Dietary Treatment. Recommendations about the benefit of dietary treatments, in general, and the substitution of hypoallergenic formula for cow's milk, in particular, deviate from the conclusions drawn by Wolke in an earlier report.[16] Although the review by Lucassen et al[29] includes 2 studies that were not included in the review by Wolke, this data[44, 45] alone do not account for the divergent conclusions. Rather, the conflict comes from different interpretations of the *same* data. The critical issue is that, although Lucassen and colleagues describe their report as an evaluation of the **effectiveness** of treatments for colic or prolonged crying, their work actually explores the **efficacy** of treatments.[29] Further, when the literature on prolonged crying is examined to determine the **effectiveness** of treatments, behavioral management interventions tend to have more positive effects for more individuals than do dietary change treatments.

An **efficacy** study tests a treatment under optimal experimental conditions. It evaluates whether the treatment *can work*.[39] In contrast, an **effectiveness** study assesses a treatment that has been implemented in practice under less-than-optimal circumstances. It evaluates whether the *treatment works in the field*.[46-51] Recall that the scoring system employed by Lucassen and colleagues rated trials based on randomization, double-blindness and completeness of follow-up.[29] Thus, the trials they deemed acceptable were rated high on these factors. Therefore, they were studies of the **efficacy** of treatment.

Positive effects for intervention were not found for all of the "acceptable" studies identified by the Lucassen group.[29] In fact, of the 6 "sufficient" dietary trials, only 3[44, 45, 52] report a positive effect. These 3 studies are flawed in ways that weaken the argument that dietary interventions are generally effective treatments for excessive crying and colic. Note also that the original studies that led to widespread treatment of colic with hypoallergenic formulations were not considered acceptable for inclusion in the review by Lucassen et al because of methodologic limitations.[53-60]

Full details of each study can be found in the original reports,[44, 45, 52] and a more lengthy discussion of the problems with each is presented elsewhere.[16, 60] A brief analysis of the most important issues will suffice for the present evaluation of the **effectiveness** of dietary interventions. Summary information about each of the 3 dietary trials deemed sufficient by Lucassen and colleagues,[29] as well as one dietary treatment trial[61] completed after their report was done, is presented in Table 1.

Examining each trial for evidence that the particular dietary treatment studied was effective, it was found that while each study described some success, it was usually limited. For example, the trial by Forsyth[52] reported improvements in crying and colic symptoms early on; however, this positive effect was no longer significant by the end of the study. Further, very few individuals (1 or 2) showed constant improvement over the course of the trial. In their intervention study, Hill and colleagues reported a significant, but generally small, effect for the total treatment group.[45] Crying was reduced by 25% or more in 61% of the infants in the treatment group and in 43% of

Table 1. The 4 "Best" Trials of Dietary Intervention[44, 45, 52, 61]

Study	Effect size	Effective by intention-to-treat	Verdict
Forsyth (1989)[52]	0.25 (0.07 to 0.44)	No	• Good study • Only 1 or 2 infants showed constant improvement
Hill et al (1995)[45]	0.18 (0.01 to 0.36)	No	• Mixture of 2 treatments • Effect limited to infants <6 weeks of age • Control and treatment mothers report same level of improvement
Campbell (1989)[44]	0.63 (0.29 to 0.97)	?	• Unclear exclusions • Preselected samples of atopic parents
Kearney et al (1998)[61]	0.44 (?)*	?	• Colic infants? • Unclear re: cry recording • Small sample

*Cannot be computed; no SD or SE reported; reduction, 1.14h/day (95% CI: 0.23-2.05).

the control-group infants. These seemingly positive results are undermined, however, because treatment effects differed according to age and feeding type. Only breastfed infants younger than 6 weeks of age showed a significant reduction in distress. Also, when asked whether infant colic had improved, mothers in the active-diet groups did not report improvement at levels greater than did mothers in the control groups. Campbell reported high levels of improvement for several infants who were switched from a cow's milk formula to a soy-based formula; however, 11 of 19 subjects had a family history of atopy, suggesting that the sample was not representative of the population of infants crying for prolonged periods.[44] Finally, in the study that was *not* reviewed by the Lucassen group,[29] Kearney and colleagues found that infants who were given lactase drops in their milk showed a reduction in crying of 1.14 hours per 24-hour period (95% CI: 0.23-2.05).[61] Because infants in the placebo group cried at levels similar to the average crying amount of infants in the general population,[62-64] it is unclear whether the subjects in the study fulfilled the adapted Wessel criteria. If these infants were not prolonged criers, the generalizability of the results to true prolonged criers may be compromised.

A problem common to all of these studies concerns subject attrition. Subjects who dropped out should be considered "treatment failures." Analysis that ignores subjects who do not complete a study yields biased results that usually overestimate treatment effectiveness. Clearly, parents whose infants are responding positively to treatment are more likely to complete a clinical trial than are parents whose children are not improving; thus, an analysis that does not account for dropouts is more likely to exclude treatment failures than treatment successes. To avoid biases that inflate treatment effects, it is standard practice to analyze results on an *intent-to-treat* basis[65] in which withdrawals or dropouts are considered treatment failures, just as they would be in a practice setting. Two of the studies[44, 61] do not provide enough information to complete an intent-to-treat analysis. Neither the data from Forsyth[52] nor that of Hill and colleagues[45] stands up to an intent-to-treat analysis. That is, no evidence for the effectiveness of their specific dietary interventions is found when dropouts are treated as treatment failures.

Parenting (Behavioral) Interventions. Of the 27 trials initially identified by Lucassen and colleagues,[29] 5 were studies of behavioral intervention.[22, 36, 40, 42, 43] A systematic database search identified one additional study.[66] Table 2 summarizes the results of these 6 behavioral trials.

All trials used a parallel-group design comparing treatment with either an alternative treatment or a no-treatment control group. Five of the 6 trials included some form of behavioral management as the primary treatment of colic,[36, 40, 42, 43, 66] and one employed increased carrying.[22] Four of the 6 trials were effective in reducing prolonged crying or colic.[36, 40, 42, 66] In these 4 trials, the dropout rates were very low (0% to 18%), compared with the dropout rates reported for the unsuccessful trials and, in particular, for the dietary trials reported previously.[44, 45, 52, 61] Further, the low dropout rate means that

Table 2. The 6 "Best" Trials of Behavioral Intervention[22, 36, 40, 42, 43, 66]

Study	Effect size	Effective by intention-to-treat	Verdict
Barr et al (1991)[22]	0.12 (-0.03 to 0.27)	No	• Good study • Increased carrying not effective
McKenzie (1991)[42]	0.48 (0.23 to 0.74)	Yes	• No colic definition • No test colic resolved
Parkin, Schwartz, Manuel (1993)[43]	-0.37 (-0.69 to -0.05)	No	• Small subgroup sizes • Not effective • No test colic resolved
Wolke, Gray, Meyer (1994)[40]	0.16 (0.02 to 0.30) 0.24 (0.03 to 0.47)*	Yes	• Controlled therapist effects • Not randomized
Taubman (1984)[36]	0.30 (0.06 to 0.55)	Yes	• Colic definition: crying >2h/d • No no-treatment control
Dihigo (1998)[66]	0.92 (0.25 to 1.50)	Yes	• Small sample size • Effective • Colic definition: crying >2h/d

*Colic resolved according to modified Wessel criterion (MWC): Experimental Group 2 (Behavioral management: 66.7%) versus No-treatment control group (43.2%). Based on reanalysis of data applying MWC rather than the criterion used in the original publication[40] of "crying on average less than 3 hours per day during the past week."

analysis by intent-to-treat does not nullify the reported positive results for behavioral treatment. Although the behavioral management trials were not without methodological weaknesses, the fact that many report positive results, even when data from dropouts are analyzed, suggests that behavioral methods are generally effective for managing prolonged crying.

The issue of generalizability is critical for rating the effectiveness of treatments.[59] Although certain individuals, such as those with a family history of atopy, may benefit greatly from dietary intervention, the effectiveness of such treatment for this small group does not necessarily translate into an effective treatment for the entire population of infants who cry for prolonged periods. Further, even if a treatment has high efficacy and has been shown to work in a laboratory setting, the treatment will be effective only to the extent that it is implemented properly, it is accessible to the target population and it is acceptable to this population.[48, 50, 67] Again, results with behavioral management techniques exceed those with dietary manipulations. The low dropout rate for behavior trials, compared with dietary trials, shows that, in general, parents are more amenable to this type of intervention. Dietary trials seem especially likely to fail when breastfeeding mothers are required to make major changes to their diets to be able to continue breastfeeding.[45] Parents are not the only adults who must comply with treatment guidelines if a treatment is to be effective. Clinicians, too, must be amenable. Many would find the advice of Lucassen and colleagues[29] to "start a one-week trial of hypoallergenic formula to treat colic" troubling, as it requires that mothers give up breastfeeding, which has proven benefits, for a trial of bottle-feeding with unproven benefit.[3, 68] Offering advice that makes breastfeeding more manageable for mothers,[69] rather than encouraging them to switch to bottle-feeding, is the preferred option of many clinicians and is in accord with public health strategies.[70] Another concern focuses on "labeling": Once an infant is labeled as "allergic," he or she may be incorrectly considered to be more vulnerable, in general. Further, subsequent behavior problems may be falsely attributed to the allergy.[71, 72]

Overall, the latest information on dietary and behavioral interventions for prolonged crying suggests that the latter type of treatment is more effective. Compared with dietary-change techniques, behavioral management treatments are more strongly associated with reduced crying and are more likely to be accepted by parents. In addition, they do not require mothers to discontinue breastfeeding. Why, then, did Lucassen and colleagues[29] recommend that dietary interventions be implemented as the first treatment step?

Recall that the review by Lucassen et al[29] scored studies based on the extent to which they met 3 criteria: randomization, double-blinding and completeness of follow-up. Adequate attention to these factors minimizes the likelihood that bias will influence a study's results. Although these criteria are useful for judging the efficacy of pharmacologic trials, their application to behavioral and psychotherapeutic interventions may not be appropriate.[1] Specifically, it may not be possible to design a double-blind, completely randomized study.

Double-blindness[73] requires that both the subject receiving treatment (or, for infants, their parents) and the therapist providing it are "blind" to the treatment. While double-blinding is a valuable tool to reduce and assess bias (such as placebo effects) in drug trials, it is impossible to do so in most areas of medicine or behavioral treatment. The absurdity of this is clear when we consider a surgeon or counselor who is unaware of what he or she is doing. Although parents can be partially blinded by not being informed about treatment details, they cannot be completely unaware of the treatment interventions because they are generally involved in implementation. Because double-blinding is not possible, it is inappropriate to use it as a quality criterion for certain behavioral and psychotherapeutic interventions.[48, 74, 75]

Of course, the elimination of bias remains an important issue. For this reason, alternative strategies for eliminating or estimating performance bias have been developed. These include the investigation of generalized placebo effects in which a treatment is compared with an alternate treatment condition as well as a no-treatment condition. The difference between an alternate treatment and no treatment indicates the generalized placebo effect (or how receiving attention alone leads to improvement). One technique used to control for therapist differences is to have the same therapist deliver the different types of treatment.[40] Complex designs, including groups primed with expectations of success of a placebo treatment, have been proposed.[16]

Randomization is used to guard against selection bias. If randomized assignment to treatment groups is not possible, alternate safeguards for the comparability of groups can be utilized. Crossover designs (such as in the dietary study by Forsyth[52]) expose all subjects to all treatment conditions. Trials in which assignment to treatment groups is not random, but which include measures of many baseline indicators, enable investigators to confirm pretreatment comparability of groups. Under certain circumstances, differences in baseline factors can occur despite randomization. When a sample is small, an outlier in any group can skew results, leading to "bias-in-effect" sizes. Some authors have suggested that in small, parallel-group trials, nonrandomized, but carefully balanced, groups may be as internally valid as randomized groups.[40, 45, 76]

In sum, although double-blind and randomized study designs are desirable, they are not always possible, or even necessary. Rather than categorically downgrading behavioral interventions that were not double-blinded and/or randomized, Lucassen and colleagues[29] should have considered whether other safeguards for bias were employed.[1]

Conclusions

When design features, efficacy and effectiveness are considered, then none of the studies for the treatment of colic, whether dietary or behavioral, fulfill all quality criteria. Also, the effect sizes in favor of treatment are usually small to moderate, rather than large. Small changes in cry/fuss amounts do not seem to make much difference to parents' perceptions of colic.[45] There is still little evidence about the effectiveness of treatments in clinical practice, although some results are encouraging.[40]

This review of the literature suggests that behavioral management should be the first course of treatment because it has been shown to be effective in efficacy studies, it tends to be accepted by parents and it does not require mothers to stop breastfeeding. If behavioral management does not lead to a change in symptoms, or if the family has a history of atopic illness, then dietary treatment may be indicated. In this context, it is of interest to note that a recent systematic review of sleeping problems in young children reached a similar conclusion. Ramchandani and colleagues stated, "Behavioural interventions are more likely to be both effective in the short term and to have continuing benefit in the longer term."[77]

A Behavioral Management Approach to Treatment

A biobehavioral model of the regulation of crying and sleeping that I practice[78] follows, along with specific behavioral interventions to help reduce prolonged crying in early infancy and to prevent sleeping problems in later infancy. A more-detailed description of this treatment approach, which extends to sleeping problems, feeding problems and temper tantrums, is presented elsewere.[16, 79-84]

A Behavioral Model of Factors that Lead to and Maintain Problems in Early Infancy

Several behavioral models have been proposed to explain the development or maintenance of regulatory problems, such as prolonged crying or night waking. These include psychodynamic approaches,[85] strict behavioral approaches,[38] behavioral-cognitive approaches[80, 86-88] and complex-system models.[89] To date, behavioral management has received the most thorough empiric evaluation.[77, 90] According to the behavioral management approach,[40, 80, 83] prolonged crying in the first 4 months to 6 months of life is due to inappropriate development of self-competence for internal regulation of behavior. Because the development of the infant's internal control mechanisms is not supported properly, inadequate internal behavior regulation is maintained. According to this model, there are *no* easy solutions that are effective for all babies. Rather, there are **principles of treatment** that must be individualized for each family.

Because very young infants lack neurologic, physiologic and cognitive prerequisites for the recognition of complex contingencies, classical and operant learning theory is only partly applicable to children in the first months of life. The separation and recognition of inner and outer stimuli and their qualities are just developing. In the first 3 months of life, withdrawal of attention (operant conditioning) when a child is crying leads to no change in crying behavior.[91] This is because the infant's behavior is biologically meaningful—helping to secure survival—rather than learned. In contrast, persistent crying is maintained or reinforced by parenting behavior that inhibits the infant's acquisition of behavioral self-control.

Beginning at approximately 6 months to 8 months of age, paroxysmal crying and sleeping problems can be explained more fully by classical and operant learning models. This is because cognitive changes have occurred that allow the child to internally represent the primary caretaker, to begin to understand cause and effect and to understand the intentions of others. These new skills influence interactions with people: For example, infants often engage in games such as dropping a spoon, watching the spoon and looking at the mother to pick it up. Infants are happy to repeat those games again and again. A clear association between the infant's action and the mother's behavior has occurred. In much the same way, crying, including tantrums, can be used to reach certain goals, such as receiving attention. Treatments for children under and over 6 months of age thus differ somewhat, however. The focus here will be on the younger infants, but information about treating older infants is available elsewhere.[79, 80, 83]

Parents of infants who have crying problems may use strategies that are not appropriate for the individual self-regulation abilities of their child. Instead, parents may provide external behavioral regulation that is not developmentally adaptive. For example, many mothers induce sleep by breastfeeding until the infant falls asleep.[70, 92] The baby is then gingerly transferred into the bed, and the parents tiptoe out of the room. If this is the regular pattern, infants do not learn to fall asleep by themselves. In this way, infants have no opportunity to learn strategies to settle themselves if night wakening occurs. Their only recourse is to cry for the parent, who then feeds them back to sleep.

Diagnosing the Problem. The course of the diagnostic process is influenced by several factors. The intensity of the diagnostic workup depends on whether the major complaints are limited to crying problems or whether additional sleeping, feeding or growth problems exist.[84, 93] Clinicians need to determine whether a face-to-face consultation is necessary or whether treatment can be completed via telephone and written material. At the initial contact, parents should always be asked how distressed they are by the child's behavior problem. If the diagnostic information indicates complex familial problems, such as psychiatric illness or risk of child abuse, then face-to-face contact is necessary. However, when appropriate, diagnosis based on diaries and questionnaires completed by the parents and feedback via telephone are time-saving and cost-effective ways of delivering primary care.[40, 94]

There are 2 main components in the diagnostic process. Initially, the clinician takes a history of somatic problems. All parents should be asked whether the family physician has recently examined the infant to rule out organic reasons for the problem behavior. Such cases are rare, but occasionally crying problems are associated with organic problems such as otitis media, urinary tract infections or severe esophageal reflux. In this first phase, parents complete a 7-day diary of infant crying, sleeping and feeding behaviors.

In the next stage of the diagnostic process, parents complete The Baby Questionnaire and The Parent Questionnaire.[40] (Note: The Baby Questionnaire and The Parent Questionnaire are available from the author.) The Baby Questionnaire includes questions about the behavioral style of the child in order to evaluate temperament and other problems such as feeding. The pregnancy and birth histories are briefly assessed. Also, parents are asked to describe their perception of their child's crying; that is, do they view it as painful or rejecting? They are also asked to give reasons why they think their child has a crying or sleeping problem. Also in The Baby Questionnaire, parents are asked how often they let the child "cry it out," and how often they reach the limit of their coping abilities. The Parent Questionnaire assesses demographic characteristics of the family, including living conditions and parental work routines. It includes screening instruments to assess maternal depression, partner relationships, social support systems and isolation. Often, living conditions and the social-psychologic situation of the family help determine the treatment option that presents the best choice for the family.

The information collected in these 2 stages is reviewed by the clinician, and hypotheses are formulated about the conditions that maintain the infant's crying problems. At this point, the probability of child abuse should be estimated, and in very rare cases admission to the clinic for a few days to relieve distress may be indicated.[42]

Treating Crying Problems. After all diagnostic information has been collected, the clinician's hypotheses are discussed with the parents, and the treatment is planned jointly with them. Parents are treated as *competent partners* in the treatment. During the first treatment meeting, the diary is discussed and used as a source of information about the parents' experiences and the infant's problems. By completing the diary, parents often have an accurate picture of the type and severity of the problem. In fact, they have often already formulated hypotheses about the etiology of the crying problem. The therapist suggests some hypotheses and probes whether the parents agree or disagree.

During the initial treatment session, the clinician should candidly discuss the stress that may arise from treatment itself. Parents must be warned that changes in caretaking behavior and routines are often necessary, and that this can be especially difficult at first. If the clinician's suggestions are not acceptable to the parents, it is often better not to even try to implement certain treatments. Alternative management principles should be discussed.

The consequences of therapeutic success should also be discussed with parents. While having an end to prolonged crying would seem to be a wholly positive treatment outcome, in some cases the negative infant behavior has covert benefits for parents. For example, social contacts may be facilitated when parents discuss their child's crying problems with other parents. A therapy success could mean the loss of such opportunities.

Lastly, the diary is used to learn details about the child's problem. For crying, clinicians determine how much crying actually occurs and whether there is a regular cry/fuss pattern. The diary provides information about the parents' behavior, too, showing whether they provide a consistent, predictable daily schedule for the infant and whether over- or understimulation occurs. The coping strategies parents have tried, and their successes or failures can be documented as well.

Using this information, concrete strategies for treatment are chosen. Therapy must be individualized for each family. The diary information makes this possible. Also, the therapeutic approach must be appropriate for the developmental level of the child. Lastly, the treatment strategies must support the development of the child's own internal behavior control. The behavioral techniques are designed to help the child learn to regulate crying; that is, to soothe with reduced levels of intervention.

At first, the clinician should provide parents with information about the normal development of crying patterns. Parents should understand that there is a variation among infants. In order for parents to develop realistic expectations for their infant, they should also be taught to observe their infant for "good" behavior. Many parents who have a "cry baby" are highly attuned to fussing and crying behavior, which represents negative behavior. When the child stops crying, such positive behavior is often ignored. Parents use these periods to recover from the long periods of negative behavior. It is important that parents learn to focus on positive behavior and to react to the infant with increased attention and positive expression during positive-behavior periods when their baby is showing adequate behavior control. Parents must increase their sensitivity, too, in order to determine the reason for a child's crying or fussing. Not every cry bout requires immediate parental reaction. No rules dictate how long a parent should wait; rather, caregivers should react according to the particular situation. In some circumstances, it may be appropriate to wait for up to 2 minutes to allow the infant to try to calm him- or herself.

Parents of "cry babies" may have lost their intuitive awareness of different causes of crying. Instead, they react very quickly, in an agitated manner, using a variety of overstimulating interventions.

Overstimulation, due to rapid changes between carrying, swaddling and talking to the infant, should be reduced. Infants exposed to these quickly changing activities are not calm and they have no chance to calm down. These infants are often overtired and react with irritability to the high level of stimulation. Rather, each of these parenting behaviors can be helpful if applied calmly and given time to work.

The lack of a predictable schedule and an underdeveloped sense of day and night may also contribute to poor self-control. To develop self-control skills, infants require a regular, predictable schedule, which includes specific times for feeding, sleeping, playing and outings. Parents should not consistently use "quick fixes" or "tricks." Car rides may provide a short-term solution for soothing a crying baby, insofar as rocking movements and the sound of the engine do calm some babies. However, many awake again when the engine stops. In the long term, the infant acquires no skills of soothing him- or herself, for example, to be able to fall asleep unaided.

Similarly, the difference between daytime and nighttime should be maximized. Young infants need to be fed during the night, but these feedings should differ substantially from daytime feedings. At night, feeding is for nutritional purposes only, with just minimal eye contact or talking. Lights should be off. Some clinicians have also suggested "focal feeds" at night.[69] In this technique, the infant is put to bed at a reasonable time and is awakened for feeding later, before the mother goes to bed. In this way the mother takes control of the feeding process in an attempt to prolong the period until the next feed.[69]

It is essential that clinicians follow up with all infants and their families to learn from their experiences and to determine whether the intervention helped resolve the infant problem.

Conclusions

Prolonged crying in infancy may lead parents to seek the assistance of a clinician. This problem often results from *disturbances of regulation and integration* of infants' biologic and social functioning. Crying has primary biologic functions, and the etiologic factors and methods of treatment for crying problems differ according to the age and developmental stage of the child. Several treatment approaches have been evaluated, and differing degrees of effectiveness have been observed. Dietary treatment may be successful for a minority of children with crying problems, but behavioral management has been shown to help more infants and to be better accepted by parents who must manage early infant crying.

References

1. Wolke D. Treating children with sleep disorders. Treatment of child sleeping problems and the quality of trials are important [letter]. *British Medical Journal.* 2000;320:1668.
2. Illingworth RS. Infantile colic revisited. *Archives of Disease in Childhood.* 1985;60:981-985.
3. Crowcroft N. Effectiveness of treatments for infantile colic. Findings apply only to the most severely affected infants [letter]. *British Medical Journal.* 1998;317:1451-1452.
4. Barr RG. Colic and crying syndromes in infants. *Pediatrics.* 1998;102(suppl E):1282-1286.
5. St. James-Roberts I. Persistent infant crying. *Archives of Disease in Childhood.* 1991;66:653-655.
6. St. James-Roberts I. What is distinct about infants' "colic" cries? *Archives of Disease in Childhood.* 1999;80:56-62.
7. Zeskind PS, Barr RG. Acoustic analysis of cries of infants with and without colic. Paper presented at: Conference on Human Development; 1992; Atlanta, Ga.
8. Zeskind PS, Parker-Price S, Barr RG. Rhythmic organization of the sound of infant crying. *Developmental Psychobiology.* 1993;26:321-333.
9. St. James-Roberts I, Plewis I. Individual differences, daily fluctuations, and developmental changes in amounts of infant waking, fussing, crying, feeding, and sleeping. *Child Development.* 1996;67:2527-2540.
10. Hyams KC. Developing case definitions for symptom-based conditions: the problem of specificity. *Epidemiologic Reviews.* 1998;20:148-156.
11. Wessel MA, Cobb JC, Jackson EB, Harris GS, Detwiler AC. Paroxysmal fussing in infancy, sometimes called "colic." *Pediatrics.* 1954;14:421-435.
12. Barr RG, Rotman A, Yaremko J, Leduc D, Francoeur TE. The crying of infants with colic: a controlled empirical description. *Pediatrics.* 1992;90:14-21.
13. St. James-Roberts I. Measuring infant crying and its social perception and impact. *ACPP Review & Newsletter.* 1992;14:130-133.
14. St. James-Roberts I, Wolke D. Bases for a socially referenced approach to temperament. In: Kohnstamm GA, ed. *Temperament Discussed: Temperament and Development in Infancy and Childhood.* Berwyn, Ill: Swets & Zeitlinger; 1986:17-26.
15. Wolke D. Schwierige Säuglinge: Wirklichkeit oder Einbildung? In: Pachler JM, Straßburg HM, eds. *Der Unruhige Säugling. Fortschritte der Sozialpädiatrie.* Vol 13. Lübeck, Germany: Hansisches Verlagskontor;1990:70-88.

16. Wolke D. The treatment of problem crying behaviour. In: St. James-Roberts I, Harris G, Messer D, eds. *Infant Crying, Feeding, and Sleeping: Development, Problems, and Treatments.* Hemel Hempstead, England: Harvester Wheatsheaf; 1993:47-79.
17. Wolke D, St. James-Roberts I. Maternal affective-cognitive processes in the perception of newborn difficultness. In: Kohnstamm GA, ed. *Temperament Discussed: Temperament and Development in Infancy and Childhood.* Berwyn, Ill: Swets & Zeitlinger; 1986.
18. Wolke D, St. James-Roberts I. Multi-method measurement of the early parent-infant system with easy and difficult newborns. In: Rauh H, Steinhausen H-C, eds. *Psychobiology and Early Development.* Amsterdam, Holland: Elsevier Science Ltd; 1987:49-70.
19. Vaughn BE, Bradley CF, Joffe LS, Seifer R. Maternal characteristics measured prenatally are predictive of ratings of temperamental "difficulty" on the Carey Infant Temperament Questionnaire. *Developmental Psychology.* 1987;23:152-161.
20. Zuckerman B, Bauchner H, Parker S, Cabral H. Maternal depressive symptoms during pregnancy, and newborn irritability. *Journal of Developmental and Behavioral Pediatrics: JDBP.* 1990;11:190-194.
21. Parker SJ, Barrett DE. Maternal Type A behavior during pregnancy, neonatal crying, and early infant temperament: do type A women have type A babies? *Pediatrics.* 1992;89:474-479.
22. Barr RG, McMullan SJ, Spiess H, et al. Carrying as colic "therapy": a randomized controlled trial. *Pediatrics.* 1991;87:623-630.
23. St. James-Roberts I, Hurry J, Bowyer J. Objective confirmation of crying durations in infants referred for excessive crying. *Archives of Disease in Childhood.* 1993;68:82-84.
24. Barr RG, Kramer MS, Boisjoly C, McVey-White L, Pless IB. Parental diary of infant cry and fuss behaviour. *Archives of Disease in Childhood.* 1988;63:380-387.
25. Barr RG, Yang H, Platt RW, Calinoiu N. Diary recording of infant behaviors: Is there a "first day" effect? Paper presented at: Society for Research in Child Development Biennial Conference; April 17, 1999; Albuquerque, NM.
26. Neisser U, ed. *The Rising Curve: Long-Term Gains in IQ and Related Measures.* London, England: American Psychological Association; 1998.
27. Wolke D, Ratschinski G, Ohrt B, Riegel K. The cognitive outcome of very preterm infants may be poorer than often reported: an empirical investigation of how methodological issues make a big difference. *European Journal of Pediatrics.* 1994;153:906-915.
28. Wolke D, Söhne B. Wenn der Schein trügt: Zur kritischen Interpretation von Entwicklungsstudien. Teil 1: Studienplan, Stichprobenbeschreibung, Probandenverluste und Kontrolgruppen. *Monatsschrift fur Kinderheilkunde.* 1997;145:444-456.
29. Lucassen PLBJ, Assendelft WJJ, Gubbels JW, van Eijk JTM, van Geldrop WJ, Neven AK. Effectiveness of treatments for infantile colic: systematic review. *British Medical Journal* 1998;316:1563-1569.
30. Treem WR. Infant colic. A pediatric gastroenterologist's perspective. *Pediatric Clinics of North America.* 1994;41:1121-1138.
31. Lehtonen L, Korvenranta H. Infantile colic. Seasonal incidence and crying profiles. *Archives of Pediatrics & Adolescent Medicine.* 1995;149:533-536.
32. Weizman Z, Alkrinawi S, Goldfarb D, Bitran C. Efficacy of herbal tea preparation in infantile colic. *The Journal of Pediatrics.* 1993;122:650-652.
33. Markestad T. Use of sucrose as a treatment for infant colic. *Archives of Disease in Childhood.* 1997;76:356-358.
34. Barr RG, Young SN, Wright JH, Gravel R, Alkawaf R. Differential calming responses to sucrose taste in crying infants with and without colic. *Pediatrics.* 1999;103:e68.
35. Wiberg JM, Nordsteen J, Nilsson N. The short-term effect of spinal manipulation in the treatment of infantile colic: a randomized controlled clinical trial with a blinded observer. *Journal of Manipulative and Physiological Therapeutics.* 1999;22:517-522.
36. Taubman B. Clinical trial of the treatment of colic by modification of parent-infant interaction. *Pediatrics.* 1984;74:998-1003.

37. Hunziker UA, Barr RG. Increased carrying reduces infant crying: a randomized controlled trial. *Pediatrics*. 1986;77:641-648.
38. Rickert VI, Johnson CM. Reducing nocturnal awakening and crying episodes in infants and young children: a comparison between scheduled awakenings and systematic ignoring. *Pediatrics*. 1988;81:203-212.
39. Jaddad A. *Randomized Controlled Trials*. London, England: British Medical Association; 1998.
40. Wolke D, Gray P, Meyer R. Excessive infant crying: a controlled study of mothers helping mothers. *Pediatrics*. 1994;94:322-332.
41. Oggero R, Garbo G, Savino F, Mostert M. Dietary modifications versus dicyclomine hydrochloride in the treatment of severe infantile colic. *Acta Paediatrica*. 1994;83:222-225.
42. McKenzie S. Troublesome crying in infants: effect of advice to reduce stimulation. *Archives of Disease in Childhood*. 1991;66:1416-1420.
43. Parkin PC, Schwartz CJ, Manuel BA. Randomized controlled trial of three interventions in the management of persistent crying of infancy. *Pediatrics*. 1993;92:197-201.
44. Campbell JPM. Dietary treatment of infant colic: a double-blind study. *Journal of the Royal College of General Practitioners*. 1989;39:11-14.
45. Hill DJ, Hudson IL, Sheffield LJ, Shelton MJ, Menahem S, Hosking CS. A low allergen diet is a significant intervention in infantile colic: results of a community-based study. *The Journal of Allergy and Clinical Immunology*. 1995;96:886-892.
46. Hauser-Cram P. Designing meaningful evaluations of early intervention services. In: Meisels SJ, Shonkoff JP, eds. *Handbook of Early Childhood Intervention*. Cambridge, Mass: Cambridge University Press; 1990:583-602.
47. Eysenck HJ. Problems with meta-analysis. In: Chalmers I, Altman DG, eds. *Systematic Reviews*. London, England: British Medical Journal Publishing Group; 1995:64-74.
48. Wolke D, Schulz J. Methoden und Kriterien entwicklungsorientierter Evaluation. In: Oerter R, von Hagen C, Röper G, eds. *Klinische Entwicklungspsychologie*. Weinheim, Germany: Beltz PVU; 1999:522-556.
49. Nutbeam D, Smith C, Catford J. Evaluation in health education. A review of progress, possibilities, and problems. *Journal of Epidemiology and Community Health*. 1990;44:83-89.
50. Rossi PH, Freeman HE. *Evaluation. A Systematic Approach*. London, England: Sage Publications; 1989.
51. Sackett DL, Richardson WS, Rosenberg W, Haynes RB. *Evidence-Based Medicine: How to Practice and Teach EBM*. New York, NY: Churchill Livingstone; 1997.
52. Forsyth BWC. Colic and the effect of changing formulas: a double-blind, multiple-crossover study. *The Journal of Pediatrics*. 1989;115:521-526.
53. Jakobsson I, Lindberg T. Cow's milk as a cause of infantile colic in breast-fed infants. *Lancet*. 1978;2(8087):437-439.
54. Jakobsson I, Lindberg T. Cow's milk proteins cause infantile colic in breast-fed infants: a double-blind crossover study. *Pediatrics*. 1983;71:268-271.
55. Lothe L, Lindberg T. Cow's milk whey protein elicits symptoms of infantile colic in colicky formula-fed infants: a double-blind crossover study. *Pediatrics*. 1989;83:262-266.
56. Lothe L, Lindberg T, Jakobsson I. Cow's milk formula as a cause of infantile colic: a double-blind study. *Pediatrics*. 1982;70:7-10.
57. Carey WB. Colic: exasperating but fascinating and gratifying. *Pediatrics*. 1989;84:568-569.
58. Carey WB. The effectiveness of parent counseling in managing colic [commentary]. *Pediatrics*. 1994;72:268-271.
59. Sampson HA. Infantile colic and food allergy: fact or fiction? *The Journal of Pediatrics*. 1989;115:583-584.
60. Hill DJ, Hosking CS. The colic debate. *Pediatrics*. 1995;96:165-166.
61. Kearney PJ, Malone AJ, Hayes T, Cole M, Hyland M. A trial of lactase in the management of infant colic. *Journal of Human Nutrition and Dietetics*. 1998;11:281-285.

62. Brazelton TB. Crying in infancy. *Pediatrics.* 1962;29:579-589.
63. Barr RG. The normal crying curve: what do we really know? *Developmental Medicine and Child Neurology.* 1990;32:356-362.
64. St. James-Roberts I, Halil T. Infant crying patterns in the first year: normal community and clinical findings. *Journal of Child Psychology and Psychiatry, and Allied Disciplines.* 1991;32:951-968.
65. Stewart LA, Parmar MKB. Bias in the analysis and reporting of randomized controlled trials. *International Journal of Technology Assessment in Health Care.* 1996;12:264-275.
66. Dihigo SK. New strategies for the treatment of colic: modifying the parent/infant interaction. *Journal of Pediatric Health Care.* 1998;12:256-262.
67. Black MM, Holden EW. Longitudinal intervention research in children's health and development. *Journal of Clinical Child Psychology.* 1995;24:163-172.
68. Buchanan P. Effectiveness of treatments for infantile colic. Trial of hypoallergenic milk is not supported by strong enough evidence [letter]. *British Medical Journal.* 1998;317:1451-1452.
69. Pinilla T, Birch LL. Help me make it through the night: behavioral entrainment of breast-fed infants' sleep patterns. *Pediatrics.* 1993;91:436-444.
70. Wolke D, Söhne B, Riegel K, Ohrt B, Österlund K. An epidemiologic longitudinal study of sleeping problems and feeding experience of preterm and term children in southern Finland: comparison with a southern German population sample. *The Journal of Pediatrics.* 1998;133:224-231.
71. Forsyth BWC, Canny PF. Perceptions of vulnerability 3 1/2 years after problems of feeding and crying behavior in early infancy. *Pediatrics.* 1991;88:757-763.
72. Warner JO, Hathaway MJ. Allergic form of Meadow's syndrome (Munchausen by proxy). *Archives of Disease in Childhood.* 1984;59:151-156.
73. Jaddad AR, Moore RA, Carroll D, et al. Assessing the quality of randomized clinical trials: is blinding necessary? *Controlled Clinical Trials.* 1996;7:1-12.
74. Howard KI, Moras K, Brill PL, Martinovich Z, Lutz W. Evaluation of psychotherapy. Efficacy, effectiveness, and patient progress. *The American Psychologist.* 1996;51:1059-1064.
75. Lipsey MW, Wilson DB. The efficacy of psychological, educational, and behavioral treatment. Confirmation from meta-analysis. *The American Psychologist.* 1993;48:1181-1209.
76. Greenhalgh T. *How to Read a Paper: The Basics of Evidence Based Medicine.* London, England: British Medical Journal Books; 1999.
77. Ramchandani P, Wiggs L, Webb V, Stores G. A systematic review of treatments for settling problems and night waking in young children. *British Medical Journal.* 2000;320:209-213.
78. Wolke D. Feeding and sleeping across the lifespan. In: Rutter MF, Hay D, eds. *Development Through Life: A Handbook for Clinicians.* Oxford, England: Blackwell Science Inc; 1994:517-557.
79. Wolke D. Frequent problems in the infancy and toddler years: excessive crying, sleeping and feeding difficulties. In: Bergmann KE, ed. *Health Promotion in the Family.* Berlin, Germany: Springer-Verlag. In press.
80. Wolke D. Probleme bei Neugeborenen und Kleinkindern. In: Margraf J, ed. *Lehrbuch der Verhaltenstherapie.* Vol. 2. Heidelberg, Germany: Springer-Verlag; 1996:363-380.

81. Wolke D. Die Entwicklung und Behandlung von Schlafproblemen und exzessivem Schreien im Vorschulalter. In: Petermann F, ed. *Kinder-Verhaltens-Therapie: Grundlagen und Anwendungen.* Baltmannsweiler, Germany: Schneider-Verl. Hohengehren; 1997:154-203.
82. Wolke D. Sleep problems in infants and toddlers. *Health Professional Digest.* 1997;5:84.
83. Wolke D. Interventionen bei Regulationsstoerungen. In: Oerter R, von Hagen C, Röper G, eds. *Klinische Entwicklungspsychologie.* Weinheim, Germany: Beltz PVU; 1999:351-380.
84. Wolke D, Skuse D. The management of infant feeding problems. In: Cooper PJ, Stein A, eds. *Feeding Problems and Eating Disorders in Children and Adolescents.* Philadelphia, Pa: Harwood Academic Publishers; 1992:27-59.
85. Daws D. *Through the Night: Helping Parents and Sleepless Infants.* London, England: Free Association Books; 1985.
86. Ferber R, Kryger M, eds. *Principles and Practice of Sleep Medicine in the Child.* Philadelphia, Pa: WB Saunders Co; 1995.
87. France KG. Fact, act and tact: a three-stage approach to treating the sleep problems of infants and toddlers. *Child and Adolescent Psychiatric Clinics of North America.* 1996;5:581-599.
88. Sarimski K. Aufrechterhaltung von schlafstörungen im frühen kindesalter: entwicklungspsychopathologisches modell und pilot-studie. [Sleep disorders in early childhood: developmental phychopathologic model and pilot study]. *Praxis der Kinderpsychologie und Kinderpsychiatrie.* 1993;42:2-8.
89. Papoušek M, Papoušek H. Infant colic, state regulation, and interaction with parents: a systems approach. In: Bornstein MH, Genevro JL, eds. *Child Development and Behavioral Pediatrics: Towards Understanding Children and Health.* Hillsdale, NJ: Lawrence Erlbaum Associates; 1996:11-33.
90. Wolke D, Messer D. Development of sleeping problems and their treatment in childhood. *Journal of Psychosomatic Research.* In press.
91. Hubbard FOA, van Ijzendoorn MH. Maternal unresponsiveness and infant crying across the first 9 months: a naturalistic longitudinal study. *Infant Behavior and Development.* 1991;14:299-312.
92. Wolke D. Disturbed attachment, behavioral strategies, breastfeeding and sleeping difficulties – a commentary. *Association of Infant Mental Health (UK) Newsletter.* 2000;2:12-13.
93. Wolke D, Meyer R, Ohrt B, Riegel K. Co-morbidity of crying and feeding problems with sleeping problems in infancy: concurrent and predictive associations. *Early Development and Parenting.* 1995; 4:191-207.
94. Angel S, Nicoll J, Amatiello W. Assessing the need for an out-of-hours telephone advisory service. *Health Visitor.* 1990;63:225-227.

Behavioral Management of Early Infant Crying in Irritable Babies

Professor Dymphna C. van den Boom

Introduction

Troublesome infant crying is one of the most common reasons parents seek the help of healthcare professionals in the child's first year of life.[1, 2] For this reason, studies that evaluate treatments for excessive crying provide important information for healthcare practice. Various explanations exist for excessive crying, and proposed treatments vary depending on the presumed cause of the condition.

For a long time, excessive crying in infants, also widely known as "colic," was considered to be a clinical or pathological condition.[3, 4] A diagnosis of colic was based simply on the amount of crying or on parental complaints about the crying.[5] More recent evidence, however, suggests that only one third of the infants selected using Wessel's criteria[4] exhibit colic behavior, while two thirds do not show any colic behavior at all.[6] Further, evidence suggests that no abnormalities of intestinal function or of any other aspect of metabolism can explain the colicky behavior of the infants.[3, 7, 8]

Within this clinical-pathologic framework, pharmacologic and dietary treatments have been suggested for colic. Of the pharmacologic agents tested, only dicyclomine hydrochloride has been reported to reduce excessive crying.[9, 10] However, this drug may act on several systems and there is no evidence that it has an intestinal effect. Its suitability as a treatment for excessive crying is questionable.[11] Most importantly, the drug has been withdrawn as a treatment for infants because of reported side effects[3]; in the US, it is contraindicated for infants younger than 6 months of age. Dietary treatment for cow's milk protein intolerance (CMPI) reduces crying significantly, but only in a very small percentage of infants with colic.[12, 13] Because CMPI appears to be rare, it seems unlikely that diet modification will provide a general solution for all excessively crying infants. Clearly, clinical-pathologic causes for excessive crying exist, but they do not explain all cases.

Alternative explanations of persistent infant crying have focused on parental shortcomings, with the assumption that social-regulatory processes influence crying more as age increases.[14, 15] The term "difficultness" is used in temperament research to designate prolonged crying, often with additional features, such as irregularity, withdrawal, difficulty adapting and intensity of response. Although one often hears of the difficult *child*, temperament theorists propose that difficult behavior is best thought of as the result of less-than-optimal interactions between individuals, rather than as a character trait of any one person.[16] The concept of "goodness of fit" describes this meshing of behavior of interactive partners. According to this approach, difficult infants are especially demanding interactive partners, and their prolonged and unremitting crying may render them particularly unresponsive to parental soothing efforts. This, in turn, may have a negative effect on the way infants and their caregivers build their relationship. Of course, parents differ in their abilities to interact with infants, so they, too, contribute to the quality of the relationship.

Attachment theorists also endorse an interactional perspective in which variations in the security of infant-caregiver attachment evolve as a function of individual differences in infant signaling behavior and in maternal responsiveness to those signals. Behaviors through which an infant promotes proximity to, and contact with, the caregiver are called "attachment behaviors".[17-19] Crying is one of the most salient of these behaviors. Viewed from this perspective, infant crying serves as a stimulus to attachment. Those studies that report higher infant crying in the early months among subsequently securely attached infants, in comparison with their insecure counterparts, are particularly informative.[20-22] According to this theory, an infant who cries frequently contributes to the construction of the attachment relationship by using a clear signal to promote and maintain the close caregiver contact that is essential for the development of a secure attachment. Whether this explanation also holds for infants who cry excessively, rather than just frequently, during the early months of life remains to be seen.

Interventions informed by this interactionist view of excessive crying focus on stress management training for parents.[23] Biodesensitization training has been used to change perceptions and physiologic responses to infant crying. Such training is effective in dramatically reducing arousal both physiologically and perceptually. Studies to date have targeted parents-to-be; therefore, it remains to be determined whether the training remains effective when these young adults are parents and are actually coping with their own infant who cries excessively. Taubman found that asking parents to increase the flexibility and amount of care and stimulation they provided was more successful than reducing stimulation[24] or than eliminating soy or cow's milk.[13] In contrast, McKenzie found that hospital admission and decreased stimulation reduced crying problems in a subgroup of infants referred for excessive crying.[25] Clearly, results are mixed for these types of intervention studies.

Other investigators suggest that excessive crying is a consequence of normal maturational and developmental processes that occur in all infants, rather than a distinct clinical condition seen in only a minority of infants.[26, 27] This conclusion is based on community studies that identified an infant crying "peak" at approximately 6 weeks of age in families using Western[26] and non-Western[28, 29] approaches to care. Also, several investigations have shown that infant crying during the first 3 months of life differs in its causes and functions from crying at older ages.[30-32] Studies that measure the contribution of parenting to infant crying are of central importance both for testing and refining the developmental framework.[33] To date, the work has provided mixed results, as some investigations demonstrate that irritable newborns become less irritable with age if their mothers are sensitive and responsive,[34] while other studies show the opposite effect.[35, 36]

Some interventions have been implemented that directly target parental interaction styles. Again, there are contradictory results. For example, Hunziker and Barr[37] found that supplementary carrying from 3 weeks of age resulted in substantially reduced levels of fussing and crying, but this finding was not replicated in a similar study by St. James-Roberts and colleagues.[38] Barr and colleagues[28] demonstrated that carrying was ineffective as a treatment for persistent crying once the crying had started. Wolke, Gray and Meyer[39] compared the effectiveness of empathy and behavioral management treatments by lay counselors for parents of excessively crying infants. They found the latter intervention strategy of behavioral management to be more effective in reducing fussing/crying than talking with the mother about the problem or simply waiting for spontaneous remission. Here, too, the findings obtained are inconsistent.

Several factors contribute to the inconsistencies observed in these investigations. In the majority of cases, measures of maternal behavior are confounded with infant characteristics. If infants are selected and studied after they have started crying excessively, parental behavior may have already changed in response to the crying.

Another problem concerns the outcome measures used in intervention studies. In most cases the outcome of interest is reduced crying, but this measure tells us little about the long-term effects of the intervention on the quality of the parent-child relationship. Certainly, several techniques may reduce the amount of infant crying, including some that seem to be complete opposites, such as ignoring[40] and being especially responsive[41] to the crying infant. The truly relevant measure, though, is long-term quality of the parent-child relationship. Interventions aimed solely at reducing the amount of crying ignore the complexity of the interactional system through which infant and caretaker build their relationship. By changing the response to crying, other aspects of the relationship change as well; therefore, it seems crucial to include other parental behaviors, besides soothing, in the intervention. For example, behavioral management might be necessary. A study completed by Hoeksma and I[42] demonstrated that dyads with irritable versus nonirritable babies differed not only in the management of crying and fussing, but in other interactive behaviors, as well.

Some previous intervention techniques appear to be based on the assumption that there exists some automatic and universal pairing of child signal and adult response. On the contrary, individual differences exist: One infant's distress may be relieved by carrying, rocking, cuddling and other forms of physical contact, while another infant may require toys, food and visual distraction. An appropriate parental response in one case of excessive crying may not be a proper response in other cases. Further, cultural requirements dictate appropriateness: A Japanese mother, for instance, is more likely to respond to her infant's signals by physical, rather than by verbal, means. The parent-child system is sufficiently flexible to permit such variations. The judgment of what makes an intervention appropriate must make full allowance for individual differences and cultural norms.

The Present Study

The present intervention was developed to apply both interactionist and developmental approaches to the study of excessive infant crying. The intervention aims to increase the sensitivity of parenting behavior, with "security of attachment" being the long-term outcome measure. First, a detailed observational study determined the specific ways in which parental insensitivity manifests itself with babies of different ages.[42] If the behavioral manifestations of insensitivity vary as a child develops, then appropriate interventions should vary as well. Based on the results of this observational study Hoeksma and I decided to implement the present intervention at 6 months of age. Our observational study revealed that patterns of interaction among irritable dyads clearly started to diverge around 5 months of age; some mothers learned to cope without intervention, while others clearly needed help. For this reason, we anticipated that mothers would be highly motivated to participate in an intervention when infants were about 6 months old. A previous study has shown that motivation is an important factor in obtaining positive results from treatments.[43]

A standardized test procedure was used to identify irritable infants shortly after birth in order to minimize the potential bias of parental report instruments. Clearly, methodologically independent appraisals of maternal and infant characteristics are necessary to evaluate the degree to which each domain affects attachment outcomes. This report will focus on measures of the quality of interaction between mother-child dyads and, to a lesser extent, on peer-child dyads, rather than on the characteristics of the individuals involved.

Methods

One-hundred mother-child pairs were observed at infant ages 6, 9, 12, 18, 24 and 42 months.[44] At 6, 9 and 12 months complete data were available on all measures used. At 18 and 24 months data were available for 82 of the 100 infants. At 3^1/$_2$ years of age, 79 of the 100 families recruited in the first year participated again. For details about drop-out rates and the absence of selective attrition, please see van den Boom.[44]

At the time of the children's births, nearly all families were intact. Only 3 mothers were single. The mother was the primary caretaker in all cases. All infants were Caucasian, firstborn and from low-socioeconomic-status (SES) families, assigned according to the 1971 social group division of the Netherlands Central Bureau of Statistics.

All infants were carried to term and had normal birth weights (>2500 grams). Pregnancies were uncomplicated and deliveries were normal, with mothers receiving no more than routine medication during delivery. APGAR scores were at least 7 at 1 minute and 8 at 5 minutes. The families were located through the birth register of the Department of Obstetrics and Gynecology of the Leiden (Holland) University Hospital and through midwives. Maternal age ranged from 19 years to 33 years. The infants were selected on irritability on the 10th day and the 15th day after birth with the Neonatal Behavioral Assessment Scale (NBAS).[45] The degree of irritability was determined through scores on the *peak of excitement, rapidity of buildup* and *irritability* items that were combined to form the neonatal irritability measure identified by Kaye.[46] Infants whose mean scores from both exams on these 3 items were 6 or higher were considered irritable; those whose mean scores were below 6 were considered nonirritable. The NBAS was administered to 588 infants to find the predetermined number of 100 irritable infants. Thus, 17% of infants from low-SES families proved to be irritable according to the criterion used in this study.

Study Design

Subjects were randomly assigned to the intervention and control groups, resulting in 50 dyads who received the intervention and 50 dyads who did not. All 100 dyads received an immediate posttreatment assessment (mother-infant interaction) and delayed posttreatment assessments (attachment security, mother-infant interaction and peer interaction).

Half of the intervention subjects and half of the control subjects received a pretreatment assessment and half did not, creating a factorial design with 2 treatment conditions (control and intervention) and 2 pretest conditions (pretest and no pretest). This 4-group design enables assessment of pretreatment differences between the intervention and control groups.[47] It also enables assessment of the interaction of pretreatment testing with the intervention. The pretested control group was observed as often as the intervention groups were visited to control for the possibility that being observed, in and of itself, would affect maternal behavior. In the second year, the intervention group consisted of 43 subjects and the control group comprised 39 subjects. The 3-year intervention group consisted of 39 subjects and the control group comprised 40 subjects.

Procedures

A detailed description of the procedures administered at the newborn and 6- through 42-month age periods may be found in studies that I have published.[44, 48] A brief summary will be presented here describing the pretreatment assessment, the intervention itself and the posttreatment evaluations.

Pretreatment Assessment

The pretreatment assessment at 6 months of age consisted of observation of the quality of mother-infant interaction. Fifty of the 100 dyads participated in this phase of the study. It consisted of 2 home visits, during which mother-infant interaction was observed in routine family contexts (feeding, bathing, playing, etc). Mother and child behaviors were recorded at 6-second intervals by trained observers. Maternal behaviors were coded and sorted into categories reflecting dimensions of maternal behavior related to later quality of attachment; specifically, affective, attentive, supportive, soothing and stimulation behaviors. Also, the coded observational data were used to define a more conceptually complex measure of responsiveness in which the contingencies between infant and maternal behaviors were analyzed. In this analysis, each infant behavior was linked to a maternal behavior in the same or the next 6-second period. The appropriateness of the maternal response was noted. Responsive behaviors, such as coming to the infant, looking at the infant or verbalizing to the infant in response to an infant vocalization, were circled on the coding sheet; unresponsive behaviors were not.

Intervention

The intervention began 3 weeks after pretreatment assessments. Mothers were asked if they wished to participate in a program in which first-time mothers could talk with the study staff about their child-rearing concerns. Mothers were not told about their infants' irritability classification because such labeling could create a self-fulfilling prophecy.[49] Three intervention sessions were scheduled for the dyads of the intervention groups while the infants were between 6 months and 9 months of age (ie, one session every 3 weeks). During the entire 3-month intervention period, I implemented the interventions. All visits took place in the home and lasted approximately 2 hours. The intervention focused on enhancing sensitive maternal responsiveness within the context of everyday interactions. The goal was to help the mother adjust her behavior in response to her infants' unique cues.

Any response process consists of 4 stages: perceiving a signal, interpreting the signal correctly, selecting an appropriate response and implementing the response effectively. Because maternal insensitivity could result from a deficiency at any of these stages, the intervention targeted all 4 parts of the reception-response sequence. For example, "response selection" was enhanced with direct suggestions from the researcher. Soothing of a crying infant was suggested if a mother did not spontaneously respond this way. If the mother attempted to soothe through close physical contact, but this proved ineffective, the researcher would suggest other soothing techniques. The goal was to individualize the intervention so that the mother would "implement effective responses" for her particular infant. Further details are presented in a paper I published in 1994 in *Child Development*.[48]

Posttreatment Evaluations

There were 2 kinds of posttreatment assessments, which, together, measured the quality of mother-infant interaction, of attachment and of peer interaction. The immediate posttreatment assessment occurred at 9 months and consisted of 2 home visits in which the quality of mother-infant interaction was observed using the same observational system as at 6 months. The delayed posttreatment assessments measured attachment, mother-child interaction and peer interaction. Each dyad was videotaped in the Ainsworth and Wittig[50] Strange Situation at ages 12 months and 18 months. Attachment classifications were assigned according to the secure (B),[51] insecure avoidant (A),[51] insecure resistant (C)[51] and insecure disorganized/disoriented (D)[52] groups. Then, at 24 months, mother-child interaction was observed at home during free play, during everyday interactive situations and in the laboratory during problem-solving interactions. In a 1995 paper in *Child Development*,[44] I detailed the many types of behavior that were coded and the various measures that were employed in other publications. Because many variables were involved, factor analyses were completed to improve subject-variable ratios. Factor analysis refers to a family of analytic techniques designed to identify factors or dimensions that underlie the relations among a set of observed variables. Factor analysis is applied to the correlations among these observed variables. An estimate of the relation between each variable and a factor—referred to as "factor-loading"—is obtained. The higher the factor-loading, the more meaningful that variable is for a factor.

First-order factors derived from analyses of infant and maternal behaviors in the home and lab contexts were subjected to second-order factor analyses to generate indices of child and maternal interactive behavior across situations and across different types of measures. This second-order factor analysis on *child interactive behavior* extracted 5 factors. (To differentiate them from first-order factors, names of second-order factors will have initial capital letters and be set in bold.) The first factor is called **Affect** (positive affect, positive contact), the second is **Cooperation** (verbalization, cooperative behavior), the third is **Problem-Solving** (problem-solving, curiosity), the fourth is **On-Task Behavior** (task involvement, task orientation, affect [loaded negatively]) and the fifth is **Negativism** (negative behavior). Collectively, the factors account for 66% of the variance.

A second-order factor analysis on *maternal interactive behavior* identified 6 factors. The first factor reflects **Maternal Teaching** (structure, support, encouragement), the second reflects **Responsiveness In Communicative And Agonistic Contexts** (responsiveness, control), the third reflects **Support** (attention, help), the fourth reflects **Off-Task Sensitivity** (sensitivity, task orientation [loaded negatively]), the fifth reflects **Monitoring** (visual contact, failure in task involvement [loaded negatively]) and the sixth reflects **Uninvolvement** (involvement [loaded negatively]). Together, these factors account for 71% of the variance.

At 42 months, 4 sets of measurements were taken. The first pertained to the quality of parent-child interaction at dinnertime, the second to security, the third to behavior problems and the last to the quality of peer interaction. Again, second-order factor analyses were conducted on all measures obtained, resulting in the factors that follow. The second-order factor analysis on *maternal interactive behavior* extracted 2 factors. The first factor is called **Responsiveness** (control, responsiveness) and the second is **Assistance** (structure, support). The second-order factor analysis on *child interactive behavior* toward the peer extracted 4 factors. The first factor is called **Absence Of Peer Contact** (solitary play, interaction and sociability [loaded negatively]), the second is **Cooperation** (sharing, contact seeking), the third is **Reactive Aggression** (avoidance, conflict) and the fourth is **Proactive Aggression** (negative contact). Together, these factors account for 75% of the variance.

A second-order factor analysis on *child behavior toward mother* identified 3 distinct factors, accounting for 75% of the variance. The first factor is called **Reliance On Mother** (dependency, affect), the second is **Security** (security, behavior problems [loaded negatively]) and the third is **Initiation Of Interaction** (negative and positive initiatives).

A second-order factor analysis on *interactive behavior of the peer* yielded 3 factors that accounted for 69% of the variance. The first factor is **Contact Seeking** (initiate interaction, focal child contact, solitary play, interaction and sociability [loaded negatively]), the second is **Interaction** (sharing, conflict) and the third is **Absence Of Adult Contact** (seek contact with focal child's mother [loaded negatively]).

Results

Results are presented in 2 sections: First, *immediate* posttreatment effects are described, then *delayed* posttreatment effects are given. Preliminary analyses established the initial equality of the groups. Only one statistically significant difference was found for maternal interactive behavior: Mothers in the intervention group showed lower rates of effective stimulation than mothers in the control group. Pretreatment infant interaction rates did not differ significantly between the intervention and control groups on 5 of the 7 variable sets: Control-group infants scored higher than intervention-group infants on positive social behavior and mobility. No sex differences were obtained in separate analyses of the pretreatment variables. All data, therefore, will be reported for the sexes combined.

No specific details of the statistical analysis are provided here, but summaries of findings are included. More detailed information about these analyses can be obtained from the paper that I published in 1994 in *Child Development*.[48]

Immediate Posttreatment Effects

At 9 months of age the effects of the intervention on the quality of interactive behavior were estimated. Maternal and infant interactive behaviors were analyzed separately to document changes in each partner's behavior. To assess the effectiveness of the intervention, a 2 x 2 MANOVA (pretest: yes versus no; intervention versus control) was carried out on the 4 maternal components: responsiveness, stimulation, visual attentiveness and control.

Results suggested that the combined dependent variables were affected significantly by intervention and by the interaction between pretest and intervention. There was no significant main effect of pretest. Univariate tests indicated that intervention mothers, compared with the control mothers, were significantly more responsive, more stimulating, more visually attentive and more controlling of their infants' behavior. The interaction effect for intervention X pretest was significant only for visual attentiveness. Post hoc comparisons indicated that the pretested control group had significantly lower mean factor scores on visual attentiveness than did the control group that was not pretested. No significant differences were found between the 2 intervention groups.

In sum, mothers who participated in the intervention differed in meaningful ways from control group mothers. Intervention group mothers generally demonstrated a more responsive and stimulating orientation toward their infants.

The same analyses were performed on infant behavior, with significant main effects of intervention and pretest observed. There was no significant intervention X pretest interaction. Univariate tests indicated that infants in the intervention groups were significantly more sociable, more self-soothing and more exploratory compared with control group infants. The effect for pretest was significant only for social behavior and self-soothing behavior, with pretested intervention infants being more sociable and more self-soothing compared with the pretested control group infants.

All infants who participated in this study were irritable infants who have been shown to fuss and cry more and to exhibit fewer positive social behaviors than do nonirritable infants.[53] Our interest in these specific behaviors led to examination of changes from pretreatment to posttreatment for the variable sets of positive social behavior and negative emotionality. ANOVAs yielded significant differences for intervention and control infants on each of these variable sets. These differences indicated that intervention infants displayed more positive social behavior directed to the mother and less negative emotionality during interactions than did control infants. For each of these variable sets, my colleagues and I found a main effect for pretest condition. The interaction between intervention and pretest was also significant for each variable set. Contrary to our expectations, post hoc comparisons revealed that the control group that did not receive a pretest displayed higher mean factor scores on positive social behaviors than did the pretested control group. No differences emerged between the pretest and no-pretest intervention groups. On negative emotionality, infants in the intervention group who did not receive a pretest scored higher than infants in the intervention group who received a pretest, but there were no differences between infants in the pretest group and the no-pretest control group.

Analyses predicted differences that favored intervention groups over control groups on several aspects of infant interactive behavior, including more positive social behavior, less fussing and crying and more exploration. On posttreatment observations, intervention-group infants were consistently more sociable, better able to soothe themselves and explored more compared with control group infants.

Delayed Posttreatment Effects

Attachment. Log-linear analyses were conducted to examine the relation between infant-mother attachment by treatment group at 12 months. Because of the small number of subjects in the insecure-resistant and insecure-disorganized/disoriented attachment categories, all 3 "insecure" categories were collapsed for subsequent data analysis into one insecure category. Together, insecure infants were compared with infants who were classified as securely attached. Fully 78% of control infants were classified in the insecure categories, compared with 38% in the intervention group. Only 22% of all control infants were assigned the traditional "secure" classification, compared with 62% of the infants in the intervention group. Infants in the control groups were most likely to be classified as insecure avoidant (52%), not insecure resistant, as would be expected from previous research with irritable infants.

At 18 months of age, 74% of untreated infants were classified as insecurely attached as compared with 28% in the treated groups. Therefore, only 26% of untreated irritable infants were assigned to the traditional secure classification, compared with 72% of the treated infants. Similar to findings at 1 year, 18-month-old toddlers in the control groups were most likely to be classified as insecure avoidant (51%).

Second-year Coded Behavior. Three separate one-way MANOVAs (intervention versus control) evaluated 3 sets of dependent variables: 18-month play ratings, 24-month coded child behavior and 24-month coded maternal behavior. In all analyses, significant differences were identified in 18-month ratings, 24-month second-order child factors and 24-month second-order maternal factors.

Univariate tests demonstrated that mothers in the intervention group were more accepting, more accessible, more cooperative and more sensitive than control group mothers. Univariate analysis of second-order child components showed that intervention children were significantly more cooperative than control group children. Finally, univariate tests done on second-order maternal components indicated that intervention-group mothers were significantly more responsive in communicative and agonistic contexts and that they exhibited significantly more off-task sensitivity compared with control mothers.

Third-year Coded Behavior. Six separate one-way MANOVAs (intervention versus control) were used to study 6 sets of dependent variables: maternal, paternal, child-mother, child-peer, peer-child and dyadic behavioral components. Significant effects were obtained for all but 2 (peer-child and dyadic components) dependent variables (second-order maternal factors, first-order father factors, second-order child-peer factors, second-order child-mother factors).

Univariate tests showed that intervention-group mothers were more responsive and more helpful to their children during peer play than were control-group mothers. Husbands of mothers who participated in the intervention were also more responsive toward their children than were husbands of control-group mothers. Intervention-group children were more cooperative than were control-group children with regard to child-peer behavior. Follow-up univariate ANOVAs on child-mother behavior suggested that children of mothers who participated in the intervention were more secure compared with children of control-group mothers.

Discussion

First-year findings indicated that the intervention was effective in enhancing maternal responsiveness, stimulation, visual attentiveness and control. Intervention-group infants were more sociable, better able to soothe themselves and engaged more frequently in cognitively sophisticated types of exploration than were control-group infants. The intervention promoted substantial improvement in the quality of the mother-infant interaction. Follow-up 3 months later revealed that significantly more intervention-group infants than control-group infants were securely attached.

Second-year findings confirmed that toddlers whose mothers participated in the intervention were more likely to be securely attached than were toddlers whose mothers did not receive the intervention. The benefits of the intervention were demonstrated at 24 months by assessments of the quality of mother-child interaction across multiple domains. Compared with control-group mothers, intervention-group mothers were more responsive to positive and negative child initiatives, displayed more sharing of interest in objects and activities, were more likely to use verbal commands in an age-appropriate way, were more likely to allow their toddlers sufficient autonomy and issued fewer direct instructions. This more sensitive mothering is associated with differences in child behaviors towards their mothers. Intervention-group children exhibited more orienting toward their mothers, they displayed more cooperation and engaging in meaningful activities and verbal interactions and they showed more imitation of their mothers' actions and comments compared with children in the control group.

In the third year, my colleagues and I found evidence of sustained effects of the first-year intervention program. Treatment-group mothers continued to use responsive interventions and offered their children guidance during initial encounters with peers to a greater extent than did control-group mothers. Husbands of mothers who participated in the intervention showed this responsive attitude, as well. Intervention-group children remained secure in their relationships with their mothers, exhibited fewer behavior problems and were better able to maintain positive relationships with peers than did the control-group children.

The treatment effects on maternal responsiveness and child cooperation are direct effects of the intervention, whereas the other observed effects are mediated by the child's history of security. Apparently, the intervention was effective at increasing parental sensitivity to the child's developmental level and to the changing meaning of child behavior at different developmental levels. This suggests that mothers were learning how to interpret children's signals, in general, and their own baby's signals, in particular, as a result of the intervention.

This work has important theoretical implications. Data presented here support the existence of a relationship between neonatal negative emotionality, quality of mother-infant interaction and attachment classification for irritable infants. Attachment theorists have stated that security is the functional goal of infant attachment behavior.[54, 55] The behavior required of mothers to effectively foster feelings of security in their infants in most situations varies across infants.[56] The high rate of insecurity in the control groups may be related to the dual risk status in our sample. In addition to being preselected on irritability, the infants were raised in lower-class families where relatively high rates of insensitivity predominate.[57] The current data suggest a more complex process than the often-assumed direct path between neonatal irritability and (Strange Situation) resistance-attachment behavior. Neonatal irritability may predispose infants who are at risk for insecure relationships for other contextual reasons toward insecurity, but it is not directly predictive of the type of insecurity. Belsky and Isabella[20] also found that rates of insecurity increased with elevated risks.

Infant irritability clearly influences the relationship between mother and infant in the first year of life. It may be difficult for mothers to adjust their actions to their child's disposition. Data presented here suggest that mothers can be taught to sensitively modify their behaviors to best suit the characteristics of their individual mother-infant dyads. Maternal responsiveness is increased, as is infant exploratory behavior.

These results are encouraging; however, replication studies with other samples of irritable infants are necessary. To date, there are very few intervention studies with irritable infants, and even their results are not consistent.

The intervention described here was framed within a developmental approach. Future interventions should be developed only after initial detailed observational studies specify the behaviors that constitute insensitivity with irritable babies. Behavioral specification is necessary because the concept of sensitivity is too abstract and too coarse to capture subtle nuances of parental behavior and it lacks sufficient contextual anchorage. Also, insensitivity may be manifested differently depending on the particular child problem investigated and the child's stage of development. The observational study done by Hoeksma and I showed that during the first 2 months of life insensitivity consisted of soothing the infant in an erratic fashion and refraining from playful interaction when the infant was in a positive mood.[42] However, at older ages (4 months to 5 months), insensitive mothers refrained from interacting with their infants altogether, or they responded inconsistently to both positive and negative infant signals. Behavioral manifestations of unresponsiveness may change during the course of infant development. Consequently, as babies grow older, mothers likely develop different ways of coping with problem behavior. Intervention programs must take into account age-related changes in unresponsive maternal behavior, and they must also include the possibility that maternal unresponsiveness manifests differently in different risk groups. Proper development of an effective intervention program, then, should be preceded by an observational study.

There seem to be threshold effects in parental interactive behavior. This may impact on the development of effective intervention programs. The majority of research on mother-child interaction is limited by an almost exclusive reliance upon linear relations, which presume that more of a good thing is always in the best interest of the child. There may be a point of diminishing returns, however, as suggested by a few studies that have documented curvilinear relations between indices of the parent-child relationship and child competence. These investigations have demonstrated that systems with strong maturational components typically exhibit threshold effects—that is, very low levels of one variable result in deficits in the second variable—and crossing this threshold results in a rapid rise in levels of the second variable, followed by a plateau in which further increases of the first variable have little effect on the second.[58]

Such results have important implications for the development of intervention programs and suggest that the level of intensity of the intervention should vary depending on the relation between a particular dimension of parenting behavior and the child outcome measure to be assessed. With maternal warmth and child competence as an example, the threshold characteristic of the relation between these 2 variables suggests that after the plateau is reached, further increases in maternal warmth will have little effect on child competence. In this case, mother-child interaction research based on nonlinear models more accurately reflects the nature of developmental phenomena. Building explicit models of outcomes can serve as a powerful heuristic for the development of effective intervention programs by considering the process character of interactive behaviors. Such inquiries also help identify the optimal timing for intervention.

In sum, we have shown the importance of a developmental approach to intervention. Changes over time in infant irritability and subsequent maternal response suggest that one type of intervention is not likely to be successful with all infants who cry excessively. The age of the infants and the underlying reasons for the crying are at least 2 factors that will influence the appropriateness of a particular intervention. Finally, findings from observational studies on mother-child interaction during the course of early development contradict some long held beliefs about early childhood intervention. Specifically, "the more, the better" and "the sooner, the better" seem to be untenable in light of recent research findings. Further research into excessive crying and its effects on long-term maternal and infant outcomes is necessary. Developmental issues should be considered in the design of future intervention studies.

References

1. St. James-Roberts I, Halil T. Infant crying patterns in the first year: normal community and clinical findings. *Journal of Child Psychology and Psychiatry, and Applied Disciplines.* 1991;32:951-968.
2. van der Wal MF, van den Boom DC, Pauw-Plomp H, de Jonge GA. Mothers' reports of infant crying and soothing in a multicultural population. *Archives of Disease in Childhood.* 1998;79:312-317.
3. Illingworth RS. Infantile colic revisited. *Archives of Disease in Childhood.* 1985;60:981-985.
4. Wessel MA, Cobb JC, Jackson EB, Harris GS, Detwiler AC. Paroxysmal fussing in infancy, sometimes called "colic." *Pediatrics.* 1954;14:421-433.
5. Barr RG, Rotman A, Yaremko J, Leduc D, Francoeur TE. The crying of infants with colic: a controlled empirical description. *Pediatrics.* 1992;90:14-21.
6. St. James-Roberts I, Conroy S, Wilsher K. Bases for maternal perceptions of infant crying and colic behavior. *Archives of Disease in Childhood.* 1996;75:375-384.
7. Miller AR, Barr RG. Infantile colic. Is it a gut issue? *Pediatric Clinics of North America.* 1991;38:1407-1423.
8. Treem WR, Hyams JS, Blankschen E, Etienne N, Paule CL, Borschel MW. Evaluation of the effect of a fiber-enriched formula on infant colic. *The Journal of Pediatrics.* 1991;119:695-701.

9. Hwang CP, Danielsson B. Dicyclomine hydrochloride in infantile colic. *British Medical Journal Clinical Research Edition.* 1985;291:1014.
10. Weissbluth M, Christoffel KK, Davis AT. Treatment of infantile colic with dicyclomine hydrochloride. *The Journal of Pediatrics.* 1984;104:951-955.
11. St. James-Roberts I. Persistent crying in infancy. *Journal of Child Psychology and Psychiatry, and Allied Disciplines.* 1989;30:189-195.
12. Forsyth BWC. Colic and the effect of changing formulas: a double-blind multiple-crossover study. *The Journal of Pediatrics.* 1989;115:521-526.
13. Lothe L, Lindberg T. Cow's milk whey protein elicits symptoms of infantile colic in colicky formula-fed infants: a double-blind crossover study. *Pediatrics.* 1989;83:262-266.
14. Carey WB. "Colic"–primary excessive crying as an infant-environment interaction. *Pediatric Clinics of North America.* 1984;31:993-1005.
15. Taubman B. Parental counseling compared with elimination of cow's milk or soy milk protein for the treatment of infant colic syndrome: a randomized trial. *Pediatrics.* 1988;81:756-761.
16. Chess S, Thomas A. *Origins and Evolution of Behavior Disorders: From Infancy to Early Adult Life.* New York, NY: Bruner/Mazel; 1984.
17. Ainsworth MDS. *Infancy in Uganda: Infant Care and the Growth of Love.* Baltimore, Md: Johns Hopkins University Press; 1967.
18. Bowlby J. The nature of the child's tie to his mother. *International Journal of Psychoanalysis.* 1958; 39:350-373.
19. Bowlby J. *Attachment.* New York, NY: Basic Books; 1969.
20. Belsky J, Isabella R. Maternal, infant, and social-contextual determinants of attachment security. In: Belsky J, Nezworski T, eds. *Clinical Implications of Attachments.* Hillsdale, NJ: Lawrence Erlbaum Associates; 1988:41-94.
21. Bradshaw D, Goldsmith HH, Campos JJ. Attachment, temperament, and social referencing: interrelations among three domains of infant affective behavior. *Infant Behavior and Development.* 1987; 10:223-231.
22. Kiser LJ, Bates JE, Maslin CA, Bayles K. Mother-infant play at six months as a predictor of attachment security at thirteen months. *Journal of the American Academy of Child Psychiatry.* 1986;25:68-75.
23. Tyson PD. Biodesensitization: biofeedback-controlled systematic desensitization of the stress response to infant crying. *Biofeedback and Self-Regulation.* 1996;21:273-290.
24. Taubman B. Clinical trial of the treatment of colic by modification of parent-infant interaction. *Pediatrics.* 1984;74:998-1003.
25. McKenzie S. Troublesome crying in infants: effect of advice to reduce stimulation. *Archives of Disease in Childhood.* 1991;66:1416-1420.
26. Barr RG. The normal crying curve: what do we really know? *Developmental Medicine and Child Neurology.* 1990;32:356-362.
27. St. James-Roberts I. Persistent crying in infancy. *Journal of Child Psychology and Psychiatry, and Allied Disciplines.* 1989;30:189-195.
28. Barr RG, Konner M, Bakeman R, Adamson L. Crying in !Kung San infants: a test of the cultural specificity hypothesis. *Developmental Medicine and Child Neurology.* 1991;33:601-610.
29. St. James-Roberts I, Bowyer J, Varghese S, Sawdon J. Infant crying patterns in Manali and London. *Child: Care, Health and Development.* 1994;20:323-337.
30. Fisichelli VR, Karelitz S, Fisichelli RM, Kardelitz S, Cooper J. The course of induced crying activity in the first year of life. *Pediatric Research.* 1974;8:921-928.
31. Gekoski MJ, Rovee-Collier CK, Carulli-Rabinowitz V. A longitudinal analysis of inhibition of infant distress: the origins of social expectations? *Infant Behaviour and Development.* 1986;6:339-351.
32. Gustafson GE, Green JA. Developmental coordination of cry sounds with visual regard and gestures. *Infant Behaviour and Development.* 1991;14:51-57.

33. St. James-Roberts I, Conroy S, Wilsher K. Links between maternal care and persistent infant crying in the early months. *Child: Care, Health and Development.* 1998;24:353-376.
34. Fish M, Stifter CA, Belsky J. Conditions of continuity and discontinuity in infant negative emotionality: newborn to five months. *Child Development.* 1991;62:1525-1537.
35. Hubbard FOA, van Ijzendoorn MH. Maternal unresponsiveness and infant crying across the first 9 months: a naturalistic longitudinal study. *Infant Behaviour and Development.* 1991;14:299-312.
36. Landau R. Infant crying and fussing. *Journal of Cross-Cultural Psychology.* 1982;13:427-443.
37. Hunziker UA, Barr RG. Increased carrying reduces infant crying: a randomized controlled trial. *Pediatrics.* 1986;77:641-648.
38. St. James-Roberts I, Hurry J, Bowyer J, Barr RG. Supplementary carrying compared with advice to increase responsive parenting as interventions to prevent persistent infant crying. *Pediatrics.* 1995;95:381-388.
39. Wolke D, Gray P, Meyer R. Excessive infant crying: a controlled study of mothers helping mothers. *Pediatrics.* 1994;94:322-332.
40. Gewirtz JL, Boyd EF. Does maternal responding imply reduced infant crying? A critique of the 1972 Bell and Ainsworth report. *Child Development.* 1977;48:1200-1207.
41. Bell SM, Ainsworth MDS. Infant crying and maternal responsiveness. *Child Development.* 1972;43:1171-1190.
42. van den Boom DC, Hoeksma JB. The effect of infant irritability on mother-infant interaction: a growth-curve analysis. *Developmental Psychology.* 1994;30:581-590.
43. Lieberman AF, Weston DR, Pawl JH. Preventive intervention and outcome with anxiously attached dyads. *Child Development.* 1991;62:199-209.
44. van den Boom DC. Do first-year intervention effects endure? Follow-up during toddlerhood of a sample of Dutch irritable infants. *Child Development.* 1995;66:1798-1816.
45. Brazelton TB, Nugent JK, eds. *Neonatal Behavioral Assessment Scale.* 3rd ed. Philadelphia, Pa: JB Lippincott; 1973.
46. Kaye K. V. Discriminating among normal infants by multivariate analysis of Brazelton scores: lumping and smoothing. *Monographs of the Society for Research in Child Development.* 1978;43:60-80.
47. Solomon RL, Lessac MS. A control group design for experimental studies of developmental processes. *Psychological Bulletin.* 1968;70:145-150.
48. van den Boom DC. The influence of temperament and mothering on attachment and exploration: an experimental manipulation of sensitive responsiveness among lower-class mothers with irritable infants. *Child Development.* 1994;65:1457-1477.
49. Aber JL, Baker AJL. Security of attachment in toddlerhood. In: Greenberg MT, Cicchetti D, Cummings EM, eds. *Attachment in the Preschool Years: Theory, Research, and Intervention.* Chicago, Ill: University of Chicago Press; 1990:427-460.
50. Ainsworth MDS, Wittig BA. Attachment and exploratory behavior of one-year-olds in a Strange Situation. In: Foss BM, ed. *Determinants of Infant Behavior.* Vol. 4. London, England: Methuen; 1969:113-136.
51. Ainsworth MDS. *Patterns of Attachment.* Hillsdale, NJ: Lawrence Erlbaum Associates; 1978.
52. Main M, Solomon J. Discovery of an insecure-disorganized/disoriented attachment pattern. In: Brazelton TB, Yogman M, eds. *Affective Development in Infancy.* Norwood, NJ: Ablex; 1986:95-124.
53. van den Boom DC. *Neonatal Irritability and the Development of Attachment: Observation and Intervention* [dissertation]. Leiden, The Netherlands: University of Leiden; 1988.
54. Ainsworth MDS. The development of infant-mother attachment. In: Caldwell B, Ricciuti HN, eds. *Review of Child Development Research.* Vol 3. Chicago, Ill: University of Chicago Press; 1973:1-94.
55. Waters E. Traits, behavioral systems, and relationships: three models of infant-adult attachment. In: Immelman K, Barlow GW, Petrinovich L, Main M, eds. *Behavioral Development.* Cambridge, Mass: Cambridge University Press; 1981:621-650.

56. Thompson RA. Temperament, emotionality, and infant social cognition. In: Lerner JV, Lerner RM, eds. *Temperament and Social Interaction During Infancy and Childhood.* San Francisco, Calif: Jossey-Bass; 1986:35-52.
57. Mey JTH. *Sociale Ondersteuning, Gehechtheidskwaliteit en Vroegkindelijke Ompetentie-Ontwikkeling [Social Support, Quality of Attachment, and the Early Development of Competence]* [dissertation]. Nijmegen, The Netherlands: University of Nijmegen.
58. Roberts WL. Nonlinear models of development: an example from the socialization of competence. *Child Development.* 1986;57:1166-1178.

The REST Regimen: A Conceptual Approach to Managing Unexplained Early Infant Irritability

Maureen R. Keefe, RN, PhD

Introduction

Unexplained early infant crying, which has been historically referred to as "infantile colic," is one of the most commonly encountered problems in the first year of life. It is particularly frustrating to parents and healthcare providers alike, as no single cause or etiology has been found to explain the persistent fussiness and recurrent crying episodes. This type of unexplained early infant crying and fussing is reported to occur in approximately 15% to 35% of all full-term healthy infants. The onset ranges from 1 week to 2 weeks of age, and its resolution may be abrupt or gradual at approximately 3 months to 4 months of age. Although the crying and fussing episodes can, and often do, occur throughout the day and night, unexplained early infant crying has a characteristic diurnal pattern with increased intensity and duration during the evening hours. It appears to be equally distributed among races and sexes.[1-6] A major challenge for families under the best of circumstances, persistent infant crying has been implicated as a major predisposing factor in cases of infant abuse and neglect for families who have limited resources and support systems.[7-9] This paper will approach the topic of the management of unexplained early infant crying from 2 interwoven perspectives: the nursing perspective and a conceptual perspective, grounded in the tenets of developmental psychobiology.

The nursing perspective is often described as holistic and contextual. This perspective allows nurses to focus on the infant's behavior as well as the infant's effect on all members of the family constellation. Through their frequent contact with these families, nurses may quickly garner their confidence and help them as they struggle with many unanswerable questions. The nurse often encounters profoundly frustrated and overwhelmed parents struggling with the unrelenting crying of an irritable infant. One mother stated, "Caring for my colicky baby was the hardest thing I've ever done. Many times I said, 'I can't do this anymore. I don't want to do this anymore.' I cried for probably three months. It was intense."[10]

Parental distress and concerns are frequently shared with nurses practicing in a variety of settings: the newborn nursery, the visiting nurses/home-health agency, an ambulatory care clinic or private practice setting. Like other healthcare providers, nurses try to provide parents with effective information and support. However, the current lack of knowledge regarding the etiology and underlying mechanisms of the irritable infant's behavior remains frustrating. Parental distress is further exacerbated by our inability to identify the cause of the persistent crying and by the random approach to treatment regimens and suggestions based on hearsay and anecdotes rather than on scientific evidence and sound rationale. While we have an incredible opportunity to assist and educate parents about their infant's behavior, in practice we fall short in our approach to the management of the irritable or colicky infant. At best we are ineffective and happenstance, and in the worst cases our efforts may actually prove detrimental.[11, 12]

This paper outlines the development of a new, conceptually based intervention for managing infant irritability that may prove more useful than previous approaches. This management strategy is based on a theoretical model, first published in 1988, that conceptualizes infant colic as a state regulation or developmental sleep disorder more appropriately termed "irritable infant syndrome."[11] Infant irritability or irritable infant syndrome was defined as a behavior disorder that is characterized by recurrent episodes of fussiness, crying, restlessness and diminished "soothability." Additional associated behaviors include increased motor tone or muscular activity, an inability to fall asleep, agitation and increased sensitivity to stimuli. The process underlying the observed behavioral manifestations was proposed to be a dysfunction in the infants' ability to self-regulate their state or sleep-wake cycles coupled with parental noncontingency. Irritable infants appear to become overstimulated by a busy, chaotic environment and yet, while overly tired, cannot self-soothe or reduce their arousal level sufficiently to fall asleep. The parent, while very concerned, may actually be reinforcing the irritable behavior pattern by disruptive and inconsistent attempts to respond to the infant's unclear cues. Infant irritability, conceptualized as an infant developmental state-regulation disorder that disrupts the synchrony of the parent-infant dyad, calls for an approach that provides support for the parents and a restructuring of the infant's animate and inanimate environments.[11]

Previous Research

A series of studies has been conducted to test and refine this model in an effort to develop an individualized nursing intervention program based on this theoretical perspective of colic or infant irritability. The program elements evolved out of previous research that was conducted by an investigative team over a period of 12 years. In the first qualitative study, interviews with 15 mothers of irritable infants revealed the daily challenges of living with an irritable infant.[10] Mothers who received reassurance regarding their competency and their infant's health, as well as empathy and support, rather than routine advice, were found to be managing their difficult situation with more resourcefulness and insight. In a study of newborn behavioral predictors of infant irritability, 13 of 60 infants who went on to become irritable at 1 month of age were more responsive to stimuli and exhibited more active motor behavior during their Brazelton Neonatal Behavioral Assessment Scale (NBAS) exam.[13] Twenty irritable and 20 nonirritable infants were studied over their first 4 months of life. My colleagues and I found that irritable infants spent less time asleep, particularly in the quiet sleep state.[14] They spent more time in a restless indeterminate state and cried an average of 4.25 hours, compared with 1.25 hours for nonirritable infants. During feeding observations at 7 weeks of infant age, we noted nonsynchronous behavior between mothers and infants in the irritable infant group.

The REST Regimen Intervention Program

The individualized nursing intervention model provided by Froese-Fretz, Kotzer and I, referred to as the **REST** Regimen for Infant Irritability, has 2 components: one for infants and one for parents (Fig 1).[15] The 4 concepts guiding the intervention for infants are **R**egulation, **E**ntrainment, **S**tructure and **T**ouch. The 4 concepts that guide the intervention for parents are **R**eassurance, **E**mpathy, **S**upport and **T**ime-out. There are 5 goals of this integrative approach to the management of infant irritability: promote synchrony

Fig 1. REST regimens for infants and parents.[15]

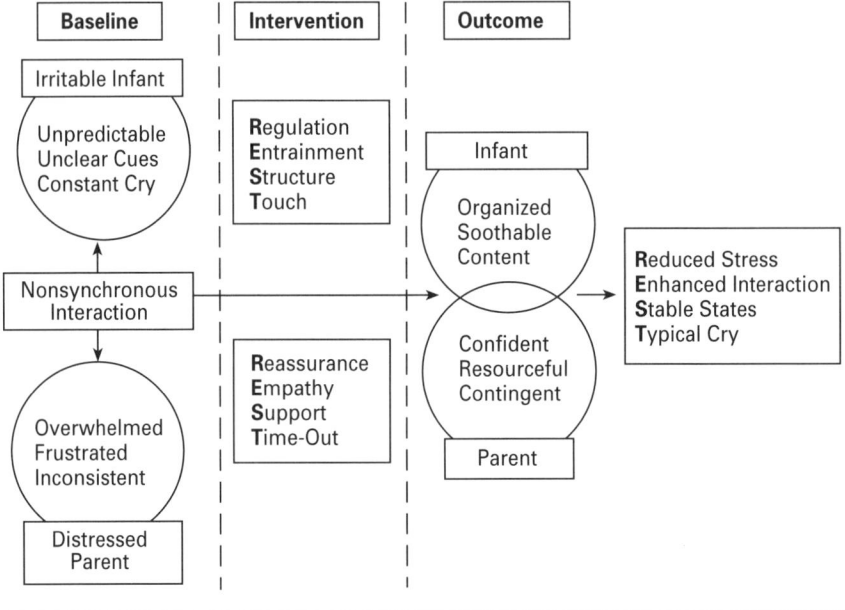

in the parent-infant dyad; decrease intensity and duration of infant irritability; promote state-regulation and organization in the infant; promote self-regulation and the use of self-soothing techniques; and provide information and support to the parents.

The 4 Concepts Guiding the REST Intervention for Infants

The REST intervention for infants[15] is composed of the following concepts (Table 1):

Regulation refers to the additional support required to assist infants in regulating their state behavior and to protect them from overtiredness and overstimulation during the first few months of life. Irritable infants are not adept at regulating their own state of arousal or transitioning from a highly aroused state. Identifying various vestibular, auditory and tactile inputs that are effective in reducing a specific infant's level of arousal and promoting shifts in

Table 1. The REST Regimen for Infants [15]

- **R**egulation
  - Prevent overstimulation
  - Prevent overtiredness
  - Watch for early warning signs
  - Assist in state transitions
  - Prevent crying jags
- **E**ntrainment: Environmental cues to synchronize sleep-wake cycles
  - Activity
  - Light
  - Noise
- **S**tructure
  - Feeding
  - Sleeping
  - Bathing
- **T**ouch
  - Firm infant hold
  - Colic carry
  - Vertical, ventral position with vestibular stimulation
  - Skin-to-skin contact

behavioral state and modulation are key strategies incorporated into the management of these irritable infants. Recommendations to parents include the following: prevent overstimulation and overtiredness, watch for early warning signs, assist in state transitions and limit crying jags by catching them early.

Entrainment is the process whereby the infant's behavior is synchronized with relevant aspects of the environment. Light, noise and activity levels must be synchronized with the infant's basic sleep-wake cycle. Parents are encouraged to adapt and utilize environmental cues to signal and regulate sleep-wake cycles. Parents are instructed to vary the light and noise levels in rooms where the infant spends time awake or asleep. Daily patterns of activity level and light and noise levels are monitored, reviewed with the nurse and modified, as needed.

Structure and repetition are also key concepts of the REST program. The goal is to create a predictably recurrent pattern of events for the infant to anticipate each day. This approach also requires increased external support from the parents, such as establishing feeding, bathing and sleeping routines that are accompanied by a predictable set of signals to initiate such activities. Daily schedules are discussed and modified to include shopping, errands and carpool arrangements, as necessary. Structured routines include bathing and playtime, as well as consistent sleeping and feeding times. Bedtime rituals, similar to those demanded by toddlers, are also incorporated into the daily routine.

Touch is also incorporated into the program. Chest-to-chest or skin-to-skin contact is used to enhance state or physiologic regulation. Various firm infant holds or colic carrying positions with good support are evaluated and adapted based on the individual infant's responses and preferences. Vertical, ventral positioning that includes vestibular stimulation, such as slow up-and-down movements, has been found to be useful in breaking through the infant's excessive crying episodes and assisting them to reduce their arousal level.

The 4 Concepts Guiding the REST Intervention for Parents

The REST intervention for parents is composed of these following concepts (Table 2):

Reassurance is focused in 2 areas; namely, the infant's health and the parents' competence. It is critical to evaluate the infant's general health status. Parents need to know that illness and an identifiable source of pain have been ruled out based on a thorough assessment. Parents also need reinforcement that they are competent and capable in their parenting roles. Reassurance that the excess irritability is a time-limited phenomenon with no known adverse sequelae is also helpful.

Empathy is provided through listening and acknowledging the challenge. Sharing the experiences of others helps overcome feelings of isolation and also normalizes the range of feelings expressed by these parents. Through listening, as well as avoiding quick fixes and pat advice, the healthcare provider acknowledges the plight of the parents, including recognizing sleep deprivation and disappointment over the lack of parenting gratification provided by their infant at this time.

Table 2. The REST Regimen for Parents [15]

- **R**eassurance
  - Infant's health
  - Parents' competence
  - Time-limited phenomenon
- **E**mpathy
  - Listen and validate
  - Acknowledge challenge
  - Sleep deprivation
  - Lack of parenting gratification
- **S**upport
  - Professional
  - Family and friends
- **T**ime-out
  - Scheduled daily
  - Out of range of infant
  - "Couple time"

Support is another element of the regimen for mothers. The healthcare provider acts as an advocate for the mother, helping her get the support she needs. Family and friends should be mobilized to provide relief for the mother. It is best to establish a network of individuals who can care directly for the irritable infant as breaks are needed. Professional support and resources are also critical and may include office or home visits and counseling or other professional referrals. Easy access to these resources and their availability by phone or personal contact are key to avoiding isolation and overload.

Time-out legitimizes the mother's critical need to take care of herself. A specific period of time-out, for at least 30 minutes to 60 minutes, is scheduled into each day. This time is designated as break time from direct caregiving and is used to rest and renew. The mother or primary caretaker must be out of the range of infant crying and must indulge in something that she enjoys or finds gratifying. A specific plan for coverage at specific times each day is negotiated within the family or immediate social support network.

"Couple time" is a major concern, as well, and parents are encouraged to go out together at least once every 2 weeks. Baby-sitter instructions and appropriate check-ins are discussed.

These concepts are applied individually and are operationalized by the nurse working in partnership with the family through an intensive 4-week home-visitation program. The program, referred to as the Fussy Baby Program, consists of weekly visits provided by a pediatric nurse specialist who has been trained in the intervention model. It includes infant behavior assessments, demonstrations, educational materials and observation guides. Parents view a video, entitled "Fussy Babies/Frantic Families," and complete accompanying worksheets between visits. The worksheets are designed to help the parents understand infant states, identify likes and dislikes, observe engagement and disengagement cues and record infant activity and home activity patterns. At nurse-specialist visits, observations and data patterns are reviewed and interpreted with the parents. An individualized daily schedule, with designated parent "time-out," is developed with the nurse's input and incorporated into the customized REST Regimen nursing intervention program. A refrigerator magnet, entitled "The Five Fuss Fixers," is developed for each infant and is revised, as needed. This list of effective cry-reducing strategies is highly visible and available for sitters, relatives and anyone interacting with, or caring for, the infant. The month-long program is followed by phone contacts and intermittent home visits, or referrals, as indicated or requested.

Outcome Measures

Upon completion of the intervention program, infant irritability, mother-infant interaction and parental stress, as well as infant state behavior patterns, are assessed for each family. In addition, the participants are asked to evaluate the program. The outcome measures selected for analysis relate to the previously stated goals of the intervention program and the desired outcomes for the REST Regimen parent-child dyad: reduced stress, enhanced interaction, stable infant states and typical cry patterns.

Unexplained early infant irritability is measured using the Fussiness Rating Scale that my colleagues and I have used in previous research. This tool is completed by the parent upon initial referral, at weekly intervals during the intervention and upon completion of the program. The Fussiness Rating

Scale was adapted originally from the Intensity Rating Scale developed by Emde.[16] The 2 dimensions of cry/fuss behavior—intensity and duration—were retained from the original scale, and an additional item was added that asked parents to estimate the amount of their infant's cry/fuss activity, as measured by the total number of hours per day the infant spends in an irritable, unexplained state. The scale defines unexplained fussiness and asks parents to rate their child's typical behavior across the following 2 dimensions: amount of fussiness and intensity of fussiness, measured on a 7-point Likert scale. In addition, the parent reports an estimated average hours per day of unexplained crying and fussing during the prior week. Reliability of the scale was assessed in previous research using mothers' and fathers' independent ratings of infant irritability at 1 month of age.[13] These independent parent ratings of unexplained infant fussiness yielded correlation coefficients among the items that ranged from $r = .72$ to $r = .91$.

Maternal-infant synchrony is defined by a pattern of coordinated exchange between the mother and infant. The degree of appropriateness that the mother maintains in her responses to the infant's cues regarding state and needs is viewed as a central component of this construct. The dyad's interaction patterns are a momentary manifestation of the dynamics of the mother, the infant and their shared environment. They are measured using the Feeding Scale from the Nursing Child Assessment Satellite Training (NCAST) tools developed by Barnard and colleagues to assess the quality of the parent-infant interaction during a teaching or feeding situation.[17] The Feeding Scale (NCAFS) selected for use in this study is an observational scale designed for use with parents and infants from birth to 1 year of age. The scale has 6 subscales; 4 to assess the parent's contribution to the interaction and 2 to measure the infant's contribution. The parent subscales are sensitivity to cues, response to distress, social-emotional growth fostering and cognitive growth fostering. The infant subscales are clarity of cues and responsiveness to parent. Internal consistency for the entire scale is reflected by a Cronbach's alpha of .86.[17] The NCAFS has been positively correlated with other measures of parent-infant communication and the infant's developmental profile.[18] For this study, feeding observations are conducted with mother-infant dyads in the home. The NCAFS is administered and scored by NCAST-certified members of the evaluation/collection team.

Parental stress is based on the theoretical premise that the total stress a parent experiences is a function of certain salient infant characteristics, parental characteristics and situational variables that are directly related to the role of being a parent. Stressors associated with parenting are thought to be related to the child's behavior style as well as the parents' expectations and feelings of being rewarded. Parental contributions to parenting stress include parent personality as well as the attachment or intrinsic investment that the parent has in the role of parent. Situational variables that may contribute to the parent's stress include the relationship with her spouse, available social support, parent health and restrictions caused by the parenting role. The Parenting Stress Index (PSI) is a validated family-system diagnostic instrument being used to assess parental coping and stress levels.[19] The short form, consisting of 36 items, is grouped into 3 subscales: parental distress, difficult child and parent-child dysfunctional interaction. It is administered 3 times during the study. In addition to evaluating each subscale score, a total parenting stress score is derived. In a study of 800 parents, alpha reliability was .91 for the total score, .87 for parental distress, .85 for difficult child and .80 for parent-child interaction.[19] Correlational analysis indicates that the total stress score of the full-length PSI and the total stress score of the short-form PSI have a correlation of .94.[19]

Infant-state stability refers to the regularity, stability or predictability of the infant's state behavior or sleep/wake cycles. Infant state is characterized by a recurrent clustering of physiological and behavioral activity patterns. These patterns reflect the infant's ability to cycle through sleeping and waking states. Increased predictability or regularity of sleep/wake cycles in an infant is characterized as a well-organized, as opposed to a disorganized, infant-state behavior pattern. A cardiac Holter monitor or DigiCorder® has been adapted for use in assessing infant-state stability or regularity of sleep-wake cycles in all infants. The DigiCorder is connected to a pressure-sensitive piece of laminated, piezoelectric fabric encased in a mattress or pad. It is a small, lightweight, nonintrusive, battery-operated recorder that is placed outside the crib. Four consecutive 24-hour recordings of infant state behavior are obtained on each infant at the beginning and end of the study. These will be analyzed for stability or regularity, and intervention and control groups will be compared. The state monitoring system was developed initially by Sander and associates,[20] and later refined by our research team in collaboration with Emergent Health Technologies Corporation. This nonintrusive system uses passive motion sensors embedded within a mattress to produce recordings of the infant's body movements and respirations. Output from the sensors is continuously monitored on a built-in system with a capacity for storage of up to 96 hours of data. The behavioral and physiological input can be printed out as respiratory and body movement analogues for categorization of the data into infant states.[20] The concurrent validity of the original LifeWatch® system was compared with live observation in a previous study using a subset of 22 infants who were observed while on the sensor mattress.[20] Minute-by-minute classifications by observers of infant state were compared with the output of the infant-state monitor. Results of the analysis showed an overall agreement of 79% for the state of the infant. Agreement for the major sleep states was 93% for quiet sleep and 85% for active sleep.[20]

A brief exit interview is conducted at the conclusion of the study to serve as a process measure. Incorporation of the intervention into the experimental group and exposure to other treatments in both groups were assessed. Other qualitative comments and observations of the infant's activity patterns and responses to treatment approaches are recorded. Program evaluation—including perceived knowledge, information and support gained by the parent—is measured by an interview and evaluation questionnaire upon completion of the intervention program. Parents in both control and intervention groups are asked to rate their satisfaction with the care they received.

Pilot Study Results

A preliminary study was conducted by my colleagues and I to refine and test this approach to the management of infant irritability.[15] Initial pilot testing was conducted using a pre- and posttest study design in a single group of 22 families referred by their pediatrician or nurse or recruited through local advertisements and flyers about the program. The families were seen on a weekly basis from the time of their referral until the resolution of irritability. The treatment program was individualized to the needs and unique features of each family. On average, families received 3 to 4 weekly clinic visits and at least one home visit with the nurse specialist. Data collected at entry into the program were compared with data collected upon completion of the program. Infant irritability was assessed weekly throughout the course of the intervention.

The mean length of unexplained fussing and crying was 4.9 hours per day at program entry and 0.9 hours at program completion ($P < .001$). The majority of participants stated that their infants' fussiness resolved by 10 weeks of age.

The mean infant age at which the parents began to note improvement was 8 weeks. The parents of infants enrolled in the intervention study reported significant improvement in their infants' irritability over time. Initially we sought infants who were between 2 weeks and 4 weeks of age. However, requests for participation in the study came from parents of infants ranging in age from 11 days to 8 weeks, and we enrolled these families in the pilot study as well. Of interest, parents who entered the program when their infants were younger adapted their approaches and appeared to be able to prevent and resolve their infants' episodes of fussiness at an earlier age as compared with parents of infants who entered when their infants were older (Fig 2).

Following the intervention, there were statistically significant decreases in the total PSI score.[15] The mean score for parents prior to enrollment was 285 ± 40 compared with 243 ± 38 after program completion ($P = .002$). Within the Child Domain subscale, significant decreases in parental perception of their infant's mood (from 17 ± 3 to 13 ± 4) and distractibility/ hyperactivity (from 27 ± 7 to 23 ± 8) were noted. The mean differences in acceptability (from 15 ± 4 to 12 ± 4) and reinforcing behaviors (from 14 ± 5

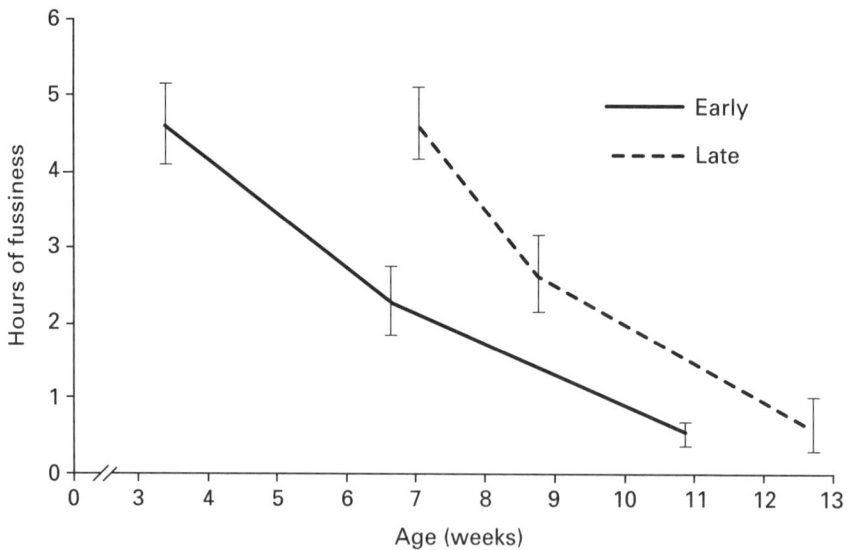

Fig 2. Fussiness hours for early and late referrals.[15]

to 9 ± 3) reflected significant improvement in these areas as well. Parent stress also decreased significantly (from 147 ± 20 to 129 ± 23; P = .005), as reflected in the mean Parent Domain subscale scores. Depression (from 26 ± 7 to 21 ± 4) and restriction of role (from 26 ± 4 to 22 ± 5) were significantly reduced over the course of the intervention, and a significant improvement in sense of competence (from 37 ± 6 to 30 ± 5) was noted (P = .001).

Overall, parents reported that the nursing intervention program was very helpful. Particular components of the program that were considered most helpful included the 24-hour activity report, the clinic and home visits, published articles on the topic and other information provided. Parents particularly valued having someone to listen to and who served as a resource for their questions. Nurse specialists shared the experiences of other parents who had irritable infants and phoned families to check on them between visits. These interactions were also perceived as very helpful. Learning about infant state behavior, infant cues and techniques to help regulate their infants' states were identified as very useful new information for these parents. Families indicated that they would be interested in establishing a phone network or support group for parents of irritable infants.[15]

Randomized Clinical Trial

Encouraged by these pilot results, we are now in the second year of a 4-year, National Institutes of Health (NIH)-funded, randomized clinical trial of the REST Regimen intervention program. This is a 2-site study being conducted in Denver, Colorado, and Charleston, South Carolina. Two hypotheses are being evaluated: Parents who receive the REST Regimen will report less parental stress and exhibit more synchrony with their infants than parents who do not receive this intervention, and infants who receive the REST Regimen will demonstrate more state stability and less irritability than infants who receive routine care. Study design is depicted in Fig 3.

A total of 160 parent-infant dyads with irritable infants between 2 weeks and 6 weeks of age are being recruited and screened for health problems and level of irritability. Families meeting study criteria are randomly assigned to either the individualized intervention or routine care. In addition to receiving routine well-child care, the intervention group infants and their parents receive the REST Regimen for a 4-week period. A separate, trained, evaluation team

Fig 3. Study design of currently ongoing 4-year, NIH-funded, randomized trial of the REST Regimen intervention program.

		Week 1	Week 2	Week 3	Week 4	Week 5	Week 6	Week 7	Week 8
Experimental	Baseline Data								
			Intervention						
	Sleep PSI NCAST				PSI NCAST				Sleep PSI NCAST
	Fussiness Rating Scale →								

		Week 1	Week 2	Week 3	Week 4	Week 5	Week 6	Week 7	Week 8
Control	Baseline Data								
	Sleep PSI NCAST				PSI NCAST				Sleep PSI NCAST
	Fussiness Rating Scale →								

of nurses collects measurements at baseline, immediately posttreatment and 1 month after completion of the intervention. Both groups are assessed in the following 4 areas: parental stress using the PSI; parent-infant interactions using the NCAFS; infant-state stability using the infant-state monitoring system; and infant irritability using the Fussiness Rating Scale.

It is too early to draw conclusions from this study; however, parents in both groups have expressed their satisfaction and benefit from the nurses (both intervention and data-collection nurses) that visit their homes. Families, nurses and pediatricians continue to express strong interest in the study, as they look for better management strategies and more accurate information.

Discussion and Conclusions

Through our studies of infants and their families, we have increased our understanding of both the infants' and the parents' contributions to the puzzling phenomenon of unexplained infant irritability. This theoretical perspective and the findings of earlier studies have led to the development of the REST Regimen, an intervention for irritable infants and their families. Our understanding regarding parental needs and maternal experiences has been incorporated into the intervention model. The basic concepts of synchrony, entrainment and support formed the core conceptual framework for the intervention strategy.

This intervention approach has been refined, and outcome measures have been identified and tested in an initial pilot study. The pilot test of the REST Regimen has suggested potential efficacy for reducing the excess unexplained crying in these infants and providing some relief for the distress seen in these families. Infants referred earlier in the course of their irritability appear to have derived the most benefit. However, the conclusions that can be drawn from this pilot study are limited due to the small sample size and the lack of a control group of irritable infants.

The efficacy of the REST Regimen in reducing excess infant irritability and providing relief from the distress seen in these families is now being examined through a systematic, randomized, clinical trial of this intervention. While the intervention program is in the process of further testing, the conceptualization of the phenomenon and the theoretically based approach to working with these families may prove useful to individuals practicing in the maternal child health arena. The treatment program emphasizes the individualized needs and unique features of each family. Irritable infants with unpredictable sleep-wake cycles and chaotic home environments may not be ideal candidates for the once popular "on demand" parenting approach, as their cues are often difficult to read and interpret.

A daily routine that reinforces regularity and predictability in sleeping and feeding may be a useful management strategy. It will be particularly important to assess the emotional and relationship impact of the infants' irritability on the mothers and the fathers.[10] Information, validation of maternal competency, opportunities to express feelings and empathetic, supportive interactions should be provided to assist parents in their own unique passage through the process of the recognition of, frustration with, understanding of and coping with an irritable infant.

Acknowledgement

This work is funded by the NIH, National Institute for Nursing Research, R01NR04661.

References

1. Barr RG, Rotman A, Yaremko J, Leduc D, Francoeur TE. The crying of infants with colic: a controlled empirical description. *Pediatrics.* 1992;90:14-21.
2. St. James-Roberts I. Infant crying levels, and maternal patterns of care, in normal community and clinically referred samples. In: Lester B, ed. *Biological and Social Aspects of Infant Crying.* New York, NY: Plenum Press; 2000. In press.
3. St. James-Roberts I, Conroy S, Wilsher K. Bases for maternal perceptions of infant crying and colic behaviour. *Archives of Disease in Childhood.* 1996;75:375-384.
4. Pinyerd BJ, Zipf WB. Colic: idiopathic, excessive, infant crying. *Journal of Pediatric Nursing.* 1989;4:147-161.
5. Stifter CA, Bono MA. The effect of infant colic on maternal self-perceptions and mother-infant attachment. *Child: Care, Health and Development.* 1998;24:339-351.
6. Gormally S, Barr RG. Of clinical pies and clinical clues: proposal for a clinical approach to complaints of early crying and colic. *Ambulatory Child Health.* 1997;3:137-153.
7. Krugman RD. Child abuse and neglect. Follow-up. *American Journal of Diseases of Children.* 1993;147:517.
8. Duncan DE, Briggs J, Bensimhon M. One deadly week. *Life.* 1996;52-58.
9. Mortimer P, Kevill F. Infant care. Frustration and despair. *Community Outlook.* 1985;8:19-22.
10. Keefe MR, Froese-Fretz A. Living with an irritable infant: maternal perspectives. *MCN. The American Journal of Maternal Child Nursing.* 1991;16:255-259.
11. Keefe MR. Irritable infant syndrome: theoretical perspectives and practice implications. *ANS. Advances in Nursing Science.* 1988;10:70-78.
12. Pinyerd BJ. Strategies for consoling the infant with colic: fact or fiction? *Journal of Pediatric Nursing.* 1992;7:403-411.
13. Keefe MR, Froese-Fretz A, Kotzer AM. Newborn predictors of infant irritability. *Journal of Obstetric, Gynecologic, and Neonatal Nursing: JOGNN/NAACOG.* 1998;27:513-520.
14. Keefe MR, Kotzer AM, Froese-Fretz A, Curtin M. A longitudinal comparison of irritable and nonirritable infants. *Nursing Research.* 1996;45:4-9.
15. Keefe MR, Froese-Fretz A, Kotzer AM. The REST regimen: an individualized nursing intervention for infant irritability. *MCN. The American Journal of Maternal Child Nursing.* 1997:22;16-20.
16. Emde RN. *Emotional Expression in Infancy: A Biobehavioral Study.* New York, NY: International Universities Press; 1976.
17. Barnard KE, Hammond MA, Booth C, Bee H, Mitchell S, Spieker S. Measurement and meaning of parent-child interaction. In: Morrison F, Lord C, Keating D, eds. *Applied Developmental Psychology.* San Diego, Calif: Academic Press; 1989.
18. Huber C. Documenting quality of parent-child interaction: use of the NCAST scales. *Infants and Young Children.* 1991;4:63-75.
19. Abidin R. *Parenting Stress Index.* 3rd ed. Charlottesville, Va: Pediatric Psychology Press; 1990.
20. Keefe MR, Kotzer AM, Reuss JL, Sander LW. Development of a system for monitoring infant state behavior. *Nursing Research.* 1989;38:344-347.

Section 4 Discussion: Empirically Based Approaches to Management: Behavioral Strategies

Moderated by Pamela High, MD
Clinical Professor of Pediatrics
Brown University School of Medicine
Providence, RI USA

High: Behavioral interventions are very much a part of what we have developed with our treatment team at Brown University School of Medicine, but we also look very closely at medical issues. Many of the children we care for are referred from the medical community and are even referred by gastroenterologists, because even after their organic issues are dealt with, there may be behavioral issues that need help as well. So I would suggest that even infants who have organic etiologies for their irritability can benefit from behavioral approaches.

Our model has been informed, in part, by the definition of behavioral disorder that Tom Anders put forth describing perturbations of normative variations in the parent-child relationship that cause normative behavioral problems. The population I see is probably far beyond the perturbation stage by the time they get to our clinic.

More of the children I see are at the disturbance level, when the parent is unable to adapt to the infant's behavioral difficulties. Many are even at the level of disorder in the parent-child relationship. This occurs when developmental milestones are disrupted and behavioral difficulties occur across several domains of functioning. The parent is not able to make the necessary adaptations, and infant behavioral disturbances may persist over time.

Our techniques of intervention include remediation, which tries to directly alter infant behavior, addressing, for example, frequent feeding behaviors or infant sleep issues. We also use redefinition, which modifies the parents' interpretation of infant signals, including the fact that many of these infants are absolutely exhausted rather than necessarily spoiled. Finally, we attempt reeducation, which alters the parent's interaction through modeling and teaching new strategies for soothing. Parents are taught that they can support self-regulation by occasionally putting their infants down. We are hearing a persistent theme—allowing the infants to begin learning self-soothing strategies.

Our approach is very family centered. A parent makes the contact. Even though all of them are referred from their pediatricians as well, it is the parent who must make the initial contact. We attempt to be incredibly responsive. Within 5 days of the parent calling us, we have scheduled an intake visit with the mental health clinician. We take a very detailed history, conducting an in-depth mental health history and looking at family functioning. The mental health clinician attempts to reduce parent stress and self-criticism by providing information about normative infant sleep patterns, as well as feeding and crying patterns. During this intake visit, we try to identify additional support for the family, so we are already beginning an intervention. We give behavior diaries to parents, and we try to obtain 3 days of diary input. It is very difficult for a family to keep 7 days of diaries before any level of treatment is provided.

We then attempt to schedule the initial treatment visit within 5 days of the intake visit. Treatment visits occur with both the behavioral pediatrician and a mental health clinician. We strongly encourage fathers to come too, and at least half the time the fathers attend. This tells you something about the height of the anxiety, frustration and stress within the family. We administer an instrument called the Infant Gastroesophageal Reflux (GER) Questionnaire, developed by Orenstein, Shalaby, and Cohn.[1] I have found this tool to be extremely helpful. We realized not only that these babies were crying, but also had very serious sleep disturbances. Many of them had difficulties with feeding as well. We also take growth parameters on the infants.

The treatment is brief and intensive. Infants are typically seen for 2 to 5 treatment visits over a 2-week to 12-week period. Parents actively participate in data collection by keeping diaries and by sharing their observations with us. We use highlighters for each behavior in the diaries. For example, sleep is pink, a very soothing color; crying is bright yellow; fussing is green. You can then visualize when the crying is occurring. We also involve the parents in creating an "individualized" (a term used by the 3 previous presenters in this section) family treatment plan. Parents are given a copy of their written individualized treatment plans at the conclusion of the session. In the individualized treatment plan, we make some typical cry intervention recommendations.

We consider just a 1-week trial of a hypoallergenic formula. If it does not work within one week, it will not work. I have mothers who are breastfeeding who are basically eating nothing but tofu and white rice. The hoops that mothers jump through trying to figure out how their breast milk is causing this irritability in their infant is ridiculous.

I believe there is a very good rationale to remove caffeine from a nursing mother's diet. A reduction in caffeine intake is a very helpful recommendation clinically. We know that in preterm infants the xanthenes in coffee increase irritability in breastfed infants. We also know that the half-life of caffeine is longer in infants than it is in mothers. Mothers may be drinking coffee simply to stay awake in order to deal with the issue of having an irritable baby.

We encourage parents to space out their daily feedings. Many of these babies are "grazing" all day. We have infants who are eating 10 or 15 times a day; in particular, the breastfed babies. We talk to parents about how much formula is appropriate, so that the babies are neither over- nor underfed. We limit feedings to 30 minutes. Many of these babies feed for 1 hour or longer, which is frustrating to their parents. We try to decrease distraction and avoid using the breast or the bottle as a pacifier. These are typical conservative recommendations for the children we have defined as having reflux difficulties. We use upright positioning and thickening with perhaps some cereal if the baby is formula-fed. These techniques do not work for nursing babies. You cannot get cereal into them. The result is a frustrated mother. We consider using a trial of an H_2 blocker. We generally use it for 2 weeks to see whether it is helpful. We use prokinetic agents with great caution and only after radiologic confirmation.

Many of our parents feel that their babies are constipated, and that constipation is the etiology of the crying. We feel that using bran is the most noninvasive way of treating this.

We also place a strong emphasis on sleep, and try to get parents to limit the duration of daytime naps to $2^1/_2$ hours each by waking and playing with the baby, make middle-of-the-night feedings boring, establish a regular bedtime, try not to allow the baby to sleep for $1^1/_2$ hours before that bedtime and develop a soothing bedtime routine. These themes are sounding familiar.

We also place a strong emphasis on family support. We ask parents to ask a trusted friend or family member to watch their children periodically. We call this time out "mom time." We also promote time together for the couple. So there are many continuities with the other presenters.

I have data on 50 subjects who were referred. These are data from a clinical sample, not a research study per se. The majority of them were 2 months old and were referred with cry problems. Infants were divided into GER-positive and -negative groups. In two thirds of these children, we felt that GER was part of the symptomatology. We treated the GER, and felt that treatment helped.

How do we diagnose GER? We use the Infant GER Questionnaire and clinical evidence. In particular, many of these children had significant feeding problems: Prolonged feeding, feeding refusal and vomiting. GER-positive infants were more likely to be male and later born. They were even difficult for experienced mothers. Parents of GER-positive infants did not differ from parents of GER-negative infants in marital status, insurance type, difficulty during pregnancy, C-section rate or maternal depression by report.

The total amount of crying in our sample is approximately 5 hours by parent diary in both the GER-positive and GER-negative groups. There was no significant difference. There was a trend toward more nursing in the GER-negative group. The GER-positive group cried during their feedings and they refused to feed 97% of the time, compared with 13% in the GER-negative group. There was significantly more spitting up. Ninety-two percent did so 2 or more times per day. Sleep problems were prevalent in both groups.

Many parents stopped keeping diaries, but they did not drop out of the clinic. The infants improved clinically, but I do not have diaries to prove that they improved. There are only 34 babies in the follow-up data relating to their behaviors and their improvement.

Breastfeeding decreased in the sample as a whole, but not because we were unsupportive. In fact, breastfeeding had decreased much more than this before we ever saw them. Spitting up decreased from 78% to 38%. At intake, 97% of parents were generally holding, rocking, stimulating and/or walking their babies to sleep at night. Only 9% were doing these at follow-up. Crying decreased from approximately $4^{1}/_{2}$ hours to less than 2 hours per day in both groups. Feedings decreased from an average of 7 to fewer than 6 per day. Sleep increased from 11.6 hours to 13.5 hours per day. This was an interesting finding because sleep time is supposed to be decreasing at this age. But

11.6 hours of sleep daily is not very much sleep. Bedtimes moved more than an hour earlier in this group. Infants slept more between midnight and 6:00 AM. In each analysis, there were no differences between the GER-positive and GER-negative groups with the exception of the number of feedings, which was greater in the GER-negative group, possibly because there were more breastfed infants in that group.

At intake, the more the baby was crying, the less the baby was sleeping. However, at follow-up, there was no association between the amount of crying and the amount of sleeping.

I want to comment on the other papers in this section. Dieter Wolke argues that behavior management of colic is more effective than dietary treatment and that parents accept this very readily. He includes sleep disturbances and hypothesizes that cry and sleep disturbances are related to a lack of the development of self-regulation in stopping crying. He also hypothesizes that parents' behavior may maintain this lack of development. This is a very important component of explaining early infant crying, and elegantly describes part of the treatment strategy.

Dymphna van den Boom designed a prospective intervention study with 100 low-income families. These data are important because the majority of colic studies are done in middle- and upper-class families. However, these low-socioeconomic status families are different from those in my clinic. Ninety-seven percent of participants from the Dutch study were married. I thought it was notable that all of the infants were firstborn. Irritability was not the general colic criterion, but rather it was reactivity in the second week of life, defined by the Neonatal Behavioral Assessment Scale or NBAS. Interventions were delivered later, were home based and were brief. Yet the effects were very long-lasting. At 24 months of age, children were more cooperative. At 42 months, mothers were responsive, as were fathers, which is a very interesting finding; and children were more securely attached.

Maureen Keefe outlined a behavioral management approach to infant cry problems, which uses a nursing perspective that is holistic and contextual. Intervention is individualized, home based and reproducible, using multiple research clinician nurses. She points out the severe amount of stress caused by excessive early crying. Maureen Keefe's point about how difficult it is to have control groups that are "clean" is an important one. If effects are not seen in control groups, we can speculate that the nurses who are collecting data in the control groups cannot help themselves but provide care. They are intervening as well.

I would like to outline what I believe are optimal treatment plans for infants who have cry problems. I am a "lumper," not a "splitter." I believe in looking at everything and using whatever I can to try to devise effective management. Treatment takes time, and that time is time well spent. Empathy is important, but empathy is not enough. The first 3 months of life is a critical period for family development—when parents are learning about themselves and their children. It is difficult for parents to "unlearn" what they learn in those first few weeks of life. Optimal treatment requires having both parents available. Treatments need to be individualized and address many levels—feeding, sleeping, crying and family support. Treatment plans should involve both parents at data collection, interpretation and devising plans of action. My colleagues and I have found that providing parents with recommendations in writing, as well as continuity, are both very helpful.

Gunnar: I find all of this absolutely amazing from an outsider's perspective. What is being described here—about how to treat sleeping and eating problems—suggests that hunter-gatherer !Kung San babies should scream forever and never sleep at all. There is a "mismatch." It may be informative if we could understand this mismatch. The !Kung San feed their babies even more often than what you are describing as detrimental in North American babies; that is, you suggest we might be causing the problems in our babies. The !Kung San do not worry about sleeping through the night. It is possible that the differences you see in the !Kung San, or in those cultures where not sleeping through the night is normative, reflect that their caregiving patterns are not in response to trying to change infant behavior that *we* find disturbing, but because it is the culturally normative behavior. What we may be suggesting is providing parents with "rules of thumb," so that they are not locked in a battle about whose will is going to triumph—baby's or mother's. Your patients are following some sensible guidelines that may tone down the distress level. Maybe that's the goal. I do not know, but there are inconsistencies between these recommendations for therapy and what is the cultural norm in other societies.

Faculty Member: I think that culture implies incredible routine. It epitomizes regularity and routine: Every day is similar to the previous day, with constant physiologic recognition of skin-to-skin, body-to-body contact. The !Kung San have powerful elements of regularity and routine. It is not chaotic.

High: That intervention would not work in our society. Carrying your baby around on your back and nursing them every 10 or 15 minutes would not work in the US.

Gunnar: But the disorders we are producing are disorders because they do not fit our ideal for infants. There is another challenge involved: A sleeping disorder is a sleeping disorder if it "disorders" the parents. But the babies are crying and screaming in one context and not in another. The outcome in terms of the baby at that moment is not as closely linked to caregiving practices as it is to other factors.

Zeskind: I think Megan Gunnar has really hit on a valuable point. In the US, we deal with Medicaid, which covers very low socioeconomic-status, poor, mostly black, families. When I say, "OK, let's deal with the colic," parents ask "Why?" It is not a phenomenon they deal with very often.

High: Well, perhaps it is more rare, but it is there. I consult in my hospital's continuity clinic, which is composed of all low-income families. Excessive infant crying presents less frequently as a problem there. More commonly, there is a problem of spitting up, which is often associated with overfeeding.

Zeskind: Perhaps our culture contributes to colic. Perhaps we have a battle of wills, and there is an element of our cultural attitude that makes us believe we need to be in control. We see this phenomenon across the domains of psychology. We create adolescents who rebel, but this is not a universal phenomenon. If there are fewer reports of colic from low-income families in the US, that is a clue. There is something to be learned from the !Kung San and others about what actually constitues colic.

High: Independently of whether it is the !Kung San, the Japanese or Americans in the United States, there is a basic cultural adaptation to the cues that a child is providing.

* * * * *

Oberklaid: Only a very small proportion of infants who cry excessively are brought for medical help. Those parents who seek help are looking for change. But we are not necessarily looking to change the infant. I have a very simple, and perhaps simplistic, notion of what constitutes infant behavioral problems. Behavioral problems as presented by a parent are a mismatch between parental expectations and the infant's behavior. That is why parents come in to see the healthcare provider. This might be considered a "dyssynchrony." Somebody once used the term "violation of maternal expectation." The goal at intervention is to restore expectations in such a way so that there is no longer a mismatch. I am drawn to Dieter Wolke's concept about offering a set of principles we know from the literature and from our personal experiences that have been shown to make a difference in this transaction. We are looking to change something, but it may not be necessary to change the behavior of the infant. It may just be parental perception that needs to change. If we give parents the information and confidence to enlist some of these strategies, then the infant's behavior will change. Then, there is no longer a mismatch between behavior and parental expectation.

Wolke: With some mothers, just giving them information is not going to change the situation. More needs to be accomplished on another issue. If you conduct a smoking cessation program, those of the lower socioeconomic class will show low participation. That low participation does not mean that they smoke less; they actually smoke more. So, conducting clinical studies will not tell us very much about the distribution of the problem. Epidemiological studies are required first.

Treem: Dieter Wolke, your presentation shows us what being on the front lines is all about. My concern is that you attempt multiple interventions simultaneously. I would also submit that you have another intervention, which is that you are paying a great deal of attention to these parents and infants. You are seeing them 5 times within a fairly short period of time for a complaint that was elicited in 15 minutes from their pediatrician who is seeing 40 patients per day. I have often wondered if the diaries used in colic studies are an intervention in and of themselves, because it causes a partnership between the pediatrician and the parent. You have elicited the mother's or the parents' help in defining the problem. They are focused: Every 15 minutes they are marking down notes, and that is a significant intervention.

High: I agree with you.

* * * * *

Leavitt: Parents may be the ones who need most of the interventions, which include, from my vantage point, some redefinition and reframing. I believe the problem is, in part, in the *ear* of the beholder, although we also need to pay attention to some infants at the high end of the spectrum based on the criteria that Siobhán Gormally and William Treem, in particular, have discussed. I believe it is the "ribbon around the box" that is ill defined.

High: I believe there is information in this crying variation that we are ignoring by arguing about cultural differences. This crying is telling us something else, and we need to listen to it. It is difficult to just say, "Chill out and let the kid develop."

* * * * *

Keefe: My personal belief is that, regardless of the cause of the fussiness, the parent learns quickly that they cannot put the baby down. So, 100% of the parents who come to us walk the floors for a long, long time before they ever put their baby down to go to sleep at night. Whatever the initial cause of the irritability, the parent has learned quickly that the baby cannot self-soothe. So, the parent will not allow their infant to *learn* how to do it, as Dieter Wolke discussed.

High: That's exactly what I see in my clinic. The babies are exhausted; Eleven hours of sleep for a 2-month-old is not enough.

* * * * *

Barr: I think that one of the concepts we are missing in clinical practice is the concept of trade-offs. There is no optimal caregiving strategy. There are dozens of strategies, and the clinician makes trade-off decisions depending on a combination of what your cultural ideologies and aims are, and what you believe that behavior is going to lead to somewhere in the future. When there is a crying problem, there are several techniques that might work. They each have different costs. The individualization does not refer to whether you recommend rest and relaxation in one case or more regulation in the other. It refers to making a decision about what the trade-offs are for any intervention. We are poor at defining what those trade-offs are, especially for these "functional" problems. It is not easy. But I believe that the concept of an optimal caregiving style for crying, poor sleeping or feeding, or for other behaviors, is a misassumption. Clinically, the difference is prescription versus options. One of the benefits of cross-cultural studies is offering choices. Mothers can be "partly" North American and "partly" !Kung San in behavior if that serves the purpose. If the crying is stressful, the mother can act like a

!Kung San mother. If it is not, and if there is no disease underlying the crying, then the mother can continue as a North American mother.

My point is not that we have no limits, but rather that the concept of trade-offs is not one that is included in many therapeutic interventions, which tend to start from presumptions about what is optimal treatment. I believe the presumptions are problematic.

* * * * *

St. James-Roberts: The notion was introduced that we need to understand the concept of "dysregulation" in order to understand, in some sense, the concept of colic. I believe that, in comparison with the concept of colic, which is difficult enough, the concept of dysregulation has no meaning whatsoever. What is meant by dysregulation? We have data that colicky infants sleep less. If the infant cries more, it sleeps less. By dysregulation, do you mean that if you look at the distribution of their behavior over the day and night, it is different from that of normal babies? Do you mean that there is greater variability? And, are you talking at a behavioral level, or are you making an assumption that there is some kind of disorganization at a physiological level that is causal of the behavioral differences? Megan Gunnar and Ronald Barr and their colleagues have shown that it is not a very simple mapping of physiology and behavior in these kinds of areas.[2-4] Do you really want us to use the concept of "dysregulation," and what do you mean by it?

Faculty Member: Thank you. I second that. I do not believe that dysregulation is a very helpful concept in this area either. But, if the term is used, we need to do some work on it.

References

1. Orenstein SR, Shalaby TM, Cohn JF. Reflux symptoms in 100 normal infants: diagnostic validity of the infant gastroesophageal reflux questionnaire. *Clinical Pediatrics.* 1996;35:607-614.
2. White BP, Gunnar MR, Larson MC, Donzella B, Barr RG. Behavioral and physiological responsivity, sleep, and patterns of daily cortisol production in infants with and without colic. *Child Development.* 2000;71:862-877.
3. Gunnar MR, Fisch RO, Malone S. The effects of a pacifying stimulus on behavioral and adrenocortical responses to circumcision in the newborn. *Journal of the American Academy of Child Psychiatry.* 1984;23:34-38.
4. Barr RG. Reflections on measuring pain in infants: dissociation in responsive systems and "honest signalling." *Archives of Disease in Childhood. Fetal and Neonatal Edition.* 1998;79:F152-F156.

New Evidence on Unexplained Early Infant Crying

Section 5:
Is There Life After Unexplained Crying?: Outcomes and Consequences

Abstracts from Section 5: Is There Life After Unexplained Crying?: Outcomes and Consequences

From Colic to Toddlerhood

Liisa Lehtonen, MD

From an extensive literature review of follow-up studies of infants with colic, it is clear that, in general, most infants with colic have good prognoses for normal physical, cognitive, and behavioral development. Differences in parental perceptions of infant behavior, however, may eventually result in negative parental views that impact parents' interactions with their children, potentially leading to negative outcomes for toddlers. Identification of families at risk for slow recovery after the resolution of colic and development of appropriate interventions for these families remain important clinical challenges.

Life After Unexplained Crying: Child and Parent Outcomes

Cynthia A. Stifter, PhD

Prospective longitudinal studies that followed infants beyond 18 months of age suggest that infant colic is a transitory condition that may be associated with temporary delays in certain developmental tasks. Colic may delay the development of self-regulatory behaviors, and it may result in feelings of maternal incompetence and affect the marital relationship. The dynamic nature of colic implies that measures of reactivity at any point are the result of both the infant's reaction and the regulatory processes involved; results presented here support the observation that differences in regulation that contribute to colic behavior may persist beyond the period of intense crying.

Clinical Perspectives on Unexplained Early Crying: Challenges and Risks for Infant Mental Health and Parent-Infant Relationships

Mechthild Papoušek, MD, Harald Wurmser, PhD and Nikolaus von Hofacker, MD

The Munich Interdisciplinary Research and Intervention Program for Fussy Babies has investigated long-term outcomes in a cohort of 60 infants with persistent crying. Infants displayed high levels of distress over prolonged periods, with lasting problems of sleep-wake organization, transient neuromotor immaturity, and difficult temperament; many of their families had multiple organic and psychosocial risks. Dynamic interactions between parent and infant promote or exacerbate parent-infant distress syndrome. As ongoing dysfunctional interactions place the parent-infant dyad at risk for lasting relationship disorders and the infant at risk for behavioral disorders, it may be critical that healthcare professionals identify families who require early intervention.

From Colic to Toddlerhood

Liisa Lehtonen, MD

Parents who bring an infant with colic to a clinician are concerned with the infant's excessive crying. They are also worried that colic could have a negative impact on the later behavior and health of their child. For this reason, the clinician's job includes providing parents with information about the long-term prognosis for infants diagnosed with colic. The behavioral syndrome of colic, or excessive crying in early infancy, is typically described as benign and self-limited, but there are reports of abuse, and even death, of infants whose crying is persistent and unsoothable.[1] Even though mortality is low and crying is unlikely to be the *only* cause, a general belief exists, and some literature suggests, that colic is associated with later morbidity, primarily behavioral problems. Some early morbidity findings, however, were based on retrospective studies and are not supported by prospective studies.

To address questions about the long-term outcomes of colic, this presentation will summarize the available longitudinal follow-up studies of cohorts of excessively crying, or colicky, infants.[2] Although these studies have limitations, and questions remain, the literature reviewed here is helpful for clinicians who counsel families of colicky infants.

Selection of Studies for Review

Follow-up studies of infants with colic are few and widely distributed in clinical, developmental and nursing journals. The MEDLINE database for 1996 to 1997 and the PsychINFO database for 1967 to 1997 were searched using the prompt words "infantile colic," "crying and infant" and "irritable and infant." From 768 papers, 59 articles that addressed outcome were selected. Analysis was limited to those studies that explicitly included infants who had the behavioral syndrome of colic and that were prospective from the time that colic status was obtained (whether by observation, diary or interview). Eleven articles met these criteria. In addition to these 11 published studies, preliminary data from a cohort of infants with colic in Turku, Finland, are discussed.

Several longitudinal studies discussed "irritability," persistent mother-infant distress syndrome, "difficult" infants or "dysregulated" infants. These groups may overlap with "colicky," or excessively crying, infants, but in this review I did not assume that they are the same group.

In 7 cohorts, comprising 236 infants with colic, diagnosis was "concurrent" with the period of excessive crying.[3-10] In an additional 5 cohorts, "recall diagnosis" was used, with colic status determined *following* the period of excessive crying.[11-16] In all groups, infants were followed prospectively from the time of diagnosis. Fig 1 presents time lines for these 12 cohorts. Large arrows indicate the time when colic status was determined, while small arrows indicate follow-up contacts.

Fig 1. Time line for 12 cohorts of infants with colic.[3-16]

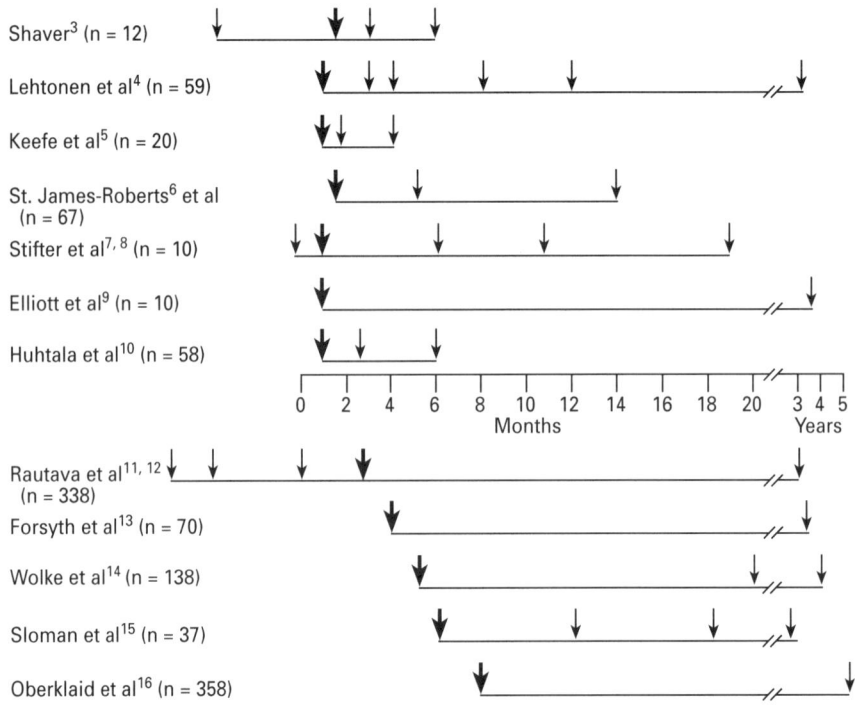

Reprinted with permission from *Developmental Medicine and Child Neurology*. Copyright 1997, Mac Keith Press.

Definitions of Colic and Biases in Longitudinal Studies

Excessive and/or persistent crying are/is the cardinal symptom(s) in most clinical descriptions of colic syndrome.[17] Specific details about the amount or quality of crying or about additional symptoms required for a diagnosis of colic remain controversial. The definitions used in the longitudinal studies reviewed here can be grouped roughly into 2 types. The definitions depend, in part, on whether a study utilized "concurrent" or "recall" diagnosis.

In "recall diagnosis" studies, the opportunity to measure actual amounts of crying has been lost. In most studies of this type, parental complaints of crying are used to define the group of colicky, or excessively crying, infants. The 2 studies that attempted to quantify crying are prone to recall bias,[15, 17] because crying was described several months after colic ended. Crying complaints should be considered more as parental perceptions of infant behavior than as representations of the behavior itself. The perception of crying problems is affected by many factors, including the personality, social situation and level of concern of the caregiver, cultural predispositions as to whether to consider crying a clinical problem and others. Parental complaint of infant crying is the *broadest* definition of colic, and a large percentage of all infants meet this definition. In the recall diagnosis studies reviewed here, 17% to 35% of all infants met this criterion, as shown in Table 1.[11, 13-16]

Table 1. Percentage of Infants Classified by Parents as Colicky in 5 "Recall Diagnosis" Studies [11, 13-16]

Forsyth et al[13]	35%
Wolke et al[14]	32%
Rautava et al[11]	28% colicky (10%, severe colic)
Oberklaid et al[16]	25%
Sloman et al[15]	17%

The "concurrent diagnosis" studies most often used Wessel's "Rule of Threes" to diagnose colic.[18] According to Wessel's definition, a "fussy [infant is one] who, otherwise healthy and well-fed, has paroxysms of irritability, fussing or crying lasting for a total of more than three hours a day and occurring on more than three days in any one week."[18] Substantial differences in the application of Wessel's rule exist among studies; thus, an infant who meets the criteria for colic in one study might be excluded from another. Specifically, some authors[7-9] use crying alone to make the diagnosis of colic while others[6, 19] include both fussing and crying as "colicky" behaviors. Further, some researchers require additional criteria, such as unsoothability[4, 20-22] or intensity of crying,[5] to capture more problematic crying and to target a more extreme group of infants with colic.

In addition to differences in defining the required amount and quality of crying, researchers approach assessment differently. Among the 12 cohorts reviewed here,[3-16] the most objective assessment technique was employed by St. James-Roberts,[6, 19] who included audio recordings and diaries. The Finnish cohorts[4, 20-22] were studied using home diaries, while other researchers utilized parent interviews.[5, 7, 8]

Some differences in the findings of these studies may result from variability in definition and assessment of colic. Referral bias is another potential confounder. If the subjects of a study had already been seen in other (often, many other) settings and/or failed other (often, many other) treatments, they were likely to have had more severe problems than infants who simply met *modified* Wessel's criteria and who were selected from nonreferred community samples. All studies that used "recall diagnosis" were cohort studies that avoided referral bias. "Concurrent diagnosis" studies avoided referral bias if they recruited infants prior to colic. Even if infants were selected prior to colic, however, most samples were biased in that they tended to draw from a white, middle-class population. Results from these studies may not be applicable to other populations, especially those that are socially disadvantaged.

Outcomes in "Concurrent Diagnosis" Studies

The earliest of the longitudinal studies reviewed here[3] assessed outcomes of 12 infants with colic and 45 control infants by interview when the infants were 3 months old and 6 months old. In this study, the colic and noncolic groups did not show reliable differences on most of the 54 outcome items, including maternal psychologic characteristics (personality, sensitivity, responsiveness and affection) and number of stress events. Mothers of infants with colic initially reported a transient decline in confidence in coping and less acceptance of their infants, but these problems resolved by 6 months. At 6 months, the infants who had earlier colic were still described as having increased irritability, increased tenseness, more feeding problems and lower overall functioning. Although this study did not define colic, making it difficult to know exactly what kinds of infants were studied, and it only poorly defined certain outcome measures, the results nevertheless seem valid, as many of them have been repeated in subsequent studies.

The next study describes one of our Finnish cohorts.[4] This cohort was followed until toddlerhood and consisted of 59 infants with colic, including a subgroup of 36 infants with "severe" colic, defined as "colicky" crying for 3 or more hours for 3 or more days per week, and 58 age-matched controls. Physical development and health (including infections, allergies and eczema) did not differ between the groups during the first year of life. Temperament was assessed at 12 months and 36 months using the Toddler Temperament Scale,[23] and no differences were found. Mothers were asked the general question of whether their infants were easier than average, average or more difficult than average at different ages. Mothers whose infants previously had colic were more likely to report their infants as more difficult than average, compared with those who didn't at 3 months (24% versus 4%),[4] 12 months (23% versus 5%)[4] and 36 months (29% versus 16%; L.L., unpublished data). The discrepancy between the *lack of difference* on all temperament subscales and the overall maternal *impression* of "difficultness" suggest that early colic may have lasting effects on maternal *perceptions* of infant difficultness despite similar infant behaviors. This theme repeats itself throughout the studies reviewed here.

Sleeping problems were investigated as well. There were *no* differences between the groups in the number of night awakenings or the duration of sleep at 8 months, 12 months or 36 months.[4] However, families in the colic group were prone to perceive awakenings as problematic. In another study,[24] my colleagues and I showed that sleep structure, studied by overnight polysomnography, was similar between infants with colic and without colic, both at 2 months and 7 months of age. Again, these data suggest that the differences between colic groups and control groups are "perceived" differences rather than actual differences.

Family interaction was assessed using taped family interviews during the colic period[25] and when infants were 12 months old,[21] and by questionnaire when infants were 36 months old.[22] The coding of interviews and questionnaires was based on constructs derived from the Beavers system model of family functioning. This model views separation and individuation as key developmental challenges, while individual functioning is seen as interrelated with family functioning.[21] Families of infants with colic showed more family interaction problems at 12 months. The severe colic, moderate colic and control groups were compared when infants were 2 months and 12 months of age. At 12 months, after colic had resolved, the severe colic group continued to have some problems. For example, families in this group showed more difficulty taking responsibility for their own actions, feelings and thoughts. Individuals in these families expressed more dissatisfaction. In addition, they showed less empathy for other family members. The level of infant crying correlated with the extent of unresolved family conflicts. In both colic groups, family functioning was characterized by less flexibility when meeting new challenges in family life.

By the time these children were 36 months old, the differences between families with colic and noncolic infants were not statistically significant; however, trends remained toward less optimal scores on the McMaster Family Assessment Scales[26] in the severe colic group. In general, colic was associated with some long-lasting problems in family interaction, which may be secondary to the significant stress caused by infant crying. Further study of nonwhite, non-middle-class samples should be done, as it is possible that the long-term impact of colic on families may differ in populations that have fewer community and economic resources. Also, the possibility that family differences may precede, rather than be caused by, colic should be explored.

The cohort, studied by my colleagues and I, showed some long-term disturbances in family functioning, but also had other problems that were transient and resolved over time. Similarly, Keefe and colleagues[5] reported problems in mother-infant interaction during colic that resolved by 12 weeks of life. By 12 weeks, there were no differences in crying or sleep behavior in the colic and noncolic groups.

St. James-Roberts, Conroy and Wilsher [6, 19] followed groups of persistent criers, evening criers and moderate criers up to the age of 15 months. In their cohort, the infants with colic (ie, persistent criers) continued to cry more than noncolic infants at 5 months of age, but this difference disappeared by

15 months. Furthermore, crying at 6 weeks of age did not predict negativity, such as fussing, crying, temper, frustration or irritability, at 15 months of age. Consistent with our Finnish data, these British mothers[6, 19] were more likely to rate infants with colic as more difficult on temperament scales at both 5 months and 15 months of age.

The most worrisome outcome in these studies was maternal depression.[6, 19] At 5 months, depression was noted in 9% of mothers in the persistent criers, group and 16% of mothers in the evening criers' group. No maternal depression was reported in the control group. The rate of depressive symptoms prior to the onset of colic is not known; thus, it cannot be known if prior vulnerability to depression manifests as such when the infant cries a lot or if depression is secondary to crying. In addition, the duration of maternal depression is unknown.

Very thorough assessments using diary measures and direct observations revealed no differences in maternal sensitivity or affection, caregiving behaviors, flexibility of caregiving or marital adjustment. Some differences were noted. Time spent carrying and soothing the infant at 5 months of age correlated with crying, so group differences were found for these measures. Also, mothers of persistent criers were slightly less likely than mothers in the control group to respond to crying. Child development, as assessed by the Bayley Scales of Infant Development,[27] was no different between the groups at 15 months of age.

Stifter, Braungart and Bono, in 2 separate studies, prospectively identified 10 infants with colic from a cohort of 100 infants and evaluated them at 5^7 months, 10^7 months and 18^8 months. At birth, prior to the onset of colic, there were no differences on measures of maternal personality and responsivity or infant reactivity (ie, crying response to pacifier withdrawal and rubber band snap to the heel). Similarly, at 5 months and 10 months, no differences were identified in negative reactivity of infants (ie, arm restraint at 5 months and toy removal at 10 months), in maternal responsiveness (ie, during a 5-minute play session), in infant development or in maternal perceptions of infant temperament. At 18 months, infants with prior colic had attachment classifications that were similar to those of infants without colic. The only difference between groups indicated decreased maternal self-efficacy at 5 months in the colic group. Although these data suggest few negative outcomes of colic, the small sample size in these studies limits the conclusions that can be drawn. Real differences may exist, but may be missed because of the limited sample size.

Elliott, Pedersen and Mogan[9] reported on another sample of 10 infants with colic. When the infants were between 2 years and 4 years of age, no differences were found on measures of child behavior, temperament, physical health and family functioning. The only difference reported was in response to a question about major family disruptions. These occurred more often in families with infants who had prior colic, but it is unlikely that these disruptions were related to colic. Again, small sample size may limit these findings.

The last longitudinal concurrent diagnosis cohort is one my colleagues and I undertook in our third cohort of Finnish infants with colic.[24] This cohort comprises 32 families of infants with colic and 31 control families. Several methods and measures were employed with this cohort, including 2 overnight polysomnographies performed at 2 months and 7 months of age diary data collected at 1 month and 6 months and temperament assessment at 6 months. No differences in sleep architecture between the colic and control groups were identified in sleep studies at 2 months or 7 months of age. As with our Finnish cohort mentioned previously, the duration of sleep in this study[24] was similar at 7 months of age, although infants with colic slept less compared with controls during the period of colic. In this cohort, there was no difference between the groups in the amount of crying at 6 months.

Outcomes in "Recall Diagnosis" Studies

Among the 5 "recall diagnosis" cohorts,[11-16] the age at which colic status was assessed (by either questionnaire or interview) ranged from 3 months[11] to 8 months.[16] As discussed previously, the diagnosis of colic in these studies was based on perceived crying problems rather than on confirmed differences in infant behavior.

The first of the 3 cohorts of Finnish infants with colic studied by my colleagues and I was part of a large follow-up study of 1443 primiparous women recruited during their first trimester of pregnancy.[11] These families were followed to 3 years postpartum.[12] Colic status was determined at 3 months postpartum by parental responses to a question about whether their infant had "quite a lot of colic" (18%) or "a lot of colic" (10%) on a 5-point scale. Colic was associated with prenatal dissatisfaction with marital life (eg, perceived worsening of the sexual relationship), more stress experiences (eg, social isolation) more stress symptoms (eg, work distress during pregnancy) and more symptoms of illness (eg, sickness during pregnancy and sick leave). There was more disappointment with the delivery (eg, with the appearance or health of the baby) reported by both parents of infants later reported to have colic. These results suggest that perceived prenatal and perinatal difficulties are associated with later perceptions about crying problems. There was no association of later colic with any sociodemographic or educational variables.

At 3 years postpartum, families that had earlier perceived their infant's crying as colic continued to be more likely to report dissatisfaction in daily family life (eg, unequal responsibility for household activities and fewer shared leisure activities), and their infants were reported to have more frequent problems falling asleep and more temper tantrums. These data do not contradict the results from our prospective cohort, as these outcomes are *perceived* problems and may not reflect actual differences in behavior. There were no other differences on measures of behavior problems (based on the Achenbach Child Behavior Checklist[28]), development (based on the Denver Developmental Screening Test[29]) or physical health, including allergies.

Forsyth and Canny[13, 30] also found that parental perceptions of their children are affected long after the colic period. Specifically, these investigators reported that infants who had crying, spitting, colic or feeding problems at 4 months of age were more likely than controls to be perceived as "vulnerable" (20% versus 11%) and as having behavioral problems (19% versus 11%) at 3½ years of age. There were no significant differences in reported prevalence of asthma (1.7% versus 4.4%) or eczema (8.8% versus 5.4%). Importantly, early diet modification increased the risk of being seen as vulnerable later in life.

Wolke and colleagues[14] followed a large (N = 432) community sample of infants in Germany from the age of 5 months to the age of 56 months. In this cohort, "actual" infant behavior *and* "perceived" behavioral problems were assessed by questionnaire. At 5 months of age, 32% of the infants were either *still having* a crying problem or had had a crying problem *before* 5 months of age. Compared with controls, parents of these children reported more night awakenings at 20 months of age (30% versus 17%, respectively) and more frequent cosleeping at 56 months of age (36% versus 23%). Regardless of these results, however, no significant association was found between crying behavior and later sleeping problems. Expressed parental *distress* about early problem behavior, rather than actual problem behavior itself, was associated with later difficulties. These results again illustrate the importance of parental perception of early behavior for subsequent child development and familial outcomes.

As part of a larger follow-up study of lead exposure, Sloman, Bellinger and Krentzel[15] interviewed mothers when their infants were 6 months old. Seventeen percent of the infants were considered to have had colic, defined as unsoothable crying for at least 1 hour per day for at least 1 month. The colic group, at 6 months of age, had lower scores on the mental and motor indices of the Bayley Scales of Infant Development,[27] and these differences were independent of several possible confounding factors. Differences were transient, however, and were not found at 12, 18 and 24 months. The authors suggested that early deficits shown by the colic group may represent a real, but transient, developmental lag, although such a lag has not been reported in other studies. Another interpretation is that the deficits shown by infants 6 months of age with prior colic reflects poor testability of the infants who were also rated as less responsive, unhappier during testing, less persistent and less able to maintain optimal functioning during the test. It is also unclear if these findings are affected by recall bias, with current negative behavior influencing reports of earlier colic.

Oberklaid and coinvestigators[16] followed a large (N = 1583) cohort of infants from 4 months of age to 8 months of age through to the preschool period (4 years of age to 5 years of age). In this study of temperament, infants' scores for colic, sleeping problems and excessive crying were summed. Children with scores in the upper quartile were considered to have *infant* behavior problems. When these children were compared with control children for preschool behavior problems, approximately 8% more of them scored high for such problems. The investigators suggest that parents' perceptions that they are raising a difficult infant may predict behavioral problems years later.

Summary

The longitudinal studies reviewed here suggest that the prognosis is good for infants with colic in relatively low-risk populations. As toddlers, their physical, cognitive and behavioral developments are comparable to those of toddlers who did not cry excessively as infants. Detailed studies reveal no differences between these children and age-matched peers on measures of temperament or sleep behavior. Transient differences reported for some cohorts at 5 months of age to 6 months of age may be related *less* to earlier colic and *more* to continued excessive crying and irritability in these children, which negatively affects testability.

The development of allergies later in life was no more common in previously colicky infants than in their noncolicky peers. This is important because the relationship between cow's milk intolerance and colic is still quite controversial. Clearly, some infants with crying problems are intolerant of cow's milk, and these children may benefit from a modified diet. Many other infants may not, however, and it is important to recall that a child who has a modified diet is at risk for being perceived as "vulnerable," even into toddlerhood.[13]

Despite few actual differences in child behavior between colic and control groups, differences in parental "perceptions" of behavior are consistently identified across cohorts. As toddlers, infants who were previously colicky are perceived as more difficult, as exhibiting more sleep problems and as more vulnerable than their peers. These negative views are potentially serious, as they may lead to behavior problems. A key issue for clinicians is the identification of, and intervention with, families prone to this negatively biased perception. A clue to this puzzle comes from comparing diagnoses of colic: A cohort with an "objective" diagnosis of excessive crying identified by audio recording in a nonreferred community sample had fewer negative outcomes. The more subjective the diagnosis of colic, the more often it is associated with negative outcomes. The tendency to "perceive" behavioral problems might be a pattern of parental behavior that becomes reinforced by increased crying by infants, leading to a vicious cycle of negative interaction. Generally, the families that a clinician would usually meet come from this group, as it is the perception of a crying problem that leads them to seek assistance.

In general, the treatment studies for colic have not been encouraging. However, elegant studies by van den Boom[31, 32] suggest that, in a group of families with irritable infants, relatively simple counseling about positive interaction improved outcomes. The follow-up study of excessively crying infants conducted by St. James-Roberts, Conroy and Wilsher showed that when mothers of highly negative 6-week-old infants held their babies more and increased their interaction with them, they were rewarded by a change from "high" to "low" infant negativity at 15 months. Another cohort of infants who fussed and cried little at 6 weeks whose mothers held and interacted with them very little exhibited highly negative behaviors at 15 months of age.[19]

Excessive crying in early infancy has been associated with problems in family interaction, maternal mood and early interaction in several cohorts. Most of these differences resolved as the crying resolved, although all cohorts were not followed long enough to show if all problems were transient. Some problems in family interaction resolved much later than the crying itself. The identification of families at risk for slow recovery represents another challenge for clinicians. Preexisting family problems may predispose some families to perceive infant crying as a problem. Controlled clinical trials should be performed with excessively crying infants to identify simple and practical interventions to help families cope during the stressful months.

References

1. Duncan DE, Briggs J, Bensimhon M. One deadly week. *Life.* 1996;52-58.
2. Lehtonen L, Gormally S, Barr RG. 'Clinical pies' for etiology and outcome in infants presenting with early increased crying. In: Barr RG, Hopkins B, Green JA, eds. *Crying as a Sign, a Symptom, & a Signal.* London, England: MacKeith Press; 2000:67-95.
3. Shaver BA. Maternal personality and early adaptation as related to infantile colic. In: Shereshefsky PM, Yarrow LJ, eds. *Psychological Aspects of a First Pregnancy and Early Postnatal Adaptation.* New York, NY: Raven Press; 1974:209-215.
4. Lehtonen L, Korhonen T, Korvenranta H. Temperament and sleeping patterns in colicky infants during the first year of life. *Journal of Developmental and Behavioral Pediatrics: JDBP.* 1994;15:416-420.
5. Keefe MR, Kotzer AM, Froese-Fretz A, Curtin M. A longitudinal comparison of irritable and nonirritable infants. *Nursing Research.* 1996;45:4-9.
6. St. James-Roberts I, Conroy S, Wilsher K. Links between maternal care and persistent infant crying in the early months. *Child: Care, Health and Development.* 1998;24:353-376.
7. Stifter CA, Braungart J. Infant colic: a transient condition with no apparent affects. *Journal of Applied Developmental Psychology.* 1992;13:447-462.
8. Stifter CA, Bono MA. The effect of infant colic on maternal self-perceptions and mother-infant attachment. *Child: Care, Health and Development.* 1998;24:339-351.
9. Elliott MR, Pedersen EL, Mogan J. Early infant crying: child and family follow-up at three years. *Canadian Journal of Nursing Research.* 1997;29:47-67.
10. Huhtala V, Lehtonen L, Heinonen R, Korvenranta H. Infant massage compared with crib vibrator in the treatment of colicky infants. *Pediatrics.* 2000;105:E84.
11. Rautava P, Helenius H, Lehtonen L. Psychosocial predisposing factors for infantile colic. *British Medical Journal.* 1993;307:600-604.
12. Rautava P, Lehtonen L, Helenius H, Sillanpää M. Infantile colic: child and family three years later. *Pediatrics.* 1995;96:43-47.
13. Forsyth BWC, Canny PF. Perceptions of vulnerability 3 1/2 years after problems of feeding and crying behavior in early infancy. *Pediatrics.* 1991;88:757-763.

14. Wolke D, Meyer R, Ohrt B, Riegel K. Co-morbidity of crying and feeding problems with sleeping problems in infancy. *Early Development and Parenting.* 1995;4:191-207.
15. Sloman J, Bellinger DC, Krentzel CP. Infantile colic and transient developmental lag in the first year of life. *Child Psychiatry and Human Development.* 1990;21:25-36.
16. Oberklaid F, Sanson A, Pedlow R, Prior M. Predicting preschool behavior problems from temperament and other variables in infancy. *Pediatrics.* 1993;91:113-120.
17. Barr RG. Colic and gas. In: Walker WA, Durie PR, Hamilton JR, Walker-Smith JA, Watkins JG, eds. *Pediatric Gastrointestinal Disease: Pathophysiology, Diagnosis, Management.* Burlington, Vt: BC Decker; 1991:55-61.
18. Wessel MA, Cobb JC, Jackson EB, Harris GS, Detwiler AC. Paroxysmal fussing in infancy, sometimes called "colic." *Pediatrics.* 1954;14:421-434.
19. St. James-Roberts I, Conroy S, Wilsher K. Stability and outcome of persistent infant crying. *Infant Behavior & Development.* 1998;21:411-435.
20. Lehtonen L. *Infantile Colic* [dissertation]. Turku, Finland: Turku University; 1994.
21. Räihä H, Lehtonen L, Korhonen T, Korvenranta H. Family life 1 year after infantile colic. *Archives of Pediatrics & Adolescent Medicine.* 1996;150:1032-1036.
22. Räihä H, Lehtonen L, Korhonen T, Korvenranta H. Family functioning 3 years after infantile colic. *Journal of Developmental and Behavioral Pediatrics: JDBP.* 1997;18:290-294.
23. Fullard W, McDevitt SC, Carey WB. Assessing temperament in one- to three-year-old children. *Journal of Pediatric Psychology.* 1984;9:205-217.
24. Kirjavainen J, Huhtala V, Kirjavainen T, Lehtonen L, Korvenranta H, Kero P. Colicky infants have normal sleep structure [abstract]. *Pediatric Academic Societies' 1999 Annual Meeting, San Francisco, Calif, 1-4 May 1999.*
25. Räihä H, Lehtonen L, Korvenranta H. Family context of infantile colic. *Journal of Infant Mental Health.* 1995;16:206-217.
26. Epstein NB, Baldwin LM, Bishop DS. The McMaster Family Assessment Device. *Journal of Marital and Family Therapy.* 1983;9:171-180.
27. Bayley N. *Manual for the Bayley Scales of Infant Development.* New York, NY: The Physiological Corporation; 1969.
28. Achenbach TM, Edelbrock C, Howell CT. Empirically based assessment of the behavioral/emotional problems of 2- and 3-year-old children. *Journal of Abnormal Child Psychology.* 1987;15:629-650.
29. Frankenburg WK, Dodds JB. The Denver developmental screening test. *The Journal of Pediatrics.* 1967;71:181-191.
30. Forsyth BWC. Colic and the effect of changing formulas: a double-blind, multiple-crossover study. *The Journal of Pediatrics.* 1989;115:521-526.
31. van den Boom DC. The influence of temperament and mothering on attachment and exploration: an experimental manipulation of sensitive responsiveness among lower-class mothers with irritable infants. *Child Development.* 1994;65:1457-1477.
32. van den Boom DC. Do first-year intervention effects endure? Follow-up during toddlerhood of a sample of Dutch irritable infants. *Child Development.* 1995;66:1798-1816.

Life After Unexplained Crying: Child and Parent Outcomes

Cynthia A. Stifter, PhD

Introduction

To date, few studies have examined the consequences of unexplained crying or infant colic. This may be because infant colic, though defined behaviorally, has come under the domain of pediatric medicine. Because infant colic is benign and ends by the third or fourth month of life it may seem insignificant, and less worthy of study, when compared with other childhood conditions and diseases. From a developmental perspective, however, infant colic provides an excellent opportunity for investigating several issues. Just as developmental psychology is informed by abnormal development, so, too, can the study of infants with colic and their contexts inform us about developmental processes.

Investigations of individual differences in infant crying have provided information about the continuity of temperament and its impact on the familial environment. Infant colic is characterized by extremes in crying and fussing, specifically in the duration and intensity of cry/fuss bouts, and by "inconsolability."[1, 2] Investigation of individual differences in infant crying has been useful in understanding the continuity of temperament and how it impacts the parenting environment. Consequently, the temperament construct most relevant to the present discussion is that of infant difficultness. Indeed, colic has been hypothesized to be one representation of difficult temperament, as difficult infants are characterized as fussy, irritable and hard to manage.[3] Moreover, maternal perceptions of difficultness have been corroborated by spectrographic analyses, which showed difficult infants' cries to be distinct from other infants' cries.[4] The negative impact of difficult/irritable infants on mothering has been well demonstrated.[5-7] For example, van den Boom showed that irritable infants are more likely than nonirritable infants to have unresponsive mothers and to develop insecure attachments.[7]

The study of infant colic—a condition that may be perceived as infant difficultness and its outcomes—may extend our current understanding of how childrens' own characteristics influence the environments in which they develop. Also, because infant colic begins and ends within the first 3 months of age, the study of colic provides an opportunity to examine how an intense and potentially stressful, but transitory, condition could have an impact on the short- and long-term behavior of both infants and parents. As may be reviewed in the text chapter by Lehtonen, currently available outcome studies suggest that infants who present with unexplained crying at 6 weeks are more likely to be perceived as having difficult temperament and sleep problems, even though their actual behavior is no different than controls. Whether these findings represent a temperament extreme is debatable, as only one study measured temperament before the onset of colic.[8] Also, the retrospective identification of colic in many studies may have influenced the report of infants' temperament at the time of measurement. The studies conducted by my colleagues and I are somewhat consistent with the aforementioned findings, and suggest that infant colic is a transitory condition, but one that may be associated with transient delays in certain developmental tasks.

Braungart,[8] Bono,[9] Spinrad[10] and I have conducted 2 longitudinal studies, which were truly prospective, as infants were assessed prior to the onset of colic, either at birth or at 2 weeks of age. All infants, those who developed colic and those who did not, were tracked for several months after the colic ended (up to at least 18 months of age in both studies). Although the investigations varied in several ways, the ages of the infants and the measures taken during the follow-up interactions were similar (Table 1). The goal of these studies was to investigate whether unexplained crying or infant colic represents a temperament extreme, is the product of maternal behavior or is a transitory condition that may or may not have consequences for later development. If infant colic were a temperamental extreme, then one would expect a continuity of reactivity regardless of developmental changes in crying. In other words, infants with colic would continue to exhibit high levels of reactivity after the colic period had resolved. If infant colic were related to parenting behavior during the colic period, assuming continuity of maternal sensitivity, one would predict negative outcomes related to maternal responsiveness, including lower maternal sensitivity and higher intrusiveness after the colic period.

Table 1. Measures Used in Study 1[8, 9] and Study 2[10]

Time of Measurement	Measure	Study 1	Study 2
3–5 weeks of age	Parent report of crying behavior	X	X
6 weeks of age	Colic and noncolic cry bouts	X	
	24-hour, 4-day cry diary		X
5 months of age	Infant reactivity (arm restraint)	X	X
	Infant regulation	X	X
	Infant temperament	X	X
	Maternal sensitivity/intrusiveness	X	X
	Maternal self-efficacy	X	X
	Marriage satisfaction (mother)	X	X
	Marriage satisfaction (father)		X
10 months of age	Infant reactivity (arm restraint)	X	X
	Infant regulation	X	X
	Infant temperament	X	X
	Maternal sensitivity/intrusiveness	X	X
	Maternal self-efficacy	X	
	Marriage satisfaction (mother)		X
	Marriage satisfaction (father)		X

Main Findings

Colic Identification

In both studies[8-10] parents were telephoned when their infants were 3 weeks, 4 weeks and 5 weeks of age and were asked questions about their infants' crying behaviors. "Colic" was not mentioned during these calls. In Study 1,[8, 9] the parents of infants identified through the phone calls as having colic, as well as parents of matched controls, completed questionnaires about the duration, intensity and consolability of their infants' cries and about the type and number of soothing techniques used. To be consistent with other studies on excessive crying Spinrad and I changed our methods slightly for Study 2,[10] asking parents to complete a 24-hour cry diary for 4 days when infants were 6 weeks old.

Through phone contacts in Study 1, 10 infants were identified as having colic. An equally sized comparison group, matched on several neonatal variables (sex, gestational age, birth weight, birth order and delivery method), was generated from the general sample. Colic was verified with descriptive data provided by the parents. As shown in Fig 1, the colic cries of the infants with colic were significantly longer and more intense than were the noncolic cries of both the colic and noncolic groups.

In Study 2 we identified 9 infants with colic based on information provided by parents during phone contacts. Because of the difficulty of applying

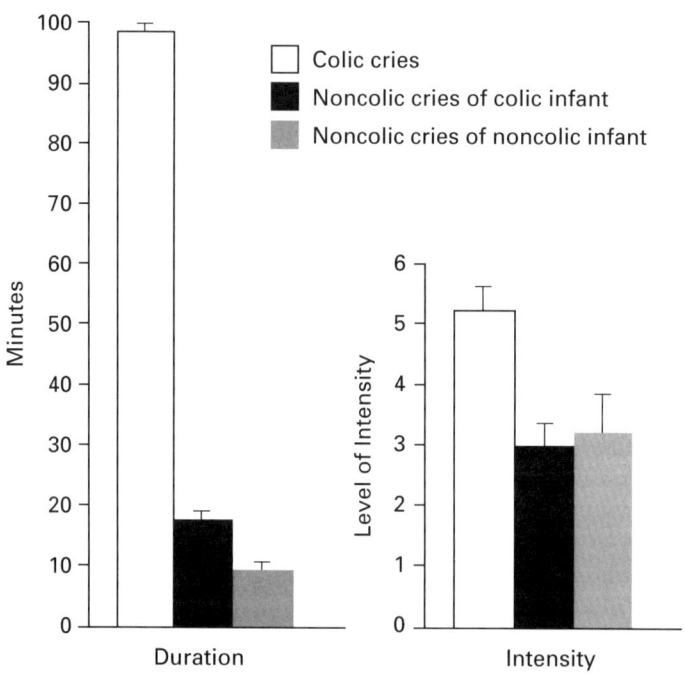

Fig 1. Cry duration and intensity for colic and noncolic infants in Study 1.[8-9]

Wessel's[1] criteria—crying of 3 hours per day for 3 or more days per week—the study sample was chosen using data reported by St. James-Roberts, Conroy and Wilsher[11] on persistent criers. In their study, infants who were persistent criers cried for 86 minutes per day, on average. This mean value was used as a criterion level for inclusion in the Study 2 colic group. All but one of the 9 infants identified previously met this criterion. (The one infant did not have complete diary data.) An additional 4 subjects who were not previously identified met the criterion for excessive crying (or colic defined this way). Finally, we included 5 infants who exhibited values above the daily mean for distress (ie, crying and fussing combined), as reported by St. James-Roberts, Conroy and Wilsher (221 minutes per day),[11] but who fell just below the cutoff value for excessive crying. Consequently, 16 children met our criteria for excessive crying (or colic). The remaining infants with completed diaries (n = 124) were considered to be typical criers. Comparisons of the means showed that excessive criers cried significantly longer and fussed significantly more frequently than typical criers. Moreover, as shown in Fig 2, the duration of daily fuss bouts for execessive criers was above the mean for fussing (135 minutes) reported by St. James-Roberts, Conroy and Wilsher.[11]

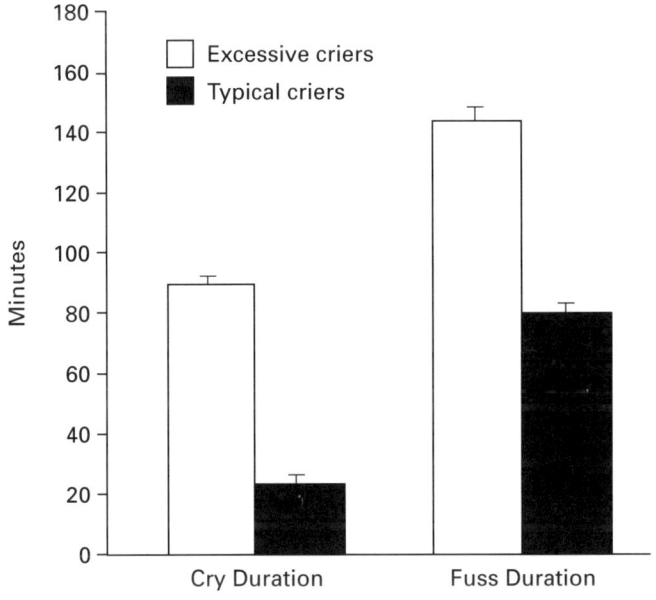

Fig 2. Diary measures of average cry and fuss durations for Study 2.[10]

Developmental Outcomes

Infant Reactivity and Regulation. The follow-up visits for both studies[8-10] were conducted in the laboratory when infants were 5 months and 10 months of age. These visits included procedures designed to elicit anger reactivity in the infants. In both studies at 5 months of age, anger reactivity was elicited using an arm-restraint procedure. At 10 months of age, anger reactivity was measured during a toy removal task in Study 1[8,9] and with arm restraint in Study 2.[10] Negative reactivity was coded from videotapes using a 5-point scale in Study 1 and a 3-point scale in Study 2. Both scales were based on the frequency and intensity of facial and vocal expressions exhibited. The infants' abilities to regulate their emotional responses to these mildly aversive tasks were also noted. Regulatory behaviors, such as reorienting, self-comforting, escape behaviors and nonnegative communicative vocalizations and gestures, were coded moment by moment, and the proportions of time spent using particular strategies were calculated. In addition to studying the infants, my colleagues and I obtained information from the mothers regarding their perceptions of their infants' temperaments by asking them to complete the Infant Behavior Questionnaire.[12]

In Study 1,[8-9] infants who had colic were compared with both the matched group and the general sample on the outcome variables. No significant differences were found between groups for anger reactivity at 5 months or 10 months of age. The matched comparison group was similar in all respects to the general sample. Because reactivity was negatively correlated with regulation, we analyzed differences in regulation controlling for level of reactivity. Interestingly, while there were no differences at 10 months of age, at 5 months of age infants in the colic group exhibited *more* regulatory behaviors than infants who had not had colic. We observed the opposite pattern in Study 2.

Study 2[10] revealed 2 important differences at 5 months of age between excessive criers and typical criers in response to arm restraint. Excessive criers were more reactive to arm restraint, and they showed fewer regulatory strategies when the level of reactivity was statistically controlled. At 10 months of age, no differences were found.

We also found inconsistent results regarding infant temperament between the 2 studies. Interestingly, the results of both studies indicated that, contrary to our expectations, mothers' perceptions of their infants' temperament mirrored observed behavior. That is, in Study 1, no differences in temperament were found at 5 months or 10 months of age between the infants with and without colic, and no differences were found between these groups for maternal report of temperament at either age as well. In contrast, in Study 2, 5 month olds in the excessive crying group showed more anger reactivity and fewer regulatory strategies than peers in the typical criers group. Again, maternal reports mirrored these results: Mothers of 5 month olds in the excessive crier group rated their children as more anger reactive (M = 3.70) than did mothers of typical criers (M = 3.16). Further, in Study 2, there were no differences in anger reactivity and regulatory strategies at 10 months of age; similarly, no differences were found in maternal reports of temperament at 10 months of age either.

In sum, infant outcome data were inconsistent across the 2 studies, with Study 1 revealing few differences between infants who had colic previously and their peers, and Study 2 demonstrating some continuity of reactivity to 5 months of age. However, no differences in infant behavior or maternal ratings of temperament were present at 10 months of age. In both studies, mothers' descriptions of their infants' temperament accurately reflected the behavioral differences, or lack thereof, between the typical and excessive criers.

Maternal Behavior. In a separate study by Fish, Belsky and I,[13] maternal behavior during a free play session was coded for sensitivity and intrusiveness. Sensitivity is a global construct, but it involves several types of behavior, including appropriate stimulation and responsiveness to infant cues. Maternal behavior scores were based on contingent, infant-centered interactions. Unfortunately, it was not possible to measure maternal behavior prior to the onset of colic, but paper-and-pencil measures of maternal personality and responsiveness to infant crying did not reveal differences between mothers whose infants developed colic and those whose infants did not.

Similarly in Study 1, we found no differences for measures of maternal behavior when infants were 5 months and 10 months old between infants with colic and the general sample. This result was replicated in Study 2. Evidence from both studies suggests that colic, or excessive crying, does not have a negative im-pact on how mothers respond to their infants.

The mother-infant attachment relationship also provides information about maternal behavior. Because attachment is proposed to reflect a history of warm, consistent and responsive social interactions with the caregiver, attachment security was used as a proxy for maternal sensitivity in our studies. We were also interested in determining, from a temperament perspective, whether infants with colic would develop insecure attachments, as noted by van den Boom.[7] Attachment was assessed in Study 1, when the infants were 18 months of age, using the Strange Situation,[14] which allows researchers to observe an infant's emotional reactions to a series of exits and entrances by the mother and a stranger when the infant is in a strange place. The infant's interest in the comings and goings—distress at departure of the mother and ability to be calmed upon her return—are used to determine the nature of the attachment between mother and child. Results of this investigation suggest that colic does not negatively affect the formation of a secure attachment relationship. Indeed, only 2 of the 10 (20%) infants with colic exhibited insecure attachment behaviors, and these were of the anxious/resistant (C) type, while 27% of the noncolic infants were insecurely attached (12 A's; 5 C's).

Maternal Self-efficacy. Mothers in both studies completed a questionnaire that assessed feelings of parental competence.[13] Results were consistent across the studies. Mothers of colicky/excessive criers were more likely to have lower self-efficacy than mothers of typical criers, as shown in Fig 3. (Recall that these measures were taken after the colic had ended.) In an earlier report[9] Bono and I hypothesized that once mothers had more positive interactions with their infants (ie, infants were more responsive to mothers' attempts to soothe), mothers would no longer have feelings of parental incompetence. To explore this idea, mothers in Study 2 completed the self-efficacy questionnaire at the 10-month visit, as well. Contrary to our hypothesis, mothers of excessive criers continued to rate themselves lower on parenting self-efficacy. The persistence of this perception, however, does not appear to be related to the infants' continued differences in regulation, as none of the correlations between reactivity and regulation and maternal self-efficacy were significant for either group or for the sample as a whole.

Marital Satisfaction. Caring for an inconsolable child not only has the potential to stress the relationship between caregiver and child, but it can also stress the caregiver's relationships with others. Studies of the transition to parenthood suggest that the introduction of a child (even one who does not cry excessively) affects both parents' perceptions of their marriage.[15] To explore this issue, measures of marital satisfaction were included in both studies.[8-10] In Study 1, mothers' marital satisfaction[16] was assessed at 5 months of age. In

Fig 3. Maternal self-efficacy at 5 months and 10 months for Study 1[8, 9] *and Study 2.*[10]

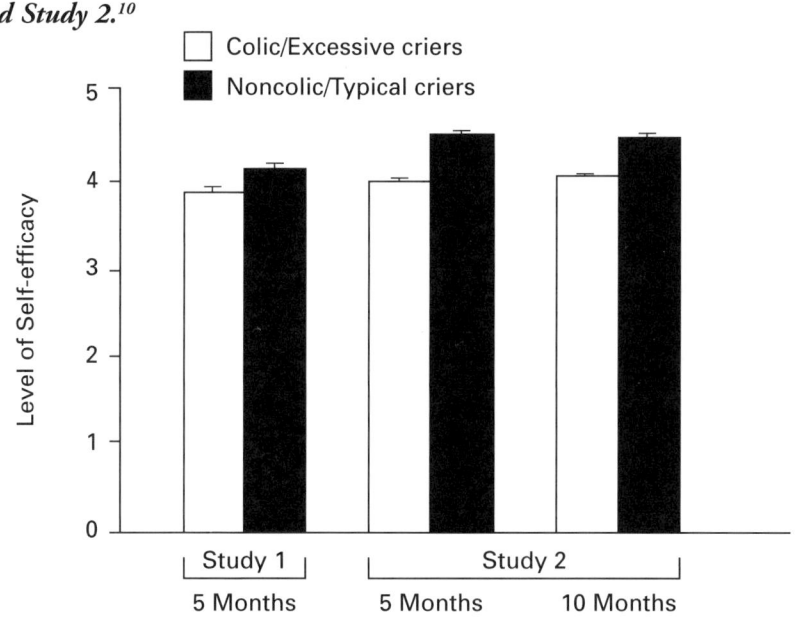

Study 2, mothers' and fathers' marital satisfaction was measured at 5 months and 10 months of age to examine the long-term effects of excessive crying in early infancy.

Mothers of infants with colic in Study 1 rated the positive (love and maintenance) and negative (conflict and ambivalence) aspects of their marriages similarly to mothers in the noncolic group. In Study 2, however, short- and long-term correlates for excessive crying were identified. Both mothers and fathers of excessive criers rated their marriages as significantly more negative at 5 months and at 10 months of age. Also, mothers of excessive criers endorsed fewer positive aspects of their marriages than mothers of typical criers at both times. Thus, it may be that the high level of reactivity of the infants has a significant impact on the relationship between the parents of excessive criers. This may involve mothers especially, since they tend to spend more time taking care of their babies. In their cry diaries, parents indicated who was caring for their infants when they were crying. As expected, mothers spent an average of 40 more minutes with their infants when they were crying than did fathers (60 minutes versus 20 minutes). The fathers' marital satisfaction may be an outcome of the mothers' dissatisfaction, as mothers' and fathers' ratings were highly correlated in both groups at both ages (r values = .34 to .63).

Discussion

The effects of infant colic or excessive crying on infant and parent outcomes are not completely clear. However, data from several reports indicate some differences between the anger reactivity and regulatory behaviors of infants with prior colic and their peers without colic, suggesting that colic may delay the development of self-regulatory behaviors. Further, maternal reports of infant temperament mirrored the infant behavior differences that were found. Mothers in the colic and noncolic groups interacted similarly with their children, and no differences in maternal sensitivity were found.

Before discussing these findings, it is important to explore the reasons why some results were inconsistent between studies. Most important among these are the results concerning infant reactivity and regulation at 5 months of age. Differences could result from methodologic differences in the creation of the Study 1[8,9] and Study 2[10] colic groups. Recall that in both studies, children with colic or excessive crying were identified by querying parents by telephone about the crying behavior of their children at 3 weeks, 4 weeks and 5 weeks of age. In Study 1, however, parents' responses were not validated with a cry diary, as they were in Study 2. Rather, parents were asked to complete forms on a noncolic cry bout and a colic cry bout.[17] Relatively recent information suggests that parents who believed their child had colic, when in fact they did not, defined colic differently than did parents whose infants developed colic.[18] For example, they did not use the characteristic of "intense crying" to define colic. It may be that some of the parents in Study 1 perceived the intensity of fussing as colic, resulting in the inclusion of infants who were fussy but not colicky. Study 2, on the other hand, used cry diaries to determine whether infants were excessive criers and excluded infants who were only extremely fussy. And, of the 9 infants identified through phone contacts, 7 were excessive criers. Despite the contrasting methods used in the 2 studies, several important results emerged regarding the possible effects of unexplained crying on parenting behavior and attitudes.

Parenting. It was hypothesized previously that the stress of caring for an infant who cries intensely and cannot be soothed would have a negative impact on mothering behavior. Two studies from our laboratory and findings from another laboratory[17] now confirm that this is *not* the case. When interacting with their infants, mothers of infants with colic looked remarkably similar to mothers of infants who did not have colic. This similarity was found whether maternal behavior was measured immediately after colic had ended[8, 17] or several months later.[8, 10] The findings about attachment provide further evidence, as secure attachment is proposed to be dependent upon a history of warm, responsive mothering. My colleagues and I found that infants who had colic were as likely to be securely attached to their mothers as infants who did not have colic.[8-10] Parental sensitivity is characterized by contingent, appropriate responses to an infant's cues. Perhaps the dramatic change from a screaming, difficult infant to one who is more quiescent and responsive allows the mother to display appropriate, sensitive behavior. It is important to note that we did not measure maternal behavior during the colic period. St. James-Roberts, Conroy and Wilsher[17] reported a modest difference between mothers of infants who had and who didn't have colic on sensitivity and affection at 6 weeks, although the majority of mothers exhibited optimum behavior. Thus, while the crying behavior of an infant with colic may contemporaneously affect maternal behavior, this effect seems to resolve once colic has remitted.

Colic seems to exert a more lasting effect on a mother's feelings of efficacy. Another consistent finding in our studies[8-10] was that mothers of infants who had colic felt less competent as parents than mothers whose infants did not have colic. This finding is not surprising when the intensity and duration of an infant's crying is considered. Such feelings may be compounded by the infant's "inconsolability." The ability to respond with success to an infant's needs forms the basis of maternal self-efficacy. Donovan and Leavitt[19] have shown that feelings of maternal incompetence are likely to develop when attempts to soothe are met with failure.

Caring for an infant who has colic also appears to affect marital relationships. This is true for both mothers and fathers. While the introduction of a child normally affects marital satisfaction, the addition of an infant who cries intensely and inconsolably may increase the strain a child places on a marriage. Mothers, who appear to do the majority of caring for the infant with colic, were dissatisfied with both the positive (love and maintenance) and negative (conflict and ambivalence) aspects of their marriages. Fathers reported increases in the negative aspects only. Cowan and Cowan[15] showed that mothers and fathers have similar ideas about who cares for a crying infant (the mother), but have very different outcomes regarding marital satisfaction. These associations appear to be dependent upon the father's involvement in childcare. For families in which fathers were more involved, mothers reported more satisfaction. On the other hand, fathers' positive feelings about their marriages were dependent upon their satisfaction with the division of labor. For parents of infants with colic, lower marital satisfaction may arise from the mother's role combined with the stress of caring for an inconsolable child. Mothers may resent fathers' lack of involvement in caring for the infant with colic, while fathers may be indirectly affected due to mothers' negative feelings. Because negative effects on the marital relationship may last well beyond the colic period, longitudinal studies of the marriage dynamics of parents of infants with colic are warranted.

In sum, the results of our longitudinal studies[8-10] suggest that excessive crying or infant colic affects maternal feelings of parenting efficacy as well as the marital relationship. It is remarkable that, despite these negative feelings, mothers of infants with colic were just as responsive to their infants as were their counterparts. It appears that mothers can effectively separate their feelings from their behavior when they interact with an infant who cries for no apparent reason.

Infant Reactivity and Regulation. The results of Study 2, but not Study 1, also suggested continuity of negative reactivity after the colic period; therefore, the following discussion is limited to the results of Study 2.[10] Infants who cried excessively at 6 weeks of age were more reactive in response to a mildly frustrating stimulus at age 5 months. Indeed, they were 5 times as likely as noncolicky peers to be highly reactive at the age of 5 months. However, at 10 months of age there was no difference in reactivity between the 2 groups. Similar findings were reported by St. James-Roberts, Conroy and Wilsher, who used diary data, rather than laboratory visits, to measure reactivity. They, too, found a high likelihood for excessive criers to be more negative than their peers at 5 months but not at 15 months of age.

Our data on infants' ability to regulate distress mirrored our findings on negative reactivity.[8-10] Infants who were excessive criers at 6 weeks of age showed less regulatory behavior at 5 months than did infants who exhibited typical crying. While this result might seem obvious, given the infants' level of distress, differences remained even when the effect of distress level was statistically controlled. It is more important to note that this difference did not persist. Excessive criers resembled typical criers on measures of both reactivity and regulation at 10 months of age.

The pattern that emerges is consistent with delayed regulation of crying, which is possibly related to excessive crying in early infancy. It has been proposed that infants may require a certain level of reactivity in order to elicit responses from the environment.[20, 21] Through sensitive interactions with the caregiver, infants learn that certain behaviors are associated with the modulation of arousal. However, at the extreme level, particularly for infants who are difficult to console,[11, 22] this associative learning may be inhibited, resulting in a delay in the emergence of self-regulatory abilities. In other words, while an infant's intense crying brings the caregiver in close contact, difficulty consoling the infant may prevent adequate soothing to the level necessary for the parent to introduce new strategies. Evidence for this idea comes from work that demonstrated that reorientation or distraction strategies are effective only at low levels of distress.[23] An alternate explanation for the apparent delay in the development of self-regulation may be that extremes in crying may prevent the infant from making the associations between the caregiver's behavior and the infant's decreased feelings of negative arousal. Studies have also shown that infant crying may inhibit memory performance.[24, 25] Thus, although parental attempts to console may be appropriate, and in some cases may lead to a reduction in arousal, infants with colic may not be able to retain the correspondence between the caregiver's behavior and the experience of regulation. Colic generally ends by 3 months to 4 months of age, thereby providing new opportunities for the caregiver and infant to experience successful soothing and associative learning. As a result, there appears to be a dramatic rise in self-regulatory behaviors at older ages, as demonstrated by the excessive criers in Study 2.

The change in negative reactivity from 5 months to 10 months of age observed in the laboratory at Penn State was confirmed by parental reports of temperament. Mothers of excessive criers rated their infants as more distressed by limitations (anger-reactive) than typical criers at 5 months but not at 10 months of age. Interestingly, this was the only temperament dimension on which the groups differed. Thus, not only were excessive criers more reactive in the laboratory context but they also exhibited more anger, and likely less regulation, in other contexts at 5 months of age. These data contrast with research findings on the convergence of laboratory and questionnaire measures, which generally indicate low agreement between behavior exhibited in the laboratory and parental reports.[26] It may be that greater agreement is achieved when extremes in behavior are observed and measured.

Conclusions

Barr and Gunnar[27] recently proposed their "transitory responsivity" hypothesis concerning the nature of colic. They provided 2 important arguments about colic that are relevant to the goals of our studies. First, these investigators suggest that infant colic is a transitory condition. The evidence they reviewed, which includes findings from our laboratory, strongly supports this position. Second, they correctly argue that measures of reactivity at any time point are likely the product of both the infant's reaction and the regulatory processes that come into play. Because of this interdependence, the present work examined differences in regulation by statistically controlling for reactivity. Our results suggest that differences in regulation may extend beyond the intense crying period observed from 1 month to 3 months.[8-10] Because parents of excessive criers appear to be sensitive and responsive caregivers, the delay in the development of self-regulatory skills may be only as long as 5 months.

The 2 studies[8-10] reviewed for this presentation have some limitations. Small sample sizes may have contributed to differences that were not statistically significant. Future studies should be conducted with larger samples before definitive conclusions can be made about the impact of infant colic, particularly on parenting behavior. Also, inconsistency across the 2 studies with regard to infant reactivity and regulation warrants further investigation of these outcome parameters. Despite these limitations, these data add to growing evidence that infant colic is a transitory condition that continues to have effects, particularly on family life, after the excessive crying has ended.

Acknowledgments

This research was supported by grants from the National Institute of Mental Health (MH44324) and the National Institute for Child Health and Development (HD27325). Special thanks go to the families that participated in both studies and to the numerous graduate and undergraduate students who assisted with the projects.

References

1. Wessel MA, Cobb JC, Jackson EB, Harris GS, Detwiler AC. Paroxysmal fussing in infancy, sometimes called "colic." *Pediatrics.* 1954;14:421-434.
2. Barr RG. The colic enigma: prolonged episodes of a normal predisposition to cry. *Infant Mental Health Journal.* 1990;11:340-348.
3. Bates JE. The concept of difficult temperament. *Merrill-Palmer Quarterly.* 1980;26:299-319.
4. Lounsbury ML, Bates JE. The cries of infants of differing levels of perceived temperamental difficultness: acoustic properties and effects on listeners. *Child Development.* 1982;53:677-686.
5. Bates JE. Temperament in infancy. In: Osofsky JD, ed. *Handbook of Infant Development.* 2nd ed. New York, NY: John Wiley & Sons; 1987:1101-1149.
6. Mangelsdorf S, Gunnar M, Kestenbaum R, Lang S, Andreas D. Infant proneness-to-distress temperament, maternal personality, and mother-infant attachment: associations and goodness of fit. *Child Development.* 1990;61:820-831.
7. van den Boom D. Neonatal irritability and the development of attachment. In: Kohnstamm GA, Bates JE, Rothbart MK, eds. *Temperament in Childhood.* New York, NY: John Wiley & Sons; 1989:299-318.
8. Stifter CA, Braungart J. Infant colic: a transient condition with no apparent effects. *Journal of Applied Developmental Psychology.* 1992;13:447-462.
9. Stifter CA, Bono MA. The effect of infant colic on maternal self-perceptions and mother-infant attachment. *Child: Care, Health and Development.* 1998;24:339-351.
10. Stifter CA, Spinrad T. The effect of excessive crying on the development of emotion regulation. *Infancy.* In press.
11. St. James-Roberts I, Conroy S, Wilsher K. Clinical, developmental and social aspects of infant crying and colic. *Early Development and Parenting.* 1995;4:177-189.
12. Rothbart MK. The measurement of infant temperament. *Child Development.* 1981;52:569-578.
13. Fish M, Stifter CA, Belsky J. Conditions of continuity and discontinuity in infant negative emotionality: newborn to five months. *Child Development.* 1991;62:1525-1537.
14. Ainsworth M, Wittig B. Attachment and exploratory behavior of one year olds in a Strange Situation. In: Foss B, ed. *Determinants of Infant Behavior.* London, England: Methuen; 1969:113-136.
15. Cowan CP, Cowan PA. Who does what when partners become parents: implications for men, women, and marriage. *Marriage & Family Review.* 1988;12:105-131.
16. Braiker H, Kelly H. Conflict in the development of close relationships. In: Burgess RL, Huston TL, eds. *Social Exchange in Developing Relationships.* New York, NY: Academic Press; 1979:79-102.
17. St. James-Roberts I, Conroy S, Wilsher K. Links between maternal care and persistent infant crying in the early months. *Child: Care, Health and Development.* 1998;24:353-376.

18. Stifter CA. Short- and long-term consequences of excessive crying: a case for differentiating perceptions of colic from more objectively-based assessments. Paper presented at: Biennial International Conference on Infant Studies; April 1998; Atlanta, Ga.
19. Donovan WL, Leavitt LA. Simulating conditions of learned helplessness: the effects of interventions and attributions. *Child Development.* 1985;56:594-603.
20. Kopp C. Regulation of distress and negative emotions: a developmental perspective. *Developmental Psychology.* 1989;25:343-354.
21. Stifter CA, Spinrad TL, Braungart-Rieker JM. Toward a developmental model of child compliance: the role of emotion regulation in infancy. *Child Development.* 1999;70:21-32.
22. White BP, Gunnar MR, Larson MC, Donzella B, Barr RG. Behavioral and physiological responsivity, sleep, and patterns of daily cortisol production in infants with and without colic. *Child Development.* 2000;71:862-877.
23. Stifter CA, Braungart JB. The regulation of negative reactivity: function and development. *Developmental Psychology.* 1995;38:448-455.
24. Ohr PS, Fleckenstein LK, Fagen JW, Klein SJ, Pioli LM. Cry-producing forgetting in infants: a contextual analysis. *Infant Behavior and Development.* 1990;13:305-320.
25. Wachs TD, Morrow J, Slabach EH. Intra-individual variability in infant visual recognition memory performance: temperamental and environmental correlates. *Infant Behavior and Development.* 1990;13:397-403.
26. Slabach EH, Morrow J, Wachs TD. Questionnaire measurement of infant and child temperament: current status and future directions. In: Strelau J, Angleitner A, eds. *Explorations in Temperament: International Perspectives on Theory and Measurement.* London, England: Plenum Publishing; 1991:205-234.
27. Barr RG, Gunnar M. Colic: the transient responsivity hypothesis. In: Barr RG, Hopkins B, Green JA, eds. *Crying as a Sign, a Symptom, & a Signal.* London, England: MacKeith Press; 2000:41-66.

Clinical Perspectives on Unexplained Early Crying: Challenges and Risks for Infant Mental Health and Parent-Infant Relationships

Mechthild Papoušek, MD, Harald Wurmser, PhD and Nikolaus von Hofacker, MD

Introduction

This report is a follow-up of 60, 1- to 6-month-old infants who were brought to the Munich Interdisciplinary Research and Intervention Program for Fussy Babies because of parental concerns about their persistent crying. Despite having passed the peak age of 6 weeks, or even the 3-month developmental shift found in the majority of cases, these infants had continued to display particularly high levels of distress for long periods of time, with lasting problems of sleep-wake organization, transient neuromotor immaturity and difficult temperament. In addition, a large proportion of these families were found to be burdened with an accumulation of organic and psychosocial risks.

By comparing these 60 infants with 45 age-matched controls at 30 months of age, our aim is to examine the factors and processes, particularly in the arena of everyday mother-infant interactions, which may maintain or exacerbate the crying problem and promote long-term unfavorable outcomes.

Responding to Parents' Concerns: The Munich Interdisciplinary Research and Intervention Program for Fussy Babies

No matter what causes or contributes to persistent unexplained crying in the early months, it exerts immediate effects on the mother's psychological state, particularly on her feelings of self-efficacy in her new role as a mother.

Converging evidence from studies using audiovisual or auditory playback of infant cries and community studies of infants with Wessel's colic[1] suggests that being exposed to inconsolable crying promotes affective arousal, autonomic signs of acute stress and feelings of helplessness, anxiety, depression, anger, ambivalence and aversive tendencies toward the baby.[2] Aggressive fantasies and guilty feelings in relation to the baby are as common as distress in the parents' relationship and problems in their transition to parenthood.

The good news for parents is that the traditional view of excessive crying as a self-limiting condition has been confirmed by several recent prospective studies reviewed thoroughly by Liisa Lehtonen in this volume. Unexplained crying is closely linked to the first 3 months of infancy and usually fades away with hardly any long-term effects that can be measured objectively. The bad news is that parents' concerns about their babies do not seem to fade away at a similar pace. On average, mothers of infants with Wessel's colic continue to perceive their child as more vulnerable and more difficult to handle and as having more problems and temper tantrums. Their family relationships also continue to be more distressed, and the mothers continue to feel less competent and less self-confident in their mothering role. Other bad news is derived from clinical reports and retrospective studies of preschoolers and school children with symptoms of attention deficit hyperactivity disorder, disorders of sensory integration and other externalizing or internalizing behavior disorders. The majority of these infants are reported to have started their careers of behavioral difficulties in the early months with excessive crying and sleeping problems.

The striking discrepancies between these good and bad news reports call for an explanation, because parents of excessively crying babies are often left alone with an immediate concern and threatening fantasies of having to raise a hyperactive, tyrannical child with imminent failures of learning and social integration. It has been argued repeatedly that long-term negative outcomes of early excessive crying may not be related to the early crying problem, per se, but to preexisting problems in the mother's psychological condition or family relationships, as evidenced, for instance, during pregnancy or prior to becoming pregnant. Such a one-sided explanation can put an additional burden on the mother and family by making them responsible for having a colicky baby, potentially with a long-term negative outcome.

One way to explore this dilemma more closely is to take a clinical perspective from the beginning and study a clinical subgroup of infants with unexplained early crying whose parents seek help from a specialized program. Such an approach allows us to:

- Review those factors in the infant's and parents' histories that may have contributed to the crying problem
- Observe and analyze the impact of inconsolable crying on maternal perception and the dynamic processes involved in the ontogeny of early interactional failures and distressed parent-infant relationships
- Identify those factors that put these infants and their mothers and families at risk for long-term negative outcomes

With this in mind, an interdisciplinary team—a pediatrician, developmental psychologist, infancy researcher and a psychiatrist—opened the Munich Interdisciplinary Research and Intervention Program for Fussy Babies in 1991 with 2 integrated goals: to offer comprehensive diagnostic and intervention services to clinically referred families with excessively crying infants and to investigate the etiology, symptomatology and immediate and long-term effects of unexplained early crying on infant behavioral development and parent-infant relationships. The program is based on a clinical model,[2] which has, at its core, the concept of intuitive parenting.[3] According to this model, early adaptational and regulatory demands, such as regulation of behavioral states, sleep-wake organization, affective arousal and attention, are coregulated within everyday parent-infant interactions. These interactions may fail or succeed depending on the dynamic reciprocities between the infant's regulatory competencies and constraints on one side and the parents' intuitive regulatory support on the other. The model takes a dynamic systems perspective in order to account for the complex network of interrelated risk factors on the part of the infant, the parents, the family and the social context, at large, which may affect each or both of the interacting partners unfavorably.

Up to the present time, 1800 families have been referred to, and diagnosed and treated in the program. To our surprise, only approximately one third of these infants were referred because of persistent crying at an age at or below 6 months. Most of the older infants (7 months to 30 months of age at the time of referral) also presented with a problem of fussiness and crying; however, these were present in relation to other problems of behavioral regulation, such as sleeping problems, feeding problems and failure to thrive, excessive clinging and social withdrawal, separation anxiety, excessive temper tantrums and early forms of aggressive behavior problems. According to a detailed diagnostic interview with the mothers, 80% of these older infants and toddlers had a history of several months of early unexplained crying. More-over, even in spite of effective early intervention, more than 40% of the 1- to 6-month-old excessively crying infants were referred again at a later age because of one or more of the behavior problems mentioned previously. These findings are concordant with other clinical retrospective reports and point to a considerable long-term risk in clinical populations.

This presentation summarizes our current evidence on whether families who seek help from specialists because of their babies' crying differ from those who are able to cope without help. Therefore, the following questions are asked: Are clinically referred infants simply more extreme in their crying problem, or do they differ in other aspects of their behavioral makeup? Are the mothers simply more vulnerable or less able to cope due to other risk factors? Can we find indices of emerging unfavorable processes in early mother-infant relationships to which both infant and parental factors contribute and which might be related to later negative outcome? The second, and larger, part of this chapter reports on a follow-up study when the infants were 30-months old.

Sample and Procedures at the Time of Clinical Referral

We report on a clinical group of 60 infants between 1 month and 6 months of age (mean age, 4.1 ± 1.5 months) referred to the Munich Interdisciplinary Research and Intervention Program for Fussy Babies because of crying problems. This group was compared to a control group (mean age 37.13 months), which was recruited from the general community by birth an-nouncements in the local newspaper and matched to the clinical group by age, sex and birth status. Both groups were reexamined at 30 months. It is noteworthy that 95% of the infants in both samples were older than age 6 weeks, and 60% had passed the age of 3 months, at recruitment.

At referral, the clinical group was divided into 2 subgroups based on parents' 24-hour diary records of the average daily amounts of infants' crying and fussing. Extreme criers (n = 30) cried and fussed for more than 3 hours per day, averaged across 5 consecutive days. Moderate criers (n = 30) also presented with a crying problem, but cried and fussed for less than 3 hours per day, on average. According to mothers' reports, 11 of the control infants (24.4%) had gone through a transient crying problem with a peak around the age of 6 weeks, but no longer presented a crying problem. In spite of retrospective assessment, the proportions of transient and persistent crying problems in the control group correspond well with reported prevalence rates in community samples.[4]

All subjects were invited for 2 sessions to undergo the same sequence of standardized diagnostic procedures. Measures, constructs and results have been reported in detail in previous publications[5-8]; individual measures[9-16] are summarized in Table 1.

At referral, a pediatrician and a psychologist conducted a semistructured neuropediatric and psychological diagnostic interview focused on pregnancy, birth and postnatal adaptation, as well as on the pediatric and developmental history of the infant and the mother's psychological status, childhood experiences, quality of marital and family relationships and social support systems. Cumulative risk scores were computed from weighted (none/moderate/severe) individual biologic and psychosocial risk factors.

The average daily amounts and diurnal distributions of crying, fussing and sleeping were computed from a 24-hour diary kept by the mother for 5 consecutive days. Mothers completed standardized questionnaires and self-rating scales to obtain information on various dimensions of infant temperament and the mother's psychological state—including her childcare attitudes, feelings towards the child, feelings of self-efficacy and signs of postnatal depression and marital dissatisfaction.

Independently, the pediatrician and psychologist in charge assessed the functional and adaptive qualities of the relationship between mother and infant on the Parent-Infant-Relationship Global-Assessment-Scale (PIR-GAS), a 9-point rating scale ranging from "well adapted" (90) to "severely impaired" (10).

Table 1. Measures and Constructs at Data Points I and II

	Measure	Construct
Data Point I (1 month to 6 months)	Semistructured neuropediatric and psychologic diagnostic interview (adapted from Esser et al[9])	Biological and psychosocial risk factors related to pregnancy, birth and postnatal adaptation, pediatric and developmental history of the infant, the psychological state of the mother, family relationships, social support systems
	5-day, 24-hour behavior diary	Average daily amounts of crying, fussing and sleeping
	Standardized questionnaires	
	– Infant Characteristics Questionnaire (ICQ[10]) for 4-month-olds	Infant temperament (difficult, unpredictable, unadaptable)
	– Einstellungen von Muettern zu Kindern im Kleinst-kindalter (Maternal Childcare Attitudes and Feelings–EMKK[11])	Maternal childcare attitudes and feelings (pleasure with infant, depressed mood, physical exhaustion, frustration, anxious overprotection, punitive tendencies, rejection, rigidity)
	– Maternal Self-Confidence Scale (MSCS[12])	Maternal feelings of self-efficacy
	– Edinburgh Postpartum Depression Scale (EPDS[13])	Postpartum depression
	– Belastungen in der Partnerschaft (Marital Distress-BELPAR[14])	Marital dissatisfaction
	Parent-Infant-Relationship Global-Assessment-Scale (PIR-GAS[15])	Quality of the parent-infant relationship
Data Point II (30 months)	5-day, 24-hour sleep diary	Average daily amounts of sleeping and night awakenings
	Standardized questionnaires	
	– Infant Characteristics Questionnaire (ICQ[10]), adapted version for 24-month-olds	Toddler temperament (difficult, unstoppable, negative adaptation, dependent, sober, irregular)
	– Child Behavior Checklist for 2- to 3-year-old children (CBCL/2-3[16])	Behavioral and emotional problems (aggressive behavior, anxious/depressed, destructive behavior, sleep problems, somatic problems, social withdrawal, internalizing, externalizing)

Expert ratings were based on all information and observations obtained during 2 assessment sessions. Cases of disagreement were discussed in an expert session until agreement was obtained.

Findings: Do infants and their mothers who seek help from specialists because of a crying problem differ from community-based controls?

In spite of having passed the peak age of 6 weeks or even the 3-month developmental shift in the majority of cases, extreme criers continued to fuss and cry for 4.6 ± 1.3 hours per day up to the age of 6 months, and moderate criers continued for 2.2 ± 0.5 hours, as compared with 1.1 ± 0.7 hours in the control group. The overall severity of the crying problem differed significantly among the 3 groups on several measures: not only by the amount and intensity of crying and fussing, but also by signs of neuromotor immaturity, the number of dysregulated behavioral domains (soothing, settling to sleep, feeding, alert waking or sleeping), the absolute duration of the problem and the proportion of undisturbed time since birth. The average amounts of crying and fussing were associated significantly with a reduction in total sleep duration and various measures of immature circadian and ultradian sleep-wake organization. In a similar vein, the 3 groups differed substantially in infant temperament: The higher the infants' daily amounts of fussing and crying, the more they were rated by their mothers as difficult, unpredictable and unadaptable.

Significant differences among the 3 groups were also found in parental and family variables: Mothers of both extreme criers and moderate criers rated themselves as significantly more exhausted, depressed and anxious than control mothers, as less self-efficacious in their maternal role and as more dissatisfied with their marital relationship. Similarly, parent-infant relationships were rated as significantly more distressed in both referred groups. The rate of clinically relevant postnatal depression (according to Edinburgh Postnatal Depression Scale [EPDS] scores above the cutoff of 12[13]) was 3 times higher in the referred groups than in the control group (25.0% versus 8.9%, respectively). These measures of maternal psychological status, marital dissatisfaction and parent-infant relationship were associated with referral status but did not differ between the groups of extreme criers and moderate criers.

In contrast, group differences in total fussing and crying were associated with significant differences in cumulative biologic and psychosocial risk scores (including unwanted pregnancy, premature labor, prenatal anxiety, lack of social support, socioeconomic problems and marital and transgenerational conflicts). Mothers of extreme criers were characterized by particularly high rates of prenatal stress and anxiety (70.0%, as opposed to 53.3% in the moderate criers and 42.2% in the controls), postnatal marital conflict (46.7%, versus 36.7% in the moderate criers and 8.9% in the controls) and maternal psychopathology (60.0%, as compared with 36.7% in the moderate criers and 2.2% in the controls).

Stepwise linear multiple regression helped identify the variables that were most strongly associated with total fussing and crying at referral. The most important single correlates of crying and fussing included the amount of distress/disturbance in the mother-infant relationship (as rated by experts on the PIR-GAS), followed by infant variables (early-night sleep deficit, difficult temperament) and maternal variables (prenatal anxiety and stress, postnatal exhaustion). This regression model accounted for 45% of the variance in total crying and fussing.

This summary of results suggests that it is not enough to identify families who are in need of help because of unexplained early infant crying simply on the basis of measures of infant behavior. On the one hand, it may be true that these infants represent no more than the extreme end of the normal distribution of crying and fussing, but their crying also tends to persist for many more weeks. On the other hand, their crying seems to occur more often in the context of subtle, but distinct, maturational and/or constitutional problems, as well as in families who have limited resources and are burdened with an accumulation of biologic and psychosocial risk factors. Dynamic interactions between infant and parental factors, often beginning during pregnancy, seem to promote and maintain what may well be characterized as *parent-infant distress syndrome* [17] reflected in our data in the overall amount of distress/disturbance in the parent-infant relationship. One may wonder who represents the "patient" in such a complex, developing system: the crying infant, the troubled parent or the severely distressed parent-infant relationship at a particularly vulnerable period of postnatal adaptation?

Therapeutic Intervention

For the referred groups, the diagnostic assessment was immediately followed by an interaction-centered therapeutic intervention. Tailored to the individual needs of the infant, the mother and the family, the treatment integrated different modules and techniques, including developmental counseling, interactional guidance, infant physiotherapy or sensory integration, focused psychodynamic individual or systemic family intervention and/or recruitment of social support. Developmental counseling focused on ultradian and circadian sleep-wake organization, reduction of overstimulation and settling to sleep. Criteria for treatment termination were: a) the infant's condition had substantially improved and/or b) the parents felt self-confident enough to cope. Diagnostic assessment and intervention together took an average of 3.4 sessions, each lasting between 1 hour and 2 hours. By the end of treatment, the pediatrician and psychologist in charge assessed the overall outcome (including effects on fussing and crying, sleep-wake organization, mothers' psychological state and mother-infant interactions) as "fully improved," "partially improved" or "unimproved" due to lack of cooperation. Full improvement was achieved in 66.7% of the referred families and in an additional 5.0% who had a relapse and were treated again, partial improvement was seen in 21.7% and the remaining 6.6% were unimproved.

Long-Term Outcomes of Early Unexplained Infant Crying

In our follow-up of the families when the infants were 30 months of age, we investigated the following questions:

- What is the long-term outcome of unexplained crying for infants and their families who received specialized intervention within the first 6 months of life?
- What factors contribute to the long-term outcome?
- What are the mechanisms and processes involved in promoting negative outcome?

Information was obtained from mailed diaries and questionnaires that focused on the toddlers' behavior.

Procedures

An initially larger sample of 83 referred and 57 control subjects was invited, by mail, to participate in the follow-up examination when the children were 30 months of age. Mothers in the aforementioned clinical (n = 60) and control (n = 45) samples consented to participate in the follow-up assessment; they represented 72.3% and 78.9% of the original sample sizes, respectively. No significant differences were found between the participating and nonresponding families in terms of the 1- to 6-month infant, maternal, psychosocial and relationship measures presented here.

At 30 months, all families were asked to complete the following instruments (also see Table 1):

Diary Record. The mother kept a 24-hour diary on the toddler's sleep behavior for 5 consecutive days. Information on average duration of nocturnal and diurnal sleep and various indices of sleep problems was extracted from the diaries and scored on 5-point rating scales (from 0 to 4) for each of the following items (adapted from Richman[18] and from Minde et al[19]): number of nights with nocturnal awakenings, average number of nocturnal awakenings per night, mean duration of nighttime awakenings, number of nights with bedtime routine problems, mean time elapsed between parents' request to go to sleep at night and actual bedtime, number of nights with sleep-initiation problems, mean time elapsed between bedtime and falling asleep and number of nights the child slept in the parents' bed. Based on data from all 105 subjects, we performed a principal components analysis with varimax rotation on the covariance matrix of these scores. This analysis yielded a 4-factor solution that accounted for 79.5% of the variance in the original scores. The 4 factors were interpreted as follows: sleep initiation problems, sleep maintenance problems, bedtime routine problem and parents' bed. All original scores had a high factor loading between 0.71 and 0.94 in absolute values. Factor scores for each subject and component were calculated from the factorial structure of the original data.

Standardized Questionnaires. Mothers completed the 24-month version of the Infant Characteristics Questionnaire (ICQ)[10] that were analyzed to obtain data on maternal perception of toddler temperament along 6 dimensions: difficult, unstoppable, negatively adapted, irregular, dependent and sober. Mothers also completed the Achenbach Child Behavior Checklist for 2- to 3-year-old children (CBCL/2-3),[16] which provides information about behavioral and emotional problems on 6 subscales (aggressive, destructive, sleep problems, somatic problems, anxious/depressed and socially withdrawn), as well as on internalizing (anxious/depressed and socially withdrawn combined) and externalizing behavior problems (aggressive and destructive combined). Data analysis on the CBCL/2-3 used the original Achenbach scales,[16] but applied normative t-scores derived from a large epidemiologic German sample of 751, 30-month-old toddlers.[20]

Main Findings at 30 Months

Toddler Temperament. The former groups of extreme criers, moderate criers and control infants continued to differ significantly in temperamental difficulty ($F_{2, 102}$ = 5.5, $P < .01$; Fig 1). Former extreme criers were also rated significantly harder to control (unstoppable) than control subjects ($F_{2, 102}$ = 4.0, $P < .05$). No group differences were found in terms of negatively adapted, dependent, irregular and sober. Low to moderate stability of temperament was also found in correlations between maternal ratings at 1 month to 6 months of age and at 30 months of age (Table 2).

Behavior Problems. The 3 groups of toddlers differed significantly on 5 of the 6 CBCL/2-3 subscales: aggressive ($F_{2, 102}$ = 3.8, $P < .05$), anxious/depressed ($F_{2, 102}$ = 5.1, $P < .01$), sleep problems ($F_{2, 102}$ = 3.6, $P < .05$), somatic problems ($F_{2, 102}$ = 4.4, $P < .05$) and socially withdrawn ($F_{2, 102}$ = 4.4, $P < .05$), as well as on the composite dimensions externalizing ($F_{2, 102}$ = 3.9, $P < .05$) and internalizing behavior problems ($F_{2, 102}$ = 6.0, $P < .005$); (Fig 2). Compared with the controls, former extreme criers obtained significantly higher T-scores on aggressive behavior, sleep problems and social withdrawal, as well as on externalizing problems, while moderate criers obtained higher T-scores on somatic problems. Both extreme criers and moderate criers had

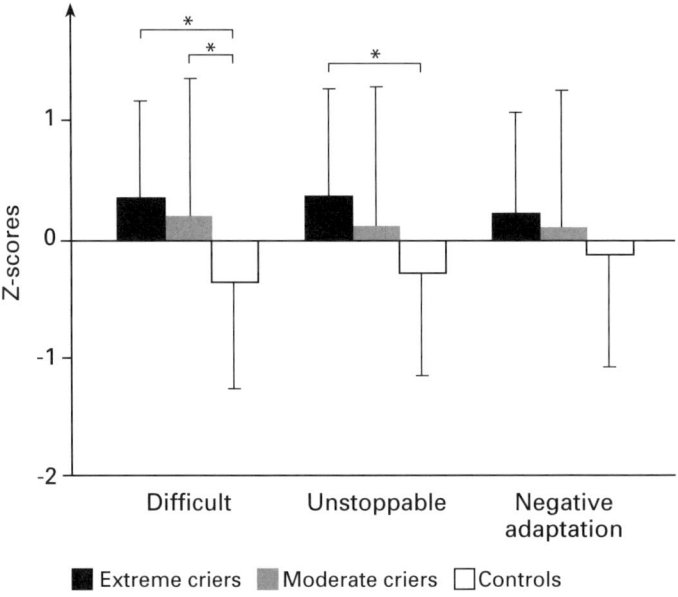

Fig 1. Temperament subscales (ICQ) at 30 months of age in extreme criers, moderate criers and control infants (means ± SD); one-way ANOVA.

*$P < .05$; 2-tailed, post-hoc, Duncan's multiple-range tests.

higher T-scores than control infants on the subscale anxious/depressed and on the composite score internalizing. No significant group differences were found with respect to destructive behavior.

In psychiatric assessments of child behavior problems, a T-score of 70 and above (corresponding to the 98th percentile) on each of the 6 syndrome scales and the 2 composite scales points to clinical disorders requiring psychiatric intervention.[20] Table 3 indicates the percentage of infants who were clinically at risk according to their individual syndrome and composite scales. The proportions of toddlers with clinically relevant behavior problems were significantly higher in the former referred group than in the control group for the following syndrome scales: aggressive (18.3% versus 4.4%; $\chi^2 = 4.6$; df = 1;

Table 2. Correlations Between Variables in Infants at 1 Month to 6 Months of Age and in Toddlers at 30 Months of Age

1 Month to 6 Months of Age	30 Months of Age										
	Toddler Temperament (ICQ)			Toddler Diary Behavior					Toddler Behavior Problems (CBCL/2-3)		
	Difficult	Negative adaptation	Unstoppable	Total sleep (min/24 h)	Sleep initiation problem	Sleep maintenance problem	Bedtime routine problem	Parents' bed	Sleep problems	Externalizing behaviors	Internalizing behaviors
Infant Diary Behavior											
Crying (min/24 h)	–	–	–	-0.26†	–	–	0.25†	–	–	–	–
Fussing (min/24 h)	0.22*	–	0.32‡	-0.24*	–	–	–	–	0.24†	0.32‡	0.35‡
Crying/fussing (min/24 h)	0.20*	–	0.29‡	-0.29‡	–	–	0.18*	–	–	0.23*	0.27†
Sleeping (min/24 h)	-0.18*	–	-0.21*	0.22*	–	-0.21*	–	–	-0.23*	–	-0.18*
Infant Temperament (ICQ)											
Difficult	0.46‡	–	0.21*	-0.28‡	–	0.21*	–	–	0.25†	0.37‡	0.34‡
Unpredictable	0.30‡	0.19*	0.24*	-0.18*	–	0.20*	–	–	0.25†	0.31‡	0.25†
Unadaptable	0.31‡	0.29‡	0.19*	-0.21*	–	–	–	–	0.25†	0.29‡	0.27‡

*$P \leq .05$; †$P \leq .01$; ‡$P \leq .005$

$P < .05$, one-tailed), anxious/depressed (18.3% versus 2.2%; $\chi^2 = 6.6$; df = 1; $P < .01$, one-tailed), socially withdrawn (11.7% versus 0%; $\chi^2 = 5.6$; df = 1; $P < .01$, one-tailed) and the composite scale internalizing behavior problems (15.0% versus 2.2%; $\chi^2 = 4.9$; df = 1; $P < .05$, one-tailed). Interestingly, 10.0% of the referred group had both clinically relevant internalizing and externalizing behavior problems, while none of the controls did (not significant).

Fig 2. Behavior problems (CBCL/2-3) at 30 months of age in extreme criers, moderate criers and control infants (means ± SD); one-way ANOVA.

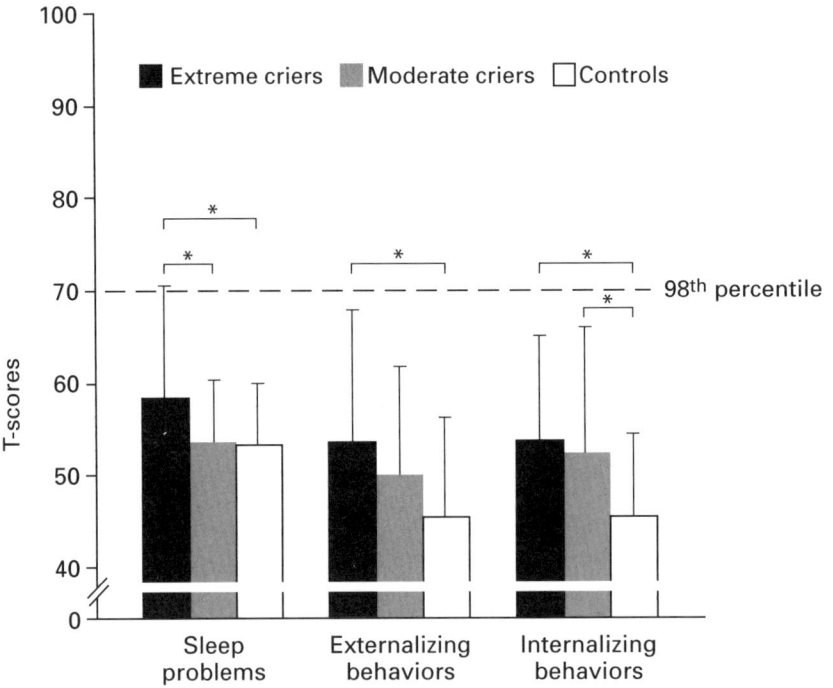

*$P < .05$; 2-tailed, post-hoc, Duncan's multiple-range tests. A T-score of 70 and above exceeds the 98th percentile that marks the clinical range on the syndrome scales.

Of the 105 toddlers studied, 26 (24.8%) had a clinically relevant behavior problem on one or more syndrome scales. We refer to these children as "clinical" rather than "nonclinical" (n = 79). Twice as many formerly referred infants than controls were assigned to the clinical group (31.7% versus 15.6%; $\chi^2 = 3.6$; df = 1; $P < .05$, one-tailed). Furthermore, 11.7% of the referred infants versus none of the control infants exceeded the 98th percentile on 3 or more syndrome scales ($\chi^2 = 6.4$; df = 3; $P < .05$, one-tailed).

Table 3. Prevalence of Clinically Relevant Behavior Problems in Former Referred and Control Infants

	Referred Group (n = 60)	Control Group (n = 45)	P*
Aggressive behavior	18.3%	4.4%	<.05
Anxious/depressed	18.3%	2.2%	<.01
Destructive behavior	6.7%	6.7%	NS
Sleep problems	10.0%	4.4%	NS
Somatic problems	11.7%	4.4%	NS
Social withdrawal	11.7%	0.0%	<.01
Internalizing behaviors	15.0%	2.2%	<.05
Externalizing behaviors	15.0%	6.7%	NS

*One-tailed χ^2-tests.

Sleeping Problems. Ninety-two sleep diaries were completed satisfactorily and were available for analysis. The former differences among extreme criers, moderate criers and controls in total sleep per 24 hours had diminished at the age of 30 months and no longer reached significance. However, extreme criers continued to sleep significantly less, on average, during the daytime than did both controls and moderate criers ($F_{2, 86} = 3.6$; $P < .05$). Stability of total sleep from datapoint I to datapoint II was low but significant ($r = 0.22$; $P < .05$—Table 2). Although the former extreme criers scored significantly higher than controls on the CBCL/2-3 subscale for sleep problems, none of the 8 diary sleep problem scales and none of the 4 sleep problem factors differentiated the 3 groups. Correlations between the CBCL/2-3 subscale score for sleep problems and both the diary-derived factor sleep maintenance problems and total sleep were moderate and highly significant ($r = 0.51$ and $r = -0.48$; $P < .005$ – Table 4).

Table 4. Intercorrelations Between Variables in Infants at 30 Months of Age

30 Months of Age	30 Months of Age										
	Toddler Temperament (ICQ)			Toddler Diary Behavior					Toddler Behavior Problems (CBCL/2-3)		
	Difficult	Negative adaptation	Unstoppable	Total sleep (min/24 h)	Sleep initiation problem	Sleep maintenance problem	Bedtime routine problem	Parents' bed	Sleep problems	Externalizing behaviors	Internalizing behaviors
Toddler Temperament (ICQ)											
Difficult	1										
Negative adaptation	0.48*	1									
Unstoppable	0.49*	–	1								
Toddler Diary Behavior											
Total sleep (min/24 h)	-0.23†	–	-0.23†	1							
Sleep initiation problem	–	–	0.23†	–	1						
Sleep maintenance problem	0.24†	–	0.20†	-0.42*	–	1					
Bedtime routine problem	–	–	–	–	–	–	1				
Parents' bed	0.18†	–	–	–	–	–	–	1			
Toddler Behavior Problems (CBCL/2-3)											
Sleep problems	0.35*	–	0.34*	-0.48*	–	0.51*	–	–	1		
Externalizing behaviors	0.73*	0.27*	0.58*	-0.34*	0.23†	0.26‡	–	–	0.44*	1	
Internalizing behaviors	0.59*	0.55*	0.32*	-0.25‡	–	–	–	–	0.41*	0.62*	1

*$P \leq .005$; †$P \leq .05$; ‡$P \leq .01$

As shown in Table 4, most of the 30-month-of-age outcome variables were significantly associated with each other. Correlations were particularly high between temperamental difficulty and unstoppable behavior on the one side and CBCL/2-3 externalizing and internalizing scores on the other. Correlations between diary sleep and temperament or CBCL/2-3 measures were weak but significant.

Factors Predicting the 30-month Outcomes

In search of antecedents for clinically relevant behavior problems at 30 months of age, we correlated early infantile, maternal and familial variables with later outcome measures (Tables 2 and 5). Early fussing and total crying/fussing were positively correlated with difficultness and unstoppable temperament and with CBCL/2-3 externalizing and internalizing behavior problems at the age of 30 months, while negative associations were found between 1-month to 6-months total sleep and both temperament and CBCL/2-3 outcome measures. Early diary measures showed only few and weak associations with later diary measures of sleep problems. Difficult, unpredictable and unadaptable temperament at 1 month to 6 months of age were also found to be correlated negatively with later total sleep and positively associated with sleep problems as assessed by CBCL/2-3 and both externalizing and internalizing behavior problems.

The psychological condition of the mother and family relationships at age 1 month to 6 months correlated significantly with later difficultness and unstoppable temperament (Table 5). Both maternal self-efficacy and quality of mother-infant relationship were negatively associated with these temperament subscales. Furthermore, maternal frustration and rejection at 1 month to 6 months of age were significantly linked to sleep problems as obtained by diary at follow-up examination. Except for maternal rejection, all measures of the mother's impaired psychological condition, marital dissatisfaction and distress in mother-infant relationship were also found to be significantly correlated with externalizing and internalizing behavior problems at 30 months of age.

Clarification of the role of potential determinants for behavior problems at 30 months of age was sought by comparing early infant, maternal and relationship variables for 2 groups of children—26 children *with* clinically

Table 5. Correlations Between Maternal/Family Variables at Datapoint I and Toddler Variables at Datapoint II.

	30 Months of Age										
	Toddler Temperament (ICQ)			Toddler Diary Behavior					Toddler Behavior Problems (CBCL/2-3)		
1 Month to 6 Months of Age	Difficult	Negative adaptation	Unstoppable	Total sleep (min/24 h)	Sleep initiation problem	Sleep maintenance problem	Bedtime routine problem	Parents' bed	Sleep problems	Externalizing behaviors	Internalizing behaviors
Maternal Psychological Condition											
Depressed mood (EMKK)	0.37*	–	0.25‡	–	–	–	–	–	–	0.34*	0.24‡
Frustration (EMKK)	0.45*	0.19†	0.34*	-0.20†	0.19†	0.21†	–	–	0.25‡	0.47*	0.34*
Exhaustion (EMKK)	0.34*	–	0.26*	–	–	–	–	–	–	0.34*	0.25‡
Rejection (EMKK)	0.20†	–	–	–	0.21†	0.22†	0.21†	0.21†	–	–	–
Self-efficacy (MSCS)	-0.42*	–	-0.33*	–	–	-0.20†	–	-0.24†	-0.27*	-0.35*	-0.29*
Family Relationship											
Marital dissatisfaction	0.35*	0.19†	–	–	–	–	–	–	–	0.39*	0.35*
Mother-infant relationship	-0.33*	–	-0.19†	–	–	–	–	–	–	-0.23†	-0.32*

*$P \leq .005$; †$P \leq .05$; ‡$P \leq .01$

relevant behavior problems (clinical group) and 79 children *without* clinically relevant behavior problems (nonclinical group) at the age of 30 months (see page 303). The daily amounts of crying and fussing at age 1 month to age 6 months had not differed with respect to the later clinical and nonclinical groups. However, significantly higher scores on early temperamental difficulty ($t^{103} = 3.6$; $P < .001$, one-tailed), unpredictability ($t^{45.0*} = 1.9$; $P < .05$, one-tailed) and unadaptability ($t^{34.0*} = 2.8$; $P < .005$, one-tailed) were found in children assigned to the clinical group than in children assigned to the nonclinical group (Fig 3).

*Adjusted t-values and degrees of freedom due to inhomogeneity of variance.

Fig 3. Infant temperament (ICQ) assessed between 1 month of age and 6 months of age in children assigned to the clinical and nonclinical groups at 30 months of age (means ± SD).

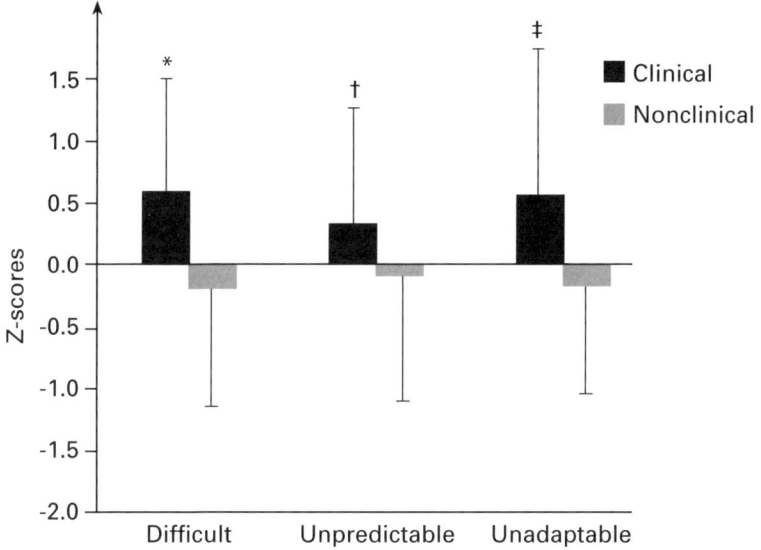

Student's t-tests: *$P < .001$; †$P < .05$; ‡$P < .005$; all one-tailed.

In a similar vein, mothers of children with clinically relevant behavior problems at follow-up had scored significantly higher on feelings of depressed mood ($t^{103} = 2.3$; $P < .05$, one-tailed) and frustration ($t^{103} = 3.7$; $P < .001$, one-tailed) and significantly lower on self-efficacy ($t^{44.8*} = -2.8$; $P < .005$, one-tailed) in the early months than mothers in the nonclinical group. They had also obtained substantially higher scores on the EPDS ($t^{103} = 2.6$; $P < .005$, one-tailed). Scores on the other maternal measures—pleasure with infant, physical exhaustion, anxious overprotection, punitive tendencies, rejection and rigidity—did not differentiate between the 2 groups. Finally, scores of accumulated psychosocial risks during pregnancy had been significantly higher in mothers of children who later developed clinically relevant behavior problems than in mothers from the nonclinical group ($t^{32.0*} = 2.1$; $P < .05$, one-tailed). Similarly significant differences were evident for marital dissatisfaction ($t^{31.6*} = 3.1$; $P < .005$, one-tailed) and for examiners' global assessment of the overall distress/disturbance in the mother-infant relationship (PIR-GAS; $t^{103} = -2.5$; $P < .01$, one-tailed).

*Adjusted t-values and degrees of freedom due to inhomogeneity of variance.

We performed stepwise multiple regression analyses with all available information about biological as well as psychosocial risk factors, and 1-to 6-month infant, maternal and relationship measures, in order to identify those factors that best predicted infant behavior problems at age 30 months. Results are depicted in Figs 4 and 5. The best regression model explaining 35% (adjusted R^2) of the variance in externalizing behaviors included only one maternal measure and 5 infant measures (Fig 4). This model comprised maternal frustration next to 3 diary measures of infant behavior (total amounts of crying, fussing and sleeping), infant difficult temperament and infant total postnatal biological risk. Conversely, with respect to internalizing behavior problems the most important single predictors were maternal depression, frustration, anxious overprotection, prenatal anxiety, distress/disturbance in the mother-infant relationship, marital dissatisfaction, and infant difficult temperament (Fig 5). This model accounted for 36% (adjusted R^2) of the variance in internalizing behavior problems. CBCL/2-3 sleep problems were best predicted by maternal depressed mood, postnatal depression, rejection, pleasure with infant and social support. Unadaptable temperament and total amount of fussing were the only infant characteristics in this regression model that explained a significant amount (27%; adjusted R^2) of the variance in sleep problems at 30 months.

Finally, a logistic regression analysis was performed to predict toddler assignment to the group with clinically relevant behavior problems on one or more CBCL/2-3 subscales. The only distinguishing regressors were infant difficultness and marital dissatisfaction ($\chi^2 = 18.1$; df = 2; $P < .001$, two-tailed).

Discussion

This report focuses on long-term consequences of early excessive crying in a clinical sample where the crying problem occurred in the midst of impaired regulatory functioning (due to temperamental difficulty and signs of central nervous system [CNS] vulnerability) and in the midst of compromised family functioning (due to an accumulation of psychosocial risks). The study was designed as a prospective longitudinal project with a community-based control group. We were unable, however, to include a control group of referred infants who did not receive our intervention. This limitation cannot be avoided for ethical reasons, and currently no such controlled data exist. The 30-month outcome data, therefore, are confounded with treatment effects.

Fig 4. Stepwise multiple regression analysis to predict 30-month externalizing behavior problems from infantile, maternal and relationship variables assessed at age 1 month to 6 months (adjusted $R^2 = 0.35$).

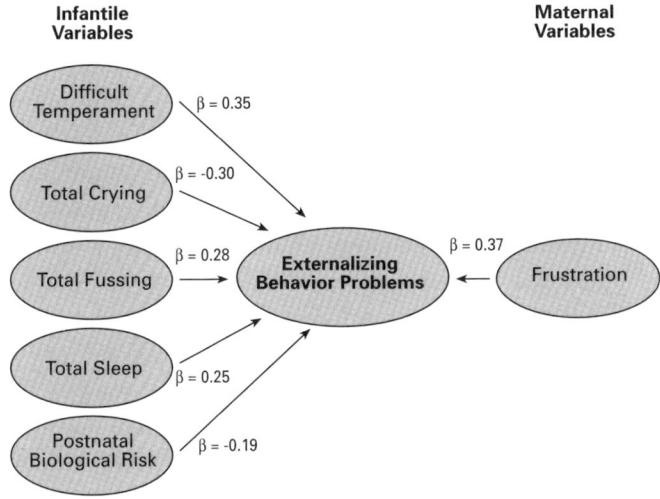

Fig 5. Stepwise multiple regression analysis to predict 30-month internalizing behavior problems from infantile, maternal and relationship variables assessed at age 1 month to 6 months (adjusted $R^2 = 0.36$).

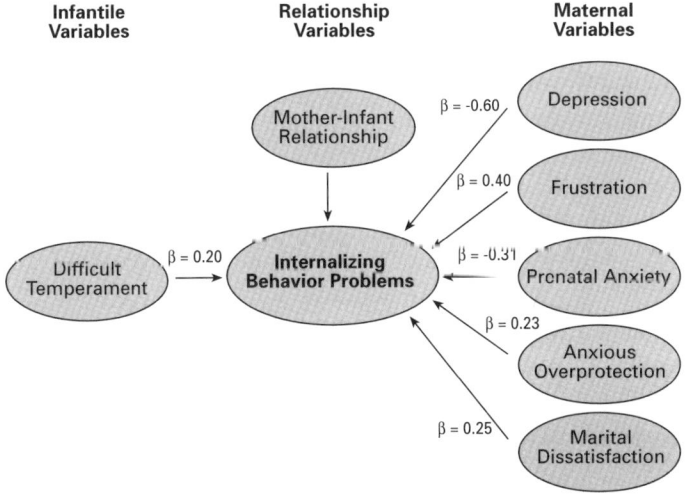

Interestingly, in view of the very high initial improvement rates in the present sample, these treatment effects did not exert a significant influence on any of the outcome findings in the long term.

Toddler Characteristics at 30 Months of Age

With this in mind, our results speak to the fact that infants whose families seek and receive help from specialists because of excessive crying continue to bear a substantially increased risk of long-term unfavorable outcome as compared with the matched community sample in the present research or with community samples of infants with Wessel's colic. According to maternal ratings on the Achenbach Child Behavior Checklist, formerly referred toddlers were significantly more aggressive, socially withdrawn and/or anxious/depressed. They exhibited more signs of sleep problems and somatic problems, and obtained higher scores on the composite dimensions of both internalizing and externalizing behavior problems than did controls. While the means in both groups were within normal limits, twice as many referred infants than controls were considered to have clinically relevant behavior problems at age 30 months. Approximately one in 3 (31.7%) of the formerly referred toddlers, as opposed to about 1 in 6 (15.6%) control toddlers, exhibited clinically relevant behavior problems in one or more domains. The latter rate in the present community control group corresponds well with rates in large normative community samples.[16, 20] Interestingly, 2 of the 7 controls who had clinically relevant behavior problems had gone through early excessive crying and were burdened with severe psychosocial risks (traumatic childhood experiences and marital conflict, respectively). Of the referred toddlers, 18% were rated as abnormally aggressive, 18% as abnormally anxious/depressed and 12% as abnormally socially withdrawn. Moreover, 12% of the referred toddlers showed clinically relevant behavior problems in 3 to 6 behavioral domains at the same time. These overall unfavorable outcomes of early excessive crying in troubled families are particularly alarming as behavioral problems within the first 3 years of life have been shown to persist in up to 62% of the cases into preschool and even school-age years.[18]

A generally positive outcome was found in both diary and CBCL/2-3 measures with respect to the toddlers' sleep. The former extreme criers continued to sleep less than the other toddlers during the daytime, but the 30-month rate of clinically relevant sleep problems and scores on the diary measures were not increased in the former referred group. This positive outcome may well be the result of our early preventive intervention, which included early support of sleep-wake organization, encouraging infants to fall asleep on their own.

It is hard to predict whether, and to what degree, the outcome would have been worse without timely intervention and a high rate of early improvement. Indirect evidence of more problematic long-term consequences comes from clinical assessments of infants who were referred to the program for the first time at an older age because of sleeping or feeding problems, excessive clinging, temper tantrums and/or aggressive behavior. In the majority of these cases the problems had started with excessive crying in the first weeks of life and had lasted ever since without any undisturbed interval and led to mutual build-up of distress in parent-infant relationships.

One may, of course, question the effectiveness of the therapeutic program over the long term. However, developmental processes may be discontinuous in nature. Following successful behavioral regulation of behavioral states, sleep-wake organization and affective arousal and attention, other adaptational demands or developmental tasks represent new challenges to be resolved in everyday parent-infant interactions, such as regulating the balance between proximity-seeking and exploration of the environment or the balance between dependency and autonomy. Even if the early regulatory demands have been mastered successfully, the system may reencounter perturbations upon transition to the next developmental stage.

Factors Predicting Outcome at Age 30 Months

CBCL/2-3 externalizing behavior problems at 30 months of age were highly correlated with difficult and unstoppable temperament at the same age, internalizing problems with difficult and unadaptable temperament, in particular. Both 30-month behavior problems and temperamental dimensions, in turn, showed low- to moderate correlations with early temperamental dimensions. These findings indicate that some stable constitutional factors may have contributed to behavioral outcome. Early temperamental attributes not only differentiate between the later clinical and nonclinical groups, but also represent an independent factor in the stepwise multiple regression analyses, contributing significantly to the prediction of both externalizing and internalizing behavior. Moreover, early temperamental difficulty was the only predictor of toddler assignment to the clinical or nonclinical group, aside from marital dissatisfaction.

As to the early diary measures, fussing, crying and sleeping were significantly related to later behavioral outcome, but did not differentiate between the clinical and nonclinical groups of toddlers. However, diary measures of crying, fussing and sleeping independently contributed to the prediction of externalizing behavior problems, next to 2 other infant factors, difficult temperament and postnatal biological risk. No similar predictors of internalizing behavior problems were found among early diary measures of behavior.

Multiple significant correlations in the low-to-moderate range were found between the mothers' psychological state, marital dissatisfaction, distress/disturbance in the mother-infant relationship and both postnatal cumulative psychosocial risk in the early months and 30-month behavioral outcome. The same variables differentiated significantly between the clinical and nonclinical groups of toddlers. However, only maternal frustration entered the multiple regression analysis of externalizing behavior problems as a single predictor next to exclusively infant variables. Conversely, in addition to temperamental difficulty, measures of the mother's psychological state, her prenatal anxiety and mother-infant and marital dissatisfaction were the main predictors of the toddlers' internalizing behavior problems.

These findings confirm what we had expected on the basis of our systemic model—that long-term outcome is accounted for by interactions among infant, maternal, relationship and psychosocial variables.

Mechanisms and Processes Involved in Long-term Negative Outcome

The present results diverge from the overall positive outcome reported from community samples of infants with Wessel's colic (see the chapter by Lehtonen in this volume). As in the majority of community studies, our data are based on maternal ratings of infant behavior on standardized, validated scales and behavior diaries kept by the mother. Similar results have often been questioned because they are mediated by, and dependent on, the mother's perception. However, this undeniable fact does not mean that they exist only in the mother's mind or that the mother's perception alone may account for any long-term consequences. It remains open to debate, particularly in the context of high-risk families, to what extent the crying, *per se*, contributes to the mother's perception and to the overall outcome. Even if the child's problem behavior exists only in the mother's mind, her perception is likely to affect the child's behavior in the context of mother-child interaction.

This is not the place to reopen the discussion of the validity of information about infant behavior obtained from mothers alone as opposed to direct behavioral observation of the child in a standard laboratory setting. Similar debates have dominated temperament research for a long time, but have come to conclude that both sources of information are needed to complement each other.

The term "perception," by itself, has been only vaguely defined in this discussion. It may refer to the mother's sensory threshold and reactivity, her expectancies and emotional appreciation of the child, her representation of the child or her feelings of self-efficacy in her role as mother to this child. Interestingly, these issues are center stage in the Intervention Program for Fussy Babies.[21] For both clinical diagnostic and therapeutic purposes, it is important to understand the intimate interrelations between the individual mother's perception and both her own behavior and her infant's behavior in interactional contexts of preverbal communication.

We and others have shown that inconsolable crying and its intrinsic negative feedback exert immediate effects on the mother's emotional state and on her feelings of self-confidence and self-efficacy as a mother.[2, 5, 22] Built on her everyday experience in interactions with her baby, she develops expectations and internal representations, or a working model, of the child and of herself in the mothering role. The mother's feelings of self-efficacy, in turn, affect her perception of her infant's behavior inasmuch as she may become hypersensitive to infant crying and may respond with increased arousal, aversive feeling and negative attitudes towards the child.[23, 24] Both the parents' hypersensitivity to crying and their negative memories related to early inconsolable crying often last well beyond the end of the crying problem.[25] We have seen many cases where the crying problem had fully resolved, but 1 or 2 years later the early experience continued to be represented in the parents' minds as a "time of horror," discouraging them from having another child in some cases.

The mother's perception may also become distorted, for instance, by an early fear of having a hyperactive or aggressive child. Such distortion may, in turn, function in the sense of a self-fulfilling prophecy. In other, more severe cases, distorted perceptions may derive from unresolved conflicts with the mother's family of origin, from traumatic experiences of child abuse or neglect in the mother's own biography and/or from various other expressions of maternal psychopathology. The infant's crying may evoke memories of herself as a child being exposed to her father's choleric spells and thus reelicit intense negative emotions. The mother's perception may get enmeshed with her past experience: She may no longer be able to disentangle her real-life interactions with her child from her representations of the past, a phenomenon that has been conclusively elucidated by Fraiberg, Adelson and Shapiro as "ghosts in the nursery."[26]

Whatever affects the mother's perception of her infant's behavior, it feeds back into the mother's caregiving behavior, it may interfere with her intuitive competencies and it contributes to interactional failures.[7] In studying and working with older infants and toddlers and their families, we observed direct paths from excessive crying in the early months to later behavioral problems. The most common path leads from the infant's early difficulty in settling to sleep and his/her exclusive reliance on parental support to lasting problems in falling asleep and sleeping through the night without intense parental intervention. Another path links the infant's early regulatory need to be carried around for most of the waking time to persisting fussiness and instrumental crying in the second 6 months of life. These infants keep protesting when being placed in the horizontal position and become highly efficient in controlling their parents' behavior by crying and fussing. As a result, they become deprived of other satisfying experiences of self-efficacy, of practicing self-initiated exploration and play and self-produced locomotion. Thus, parent-infant interactions represent the everyday arena in which some of the mechanisms and processes involved in promoting long-term negative outcome may be directly observed.

Conclusions

Excessive crying in early infancy is usually a transient condition linked to normal adaptational and maturational processes, mainly in the domains of arousal regulation and sleep-wake organization. The clinical syndrome of persistent crying, however, represents a heterogeneous group often burdened with multiple organic and psychosocial risks, including infants with temperamental difficulty or CNS vulnerability on the one side, and families with compromised parental functioning on the other.

Mother-infant communication normally functions as a primary protective resource, providing the infant with crucial regulatory and didactic support and the mother with reassuring positive feedback. However, due to the impact of inconsolable crying on the mother and the family during a vulnerable period of postpartum adaptation, persistent crying may interfere with the mother's intuitive competence, endanger the system's primary resources and push the system into vicious circles of dysfunctional interactions characterized by negative reciprocity and mutual build-up of distress. Infant mental health and the developing parent-infant relationship are affected the longer the condition persists, the more everyday domains of parent-infant interactions become dysfunctional and the more the parents' resources are drained by other factors. Dysfunctional interactions and persisting distress in the parent-infant relationship put the dyad at risk for lasting relationship disorders and the infant at risk for externalizing and internalizing behavior disorders. Because of these risks, persistent crying calls for close attention among infant mental health professionals in order to identify, at an early age, those families who are in need of specialized intervention.

Acknowledgements

This study was kindly supported by the Bavarian Ministry of Labor, Social Affairs, Family, Women, and Health; Christian Seltmann Foundation; and the Munich Child-Center.

References

1. Wessel MA, Cobb JC, Jackson EB, Harris GS, Detwiler AC. Paroxysmal fussing in infancy, sometimes called 'colic.' *Pediatrics.* 1954;14:421-435.
2. Papoušek M, Papoušek H. Excessive infant crying and intuitive parental care: buffering support and its failures in parent infant interaction. *Early Child Development and Care.* 1990;65:117-126.
3. Papoušek H, Papoušek M. Intuitive parenting: a dialectic counterpart to the infant's integrative competence. In: Osofsky JD, ed. *Handbook of Infant Development.* 2nd ed. New York, NY: John Wiley & Sons; 1987:669-720.
4. St. James-Roberts I, Halil T. Infant crying patterns in the first year: normal community and clinical findings. *Journal of Child Psychology and Psychiatry, and Allied Disciplines.* 1991;32:951-968.
5. Papoušek M. Persistent infant crying, parenting and infant mental health. In: Osofsky JD, Fitzgerald HE, eds. *WAIMH Handbook of Infant Mental Health.* Vol. 4. New York, NY: John Wiley & Sons; 2000.

6. Papoušek M, von Hofacker N. Persistent crying and parenting: search for a butterfly in a dynamic system. Early Development and Parenting. 1995;4:209-224.
7. Papoušek M, von Hofacker N. Persistent crying in early infancy: a non-trivial condition of risk for the developing mother-infant relationship. *Child: Care, Health and Development.* 1998;24:395-424.
8. Papoušek M, Papoušek H. Infantile colic, state regulation, and interaction with parents: a systems approach. In: Bornstein MH, Genevro J, eds. *Child Development and Behavioral Pediatrics.* Hillsdale, NJ: Lawrence Erlbaum Associates; 1996.
9. Esser G, Laucht M, Schmidt M, et al. Behaviour problems and developmental status of 3-month-old infants in relation to organic and psychosocial risks. *European Archives of Psychiatry and Neurological Sciences.* 1990;239:384-390.
10. Bates JE, Freeland CAB, Lounsbury ML. Measurement of infant difficultness. *Child Development.* 1979;50:794-803.
11. Engfer A, Gavranidou M. Antecedents and consequences of maternal sensitivity. A longitudinal study. In: Rauh H, Steinhausen H-C, eds. *Psychobiology and Early Development.* Amsterdam, Holland: Elsevier Science Ltd; 1987:71-99.
12. Lips NH, Bloom K, Barnett H. Psychometric evaluation of a new scale to measure maternal self-confidence. 1990. (Unpublished manuscript.)
13. Murray L, Carothers AD. The validation of the Edinburg Post-natal Depression Scale on a community sample. *The British Journal of Psychiatry; the Journal of Mental Science.* 1990;157:288-290.
14. Sarimski K. Aufrechterhaltung von Schlafstörungen im frühen Kindesalter: Entwicklungspsychopathologisches modell und Pilot-Studie [Sleep disorders in early childhood: developmental psychopathologic model and pilot study]. *Praxis der Kinderpsychologie und Kinderpsychiatrie.* 1993;42:2-8.
15. Zero to Three Task Force on Diagnostic Classification in Infancy. *Diagnostic Classification of Mental Health and Developmental Disorders of Infancy and Early Childhood.* Arlington, Va National Center for Clinical Infant Programs; 1994.
16. Achenbach TM, Edelbrock C, Howell CT. Empirically based assessment of the behavioral/emotional problems of 2- and 3-year-old children. *Journal of Abnormal Child Psychology.* 1987;15:629-650.
17. Barr RG. The enigma of infant crying: the emergence of defining dimensions. *Early Development and Parenting.* 1995;4:225-232.
18. Richman N. A community survey of characteristics of one- to two-year-olds with sleep disruptions. *Journal of the American Academy of Child Psychiatry.* 1981;20:281-291.
19. Minde K, Popiel K, Leos N, Falkner S, Parker K, Handley-Derry M. The evaluation and treatment of sleep disturbances in young children. *Journal of Child Psychology and Psychiatry, and Allied Disciplines.* 1993;34:521-533.
20. Fegert JM. Verhaltensdimensionen und Verhaltensprobleme bei zweieinhalbjährigen Kindern [Behavioral dimensions and behavior problems in 2 1/2-year-old children]. *Praxis der Kinderpsychologie und Kinderpsychiatrie.* 1996;45:83-94.
21. von Hofacker N, Papoušek M. Disorders of excessive crying, feeding, and sleeping: The Munich Interdisciplinary Research and Intervention Program. *Infant Mental Health Journal.* 1998;19:180-201.
22. St. James-Roberts I, Conroy S, Wilsher K. Clinical, developmental and social aspects of early infant crying and colic. *Early Development and Parenting.* 1995;4:177-190.
23. Lester BM, Boukydis CF, Garcia-Coll CT, Hole W, Peucker M. Infantile colic: acoustic cry characteristics, maternal perception of cry, and temperament. *Infant Behavior and Development.* 1992;15:15-26.
24. Wolke D, Meyer R, Ohrt B, Riegel K. Co-morbidity of crying and feeding problems with sleeping problems in infancy: concurrent and predictive associations. *Early Development and Parenting.* 1995;4:1-17.
25. Räihä H, Lehtonen R, Lehtonen L, Korvenranta H. Does time heal? Family functioning six years after infantile colic. *7th Congress of the World Association for Infant Mental Health,* July 2000, Montréal, Quebec, Canada.
26. Fraiberg S, Adelson E, Shapiro V. Ghosts in the nursery: a psychoanalytic approach to the problem of impaired infant-mother relationship. In: Fraiberg S, ed. *Clinical Studies in Infant Mental Health: The First Year of Life.* New York, NY: Basic Books; 1980:164-196.

Section 5 Discussion: Is There Life After Unexplained Crying?: Outcomes and Consequences

Moderated by Professor Frank Oberklaid
Director, Centre for Community Child Health
Royal Children's Hospital
University of Melbourne
Melbourne, Victoria, Australia

Oberklaid: Longitudinal studies of colicky infants reinforce the importance of increased crying as a predictor of persistent differences in the perception of behavior, not the behavior itself. Liisa Lehtonen stated that an important unresolved question is whether these difficulties were present prior to, were caused by or were moderated by the experience of having an infant with colic. I want to highlight the concept of crying as a "second hit" in a family where there may be postnatal depression or where there may be psychosocial difficulties already. Suddenly there is "violation of expectation," and the crying acts as the second hit. That is the real dilemma for clinicians. The laboratory data and group analyses are good, but what can we say about this infant in this situation to this mother?

The real challenge in Cynthia Stifter's data is how to take that design, those concepts, those laboratory measures, and use them in what I call translational research. Several studies have found colic to be related to how infants are perceived by their parents. Colicky infants were rated by their parents as temperamentally difficult well after their colic symptoms dissipated. Perhaps what was identified as colic for some of the infants was, in fact, "difficultness." We do not always ask parents about sleep and other difficult behaviors. Perhaps colic, crying and fussing are a metaphor for a more complex condition.

Dynamic interactions between persistent crying, difficult temperament and parenting factors, which compromise maternal resources and intuitive parenting, may put families at long-term risk for both relationship and behavior problems. This broadens the notion of just considering the infant into something more complex. Even if infant colic by itself may not be sufficient to put infants and their families at risk for later problems, it may do so under conditions where there are increased organic and psychosocial adversities.

In our temperament study of 1583 patients,[1] we found no relationship between ratings of difficult temperament on a validated scale and later behavior problems at 4 to 5 years of age. There is tension between subjective and objective ratings, and much of the temperament literature discusses whether the maternal ratings of temperament are truly objective compared with laboratory measures. For the purpose of this discussion, I suggest that maternal ratings of temperament on a validated scale are objective. So, there is no relationship between these ratings and subsequent problems, but there is for a maternal overall subjective rating. One can ask the mother a single question, such as "Compared to an average infant, is your infant much more difficult, more difficult?" and so on. This is a mother's "overall" subjective rating, and mothers' ratings were predictive. The best predictors were situations in which mothers perceived subjectively that the infants had difficult temperaments and perceived subjectively that the infants had behavior problems.

Another finding is that there were no strong relationships between validated ratings and perceptions. In our study, only 44 % of infants who were perceived as difficult were categorized by validated rating scales as difficult. Looking at it the other way, only 25% of infants who were categorized as difficult on objective measures were actually perceived as difficult. This suggests that when one measures "objectively" or "subjectively," one is measuring different factors. One can hypothesize a parallel situation for objective and subjective measures of colic and crying. Global impressions of crying and fussing may include influences from maternal psychological functioning as well as sociodemographic and cultural factors.

I do not want to view colic and excess crying as a function of just one variable. In real life situations, once you take that infant outside the lab and look at the 20% or 15% of mothers who report infants with colic, the situation is extraordinarily complex.

Clinically, it is very difficult to predict outcome for an individual infant. There is now good evidence of efficacy of short-term interventions, although there is no good follow-up to suggest that these interventions help in the long term. I would broaden this debate and suggest that colic may, in fact, be a marker for a whole range of other conditions. Dieter Wolke used the term "comorbidity." Perhaps if we examined not just excess crying and fussing but also a range of other infant variables, we would find the situation to be less pure then we had believed it to be.

Gunnar: I am deeply concerned that, as we try to make the translation between subjective questionnaire measures and more objective measures, we do not fall into the trap of assuming that because we brought a child into a laboratory or we have a very specific objective parameter, we have created a better index than the observational one. I am concerned that as we view one against the other, we are as rigorous about asking for repeated observations and evidence of stability and aggregation in our objective measures. We need to ask ourselves if we have reduced our error in our objective measurements so that we can look at the relationship with subjective measures, because the mother is aggregating many more instances of behavior than we typically have the opportunity to collect for lab-based measures.

Fox: From the position of the pediatrician, who is the patient? Are we treating the child by using the maternal rating, or are we treating the mother and her concerns and perceptions about the child just as much? We need to address whether it is temperament, difficult temperament or colic.

Oberklaid: That speaks to the essence of this session and its huge implications for both researchers and clinicians—namely, what does colic predict? We can look at "objective" measures and find that they do or do not predict behavior versus asking the mother and then determine whether long-term behaviors can be predicted. Are they both valid? Are we measuring different sorts of things? Certainly they have different clinical implications.

Gunnar: The point that Dieter Wolke and I are making is that if you are going to collect objective data, be sure that you have sufficient data so that you can sort out its sources. Do not automatically leap to the conclusion that what is not explained by objective data is a maternal perception issue.

Oberklaid: It is more worrisome when objective ratings suggest that a child is good or average and the mother perceives him or her as difficult. There are some suggestions in the literature that that this discrepancy is a risk factor for child abuse. In our research, we concluded that, from a clinical point of view, where ratings say a child is fine and the mother says the child is difficult, that is a red flag.

I would like to ask Ian St. James-Roberts about perception. When you go out looking for "pure colic," or "pure crying," can you get a sample uncontaminated by measurement issues or comorbidity issues? To what extent can researchers recruit a sample of pure-colic infants where perception and objective measurements coincide?

St. James-Roberts: In colic infants, defined now by the Wessel criteria for amounts of fussing and crying, there were many problems. Diaries indicated 3 or more hours of fussing and crying, confirmed by audio recordings. You are really asking for the rate of false-positive and false-negative diagnoses. We do not know. In general, in many cases, parents are correct about the amounts, the distribution, and the group differences, and they are right about age of occurrence. I agree, however, that there is more involved. Certainly, you are using the word "perception" differently than I would. I use the word "perception" to mean "as near as possible to objective reality." What you call a rating is an evaluative judgment to me; so there are difficulties of language between us. I do not believe there are difficulties in meaning, though.

Goldson: I have a question for those who conduct interventional studies. You mentioned this potential discrepancy between a mother who perceives an infant to be very difficult and crying a great deal and a diary that does not corroborate those findings. What happens after you reassure the mothers and show them that the diary indicates that the child is crying a normal amount and is not an excessive crier? Have you then gone back and looked at their perceptions? Does reassurance really help, or are you dealing with deep-seated anxiety and fear in the mother, so that the focus of concern may shift from crying to another area?

Wolke: In our study,[2] we had an empathy condition, where the parents received the same amount of contact as the other groups. The intervention was by a mother who had previously had a colic baby. She talked to the subject to help her understand that the colic would go away and this would get better. We found that the mothers rated this as being good for them, that it helped them. When we looked at the diary measure, however, it did not have an impact on the crying compared with the nontreatment group. The reason is that you have to give parents guidance to make a change. If you make them feel better, they might go to the cinema or shopping, but it does not help the child. You have to give parents strategies to actually manage the child's crying. Just reassuring them but not giving them any advice does not change the mother's behavior.

* * * * *

Barr: One wonderful aspect of dealing with crying in the first 3 months of life is that it is relatively less compromised by comorbidity than in older children. Therefore, it presents an opportunity in a developmentally compressed situation to try to understand the real determinants of behavioral change, including how well the mother and infant coregulate. What are determinants of infant behavioral state? There is a golden window of opportunity that becomes increasingly compromised as the child gets older. We need to understand mother-infant interaction better. We should look at mother-infant interaction in a way that provides insight that is impossible otherwise except by artificial mathematical modeling.

Oberklaid: So perhaps one of the constructive outcomes here is to begin to add chronological features to definitions?

Barr: Absolutely. We want to say that development does make a difference. You get a different picture of crying in the first 3 months from what you get in the last 3 months of the first year.

* * * * *

St. James-Roberts: I would like to discuss the concept of a "pure" crying baby and the notion of a regulatory disorder and what the distinction is between those two. We have studied sleeping in babies who are selected purely because of their crying. There is a well-defined inverse relationship between the amount of crying and the amount of sleeping. We have not found any evidence that the sleeping is distributed in these crying babies in a way that is different from its distribution in other babies. Crying babies simply sleep less. If you look at day/night distribution, it is the same. That leads me to believe that there is no regulatory problem involved. Liisa Lehtonen's data on sleep architecture were consistent with that concept.[3] Do we know what the measures of sleep are that support this idea of a regulatory disorder?

Zeskind: If we look at differences in "mean" regulation, the answer is no. The value of time series analysis is that you can ask not just whether the means and standard deviations and distributions differ but how those distributions are distributed over time, which is a measure of temporal organization. Time series analysis is a real measure of organization—not just of whether there are differences, but of how things work. We have ways of measuring that go beyond our relatively simplistic looks at distribution of status types of information. You can get a "state regulation" measure, and I think that would be very valuable.

* * * * *

Fox: One of the goals of the meeting was to try to understand determinants of unexplained crying, limited to the first 3 months of life. For some infants, unexplained crying may be some sort of sensory sensitivity. Some suggest that organicity and visceral sensitivity may be contributing to this phenomenon. Some of the more intriguing findings that we have heard, however, deal with early antenatal and prenatal parental perceptions and their possible contribution to subsequent parental perceptions of a child as being a "high crier." We should not ignore this issue. There is an underlying theme here. Perhaps parental perceptions—the subjective perceptions of the parent—are driving the system.

* * * * *

Zeskind: We have discussed what the parent can do for the baby, but we should not forget that parenthood also involves expectations about what the baby is going to be doing for the parent. Parental expectations are very important.

References

1. Oberklaid F, Sanson A, Pedlow R, Prior M. Predicting school behavior problems from temperament and other variables in infancy. *Pediatrics.* 1993;91:113-120.
2. Wolke D, Gray P, Meyer R. Excessive infant crying: a controlled study of mothers helping mothers. *Pediatrics.* 1994;94:322-332.
3. Kirjavainen J, Kirjavainen T, Huhtala V, Lehtonen L, Korvenranta H, Kero P. Infants with colic have a normal sleep structure at 2 and 7 months of age. *Journal of Pediatrics.* 2000;137:1-6.

New Evidence on Unexplained Early Infant Crying

Section 6:
Summary

Abstract from Section 6: Summary

What Do We Know? What Are the Implications of the Findings for Practitioners? What Do We Need to Know?

Ian St. James-Roberts, PhD

This section first summarizes the new evidence, and view of unexplained early infant crying, which emerged from this Round Table meeting. Next, the key implications of the evidence for practitioners are made clear. Lastly, some of the puzzling and unanswered questions raised by the findings are highlighted. The aim is to identify the kinds of information which are needed in order to help research and practice in this area to continue to move forward.

Summary: What Do We Know? What Are the Implications of the Findings for Practitioners? What Do We Need to Know?

Ian St. James-Roberts, PhD

What Do We Know? The New Evidence and an Emerging View.

For a generation or more, unexplained crying in young babies has been widely thought of as an acute clinical condition involving gastrointestinal disturbance and pain. The origins of this view can be traced back to three main sources: the seminal 1954 research by Wessel and colleagues,[1] which popularized the use of the term "colic"; the 1955 review by the eminent pediatrician Illingworth,[2] which endorsed the view that the crying was due to intestinal pain; the trailblazing 1960s studies by Wasz Höckert and colleagues,[3] which proposed the existence of discrete cry types, such as hunger and pain cries, which enabled the listener to discern the causes of crying.

The view of early crying which has emerged in this Round Table departs from this early work in 8 main ways:

- The evidence reviewed in Section 3 makes clear that although young babies do sometimes cry because of organic disturbances, such conditions are rare. Food intolerance can occasionally lead to gastrointestinal disturbances that cause crying, but this is just one of an array of uncommon organic conditions. It follows that practitioners need to be alert to organic disturbances as a basis for crying in young babies but that they should expect them to be rare. Organic disturbances are estimated to account for less than 10% of the cases where unexplained crying is the presenting symptom in 1- to 3-month-old babies.

- Instead of identifying a discrete abnormal condition in a subgroup of young babies, high amounts of crying in 1- to 3-month-old babies are considered to be due mainly to developmental processes that normally occur at this age.

  This conclusion reflects the weight of evidence that most babies selected because of large amounts of crying or parental complaints about crying differ from their agemates in the extent of their crying, rather than in kind. This does not preclude the need to understand individual differences or to develop strategies that help parents manage and cope with babies who cry excessively. Rather, the implication is to remove the assumption that the crying reflects a pathological condition that requires a medical cure.

- Section 2 describes extensive evidence that the first 3 months of infancy constitute a transitional period during which major maturational and developmental changes occur. It is likely that these changes are responsible for the large amount and other features of crying that generally occur in infants during this period. Variations in how and when this normal transition is accomplished are considered to be largely responsible for the individual differences in babies' crying and related behavior.

  There is growing evidence that the development of the neurologic rather than the gastrointestinal system may hold the key to an understanding of these individual differences in crying in the first 3 months. It is likely that neurologically mediated individual differences in reactivity to stimulation, or in the ability to inhibit or regulate responsiveness, are at least part of the reason for the variations in crying behavior.

- Rather than producing different "cry types" (such as "hunger," "anger" or "pain" cries), which tell the listener precisely what causes their crying, young infants' cries provide a "graded signal" that conveys the degree of an infant's arousal or distress but not precisely what may be the cause. It is not possible to determine reliably the underlying causes from the sound of the cry alone.

  It follows that when an infant cries without apparent reason in an everyday setting, it is difficult to determine if he or she is in pain and more difficult to determine the cause of the crying. In everyday circumstances, parents probably determine the causes primarily from contextual information, such as the effectiveness of a feed in resolving crying.

- Some crying bouts in 1- to 3-month-old babies have features that make the crying particularly stressful for parents. These include relatively high intensity, long bout length, resistance to generally effective soothing strategies and unpredictability. These features have been confirmed objectively. For instance, these bouts of crying are hard to soothe for trained researchers using standard soothing procedures as well as for mothers. There is reliable evidence that 1- to 3-month-old babies can have prolonged bouts of fussing and crying even with sensitive and responsive parental care.

  The hard-to-soothe nature of the crying and lack of explanation for its occurrence are central in understanding its impact on Western parents. These characteristics make the crying uncontrollable and lead parents to feel helpless and guilty about their inability to prevent their very young babies from crying.

- The impact of these crying bouts on parents depends partly on the parents' subjective characteristics, including their experience, knowledge, resilience and supports. The impact can be particularly serious when mothers are prone to depression or when parents have other vulnerabilities.

- As they grow older, infants who cry a lot in the first 3 months show the normal developmental tendency to reduce their crying, but they tend to cry more than their peers until at least 5 months of age.

- In the absence of other risk factors, prolonged crying in the first 3 months has not been found to have effects on the growth, development or behavior of children after the first year. However, the combination of excessive crying and parental or family risk factors may be associated with poor child outcomes, as discussed in Section 5.

What Are the Implications of the Findings for Practitioners?

- There is currently no clinically useful way of predicting which baby will experience prolonged bouts of hard-to-soothe crying. Factors such as birth order, demographic background and feeding method are poor predictors.

- The presenting phenomenon is parental complaints about infant crying, so parents, as well as infants, are always involved. Many parents are accurate in their judgments of crying, but some parents' perceptions may be colored by their expectations or anxieties. Therefore, accurate assessment of infant behavior should be a primary goal. The use of a diary or other instrument to measure the crying amount, pattern and nature will allow confirmation, will generate diagnostic information and may be helpful in providing parents with reassurance and insight.

Where use of a diary is not possible, interview or questionnaire measures may be substituted. The research literature contains alternative versions of these instruments suitable for use in person or over the telephone.

- To distinguish crying due to organic causes, practitioners need inclusion and exclusion criteria that allow them to identify these rare but important cases. Section 3 provides provisional protocols for this purpose. These should to be viewed as first approximations that will need amendment and qualification in the light of further use. Their strength is that they are evidence based and have been found helpful in specific locales.

- It is known that high rates of fussing and crying may occur despite responsive and sensitive caregiving by parents and others. Consequently, unless otherwise indicated, the assumption is that the parents are not to blame.

- Parents' responses to the crying will vary, and some will find it particularly difficult to cope with. The collection of information to identify maternal depression, lack of social supports and other sources of vulnerability should be a core part of the primary workup.

- Once the possibility of organic disturbance has been addressed and the infant's healthy growth and development confirmed, the focus for management should shift to providing parents with information, advice and support. Important elements are likely to be:
    - Examining the notion that crying means that there is something "wrong" with an infant of this age and introducing alternatives, such as the possibility that it signals a reactive or vigorous baby
    - Viewing the first 3 months of infancy as a developmental transition, which all babies go through more or less smoothly
    - Reassuring parents that it is normal to find crying aversive and discussing the dangers of abuse and Shaken Baby Syndrome
    - Discussing ways of containing and minimizing the crying and highlighting positive features of the baby

- Considering the availability of supports and the development of strategies that allow parents to cope, take time out and "recharge their batteries"
- Empowering parents and reframing the first 3 months as a challenge they can overcome, with positive consequences for themselves and their relationships with their infants
- Continuing to monitor the infant for emerging symptoms and signs, at least until the crying problems have resolved

What Do We Need to Know? Questions and Recommendations.

- Crying is a complex act that comprises not only vocal but facial, motor and postural components. We need to know more about how these components develop and become coordinated if we are to understand the infant phenotype during this period.
- A clearer understanding of the factors that link parents' reports of infant characteristics to infant behavior is needed. Such approaches may be more fruitful than continuing to discuss which measures are more accurate or assuming that correlations between parental characteristics and reports mean that the reports are groundless.
- Most systematic information on crying in 1- to 3-month-old babies is based on studies in North America, Canada and northern Europe. There is an urgent need for information from other geographic areas and cultures to broaden our understanding of the range of normal variations in young babies' behavior, identify caregiving practices that contribute to these variations and throw light on the relationship between parents' concepts about crying and the care they provide.
- In the Section 2 Discussion, Megan Gunnar pointed out that it is Western societies' existing dogma that infants cry to express needs that parents can identify and respond to. The view of early crying that has emerged from the Round Table—that it is sometimes ambiguous with respect to its causes and resistant to caregivers' attempts to resolve it—is at odds with this dogma and presents a puzzle. Why should behavior of this sort have evolved and what, if anything, is its purpose?

Two main approaches to this question have emerged from the discussions. First, it is possible that this behavior is an artifact of other evolutionary pressures, rather than having a specific function of its own. For example, crying during the first 3 months may be a by-product of the major reorganization of human brain systems that takes place during this period, where these neurological changes reflect other constraints on growth. This explanation tends to draw a distinction between human and other species and regards the crying as largely unavoidable.

Alternatively, the discussions in Section 2 draw attention to crying-like vocalizations in the young of other species and to the possibility that early crying in humans functions as part of an attachment-regulatory system. If this is the case, Western caregiving practices may enhance early crying, because caregivers are relatively unresponsive to infant regulatory needs.

Both cross-cultural human and cross-species studies of the regulatory systems of infants and parents are required to help resolve this issue.

- More evidence is needed about the distinction and the relationship between measures of spontaneous crying in everyday contexts and measures of responsiveness under standard, mildly challenging conditions. Some investigations have found these measures to be correlated, suggesting that high amounts of crying might reflect differences in reactivity or regulation of responsiveness between babies. Other research has not confirmed this relationship. Studies are needed to explain these inconsistencies and show whether differences in peripheral sensory, autonomic or central nervous systems underlie the differences in everyday crying.

- The importance of consolability as an infant characteristic, and of parental use of consoling and containment strategies to manage infant crying, have been highlighted by recent studies. These characteristics and their origins and interactions need to be better understood.

- A uniform set of criteria and terms, ie, a taxonomic system for describing infant crying in research and clinical settings, is needed. The desirability of abandoning the use of the word "colic" was discussed, but it is unclear whether this is possible or desirable at present; other terms in current use also have disadvantages.

To encourage the development of a uniform taxonomy, it is recommended that studies provide explicit operational definitions for the terms and detailed descriptions of the sampling and measurement methods used.

References

1. Wessel MA, Cobb JC, Jackson EB, Harris GS, Detwiler AC. Paroxysmal fussing in infancy, sometimes called "colic." *Pediatrics.* 1954;14:421-433.
2. Illingworth RS. "Three months' colic." *Archives of Disease in Childhood.* 1954;29:165-174.
3. Wasz-Höckert O, Lind J, Vuorenkoski V, Partanen T, Valanné E. *The Infant Cry.* Clinics in Developmental Medicine No. 29. London, England: Heinemann/Spastics International Medical Publications;1968.